CERAMICS FOR THE ARCHAEOLOGIST

ANNA O. SHEPARD

Publication 609

CARNEGIE INSTITUTION OF WASHINGTON

WASHINGTON, D. C.

Manuscript submitted November 1954

Standard Book Number 0—87279—620—5

COMPOSED ON PHOTON MACHINE BY MACHINE COMPOSITION COMPANY, BOSTON, MASSACHUSETTS
PRINTED OFFSET BY THE MULLEN PRINTING CORPORATION, WOBURN, MASSACHUSETTS, 1956
REPRINTED BY THE KIRBY LITHOGRAPHIC COMPANY, INC., WASHINGTON, D.C. 1957, 1961, 1963, 1965
REPRINTED OFFSET BY SAULS LITHOGRAPHIC COMPANY, INC., WASHINGTON, D.C., 1968, 1971, 1974

Foreword to Fifth Printing

Ceramic Studies, 1954 to 1964

MANY CHANGES in ceramic studies have occurred since *Ceramics for the Archae-ologist* was written in 1954. The physicists have introduced sensitive and rapid methods for compositional analysis; the availability of computers has given statistical studies great impetus; there has been renewed interest in the potter's natural resources; the classification of pottery has been pursued with fresh enthu-siasm, taking different directions in different regions; ethnologists have been inquiring into the place of pottery in the lives of village people; and the archaeol-ogist, in his turn, has been challenged to think about the cultural significance of pottery rather than content himself with its use for relative dating. A review of these developments will point toward the fundamentals in ceramic studies and suggest how the archaeologist can best obtain the aid he needs. Although this re-view is not seasoned with either humor or satire, it is brief, and the points are car-ried by illustration rather than by precept.

The physicist's contribution to ceramic studies. Physics has wrought and is working a remarkable revolution in chemical analysis by the development of new instrumental methods. In contrast to classic procedures, these methods are based on the measurement of characteristic properties, especially atomic and electronic properties. The methods are so varied that it is difficult to generalize about them, but a number require relatively little material, and some are nondestructive—con-ditions that are important to the archaeologist. They vary widely in sensitivity and specificity; some are especially useful for the identification of impurities and trace elements because of their extreme sensitivity; and some give a complete ele-mental analysis whereas others can be used only for certain elements. A number employ standards that must be prepared by classic methods, and their accuracy is therefore dependent on the accuracy of those methods. Most of them require ex-pensive instruments, but in routine industrial testing the cost may be offset by the reduced time for analysis. On the other hand, since standardization is required when unknown material is tested, more time may be needed by the new than by the standard method. In other words, the instrumental methods have great poten-tialities but must be used with judgment. Reference to a few that have been ap-plied in archaeology will illustrate their potentialities and limitations.

Emission spectroscopy is a method that has been throughly tested over many years; it offers a quick means of obtaining complete qualitative data, and its value for quantitative analysis is well established for both routine work and research. Its earlier applications in archaeological ceramics were mainly for pigment analysis, for which it is particularly well adapted. As an example, qualitative analyses of Rio Grande glazes were performed in the laboratories of the Massachusetts Institute of Technology to learn (a) whether production of glaze paint ware awaited discovery of local sources of ore or whether lead ores were initially imported from the western glaze paint centers; (b) how many sources of lead ore were known in the Rio Grande Valley, and the influence of their location on the centers of production and on trade (Shepard, 1942, p. 258).

In recent years spectrographic analysis has been used in the study of pastes, with the aim of differentiating pottery from different sources. A study of Mycenaean and Minoan pottery conducted by the Oxford Laboratory for Archaeology and the History of Art is the most extensive and successful of these. Archaeologists of the British School of Archaeology in Athens and the Ashmolean Museum outlined a sound and challenging problem of trade in the eastern Mediterranean in Late Bronze Age times (Catling, 1961), and they collected an excellent sample from sites considered centers of production in the Mycenaean-Minoan world and from sites in the eastern Mediterranean where pottery, especially Mycenaean, seemed to have been traded. Nine elements were chosen for quantitative spectrographic analysis because they had been found useful in comparing and contrasting various types of pottery (Blin-Stoyle and Richards, 1961). Initially, analysis of 40 sherds each of Mycenaean and Knossian pottery showed that the composition patterns (plot of percentages of elements) of the two were sufficiently distinct to permit assignment of origin of sherds to one or the other if there seemed to be only the two alternatives. Both the advantages and the limitations of the study are indicated in the second report (Catling, Richards, and Blin-Stoyle, 1963) and the review of archaeological interpretations (Catling, 1963). Eleven composition patterns were recognized from the analysis of more than 500 sherds. In addition, there were a few odd patterns that were not comparable to any of the others or to one another. The largest group (composition pattern A) was represented by all except a few of the Peloponnesian sherds tested. Mycenaean-like pottery from three sites in Cyprus, one in north Syria, and Tell Amarna, Egypt, as well as pottery from various sites in the Aegean, had the same pattern. The second important group (composition pattern B) occurred in most but not all the Minoan sherds. It was much less common outside Crete than the Mycenaean pattern, although there are occurrences within the Aegean area. Most of these may represent trade, but the proportion of sherds with this composition pattern in Thebes in central Greece is surprisingly high, making up nearly two-thirds of the sample analyzed. Catling comments that an intensive trade between Thebes and Crete is highly improbable, and that the occurrence in the two regions of clays indistinguishable by the analytical method employed is the more likely explanation (*op. cit.*, p. 6). Catling, Richards, and Blin-Stoyle generalize that differences in composition pattern indicate different sources but the same pattern does not necessarily prove identity of source (*op. cit.*, p. 103). The sherds with the eleven other composition patterns are more limited in distribution: two occur in Thessaly, one in a site in Attica, and two were found in each of four islands, Melos, Rhodes, and Cyprus, and the eastern end of Crete.

A disappointment in the study was the similarity of all pattern A Peloponnesian pottery analyzed. Although the sites did not give a good coverage, the area was nevertheless considered too extensive to have been dependent on the Mycenaean region alone; similarity of clays within the area is proposed as the probable explanation.

The Mycenaean-Minoan study was conducted without reference to geological and geochemical conditions. Geological formations in which the sites are located are not mentioned. It is interesting to note that the Minoan sites with type B composition patterns are in the Pliocene, which is not present in the eastern end of Crete where the principal formation is Cretaceous, and where type B pattern is rare, but two distinct patterns were found.

Although the geology of the Peloponnesus is complex, including many different formations, the four sites on which the study was based all appear from a geologic map (Renz, Liatsikas, and Paraskevaidis, 1954) to be in alluvial formations. Occurrences on the island of Melos, an important staging port for ships, is singled out by Catling as especially interesting. In addition to group A sherds, presumably imports from the Mycenaean region, two distinct composition patterns were found. One, described as "very distinct," is low in calcium (2.4 per cent); in the other group calcium (16.2 per cent) is within its range for most patterns reported. The low-calcium sherd is classed as trade of unknown source because it is indistinguishable from the Mycenaean sherds in general appearance. The high-calcium sherd, an imitation of Minoan pottery, "was certainly made on Melos" (Catling, 1963, p. 7). But the formation of Melos is Tertiary volcanic of acid composition, and consequently the local clay should be low in calcium. This observation illustrates a situation that often arises in archaeological ceramic investigations: finds from one method of study suggest re-evaluation of those obtained from an independent approach; the re-evaluation, in turn, may suggest further investigation by the first method; and so problems are solved by a repeated interplay between different methods. The question that immediately arises about Melos is the occurrence of some sedimentary formations. The geologic map shows only a small section of Cretaceous formations in the southern part, far from Phylakopi, where the sherds were collected, and shows some undifferentiated Miocene-Pliocene on the north side.

The formations plotted on a geologic map are broad guides and offer many helpful hints, but of course it would be extremely naive to expect clays of the same composition pattern to occur throughout a formation. Aside from the necessary broad generalizations of mapping, there are many factors that affect the composition of clays: composition of the parent material, the conditions prevailing during formation of the clay, and, if the clay is sedimentary rather than residual, the conditions during transport, during deposition, and subsequent to deposition. Localized conditions, such as action of hydrothermal solutions, may also have a marked effect.

Analysis of clays from production centers is a direct approach in the study of sources of fine-textured pottery. Catling, Richards, and Blin-Stoyle (1963, p. 95) dismissed this possibility because the raw clays had presumably been refined and they were dehydrated in firing. Dehydration is simply performed in analysis. Refinement of clay, which would affect relative values of some elements, would be carried out by a process of sedimentation, and the relative degree of refinement of clay and pottery could be compared optically. Since Pliocene sedimentary clay occurs in many parts of the Peloponnesus and in the Megara it would be interesting to compare the composition of clays in some of these areas with clays from the Pliocene of Minoan settlements of Crete. This would be an independent and more direct approach to the problem raised by the B pattern sherds in Thebes than reliance on pottery analyses and relative distances alone, granting that knowledge of style in the various centers is also essential.

The analysts' selection of nine elements on which to base their study was empirical; they did not consider the place of these elements in clays. Many different roles are played by chemical elements: they may be major constituents of the clay minerals, impurities in the clay, adsorbed cations, proxying atoms, and additives. The meaning of variations in amounts of elements is judged by their place in the clay. Once chemical data are studied in the light of the geological nature of ceramic materials, complementary and supplementary means of analysis will become apparent.

It is important first to have an estimate of the impurities in a sample. The calcium, magnesium, and iron are much too high in these analyses for clay minerals. Petrographic thin sections of the pottery would permit estimation of the major impurities in the pastes even though the paste is fine and presumably the clay was sedimented. I have observed particles of carbonates, iron oxides, and quartz in thin sections of classic Greek pottery. The presence of dolomite could be checked by X-ray diffraction. The significance of migratory elements, such as sodium, should also be critically evaluated. The possibility of its presence as an adsorbed cation can be checked by identification of the clay mineral; the structure of montmorillonites leads to adsorption of cations, whereas the structure of kaolinite does not. These two clay minerals can be differentiated by their silica-to-alumina ratio. Granted that silica may be present as an impurity in the form of quartz, its amount can be estimated in thin sections. Alumina was included in the analyses, but silica was omitted. The minor and trace elements may occur in the clay minerals or in the impurities of clays. The ratio of pairs of elements that are often associated may be more significant than the amounts of the elements considered individually. The values reported for nickel, chromium, manganese, and titanium are very high for clays, but they are not reported as absolute values; they are estimates conditioned by the method of analysis and are adequate for comparisons because the evaluations were consistent.

The nine elements selected for analysis are not necessarily always the most useful for differentiation. Knowledge of the geology of a region might suggest other elements that would be more significant—for instance, if alteration had taken place in areas of mineralization or in the vicinity of a hot spring, or if the formation were marine. These comments may suggest the role of geochemistry in the study of archaeological ceramics. It is a new field of application, and the theoretical frame of reference is still to be developed; but the importance of understanding the meaning of chemical composition in terms of the genesis of clays is clear.

I have commented on the Mycenaean-Minoan study in detail not only because of its importance but also because it illustrates the problems about the sources of pottery that arise when inferences are based on chemical composition alone. These comments apply equally well to results obtained by the newer methods of instrumental analysis, because they too yield chemical data. It will be sufficient to mention a few of the newer methods to suggest the difference in sample requirement, the number of elements detectable, and the differences in sensitivity.

X-ray fluorescence is a newer method than emission spectroscopy that has the advantage of adaptation to nondestructive analysis. The fact that a paint or glaze need not be removed from the surface eliminates risk of contamination and saves time as well; but quantitative results cannot be obtained if the pigment is thin or uneven. The method has been used effectively for the analysis of manganese in Greek glazes and pigments (Farnsworth and Simmons, 1963). Another application was for identification of the red color that trails beyond the lines of black paint on Urfirnis pottery (Greek Neolithic). Superficially the paint appears to change from black to red, but there is no corresponding change in surrounding surface color that would accompany a localized oxidizing effect. My experience with pottery of the American southwest led me to expect that a medium in the black mineral pigment had extended beyond it and had reacted with the clay to liberate iron. If this hypothesis is correct there should be the same percentage of iron in the red line and in the light orange body. A test of red lines and body surface with an X-ray fluorescent probe proved that the amounts of iron were the same in both. (Test made by courtesy of the U.S. Geological Survey, results unpublished.)

At present the possibilities of analysis by neutron activation are arousing interest. Spectacular results have been obtained with this method in certain specialized fields outside of archaeology. Its primary limitation lies in the number of elements it is practicable to determine. In archaeology the method has not had extensive tests comparable to those of emission spectroscopy. It was used by research workers at the Oxford Laboratory in some of their studies of differences in paste composition (Emeleus, 1958, 1960b; Simpson, 1960); they later substituted emission spectroscopy for paste analysis because it is more comprehensive and less expensive. Some pilot work in the application of neutron activation for paste analysis was undertaken in this country by E. V. Sayre and his associates (Sayre and Dodson, 1957; Sayre, Murrenhoff, and Weick, 1958). With one exception the pottery analyzed had no added nonplastics; therefore the comparisons were of clays. The exception was the only test of American Indian pottery made by Sayre; it involved comparison of tempered and untempered pastes, although allowance was not made for this condition. The most recent published report of the neutron activation method deals with tempered pottery (Bennyhoff and Heizer, 1964). The conclusions drawn from this study, which support the authors' hypothesis, are difficult to judge because of several unknown factors: the reliability of the megascopic identification of rock temper in 9 of the 11 sherds; justification for the assumption that the manganese was derived from the clay alone; and the possibility of postdepositional alteration of the sherds that might affect the percentage of the single element upon which judgment was based.

Beta-ray backscatter is a quick and inexpensive analytical method but has limited applications. It has been used effectively for the determination of lead in glazes (Emeleus, 1960a; Aitken, 1961, pp. 169–171). There are a number of other instrumental methods of chemical analysis, some of which are so new that they have not yet been used in archaeology. Those I have mentioned will suggest the wide differences in applicability and sensitivity.

Fortunately, the archaeologist does not have to rely on trial-and-error tests of new methods; he can learn from specialists in the different fields of the physical sciences the kind of results their methods give—their accuracy, their cost, the size of sample required, and whether the test is nondestructive. But first the problem must be outlined, and the archaeologist must decide which class or classes of data give the best promise of solution. This review of chemical applications in archaeological ceramics should be balanced by reference to other analytical fields.

Mineralogical analysis, the other important method of archaeological ceramic analysis, is made by means of optical mineralogy and X-ray diffraction. There are supplementary methods, morphological (electron microscope) and thermal (DTA), for example, but for our immediate purpose it is not necessary to consider them. Comparison of chemical and mineralogical methods will illustrate the necessity of evaluation and the frequent need to combine different methods in a complementary or supplementary way. The petrographic microscope has long been used for the identification of nonplastics in pottery, though far more extensively in the Americas than in the Old World. The applications of X-ray diffraction are much more recent, as is the development of the method itself. Optical mineralogy and X-ray diffraction are complementary methods because X-ray diffraction is an extremely efficient and powerful means of determining the mineralogical composition of samples too fine-grained for optical analysis. It is limited to the identification of crystalline materials, but it has shown that many materials supposed to be amorphous are actually crystalline—such as many "limonites" and most clays—but it gives no record if the material is actually amorphous. It is the essential instrument for the study of clays, and clay mineralogy has made tremendous strides since its introduction, leading to a basic classification of clays, the establishment of the relation of their properties to structure and composition, and the determination of the conditions of formation and alteration. During this period the method has been refined and elaborated. The value of X-ray diffraction in the study of clay is not matched by its applications in the study of pottery because the crystalline structure of clay is often, though not always, destroyed in firing. The problem of the identification of clay minerals in fired pottery is being investigated by a combination of methods.

Although optical crystallography is a very old method in comparison with X-ray diffraction, it, too, has undergone developments and refinements, some of which are especially advantageous in the study of pottery.

The differences between chemical and mineralogical data suggest their primary applications in archaeological ceramics: chemical methods for the analysis of paints and glazes, and fine amorphous materials; optical crystallography and X-ray diffraction for pottery with nonplastic inclusions, the natural mineral inclusions in clays, and raw clays. In the earlier years of ceramic technological investigation in the American field this distinction in application was generally followed. In recent years chemical analysis has been used more often in the analysis of pottery itself. This trend has been influenced by the physicists' interest in testing the applications of instrumental methods of analysis.

The fact that a chemical analysis, whatever its method, identifies the elements of a substance, whereas mineralogical analysis identifies minerals and rocks, means that each has its particular advantages and limitations. There is the difference in scope: all substances can be analyzed chemically, but only minerals and rocks can be identified mineralogically—which is not a serious limitation for the ceramist inasmuch as minerals and rocks are the potter's principal materials.

In contrast to scope of application is the number of distinctions that can be made by each method of analysis. In qualitative terms, chemical distinctions, on the one hand, are limited theoretically by the number of elements that it is practicable to identify, but this number may be greatly reduced by methods such as analysis by neutron activation. In mineralogical analysis, on the other hand, distinctions are made on the innumerable combinations of elements in minerals and on the combination of these again in rocks. In quantitative analysis the number of distinctions is multiplied in both methods, but, as long as chemical data alone are available, a difference in proportion of elements cannot be interpreted; it may mean differences in proportion of a constituent or a difference in constituents. An illustration will clarify this point.

In the summary of a spectrographic study of foreign pottery from Abydos (Hennessy and Millett, 1963), the authors stress the proportion of calcium: two groups of pottery were allied by very high calcium content but were otherwise quite distinct; two other pairs were very similar except for calcium. The mineralogist would immediately ask what was the source of the calcium: a calcareous clay; added calcareous temper, such as limestone—of which many varieties can be distinguished—or dolomite; shell temper; or perhaps calcareous microfossils, such as Foraminifera, in the clay, or secondary calcite deposited after discard? These questions are answered directly by optical methods.

In the study of pastes, mineralogical analysis is a more definitive means of separating pottery from distinct sources. One of the greatest advantages of mineralogical as compared with chemical analysis is that it identifies the materials the potter used, thus throwing light on the potter's techniques and also giving a clue to the source of material. The chemist can say that two pastes are similar in composition and therefore very likely came from the same source, or that they differ and consequently may have come from different sources. Chemical analysis may provide indirect means of reasoning about the kinds of materials used; but this is a geological matter, and the physicists who have been applying instrumental methods have not pursued the geological and geochemical implications of their results. The mineralogist reads the history of rock formation and subsequent alteration from the conditions and relation of the minerals.

The mineralogist will readily grant that the difficulty of analysis increases as the size of mineral grains or fragments is reduced. For refined pastes made from untempered clay, chemical analysis may represent the quicker means of establishing an arbitrary scale of comparison, but it is more than likely that chemical and mineralogical methods will complement or supplement each other in the study of most fine-grained pottery.

An illustration will suggest the potentialities of mineralogical analyses of fine pastes. Two ivory-colored sherds, one from Kaminaljuyu in the highlands of Guatemala, the other from Monte Alban in southern Mexico, appeared so similar in color, texture, and surface finish that two archaeologists who were thoroughly familiar with the pottery of Kaminaljuyu concluded that they were identical and indicated trade from one site to the other. Petrographic thin sections showed that the Kaminaljuyu sherd was distinguished by minute crystals of tourmaline. Tourmaline crystals were absent in the Monte Alban sherd, which contained abundant fine mica. These pastes would have been distinguished chemically by the presence of boron in the specimen from Kaminaljuyu, but, aside from the fact that boron has not been sought in chemical analysis of pottery, interpretation of its significance, if found, would be speculative.

In statistical studies, when a large number of sherds must be identified, optical examination of pastes with the binocular microscope for preliminary classification and comparison has a great advantage and is a valuable guide for more detailed analysis, either chemical or mineralogical. The tendency to overlook simple means of identification recalls an incident that occurred some years ago. A well known chemist in the ceramics section of the National Bureau of Standards undertook an analysis of Pueblo pottery. He thought that the clays of different river drainages might be distinguishable chemically and therefore give evidence of the source of pottery. To demonstrate the possibilities of his methods he analyzed samples of Acoma clay and Acoma pottery. The results showed that the clay and pottery were similar in composition but that something had been added to the clay, something of comparable composition. The chemist came to the conclusion that the potter had added earth from the village "in order to make the pot feel at home." Had he examined a fragment of the pottery with the binocular microscope he could have seen that it was tempered with potsherds.

Both the advantages and the limitations of the binocular microscope should be recognized. For paste analysis, it serves two main purposes: (1) to identify the custom or "tradition" of paste preparation, and (2) to distinguish the abundant from the unusual paste when a preliminary sort is made for detailed petrographic analysis with the object of distinguishing centers of production. The rapidity of classification with the binocular microscope permits sampling of sufficient size for statistical treatment of the data, and often the foreign sherds can be recognized from paste when their surface features give no suggestion that they are intrusive.

It is clear that chemical and mineralogical analyses both have their particularly appropriate applications in ceramic studies, and in many phases of investigation they supplement or complement each other. The great advantages of mineralogical analysis are that it defines the potters' materials, affords a direct guide for location of centers of production, and can be used effectively for samples of sufficient size for statistical analysis.

Use of the computer. Instrumental methods of analysis that have accelerated studies requiring chemical data are matched in statistics by computers. Even though archaeology does not demand involved mathematical calculations, the speed of operation of computers opens undreamed-of possibilities for studying correlations of features. But, to obtain meaningful answers from the computer, questions must have meaning in anthropological terms. It is clear that electronics cannot relieve the investigator of the need to exercise insight and imagination.

An excellent example of problem formulation is a study (Longacre, 1964a) of social relations in a prehistoric pueblo in eastern Arizona. Although the material objects on which archaeology usually depends give no direct information about social relations, Longacre found indirect evidence, taking as his model Pueblo Indian society in historic times, a matrilinear society in which women are the potters. He reasoned that the presence of local matrilinear groups would be reflected in ceramic decoration. He had an unusually good sample, and a computer made the statistical work practicable. His reasoning covered evidence for the use of special ritual vessels and the extent of community organization.

Although Longacre was not concerned with a study of design itself, problems of terminology arose, as in the distinction between elements and motifs, and the appropriate designation for the unit of design on which his study was based (Longacre, 1964b). Thorough, systematic analyses of design go back thirty years or more to studies that defined a careful language of design (e.g., Chapman, 1936; Kidder and Shepard, 1936; Amsden, 1936). The standards set by these pioneers in design analysis should also aid in designation of design styles; the archaeologist need not lapse into the habit of describing a style as "distinctive in feel to" a type. The difficulties of terminology will be met in Longacre's final report (personal communication), a report that will be of unusual interest as an example of problem formulation and use of the statistical method.

Ceramic ecology has been reviewed by Matson (1961), who thinks in terms of three chief elements of a ceramic technological study—physical, biological, and cultural. He discusses briefly ways in which these may affect the ceramic product. This is a holistic view of pottery for which there has long been need. Nevertheless, I will confine my remarks to the physical element. Of the three, it is the easiest to investigate directly without resort to speculation.

The importance of knowledge of the potter's materials is self-evident: the materials set limits within which the potter had to work; the status of the craft has to be judged within these limits. Furthermore, the potter's choice of materials and the ways in which he used them, together with form and style of decoration, are trade marks—our means, often powerful, of locating centers of production. This approach to the study of trade relations was illustrated many years ago with the first extensive petrographic analysis of pottery in the American field (Kidder and Shepard, 1936; Shepard, 1942; summarized, Shepard, 1965?). The location of sources of tempering material demonstrated that there was far more extensive trade in pottery than had been considered probable up to that time. The study also showed that control, by favorably located communities, of material essential for the production of glaze limited the area of production and, in turn, stimulated trade. The primary basis of the study was petrographic analysis of temper. Simple differences in the clays were recognized—for example, the occurrence of mont-morillonite in a volcanic region, and the relation of the properties of this class of clay to the production of a black carbon paint. The relation of the distribution of red- and buff-burning clays to that of red and buff pottery was also noted. These were simple observations that in no way matched the petrographic identification of nonplastic materials as sources of basic data. At that time X-ray diffraction, now recognized as the fundamental and essential method for identification of clay minerals, had not been used in archaeology.

The value of X-ray diffraction is demonstrated in a study (in preparation) of Yucatecan potters' clays (Shepard, "Technology of contemporary Yucatecan pottery"). These clays are from a seemingly monotonous limestone country, and their physical properties are similar; yet differences in their mineralogy explain unusual ceramic effects obtained by Yucatecan potters. The importance of clay mineralogy in archaeology is just beginning to be recognized, because ideas mineralogists held about clays in the early part of this century have persisted not only in the popular mind but generally outside the geologic profession, and, with them, the idea that a few simple physical tests are sufficient to define a clay.

On pages 7–10 and 374–377 three of the principal classes of clay minerals are briefly described. To this classification should be added the fibrous clay minerals palygorskite and sepiolite, which were originally omitted because they were con-sidered rare at the time of writing. The place of field studies in ceramic techno-logical investigation is strikingly demonstrated by comparing results of my Rio Grande and Yucatecan studies with those in the central and highland Maya area. In the Maya area there was little field work, and even sampling of pottery was often sketchy and spotty in consequence of the status of archaeology at the time. Field work with archaeological expeditions is an essential part of the ceramic technolo-gist's program.

The classification of pottery. Important changes in classification come about with better understanding of the objects that are being ordered, understanding that reveals new, more fundamental relationships. The history of clay mineralogy affords a clear illustration. During the early part of the century there was a welter of clay mineral names, and confusion in identification. Attempts to reach agree-ment on names would have been a poor palliative, because the fundamental prop-erties of the clay minerals were not understood. In the late twenties, with the applications of X-ray analysis, the basic structure of the clay minerals was eluci-dated and simple, logical classification developed from new fundamental knowledge.

Pottery classification has not been shaken by revolutionary ideas in recent years. Perhaps taxonomists are conservatives; they have concentrated on elaboration and extension of existing methods. Although they have remained interested in pottery primarily as a tool for establishing relative chronology, they have approached the problem of classification with different philosophies, and their results have differed even when they were trained in the same hotbed, the American southwest. The differences can be appreciated by comparison of the systems proposed for the pottery of the Sudan (Adams, 1964) and the Maya area (Smith, Willey, and Gifford, 1960). Adams' method combines analysis and synthesis. His analysis is based on five categories: fabric, form, decorative style, surface colors, and surface treatment, of which fabric, form, and style are considered sufficiently complex and regular to allow for comprehensive classification. The synthesis consists of recognizing recurring combinations of all five factors. Adams believes that such combinations of traits recurring with any frequency can only be dictated by cultural traditions together with available raw material. He reasons further that "Any one ware can nearly always be interpreted as the product of a group of people sharing a common cultural tradition and a common environment." This meaning of a basic ceramic category seems a desirable objective of classification (p. 309). I will not judge Adams' system in detail, because I have not worked with Sudanese pottery, but I believe that his combination of analysis and synthesis, his logical reasoning about the significance of features, and his clear exposition are essential for sound classification.

The system of classification that has been borrowed from the North American southwest and applied in the Maya area (Smith, Willey, and Gifford, 1960) recommends a different procedure. "Operationally, . . . one must first sort the material into ceramic units that are distinct from one another only because each represents a combination of attributes which, when observed together, is separable from some other combination of ceramic attributes" (*op. cit.*, p. 333). This is a sorting technique, and units selected are combinations of features. Although definitions for "attributes," "modes," and "features" are proposed, the reliability with which they can be recognized, their relative value for classification, and their significance for understanding the place of pottery in the culture are not discussed. Classification is by the look-feel method. The role of the archaeologist's "feel" for pottery I have discussed (pp. 97–100). I would not modify that discussion, but I hope that awareness of the limitations of pottery sense will curb the dogmatism of the classifier who relies on this means alone.

The role of ceramic taxonomy can be better understood when it is viewed in its historical setting. The intensive study of potsherds became a necessity with the development of stratigraphic excavation. Doubtless the most fortunate results of this change in ceramic studies has been the greatly extended possibilities of statistical treatment of ceramic data; and now, with the overwhelming accumulation of sherds that come from modern digs, it offers the archaeologist a means of meeting the demand for description. Nevertheless, concentration on type classification has become so intensive at times that its limitations as a means of studying pottery seem to have been forgotten. The reliability of a classification depends on distinctiveness of features, size and state of preservation of the sherd, the classifier's success in completing description of such major features as shape and decoration by comparison with those of entire vessels, and also on the attitude of the classifier. Adams' statement (*op. cit.*, p. 128) of the proportion of sherds that he attempts to classify reveals a realistic grasp of the limitations of sherd classification.

As long as the type is used only for relative chronological ordering, the percentage of error in classification that occurs with favorable samples can be tolerated. When the type is recommended as a means of pursuing broader studies, its inadequacies should be understood. Two examples will illustrate this point.

Study of the economics of pottery and of the effects of traded pottery on local ceramic development commences with differentiation of indigenous and trade pottery. Proponents of the type-variety system assume that this distinction is made in their classification. Some years of experience in pottery analysis, particularly in the Maya area, have taught me that the sherds from traded vessels are often unrecognized when reliance is placed on examination of surficial features because of absence of definitive surface characteristics or superficial resemblance to well known local types. The student who would follow the history of trade in pottery needs more conclusive evidence than that offered by the type-variety concept.

Decorative design of pottery is an attractive and open field of investigation. The difference between a study of pottery design as art and as a means of type classification is illustrated by a recent study (Grieder, 1964). Irrespective of one's evaluation of Grieder's specific conclusions, his refreshingly original and clearly presented ideas were developed without reference to the type-variety concept. The student who accepts that concept as the starting point for all ceramic studies will indeed be shackled.

The ethnologist's contribution. The stimulating ideas of the ethnologists are well illustrated by Foster (1961), who reasons about the social position of the potter in peasant societies, considering the economic status of the potter as well as the dirtiness of the work as factors. He discusses the risks of production as they affect the potter's conservatism in the practice of his craft, which is in turn reflected in his basic personality.

Foster summarizes the factors affecting the "dynamics of pottery": innovation, stabilization, and disappearance of particular styles and techniques. His arguments are fully illustrated by records from the literature as well as from his own extensive experience in Mexico. He recognizes some exceptions to his generalizations and also weighs the influence of tourist trade as it influences the market and innovation.

These are welcome ideas for the archaeologist; they should stimulate a careful study of the way some of the factors reviewed by Foster can be studied in an archaeological context. The archaeologist cannot draw direct analogies from Foster's data, because he is handicapped by dependence on material remains, and the social and economic conditions of contemporary and prehistoric potters are not the same. Foster attributes the general low social status of the potter in peasant societies in part to low economic status, pottery being less remunerative than other occupations. The extent of trade is a means of judging popularity. A distance of 150 miles is the maximum Foster gives for direct transport of pottery in various parts of the world. A systematic study of trade pottery from archaeological context would throw much light on economic conditions. As compared with Foster's 150 miles, we have evidence of airline distances of well over 500 miles for transport of well defined classes of Mesoamerican pottery such as Thin Orange and Plumbate. Exchange of pottery between communities of a region is also amenable to investigation, as I suggested with an example from Oaxaca (Shepard, 1963).

Foster suggests (1) that market demands spur innovations in styles and production techniques, (2) that a common knowledge of methods and styles leads to stability, and (3) that technical secrets and possession of incorporeal rights to stylistic features by individuals can account for the sudden disappearance of these features with the death of the individuals. These ideas about the "dynamics of pottery" should be a challenge to the archaeologist to test for evidence in archaeological contexts. Trade can be recognized, given an adequate sample and an efficient method of identification. The extent to which knowledge of a craft was shared will be more difficult to ascertain even indirectly, although Longacre's (1964a) method of investigating social structure suggests possibilities. There are other conditions that influence the history of pottery, and the archaeologist does not limit his studies to peasant societies. For example, the early introduction of painted design together with the use of several distinctive classes of pigment in Basket Maker III pottery rested on a high development of basketry design and familiarity with native dyes and body paints. Evidently, on the invention of a totally new craft, there was a period of experimentation stimulated perhaps by the unexplored possibilities of new techniques and the chance to use materials familiar from other crafts in different ways. Pueblo I to III pottery shows a dull conservatism in technique matched by diverse and fascinating developments in design. Foster describes the potter in the peasant societies as a craftsman uninterested in creative expression and refers to studies in which only one or two "artists" have been found in a community. But one or two are enough for invention, whether it be technical or artistic. The history of glaze paint ware in the southwest affords clear examples of invention and also of the controlling influence of local material. Thus, Foster's suggestions can sprout new shoots as well as branch out in various directions, provided that we study the archaeological record thoroughly.

Collaboration of archaeologist and ceramic analyst.   This sketchy review of the recent course of ceramic studies underlines the primary role of problem formulation. It is foolish to shop for the latest analytical methods just to learn what they will do with raw ceramic data, but with pertinent questions, wise choice of analytical methods, and collaborative pursuit of investigation there are untouched possibilities of obtaining answers. If I were rewriting *Ceramics for the Archaeologist* I would not change the Introduction, because it expresses concern for the place of pottery in the life of a people. Nor would I change the organization of the book by placing the chapter on classification first "because the archaeologist starts with the classification," as was suggested by one eminent critic of the original manuscript. I am as confident now as I was then that knowledge of the potter's materials and methods is needed for sound classification.

Study of ceramic evidence of the different aspects of man's life calls for a variety of specialists. On the economic side, material evidence is important. Possibilities of identifying trade pottery were sensed long ago with the recognition of "intrusives" distinguished by style. Exact methods of identifying materials tremendously extended the range of possible identifications. Ceramic contributions to the understanding of the social relations, well illustrated by Longacre's study (1964a), is a new field that requires a well defined model for a problem. Ceramic decorative art calls for a specialist trained in aesthetics, and, to study ceramic reflections of religious ideas, anthropological background is needed. But these are not isolated compartments of investigation; they are closely interwoven and interdependent. Clearly, the study of pottery in its cultural context demands close collaboration of ceramic analyst and archaeologist, a collaboration expressed in interchange of information, interplay of ideas, and cross-checking of evidence throughout a study. The custom of submitting a few "representative sherds" for technological analysis belongs to the past; obviously unsound, it has been allowed to linger in practice much too long.

The meaning of collaboration was well stated by Johnson some years ago (1951). He recalls Webster's definition of the verb to collaborate, "to labor together," and comments (quotations by permission of the University of Michigan Press):

"There can be no greater aid to a collaboration than the possession by the participants of, as a minimum, a sympathetic understanding of at least the theoretical background of the fields involved. Such an understanding indicates the range of the subject matter and the limitations of the results, and makes possible the mutual understanding of the methodology used by each participant."

I cannot express my attitude toward collaboration more effectively than Johnson has in two paragraphs:

"Another point is that an archaeologist, or any one else for that matter, should not present his collaborating colleague with a mass of samples or specimens and a sheaf of undigested field notes and expect him to answer all, or even a few, questions. To do this is to expect a miracle, and furthermore this is the opposite of the idea of collaboration. It is desirable that collaborators work together in the field. Such labors do not necessarily add specific details but they do provide an invaluable point of view. For example, when an archaeologist climbs out of his trench to spend time ranging the country with his colleague who is a geologist, the minute details in the profile appear in a perspective which enhances their significance (sometimes their insignificance) in a startling manner. It is true also that work in the field, when combined in this way, will open new lines of attack. While data are being collected, it is often possible by trial and error, if by no other way, to modify the several lines of investigation so that the field work will keep pace with steadily expanding problems. If left until the close of a field season, the analysis of several sets of field notes brings to light inevitable lacunae preventing the development of ideas which in a field collaboration would have been investigated on the spot.

"The collaboration must be carried through all the steps in the research. The participants must understand how each one processes his data and compiles the results. In each of these stages the interchange of ideas is essential, and the success of the venture depends largely upon a mutual understanding and tolerance of everyone's trials and tribulations."

These ideas are well illustrated by Johnson's own research.

Ceramics for the Archaeologist would not have been written had I doubted that archaeologists could benefit from knowledge of the nature of ceramic materials and processes, the methods of village potters, the principles and evaluation of analytical methods, and critical judgment of the objectives of analysis. But general background must be complemented by the specialized training and experience of the professional ceramic technologist. Recognizing the distinction, I omitted details of analytical procedure except for simple tests that can be performed in the field. It would have been presumptuous to offer substitutes for the formal training in geology, chemistry, physics, and mathematics that a ceramic analyst requires.

How the archaeologist is to obtain analytical collaboration is an open question. Many opportunities for interesting studies are passed by because a ceramic technologist is not available, or samples are submitted to analysts who have no special background for the work and routine results are accepted without thought of interpretation. Ideally, a ceramic technologist is a specialist with multiple skills and interests. His major fields of training are geology and ceramics. In his geological training, optical mineralogy, geochemistry, and clay mineralogy are important. In ceramics he should be familiar with methods of village potters and the effect of low firing temperatures on ceramic materials, matters with which the commercial ceramist has little concern. He should also understand the principles, possibilities, and limitations of the various methods of chemical and physical analysis, and he should have training in statistical methods. Aside from his specialties, he needs background in archaeology. A student should weigh carefully the chances of obtaining full collaboration before he enters a field with such unusual requirements.

Archaeologists have opportunities for collaboration with specialists in the fields in which the ceramic technologist should be trained. As an example, Professor Charles B. Hunt suggested that archaeologists seek the assistance of petrographers who are thoroughly familiar with the geology of the area of their excavation. There are many possibilities that will become apparent with closer collaboration of archaeologist and specialist.

Archaeological ceramic technology, having grown haphazardly, has reached a period of ferment. New analytical procedures are at our disposal. To use them effectively, we must focus our efforts on problems of broad significance, define them clearly, and choose analytical methods critically. The time for discipline has come, and the responsibility for sound development is shared by archaeologist and ceramic analyst.

Acknowledgment. I am indebted to Dr. Harry A. Tourtelott of the U.S. Geological Survey for his criticism of the first draft of the manuscript and for his stimulating discussion of the geochemistry of clays.

REFERENCES

ADAMS, W. Y.
1962 Introductory classification of Christian Nubian pottery. *Kush*, vol. 10, pp. 245–88. Khartoum.
1964 An introductory classification of Meroitic pottery. *Kush*, vol. 12, pp. 126–73. Khartoum.
AITKEN, M. J.
1961 Physics and archaeology. New York.
AMSDEN, C. A.
1936 An analysis of Hohokam pottery design. *Medallion Papers*, no. 23. Globe.
BENNYHOFF, J. A., AND R. F. HEIZER
1964 Neutron activation analysis of some Cuicuilco and Teotihuacan pottery: Archaeological interpretation of results. *Amer. Antiquity*, vol. 30, pp. 348–49. Salt Lake City.
BLIN-STOYLE, A. E., AND E. E. RICHARDS
1961 Spectrographic analysis of Mycenaean and Minoan pottery: II. Method and interim results. *Archaeometry*, vol. 4, pp. 33–38. Oxford.
CATLING, H. W.
1961 Spectrographic analysis of Mycenaean and Minoan pottery: I. Introductory note. *Archaeometry*, vol. 4, pp. 31–33. Oxford.

1963   Minoan and Mycenaean pottery: Composition and provenance. *Archaeometry*, vol. 6, pp. 1–9. Oxford.

——, E. E. RICHARDS, AND A. E. BLIN-STOYLE

1963   Correlations between composition and provenance of Mycenaean and Minoan pottery. *Annual of the British School of Archaeology at Athens*, vol. 58, pp. 94–115.

CHAPMAN, K. M.

1936   The pottery of Santo Domingo Pueblo. *Mem. Lab. Anthropol.*, vol. 1. Santa Fe.

EMELEUS, V. M.

1958   The technique of neutron activation analysis as applied to trace element determination in pottery and coins. *Archaeometry*, vol. 1, no. 1, pp. 6–16. Oxford.

1960a   Beta ray backscattering: A simple method for the quantitative determination of lead oxide in glass, glaze and pottery. *Archaeometry*, vol. 3, pp. 5–9. Oxford.

1960b   Neutron activation analysis of Samian ware sherds. *Archaeometry*, vol. 3, pp. 16–19. Oxford.

FARNSWORTH, M., AND I. SIMMONS

1963   Coloring agents for Greek glazes. *Amer. Jour. Archaeol.*, vol. 67, no. 4, pp. 389–96. New York.

FOSTER, G. M.

1961   The sociology of pottery: Questions and hypotheses arising from contemporary Mexican work.   *Wenner-Gren Foundation for Anthropological Research. In* Ceramics and man, F. R. Matson, editor (in press). Chicago.

GRIEDER, T.

1964   Representation of space and form in Maya painting on pottery. *Amer. Antiquity*, vol. 29, pp. 442–48. Salt Lake City.

HENNESSY, J. B., AND A. MILLETT

1963   Spectrographic analysis of the foreign pottery from the royal tombs of Abydos and early bronze age pottery of Palestine. *Archaeometry*, vol. 6, pp. 10–17. Oxford.

HODGES, H. W.

1964   Artifacts: An introduction to early materials and technology. Praeger. New York.

JOHNSON, F.

1951   Collaboration among scientific fields with special reference to archaeology. *In* Essays on archaeological methods, J. B. Griffin, editor. *Anthropol. Papers*, no. 8, pp. 34–50. Ann Arbor.

KIDDER, A. V., AND A. O. SHEPARD

1936   The pottery of Pecos, vol. 2. New Haven.

LONGACRE, W. A.

1964a   Archaeology as anthropology: a case study. *Science*, vol. 144, no. 3625, pp. 1454–55. Washington.

1964b   Sociological implications of the ceramic analysis. *In* Paul S. Martin, Chapters in the prehistory of eastern Arizona, II. *Fieldiana: Anthropology*, vol. 55, pp. 155–170. Chicago.

Matson, F. R.
   1961   Ceramic ecology: An approach to the study of the early cultures of the Near
          East. *Wenner-Gren Foundation for Anthropological Research. In* Ceramics and
          man, F. R. Matson, editor (in press). Chicago.
Renz, C., N. Liatsikas, and Il. Paraskevaidis, compilers
   1954   Geologic Map of Greece. The Institute for Geology and Subsurface Research.
Sayre, E. V., and R. W. Dodson
   1957   Neutron activation study of Mediterranean potsherds. *Amer. Jour. Archaeol.*,
          vol. 61, p. 35. New York.
——, A. Murrenhoff, and C. F. Weick
   1958   The nondestructive analysis of ancient potsherds through neutron activation.
          Brookhaven Nat. Lab., Pub. 508. New York.
Shepard, A. O.
   1942   Rio Grande glaze paint ware: A study illustrating the place of ceramic techno-
          logical analysis in archaeological research. *Carnegie Inst. Wash.*, Pub. 528, Con-
          trib. 39. Washington.
   1963   Beginnings of ceramic industrialization: An example from the Oaxaca Valley.
          Notes from a Ceramic Laboratory, 2. *Carnegie Inst. Wash.* Washington.
   1965? Rio Grande glaze-paint pottery: a test of petrographic analysis. *Wenner-Gren
          Foundation for Anthropological Research. In* Ceramics and man, F. R. Matson,
          editor (in press). Chicago.
Simpson, G.
   1960   Notes on Gaulish Samian pottery and its analysis by neutron activation. *Archae-
          ometry*, vol. 3, pp. 20–24. Oxford.
Smith, R. E., G. R. Willey, and J. C. Gifford
   1960   The type-variety concept as a basis for the analysis of Maya pottery. *Amer.
          Antiquity*, vol. 25, no. 3, pp. 330–39. Salt Lake City.

Anna O. Shepard

June 1965

Preface

THE CERAMIC technologist who attempts to write a general book on ceramics finds himself in the position of a leopard who would like to hide his spots. The high degree of his specialization makes him acutely aware of the need for placing his own interests in proper perspective and establishing a ground of common understanding with the archaeologist. The archaeologist, for his part, also tends to become a specialist when he turns his attention to pottery because he deals primarily with potsherds and he uses them in the main to establish time-space frames of reference. As long as ceramic research is divided between archaeologist and ceramic technologist, it is highly desirable—I am tempted to say imperative— that both understand the fundamentals of ceramics, the principles and limitations of analytical methods, and the objectives of archaeological research. If it is important for the archaeologist to understand the nature of ceramic materials and techniques, it is no less important for the technologist to know the archaeological context of the pottery submitted to him and to understand the problems the archaeologist is trying to solve, the reconstructions he desires to make, in order to recognize how his data fit into the human picture. Archaeologist and technologist cannot remain within the shells of their respective specialties when they join efforts because they share problems and their means of investigation are complementary. If they are to work together efficiently, they must have a common pool of knowledge and understand each other's methods and sources of information. It is the aim of this book to contribute to this pool of common interest and understanding.

Since I entered the ceramic field by way of archaeology and have never forgotten the sense of hopelessness I experienced on opening a book on optical crystallography for the first time, I can understand the archaeologist's attitude toward the physics and chemistry of pottery. It is not surprising if he doubts that he can acquire, in the time available to him, the background of information and the experience that will enable him to grasp the significance of technological questions and recognize when analysis is needed and what it can contribute. He learns something by making pottery himself, particularly if he follows primitive methods and tries to reproduce prehistoric wares, and he can also learn much by observing present-day prewheel potters at work. It is desirable that he do both of these things, but these alone are not enough. Unguided practice is slow and uncertain; the primitive potter can demonstrate how certain effects are obtained, but cannot explain their causes or teach underlying principles. Principles are explained in ceramic literature, but much of this literature presupposes training in chemistry and physics. It is also heavily weighted with discussions of modern commercial applications and does not touch on many questions relating to low-fired ware. Hence the need for a book written for the archaeologist, one that presents the essential facts regarding ceramic materials and processes, makes the properties of pottery more meaningful, and evaluates methods of analysis and description in terms of archaeological objectives. This demands that at times the technologist step out of his role of specialist.

The first section of this book, devoted to the properties and sources of ceramic material, is an attempt to summarize present knowledge in so far as it is relevant to the archaeologist's interests. This section has been difficult to put in simple, readable form because the modern concept of clay rests upon extensive research in chemistry, crystallography, and physics. Moreover, scientific and technical writing cannot always be translated satisfactorily into a popular vocabulary, nor can particular ideas be abstracted and fully comprehended without knowledge of the principles upon which they rest. Yet this tough part of our survey cannot be sidestepped because there are many facts about clay which we need to know in order to understand and explain the characteristics of pottery. Consequently, the reader will find between the lines of this section a plea for his patience and co-operation.

In the second section, on ceramic practices, I have drawn largely on the methods of present-day prewheel potters for illustration because they offer many parallels to prehistoric practice and often suggest observations which can be made in the study of prehistoric techniques. I have also attempted to indicate how knowledge of ceramics will aid the ethnologist in making more complete and useful records.

The third section, devoted to ceramic analysis, requires some explanation. In the first place, I have tried to make it inclusive and have therefore treated pottery shape and decoration as well as physical properties, composition of materials, and techniques of manufacture. Pottery style, no less than paste composition or firing method, affords opportunities for experimental work and analytical approach. Equally important is the fact that we should attempt to grasp the task of pottery analysis as a whole and to realize how the study of one feature may aid in interpreting another. The microscopic examination of pastes and the description of design may appear to be unrelated tasks; but the paste was prepared and the design painted within the same cultural milieu, and each throws some light on the practices, traditions, and tastes which guided them. Only as we study these features together and give due heed to their interrelations can we appreciate fully their meaning.

As for the technical parts of the section on analysis, I have attempted to indicate the observations, tests, and interpretations that it is practicable for the archaeologist himself to make. I have also given an explanation of laboratory methods that is intended to aid the archaeologist in judging the kind of questions that can be answered, what to expect, and what is required for analysis. I have intentionally avoided set outlines and procedures because I believe that the nature of our materials and the continual progress of the sciences on which we are dependent render fixed procedures hampering. The questions that pottery raises are constantly being formulated in new contexts and the features of pottery never have the same relative importance; furthermore we have every reason to believe that methods of analysis will continue to be refined and extended, even though the value and wide usefulness of certain methods have been well established. The important thing is to understand the principles and purposes of analysis. Methods must be kept flexible, and the student must ever be alert to new evidence. Pasteur has said, "in the field of observation, chance only favors the prepared mind." The prepared mind is not one conditioned by routine.

The last section, on the evaluation of ceramic data, I have approached with some hesitancy because the archaeologist is better prepared than the ceramic specialist to write a general critique. Perhaps my principal excuse for attempting it is that I believe it is so important that we can afford to consider the viewpoint of anyone who will make a serious, independent evaluation.

In writing this book I have drawn on the experience of a number of years. As I think back over those years, the names of people to whom I am indebted come as a flood into my mind. The list is too long to name them all individually and they cannot be separated arbitrarily by degrees of importance. Therefore, I shall simply acknowledge the debts. First, there was the demand for analysis by scientific-spirited archaeologists, men who were fully alert to the possibilities of new and more exact methods, men whose interest and eagerness burned with a bright and steady flame. Then followed the unstinted and unremitting help of scientists, the advice, the assistance, the encouragement and criticism of men in many branches of science, men of the Carnegie Institution's Geophysical Laboratory, the U. S. Geological Survey, the National Bureau of Standards, university faculties, and many others. But these could only have built castles in the air had it not been for the support of institutions whose policy it is to venture into new fields. Finally, there has been the opportunity to test the value and significance of methods, an opportunity contributed to by all archaeologists who have submitted material, whether that was done hopefully or skeptically. Archaeologists, geologists, chemists, and physicists have all played a role in building this branch of archaeology; sometimes they have played it unwittingly, more often they have played it consciously and enthusiastically. Their efforts have been generous, at times self-sacrificing. I would not single out one from another. They constitute a whole.

Direct contributions in the preparation of the book call for acknowledgment. The illustrations were drawn by Miss Ann Trucksess, who also participated in testing methods of classification and composed experimental figures 50d,e, 51, and 52a. The greater part of the stenographic work was done by Mrs. Mary McKinstry and Mr. Lloyd Baysdorfer. Mrs. McKinstry brought to a tedious chore the lively interest of a student's mind. Mr. Baysdorfer bent unusual qualifications to the task of proofreading, and I am indebted to him for many reminders of the reader's point of view. An early draft of the manuscript was read by Drs. James B. Griffin, Emil W. Haury, A. V. Kidder, H. E. D. Pollock, and Gordon R. Willey, for whose comments and criticisms I am grateful. I am indebted to Mrs. W. H. Harrison for the interest and understanding that she brought to her task. Many times she has exceeded her duty as editor of the Department of Archaeology. It is with deep appreciation that I acknowledge the encouragement that Dr. Pollock has given me in the preparation of the book. The role that his interest in scientific method and his confidence of its value in archaeology have played in the undertaking cannot be measured, but when I recall the many times they acted as a stimulant and how often they carried me over rough spots, I know that they were indispensable.

Anna O. Shepard

November 1954

Contents

Illustrations

Tables

Introduction

THE FACT that the archaeologist draws his knowledge of prehistoric cultures largely from the remains of material things places him in a unique position with relation to the physical sciences. Although he works in the field of the social sciences, he can apply the methods of analysis which the laboratory sciences offer, and he has long shown readiness to avail himself of the opportunity. For their part, scientists in other fields have taken keen interest in archaeological materials. Thus, chemical analyses of metal objects were made as early as 1796, long before archaeology had become a systematic discipline; petrographic analyses of thin sections of pottery were published in 1893, only 31 years after transparent sections of rock were first prepared and the microscope was adapted to their study; and investigation of the value of carbon[14] for dating archaeological material followed close on Nagasaki and Hiroshima. It may be said that the attitude of the archaeologist is in part a reflection of the conditioning of our minds in this age; we are predisposed to look to the sciences for short cuts and new solutions. But psychological climate is not an adequate explanation. Materials must lend themselves to the laboratory and the results of analysis must have meaning in terms of culture history to command the archaeologist's attention.

The relation of archaeology to certain of the sciences is so intimate that their individual contributions can hardly be separated and evaluated independently. One of the most telling examples of this interplay of disciplines is the correlation of geological and archaeological data in the study of Early Man. Despite the archaeologist's fortunate position in relation to the sciences, however, much of the analytical work he requires is on the level of identification and is farmed out to different specialists—animal bones to the zoologist, shells to the conchologist, plant remains to the botanist, rocks to the petrographer, metals to the metallurgist, and so on. When, as in these cases, the archaeologist does not have an opportunity actually to participate—does not formulate questions and follow developments—it is difficult for him to interpret results and relate them to archaeological problems, and the instances in which raw data serve as springboards for further investigation are all too infrequent. Furthermore, the routine analysis demanded for identification is not stimulating to the analyst. His contribution is far short of what it could and should be. Consequently, those problems that demand more of scientific method than mere identification offer advantages to both the archaeologist and the analyst.

Pottery presents such problems. The archaeologist not only needs to know the composition of paste and paint, he also wants to learn as much as he can about the potter's techniques, and then he goes beyond this to judge technical development and to consider its causes and relations to development in other fields of human activity. Since he is dealing with something that at times was traded, he has occasion to separate indigenous from foreign pottery, and he should be prepared to recognize when imports influenced local practices.

There is another and quite different reason why ceramic study demands more than routine identification. Composition of material and nature of techniques combine to make pottery one of the most complex artifacts that early man has left. The range in properties of clays alone is very great, and their chemistry and mineralogy are intricate. To recognize the potter's methods is likewise a challenge because techniques are diversified and even more because clay is changed to a different kind of material in firing.

The qualities of an artifact—its usefulness, durability, beauty—are determined by its material and method of manufacture. A study that neglected method of production would indeed be superficial. In reporting on a textile, it is not considered sufficient to describe color, texture, and feel; fibers and weaves are identified. Methods of making stone tools have been the subject of experimentation designed to establish characteristic marks of various processes. Metal tools are analyzed to determine composition and to check for evidence of alloying, casting, and annealing. The student of pottery goes no further when he determines the nature of paste and paint, and seeks evidence of the methods of forming, finishing, decorating, and firing.

The fact that the technological aspects of pottery are not fully explored can be attributed in no small measure to the complexity of the problems that are presented and the need for laboratory investigations. The role of instrumental analysis in the study of a craft technique bears a direct relation to the nature of materials and techniques and to the development of the craft. The more complex the material and the more involved the technique, the greater the opportunities to apply laboratory methods. This fact, together with the abundance in which pottery occurs, means that more analytical work is required than interested scientists can handle in their spare time; consequently, ceramic technology has come to be recognized as a specialized field within archaeology. It does not follow from this circumstance that ceramic technology is something to be set apart as the domain of the specialist. It is the interest and concern of everyone who deals with pottery. Moreover, the observations and deductions of the archaeologist who possesses an understanding of the nature of ceramic materials and processes can constitute an essential contribution. From the start, therefore, we should think of technology as an integral part of ceramic studies and not merely as the responsibility of the specialist.

It may be well to recall how greatly the course of development of archaeological field methods has influenced the trend of ceramic studies. The excavator's spade determines the kind of ceramic material with which we work. The early explorers sought specimens that could grace a museum shelf. They paid little attention to potsherds and, when they discussed pottery, they were likely to speculate on the functions of particular shapes, the symbolism of designs, and how the first pot came to be made. A great change took place when stratigraphic methods of excavation were introduced because the trenching of refuse heaps resulted in the collection of great quantities of sherds but few entire vessels, hence the archaeologist was forced to use pottery in its fragmentary condition in order to compare the content of one level with that of another. Dependence on sherds forced him to give more attention to secondary features, such as rim shape, and to physical properties that can be judged by inspection, such as surface color, hardness, and luster, and paste texture and color. Many of these properties are difficult to describe adequately because they exhibit a wide and continuous range of variations and our vocabulary is not precise enough to designate the distinctions that should be made. Moreover, one man's impressions differ from those of another since judgment is influenced by experience. To meet these difficulties, much attention has been given to nomenclature and to the criteria by which pottery types can be established.

These developments were coupled with a shift in interest and purpose. The study of stratigraphic material demonstrated that pottery is an extremely useful tool for seriating and correlating finds and establishing relative chronologies. As its value in cultural correlation became apparent, it received less attention as a facet of culture. As an object apart from its original purpose, it became a tool, a marker for a period of occupation, and the paleontologist's term "index fossil" was borrowed for the pottery type having a short vertical range, indicating a short period of manufacture.

Technological analysis was a logical development in a period of intensified interest in pottery and concentration on the features that can be judged from sherds. Laboratory methods offer an attractive precision of results, and generally they can be applied to stratigraphic and surface survey collections as satisfactorily as to whole vessels. For example, the sherd that gives only a hint of decoration and leaves one guessing the shape of the vessel is perfectly adequate for petrographic analysis of paste. Consequently, technology has tied in with the current trend in ceramic studies and has aided in the refinement of descriptive methods. Among other things, the technologist has proposed reference standards for color, hardness, and texture, and has pointed out the value of composition of paste and paint and of various techniques of manufacture as criteria of identification. The soundness of systems of classification has concerned him, particularly the selection of criteria directly related to the purposes of a system and the rejection of those irrelevant criteria which attract by their conspicuousness and ease of application. Nevertheless, serving as a supplement to taxonomy has not been the principal objective of ceramic technology. The scope and aims of the two disciplines, as well as their procedures, differ. The basic purpose of ceramic technology is to study pottery in terms of its materials and methods of manufacture. Early in the course of technological research, the value of data on source of raw material for the identification of traded pottery became apparent. Such evidence throws light on trade relations, contacts of people, and interactions of cultures; and it is also fundamental in pottery classification. This interplay of approaches shows that ceramic technology cannot be narrowly compartmentalized.

The specialization that followed from detailed study of the potsherds turned out in stratigraphic excavation and collected in surface survey has not gone unchallenged. Some anthropologists, observing the enthusiasm with which the naming and description of types has been pursued, have feared that taxonomy might become an end in itself. Moreover, such expressions as "ancestral type," "hybrid type," and "mutation" have been used often enough to give the impression that the role of the potter was being forgotten. I suggest that what the technologist can do to offset the restricting effect of dependence on sherds is more important than his contribution to taxonomic methods. The possibility that a specialist can help counteract a trend toward over-specialization may seem paradoxical, but the reason is simple. Since the technologist is concerned with the way pottery is made, he must study what potters did and how they did it. The person who thinks of laboratory procedures as mechanical may be surprised by the suggestion that technological analysis constantly reminds one of the role of the potter, but actually there is a direct and inevitable relation. The technologist must go beyond outward appearance to the causes of properties, and he would argue that to ignore the potter's technique is to skip the most important preparatory step in any ceramic inquiry, because it leaves the student without adequate basis for differentiating fundamental from incidental properties or intrusive from indigenous products; and he therefore is unprepared to sift data for clues to the part played in ceramic development by properties of materials, custom, individual inventiveness, and foreign influence. In stating the role of ceramic technology, I am inclined, therefore, to stress, not its accuracy and reliability, not the data it recovers, not even the special advantages it offers for determining the sources and relationships of pottery, for these contributions are recognized, in some measure at least. Rather,

I would bring out the fact that ceramic technology places the human factor in proper perspective.

Awareness of the potter's role means interest in pottery as a product of human skill and intelligence and as a facet of culture. The technologist's leaning toward the study of the origin and relationships of pottery techniques and the history of ceramics in relation to the total culture is not difficult to explain. We have only to recall the unique place that ceramics holds among our industries. Consider the history of tool manufacturing. Man started with stone, bone, and wood. Then he discovered metals, and all these other materials became obsolete for tools. The lithic industry has no ties with the present; it marks a stage in cultural development on which the curtain was rung down long ago. But ceramics has an unbroken history from its beginning to the present, for clay has piqued man's curiosity and nurtured his ingenuity through the ages. At first he learned only by the painfully slow process of trial and error, thus gradually building a lore of the craft which expanded from age to age as new effects were obtained by happy accident or persistent effort. Then, finally, with the rise of science, he began to understand something about the way in which clay originates and to generalize about its properties. But he still could not explain satisfactorily such fundamental properties as plasticity, and the variety of ill-defined clays he had named was confusing. Only during the past 25-30 years have we begun to gain a clearer concept of the nature of clay through research employing new methods of the physical sciences, and even now much remains to be learned.

The complexity of clay—the fact that it is not a single mineral substance but may be any one of several, or a mixture of them, and that it practically always carries impurities which affect its properties markedly—has much to do with the fact that it has long been a challenging thing to investigate. Beyond this is the ease with which man can completely alter its constitution and its properties, not in a single well-defined way but in innumerable ways. In most primitive industries, the process of artifact making is a simple mechanical one—the stone is chipped, pecked, or ground; the plant stem is peeled and split; the hide is scraped and kept pliable by dressing—but when clay is fired it becomes a different substance and not one change but many take place. Something entirely new has been created, and thus the first potter can be called one of the first chemical engineers.

I. Ceramic Materials: Their Composition, Sources, and Properties

CLAYS

W E ARE today drawing upon the most recent methods of analysis in the study of pottery made by people who knew no more about clay than what they learned by searching for it and working with it. This situation is not as paradoxical as it may seem, for we need to understand the origin, constitution, and properties of clay in order to discover how potters obtained their results and what the differences in pottery mean. It is fortunate, therefore, that we can turn to the various fields of science for aid. In fact, this is a particularly opportune time to review the basic facts of ceramics because great progress has been made during recent years in fundamental clay research.

Clay is difficult to define precisely because the term has been applied to a variety of materials differing in both origin and composition. It is broadly defined as a fine-grained, earthy material that develops plasticity when mixed with water. Its essential chemical components are silica, alumina, and water; frequently it also contains appreciable amounts of iron, alkalies, and alkaline earths. The term "clay,".however, has been applied to materials that have some but not all of these properties. It has also been used as a particle-size designation for the smallest fraction of soil.

The primitive potter utilized two of the most distinctive properties of clay, plasticity when wet and hardening when subject to heat. Fineness of texture or the "unctuous" feel must also have been noticed from the beginning. Moreover, prewheel pottery shows many interesting effects obtained by simple trial or by chance. Yet it was only with the rise of the sciences that clay began to be understood fundamentally. The geological sciences showed that it is a product of rock alteration, and chemical analysis suggested the main steps in the process of its formation. Kaolinite, which forms fine crystals, was identified as the principal mineral of china clay at a time when common clays were still ill-defined. This is not surprising, for most of them are so fine-grained that the microscope does not reveal their form and, with rare exceptions, they carry a variety of impurities which modify their properties and are difficult to separate. Many concepts of the nature of clay have been advanced in the past, and conflicting ideas were maintained as long as the means of investigating the structure of very fine materials were lacking. Two of the early concepts may be mentioned because they persist to some extent in the popular mind, and also because they serve by contrast with present ideas to emphasize the remarkable advance that has been made in knowledge of the constitution of clays. One of the most prevalent of the older concepts assumed that there is a single pure clay substance, kaolinite. The great differences in the properties of clays were attributed to variations in their impurities. Acceptance of this theory is understandable because kaolinite, unlike other important clay minerals, occasionally occurs in crystals large enough for microscopic study which permits collection of pure samples for analysis. This concept of clay was once widely held by geologists. Many early soil investigators, on the other hand, believed that the essential component of clay was an amorphous complex of extremely fine-grained substances. But clay research of the last three decades has shown that the vast majority of clay materials are crystalline, having distinct structural patterns that directly influence their properties.

The structure and relationships of the principal clay minerals have been established during the last three decades by use of the newer methods of physical analysis in conjunction with chemical and petrographic analysis. The results of this research have been something of a triumph. In place of many loosely defined types of clay—the number that had been named but not adequately identified or described was bewildering—scientists now recognize definite clay minerals which, by the similarities of their atomic structure, can be classed in a few groups. Such classification is fundamental, whereas previous classifications were based on the specific interest or purposes of the classifier. For example, geologists classed clays by their origin and occurrence: residual, and transported; marine, alluvial, glacial, aeolian, etc. Ceramists classed them by their firing properties: white-burning, high refractory; red-burning, low refractory, etc.; or by their uses: china clay, fire clay, stone ware clay, etc. These classifications still have their uses but they are not basic as is the modern mineralogical one.

It may seem strange to speak of clay minerals, for the word "mineral" suggests a well-crystallized substance, whereas the minute particles of earthy clay generally show no regular form that can be detected by the unaided eye. But minerals are essentially composed of definite proportions of elements combined in regular patterns of arrangement. It is these patterns of arrangement rather than the outward form that define crystalline structure. X-ray diffraction, a powerful tool for investigating the structure of fine-grained materials, has made a major contribution to the definition of clays by showing the presence of such arrangements in the essential constituents of clay. Many other analytical methods have played a role in modern clay research. Chemical analysis has been indispensable in establishing the composition of these minerals and testing the purity of samples, which is essential in order to interpret the data obtained by other methods. The petrographic microscope has also been used to test purity, as well as to investigate optical properties which are conditioned by atomic arrangement. Colloidal chemistry, because it deals with matter in a very fine state, has had a direct bearing on clay research and contributed to the explanation of basic properties. Differential thermal analysis (see p. 145) has aided in the study of the role of water in clay and proved to be a useful means of identifying the clay minerals. Finally, the electron microscope has shown the external form of these submicroscopic minerals.

This research has clarified the modes of formation and the properties of clay; moreover, it has had important applications, not only in the ceramic industry, but also in agriculture and in engineering. It cannot be said to have made the study of clay simple but it has certainly clarified it and made it vastly more interesting. It is research in progress, but enough has been learned to establish basic concepts and to afford a broad frame of reference. To follow the history of this research in detail arouses one's pride in man's power to learn the nature of things and awakens us to the marvel of the minute and orderly patterns of matter which, though hidden to our eyes, condition what we can do with it.

The basic structural units of the clay minerals are sheets. The constitution of these sheets and the manner in which they are combined have an important bearing on the properties of clay. It is therefore worthwhile for the student of pottery to have a general idea of this structure and of the characteristics of three important classes of clay minerals, the kaolinite group, the montmorillonite group, and the illites. These are described in Appendix B. It will be sufficient to introduce them briefly here.

Kaolinite is the chief member of the kaolin group and also the chief constituent of most high-grade clays. Chemically it is a hydrated aluminum silicate and, when well crystallized, it forms minute plates roughly hexagonal in outline. Crystalline form is clearly shown by the electron microscope, even in very fine-textured material (fig. 1b); and the larger crystals, which not infrequently form vermicular aggregates, are of microscopic dimensions (fig. 1a). Montmorillonite, the chief mineral of the group that bears its name, is the constituent of bentonite, which often is formed from the decomposition of volcanic ash. Montmorillonite, also a hydrous aluminum silicate in which part of the aluminum is replaced by another ion, generally magnesium, likewise has a platy structure. Owing to its distinctive atomic structure, it adsorbs water between its molecular layers. Each particle is then like a club sandwich. This accounts for its characteristic excessive swelling

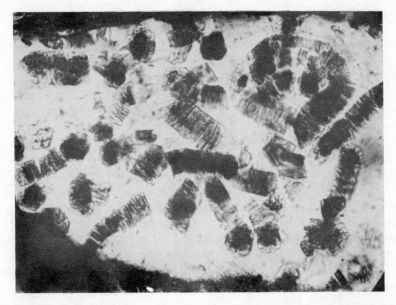

a

b

FIG. 1—KAOLINITE CRYSTALS

a: Vermicular crystals of kaolinite from Calhoun County, Arkansas, typical of those in many deposits. Magnification 350 diameters. (From U.S. Geol. Survey, Prof. Paper 165-E.) *b:* Electron micrograph of kaolinite crystals. 43,300 times natural size, original magnification 20,000. The shadow is three times the thickness of the crystal. (Reproduced by courtesy of Dr. Walter East. Taken by C. E. Hall, Massachusetts Institute of Technology, Cambridge, Mass.)

when wet. The plates also adsorb from soil water soluble salts, which modify the properties of the mineral. Montmorillonite is widely distributed in clays and soils. The illites, micaceous clay minerals (hydrous aluminum silicates with magnesium, iron, and potassium included in the molecule), are similar to muscovite in structure. They are important constituents of many clays but they were the last of the three groups to be investigated.

The simplest potter is aware of the vast differences in clays, in sandiness and plasticity, in the color and degrees of hardness and strength they attain on firing —in properties that determine how they must be handled and how useful they will be when fired. Just as the soils of the earth run a gamut of texture and fertility that enables man to find those especially adapted for each of his crops, so clays by virtue of their variability are individually suited for making flowerpots or porcelain, terra cotta or fire brick. What are the causes of this wide variability? Differences in structure, chemical composition, physical state, and impurities all contribute. The origin and occurrence of clays further explain the wide range in their properties and condition.

ORIGIN AND OCCURRENCE OF CLAY

The minerals of the earth's crust are constantly undergoing change as they are subjected to physical forces, chemical processes, and biochemical action. Expansion and contraction due to temperature variation slowly cleave rock, and attrition by water- and wind-borne sand pulverizes grains, making them more subject to the solvent action of water. During the course of decomposition, soluble constituents are carried away in solution and new minerals crystallize. It is a dynamic and intricate picture of reduction, alteration, separation, redistribution, and recrystallization.

A few important minerals form the chief constituents of the common igneous rocks which are the parent materials of other rocks and soils. Primary among these minerals are the feldspars, a family of closely related basic aluminum silicates, including potash feldspars (orthoclase and microcline) and the soda-lime series (the plagioclases). Rock minerals differ greatly with respect to stability and to the conditions which will cause their decomposition. The feldspars are among those that alter readily, and the clay minerals are common alteration products. In the process, the alkali is removed and hydrous aluminum silicate minerals form in very fine crystals, but the mode of transformation varies, depending on composition of the parent rock and chemical environment. The opaque, chalky appearance of feldspar crystals is evidence of the form of alteration known as kaolinization.

When clay remains in contact with the igneous rock from which it was formed, it is classed as primary or residual. Such clay contains grains of the more stable minerals of the parent rock, especially quartz and micas, and these deposits show a transition from clay through partially altered to fresh rock on passing downward. Such beds vary widely in their extent, properties, and usefulness. They may be formed from extensive rock masses or from narrow veins as of pegmatite. They are often formed by weathering under normal temperatures. Since this action is very slow, they are seldom of great depth. Alteration may also take place through the action of hot, mineralized waters rising in veins. These deposits may have considerable depth, but they are often narrow and therefore of no commercial interest. China clay, used in the manufacture of white ware and porcelain, is a residual clay, but not all residual clays are of this quality. Some are red and of low commercial grade, an example being the brown highly micaceous clay used by Picuris Indians of New Mexico for beanpots.

Clays and the minerals from which clays form are carried from their place of origin by water and redeposited under many conditions. Sedimentary clay beds vary in extent and in properties, depending on their source, the conditions of deposition, the amount of intermixture with other materials during transport, and changes occurring in them after deposition. The most extensive sedimentary beds are marine. Clays deposited in the ocean vary in texture and composition, depending on how far they are carried from shore. Deposits formed at considerable depth are extensive and fine in texture. They may vary laterally in composition as material is carried in from different drainages. Clays deposited in shallow sea water between high and low tide, or in narrow arms of the sea, are coarser in texture, may show cross-bedding, and often contain organic material. Clays deposited by streams and on flood plains are often sandy or interbedded with sand and silt. They are of low grade and seldom attain great depth. Lake and swamp clays form basin-shaped deposits that become thinner and more sandy toward the margin. Glacial clays are highly variable in composition and are unsorted. The bentonites formed from the decomposition of volcanic ash are deposited over great areas of land and sea.

Shales are clay deposits that have been consolidated by pressure. Although many are low in plasticity or are nonplastic unless ground, they often weather to a plastic clay. Some are silty; others ferruginous, calcareous, or carbonaceous; consequently, they vary greatly in their properties and usefulness. Many form extensive beds and some have commercial value for structural products such as hollow block, face brick, and sewer pipe.

This sketchy review is intended only to suggest the wide range in qualities of clay that may be expected from its varied modes of deposition. The chemical conditions that favor the formation of one clay mineral over another are no less diverse than the physical conditions of deposition. Many clays have had such a varied history that the physical and chemical environment of the successive stages of their formation is not easily determined. In other instances the conditions of formation are sufficiently clear to indicate plainly the factors that brought about alteration. The two primary factors affecting the formation of clay are chemical composition of the parent rock and the chemical environment to which it was subject. Rocks characterized by the alkali feldspars, particularly granites and pegmatites, tend to alter to kaolinite, whereas rocks characterized by calcic plagioclase, such as the basalts and rocks high in calcium, magnesium, and iron, tend to alter to montmorillonite. But the product of decomposition cannot be predicted from the composition of the parent rock alone. The physical and chemical conditions of formation also play a primary role. Kaolinite forms in an acid environment or under neutral conditions that are strongly leaching. Under both conditions bases are removed, and this seems to be the controlling condition. Montmorillonite forms under a wide range of conditions, but the presence of magnesium and other essential bases seems to control its formation, and reducing conditions or conditions that are not actively oxidizing favor the formation of minerals of the montmorillonite group. The clay minerals themselves vary in stability. Kaolinite appears to be the most stable. Montmorillonite is decomposed when the bases are leached from it and it may alter to kaolinite.

The geological field study of clay deposits gives some idea of their general mode of formation, their homogeneity, impurities, and texture. The determination of clay mineral composition gives more specific data which have direct applications because the different species of clay vary greatly in their physical properties and firing behavior. To date, clay research has been directed largely to the definition of these minerals from relatively pure samples. When intensive studies are made of the impure and mixed minerals used in industry, many practical applications, as well as a much clearer understanding of these materials, can be expected.

PHYSICAL PROPERTIES OF CLAY

Texture.   When we consider the unconsolidated materials of the earth's surface in terms of the sizes of their particles, we find clay occupying the fine end of the scale. And if we look at the exposure of a stream bank or a road cut, the first feature that makes us suspect the presence of clay is fineness and homogeneity. But even though all clays are very fine in relative terms, they differ greatly among themselves in the size and grading of their particles. These textural differences can be demonstrated very quickly and simply by stirring samples of clay in water and watching them settle. Some clays settle quickly, leaving the water nearly clear above the sediment. Often the sediments will show layers of different texture, beginning at the bottom with the silty inclusions that deposited first and becoming progressively finer toward the top. Other clays will remain in suspension for hours, or even months or years. It is not surprising, therefore, that in common usage a clay suspension is often referred to as a solution of clay. But the difference between a solution and a suspension is fundamental and they should not be confused. A soluble substance is one which, when mixed with a liquid, will separate into simple chemically defined units: molecules, atoms, or ions. A substance that forms a suspension is composed of particles in a size range between molecules and grains that can be seen with a microscope. This is the colloidal range of matter. Matter in this state is characterized by special properties, one of which is the formation of suspensions. Clays are not soluble but they generally contain some colloidal material, and some are entirely colloidal. In judging the particle size of a clay, one must remember that all clays are not readily dispersed, that is, separated into individual particles in water. The fine particles of some remain as aggregates or flocks, which will settle like the coarser particles.

One cannot set arbitrary limits for the size of clay particles, but some idea can be gained of the range from sedimentation studies and from measurement on electron micrographs. Crystals of kaolinite in finer clays measure from 0.05 to 0.15 microns in diameter (0.00005 to 0.00015 mm.). The largest kaolinite crystals in a series of samples studied with the electron microscope measured 3.51 microns. Sedimentation studies show some clays to have no material coarser than 10 microns, others may have a fraction as coarse as 0.1 mm. or above (see Norton, 1952, p. 28, for a comparison of textures of various natural clays).

Fineness of texture is an important property of clay because it affects its workability and firing behavior. Since it is the finer fraction of clay that is most active and has the greatest effect on plasticity and fusibility, it will be worthwhile to consider the characteristics of the colloidal state.

The colloidal state. Colloids are not a particular substance or group of substances, but a degree of subdivision which may be attained by any substance. The word colloid refers to a range of particle sizes, between microscopic particles and molecules. The upper limit is generally placed at 5 microns and the lower limit at 1 millimicron. Colloids are too fine to be visible with the microscope, but their movements in a liquid medium can be seen by their reflection of light in a dark field.

There is, of course, no sharp boundary between particles of microscopic size, colloids, and molecules; it is an unbroken range. Why then should the range of colloids be singled out for special study? Why do substances in this general size range possess properties they lack in other size ranges? The explanation lies in the greatly increased surface of colloids and the consequent prominence of surface phenomena. An example will serve as a reminder of the increase in surface area as the particle size of a solid mass is reduced. If a cube having a volume of 1 cu. cm. is subdivided into cubes of colloidal dimension, with volumes of 1 cu. mμ, the total surface area is increased from 6 to 600,000 sq. cm., although there is no change in total volume. The importance of the surface of small particles rests on the fact that ions at the surface of a solid, unlike those in the interior, are not entirely surrounded by other ions and consequently their charge is not fully satisfied. If the particle is large, the surface charges are insignificant in relation to size, but when particles are reduced to colloidal dimensions, the charges become strong enough to exert an influence on the properties of the particles, and matter becomes more active in this state. The effect of the charges is shown when an electric current is passed through a colloidal suspension. The particles act like ions, migrating to one pole or the other according to the sign of their charge. Colloidal particles attract ions from solution and are prevented from coagulating by the repulsive forces of like charges. This property is important in the formation of slips, since it slows the rate of settling. Certain colloids attract molecules of water to their surface, forming a "water hull." Clay colloids are of this class, and the characteristic has a relation to plasticity.

Particle shape. The shape of clay particles is of interest because it affects the way in which they will pack. The hexagonal outline of coarse crystals of kaolinite has long been recognized, and the electron microscope has shown that this shape is retained even in very fine clay. There are variations in form, however, and some crystals have a tendency toward elongation in one direction. From the measurement of shadows, the thickness of plates is found to be 8–10 per cent of their diameters. Electron micrographs of halloysite show elongated forms that are believed to be elongated plates rolled into tubes. Montmorillonite, though platy, has no regular outline; boundaries are ragged or fuzzy in appearance. Nontronite, the iron-bearing member of the montmorillonite group, has a lathlike structure, despite the fact that it is poorly crystallized.

Evidences of the platy form of clay can often be recognized in thin sections of pottery that has not been fired high enough to destroy the crystalline structure of the clay mineral. A slip, for example, will act as a unit optically when the plates of clay have been aligned with the surface and pressed into parallel position in the process of smoothing and polishing.

Plasticity. Everyone is familiar in a general way with plasticity—that property of a water-clay mixture that allows it to be pressed into a shape without returning to its original form when pressure is released. Although the potter can judge plasticity reliably for practical purposes by simply working a lump of clay in his fingers, this basic property has been difficult to measure exactly, and its mechanism has been the source of much speculation and many theories. In recent years colloidal chemistry has contributed to our understanding of it because fineness of particle size and the layers of adsorbed water surrounding particles are among the primary factors that affect it. The water film acts as a lubricant allowing the minute plates to glide over one another. This effect can be tested by pressing two plates of wet glass tightly together. They will slide across one another although considerable force is required to pull them apart. Clay particles are readily wet; furthermore, they adsorb water, that is, hold it on their surfaces by ionic forces. This water hull that surrounds and separates them is thin enough to allow attractive forces to operate. These forces and the surface area subject to lubrication are both increased as particle size is reduced. Adsorption and particle size are related to the great difference in water of plasticity of clays (water required to develop maximum plasticity). But the clay minerals themselves vary greatly in plasticity even when their size range is identical because of differences in the adsorptive properties of the surfaces of their plates resulting from their distinctive atomic structures (see Appendix B). This fact explains the great difference in plasticity between kaolin and bentonite.

The plastic flow of a wet clay begins at a definite point (the yield point). Up to this point, the clay has elastic flow when subject to shearing force. After the yield point is passed, a plastic clay allows considerable extension before cracks appear. A workable clay should have a high enough yield point to prevent accidental deformation before drying and a large enough extensibility to allow for forming without cracking. The two properties are not independent; the higher the yield point, the lower the extensibility; that is, the stiffer the clay paste, the sooner cracks will appear when it is pressed out. The yield point can be decreased by adding water; at the same time the extensibility will be increased. The workability of the clay can be expressed as the product of the yield point and the maximum extension. Each clay will reach its maximum workability with a certain water content. It follows from the differences in structure of the clay minerals that there is a wide range in workability of clays. A good plastic clay has both a sufficiently high yield point and good extensibility. It is believed that the force of the surface film of water which holds particles together explains the yield point. The sliding of platelike particles across each other influences extensibility.

Base exchange capacity.   In the discussion of the structure of clay minerals (Appendix B), the tendency of those of the montmorillonite group to adsorb bases on the surface of the plates is mentioned. The kaolinite minerals, on the other hand, appear to adsorb ions only on the edges of the plates. The maximum capacity of a clay to adsorb ions is called its base exchange capacity. Adsorbed ions affect the dispersion of clay particles, and therefore influence quality of slip. Base exchange capacity is expressed as milliequivalents per 100 grams of clay. An idea of the variability of clays with respect to this property can be obtained from values reported by Lewis (1951) for a series of samples. Values for kaolinites range from 1.5 to 20.4, the average of 21 samples being 6.61, whereas the mont-morillonites range from 8.5 to 160 with an average of 107.9 for 15 samples.

Color.   The color of raw clays is due primarily to two classes of impurities, organic matter and iron compounds. Clays that are relatively free from impurities are white. Organic matter makes a clay gray to blackish, depending on its amount and condition. Hematite and the hydrated forms of ferric oxide, goethite and limonite, produce reds, browns, buffs, and yellows. These are compounds in which the iron is in its highest state of oxidation. Compounds in which the iron is not fully oxidized impart a gray color. The more common minerals of this class occur-ring in clay are magnetite (ferro-ferric oxide), pyrite (ferrous sulfide), and siderite (ferrous carbonate). Silicates containing iron in the ferrous state, such as glauconite and chlorite, produce a greenish color, and the phosphates of iron give blues, greens, and reds; but these compounds are rare in clays, whereas the oxides and hydroxides are so common that a clay completely free of them is exceptional.

The effect of a particular iron compound depends not only on its composition and amount, but also on its grain size and distribution. If iron oxide occurs as a film coating the particles of clay, the texture of the clay will affect the color; that is, the finer the particles the greater their surface area and the more iron oxide required to cover them. Consequently one cannot judge the amount of iron oxide in clays by their color. Two clays of the same color may differ in iron con-tent, and clays of different color may contain the same amount. Ries (1927, p. 260) mentions a clay containing 3.12 per cent ferric oxide which has nearly the same color as one with 12.40 per cent.

The appearance of raw clay is not a reliable guide to the color it will attain on firing because carbonaceous matter, if present, may mask the effect of iron compounds and these in turn will be modified in firing. When a clay that is black owing to the presence of organic matter is fully oxidized in firing, it will change to a color in the cream to red-brown range or to white, depending on its composition. This is a simple matter of getting rid of the masking carbon by con-verting it to a gaseous compound through oxidation. The change taking place in the iron compounds may be one of dehydration, oxidation, or decomposition and oxida-tion. The yellow or brown hydrous oxides are converted to red ferric oxide by dehydration; the lower oxides, by oxidation; and the sulfides and carbonates, by decomposition and oxidation. The color that iron imparts is also affected by other compounds in the clay, a factor that is discussed under the effects of heat on clay (p. 24).

Since the color of raw clay does not enable the ceramist to predict that of the fired body, it is not of primary interest to him. When the archaeologist studies the potter's resources, he works in the opposite direction, from pottery to clay. Since there is not a simple relation between color of raw and fired clay, he cannot make definite predictions from pottery to guide him in recognizing the original clay. There are, however, a few simple generalizations which will in some cases reduce the number of clays that need be tested. Typical changes are summarized in Table 1, but there is a wide color range in each of the categories mentioned and there are no breaks between them. Also, I have not attempted to indicate all the subtle color variations found in clays.

TABLE 1—RELATION BETWEEN COLOR OF CLAY AND OF POTTERY

Pottery	Clay
White	White
	Neutral gray
	Black
Buff	Cream
	Yellow
	Neutral gray
	Black
	Gray-brown (rare)
	Brown (rare)
Red and brown	Yellow
	Red
	Brown
	Grays
	Black
Dark gray and black	All colors

It will be noted that white pottery could not have been made from a colored clay nor could colored pottery be obtained from white clay, and that buffs are not obtained from the darker-colored clays. Gray or black pottery may owe its color to carbonaceous matter or to smudging. In either case the paste should be oxidized by refiring in air in order to judge its color. The possibility that oxidized pottery was made from a carbonaceous clay must also be borne in mind, and a dark central zone in a vessel wall left by incomplete oxidation is a significant feature.

Slaking. The rate at which clay disintegrates when immersed in water is referred to as slaking. Clays differ greatly with respect to slaking time (measured on a cube of dry clay of standard dimensions), and this property affects the relative ease with which they can be brought to the plastic state.

Drying properties. Drying shrinkage is measured by change in either length or volume of a test piece. It is a property of direct concern to the potter because excessive shrinkage will cause large or heavy pieces to crack. In general, the finer and more plastic a clay, the higher its shrinkage, since contraction is caused by loss of water, and a fine clay which has a large surface area holds more water in the plastic state than does a coarse clay.

Clays vary greatly in their strength when dry. This property determines the care that must be exercised in handling ware before firing. A fine-grained clay is usually stronger when dried than a coarse-grained one.

IMPURITIES OF CLAY

It follows from the modes of formation and deposition of clays that they contain many impurities. Aside from foreign matter, different clay minerals may be mixed in the same deposit. One may be altering to another, they may be formed simultaneously from different constituents of the same rock, or they may be brought together in sedimentary clays derived from different sources. The clay minerals are generally so fine and so completely intermingled that a mixture is difficult to recognize.

The foreign matter of residual clays consists of detrital grains of the stable minerals of the parent rock. Minerals from many sources are deposited with sedimentary clays. These clays generally contain quartz, feldspars, micas, carbonates, iron oxides, titanium in several forms, and various rarer minerals. Then there are the soluble salts that are adsorbed by some clays, the organic matter that is often deposited with clay—decaying vegetable matter that settles in lakes, swamps, and estuaries, and organisms, many with calcareous shells, that die and settle with the sediments. All of these impurities affect the properties of clay and especially its reactions to heat. It is important therefore to understand their sources and characteristic effects.

Quartz and other forms of silica are among the commonest impurities of clay. The particle size ranges from that of colloidal silica through the fine silt that is common in sedimentary clays to coarse grains such as the phenocrysts of some bentonites. Mechanically, silt has the effect of reducing the plasticity of clay. Silica that is fine enough to react at high temperatures lowers the fusion point, but it does not promote vitrification within the temperature range of primitive firing.

Iron oxide, as we have noted, is the chief colorant of fired clay. The common iron-bearing minerals of clay include hematite, goethite, limonite, magnetite, pyrite, marcasite, and siderite. Iron is also a component of various silicates. In particle size these iron minerals vary from colloidal dimensions to nodules a millimeter or more in diameter. Their reactions in firing depend on particle size, chemical combination, and relation to other constituents of the clay.

Most clays contain some organic matter, but its type and condition, as well as its amount, are highly variable. Vegetable matter is common in surface clays of recent origin; bituminous and asphaltic matter occurs in shales and clays associated with coal measures; and lignite is common in Cretaceous clays. Anthracite also occurs, and some clays and shales contain organic matter that can be extracted with water or other solvents. As might be expected, the primary clays have the least organic matter. The amount in sedimentary clays is variable. Parmelee (1946, p. IV–13) states that glacial and alluvial clays contain up to 1 per cent, fire clay up to 3 per cent, and shales up to 10 per cent.

Calcium carbonate in a fine cryptocrystalline form or as fragments of calcite or of shell occurs in many clays. Calcareous clays grade into marls and clayey limestones. High-grade products cannot be made from calcareous clays, but they are often used for coarse products. For example, the average calcium carbonate content of Wisconsin brick clays is reported as 14.4 per cent and the maximum as 31.4 per cent (Parmelee, 1946, p. IV–11). The effect of lime in firing depends partly on its particle size.

These are the most common impurities. There are many others, less abundant and less frequent, including titanium and manganese compounds, that occasionally influence the color of clay. To the man engaged in clay research, impurities are a contaminant of the sample. The ceramist considers their effect on the commercial value of clay and either rejects the clay or refines it, and adopts suitable firing schedules. Primitive potters did not discriminate or have high standards, and were often restricted in choice of clay. Consequently, they utilized many impure, low-grade clays that would have no commercial value.

EFFECTS OF HEAT ON CLAY

The changes that take place in clay on firing can be considered either from the standpoint of the student of the clay minerals or from the standpoint of the ceramic engineer. The one is investigating the nature of pure materials; the other is concerned with the kind of products impure clays are suited for and how they can be fired efficiently. Even though the potter may never have an opportunity to make a vessel from pure clay, what has been learned by laboratory investigation is by no means a matter of theoretic interest only, because the clay minerals are the essential constituents and their reactions are fundamental.

Effects of heat on the clay minerals. Differential thermal analysis has been extensively used in studying the effects of heat on the clay minerals. This method (described under analytical methods, p. 145) shows the temperatures at which changes that are accompanied by either absorption or evolution of heat occur. The atomic structure of clays heated to these critical temperatures is determined by X-ray diffraction analysis. The clay minerals take up heat when water of crystallization is driven off. This loss destroys the crystal lattice. At higher temperatures new minerals begin to crystallize and heat is given off. The temperatures at which these changes take place differ for the various clay minerals depending on their structure and composition, and each has a characteristic heating curve. Kaolins begin to lose combined water at about 450°C. With constant rate of heating, dehydration takes place over a considerable range, but the peak of the curve is at about 600°C. Rate of heating causes some variation in these temperatures. The X-ray pattern of the dehydrated material shows that the crystalline structure is destroyed, but the outlines of crystals remain intact, as can be seen from electron micrographs. The material remains in this state until constituents begin to crystallize. This reaction is sudden and occurs around 1000°C. The X-ray pattern of kaolin quenched at this point shows a faint pattern of crystalline alumina. When the change is complete, mullite, a fibrous aluminum silicate mineral, is present as well as crystalline alumina. Mullite is rare in nature but common in porcelain. When amorphous alumina alone is heated, crystallization commences at a lower temperature, from which it appears that the amorphous silica in the network of the dehydrated kaolin has a retarding effect on the crystallization of alumina (Insley and Ewell, 1935).

The heating curve of montmorillonite is more complex than that of kaolinite. There is a sharp drop between 100° and 250°C when the adsorbed, interlayer water is driven off. The destruction of the crystal lattice begins at about 600°C when water of crystallization is lost. The lattice is fully destroyed by a second change occurring between 850° and 900°C. Crystallization follows immediately, and spinel, a magnesium aluminate, appears first. At about 950°C, silica commences to crystallize and at the same time some glass is formed. The glassy phase increases with temperature rise and some mullite crystallizes at 1050° to 1150°C. Samples fired at 1300° to 1400°C are largely glass with scattered crystals of mullite (Grim and Bradley, 1940).

High-grade china clay will have firing reactions similar to those of kaolin, of which it is largely composed. The changes in clays of mixed composition will be more complex, and various impurities in sedimentary clays will promote the formation of glass and lower the vitrification point.

Stages of firing. Discussion of the effects of heat on clay is simplified by reference to the major changes that take place. There are three: dehydration, oxidation, and vitrification. These do not occur in neatly separated succession, each reaction being completed before another starts. Instead, their ranges overlap; oxidation may commence before dehydration is complete and may still be in progress when vitrification starts.

The principal constituents that are dehydrated are the clay minerals themselves, and the discussion of water of crystallization covers this phase of firing.

Plasticity is generally lost during dehydration and the porosity of the body is increased. Some impurities also are dehydrated, limonite and goethite, for example.

Oxidation, unlike dehydration, is a chemical change that affects the impurities of clay, chiefly carbon and iron compounds. Minerals containing sulfur are also decomposed and oxidized, but these are less common. The oxidation of these compounds does not take place simultaneously; carbon has a greater affinity for oxygen than does iron and therefore any iron that is not in its highest state of oxidation will remain unaffected until the carbon is burned out. Under certain conditions the carbon may even rob iron oxide of some of its oxygen.

Carbonaceous matter in the clay combines with oxygen to form carbon monoxide or dioxide and passes off as gas. This reaction produces heat and raises the temperature of the ware. High content of carbonaceous matter will even cause over-firing in some cases if the rate of combustion is uncontrolled. The hardness and density of carbon, duration and temperature of firing, and density of the paste, which controls circulation of gases within the body, all affect rate of combustion. Some carbonaceous matter commences to oxidize at temperatures as low as 225°C, but even the soft carbon deposited by smudging oxidizes very slowly below 500°C and the most effective temperatures are considerably higher, generally between 700° and 800°C. Above this range, carbon may be converted to a denser form that is less easily oxidized; moreover, incipient vitrification, which impedes circulation of oxygen, may occur at these temperatures.

If carbonaceous matter is not fully removed before vitrification commences, gases will be trapped by the dense impervious surface that forms, the interior will become black and vesicular, and the wall bloated. This defect is known as black coring. It should not be confused with the black cores of low-fired pottery. These are also generally caused by carbonaceous matter, but there is no vitrification, and the cores merely indicate incomplete oxidation resulting from one or more conditions —short firing, low temperature, or insufficient oxygen in the firing atmosphere. Only occasionally does the surface of a prehistoric ware become sealed so that the defect of true black coring occurs.

Sulfur can occur in clay as iron sulfide (pyrite and marcasite), in organic matter, or in a sulfate (gypsum). Sulfur is objectionable because it unites with other substances to form salts that produce a scum on the surface of ware. Ferrous sulfate appears as a brown scum, and the sulfates of calcium, magnesium, potassium, and sodium form a white efflorescence. Sulfur compounds are not oxidized until all the carbon is burned off, and some are eliminated with difficulty. The sulfur that is sometimes associated with lignite is removed as dioxide or trioxide at temperatures between 225° and 1000°C. Iron sulfite dissociates at 350° to 800°C. Gypsum does not dissociate until a temperature of 1200°C is reached and therefore causes greatest difficulty.

The iron-bearing minerals of clay differ with respect to their state of oxidation and are therefore affected differently in firing. Hematite and the hydrous oxides can undergo no further oxidation. Other iron-bearing minerals will take up oxygen after carbonaceous matter has been burned out. Magnetite begins to oxidize when heated in air to 400°C, but the coating of ferric oxide that is formed on the surface of particles retards further oxidation. Ralston (1929, p. 57) reports that oxidation is only 95.6 per cent complete after 100 hours heating at 1000°C. Pyrite begins to decompose at 350°C forming ferric oxide or magnetite. Since the oxidation of pyrite is accompanied by a volume increase, particles of pyrite may cause popping on the surface of a ware. If there is insufficient oxygen, ferrous oxide will be present and may form a slag pocket. Siderite decomposes at 800°C and oxidizes to form ferric oxide, but decomposition is reported to occur at a considerably lower temperature in the presence of clay. Granules of siderite will cause the same defects as pyrite.

Oxidation is not the only chemical change that takes place during the intermediate temperature range of firing. Some impurities are decomposed, and the term "oxidation and decomposition range" is sometimes applied to this period of firing. The chief constituents that are decomposed are the carbonates, and of these, calcium carbonate in its many forms is by far the most common. When calcite or limestone is heated above 650°C, it begins to lose carbon dioxide, which passes off as a gas leaving calcium oxide. Although this reaction starts at a relatively low temperature, it proceeds very slowly at first. The rate increases with rise of temperature up to 898°C when it is immediate and complete in air. The rate of decomposition depends not alone on temperature but also on the amount of carbon dioxide in the kiln atmosphere. Carbon dioxide retards decomposition, and the proportion of this gas in the firing atmosphere is increased during the oxidation of a highly carbonaceous clay.

Calcium oxide, the product of decomposition of limestone and other carbonates of calcium, is a fluxing agent. If it is finely disseminated, it will promote vitrification, but this action will not take place at the lower temperatures of primitive firing. If calcium oxide does not react with constituents of the clay during firing, it will take up moisture from the atmosphere after firing, forming calcium hydroxide, a reaction accompanied by expansion, which will cause popping or spalling of the vessel surface.

These are the common impurities of clay that are oxidized or decomposed in firing. Others are rare or occur as minor constituents. Despite the wide variety of impurities and the fact that one reaction can influence another, the changes are relatively simple and each individual reaction is well known. By comparison, reactions taking place during vitrification are complex and more difficult to follow. Of primary importance is the fact that fundamental changes occur in the clay substance itself, as we have seen in the discussion of the results of differential thermal analysis; new minerals crystallize from the alumina and silica left by the decomposition of the clay, and glass begins to form. Various impurities, especially those that have a fluxing action, affect this process. Alkalis, alkaline earths, and ferrous oxide lower the vitrification point. The formation of a glassy phase is preceded by sintering or the condition in which the edges of particles soften sufficiently to adhere. In this stage the colloidal fraction of the clay plays an important role because the finer the particles, the more readily they fuse. This process may begin considerably below the vitrification temperature.

In judging a clay, the ceramist is concerned not only with the temperature of vitrification but also with its range. Clays high in fluxing impurities vitrify quickly and therefore are subject to deformation, whereas clays that vitrify slowly and over a long temperature range produce sound, dense ware.

Effects of firing on the physical properties of pottery. The changes in the physical properties of pottery that take place during firing are intimately connected with the chemical changes and changes in state that I have briefly described. When substances are dehydrated or decomposed with the formation of gas, porosity is increased. Sintering and fluxing, on the other hand, reduce porosity and cause shrinkage because particles are drawn together and bonded. Porosity is further reduced as vitrification proceeds and melted matter fills pore spaces and takes finer constituents into solution. Heat-induced changes in crystal structure of some minerals, especially quartz, are accompanied by volume change which may be opposite to that taking place simultaneously in the clay, a circumstance that increases the variability in the firing behavior of clays and renders broad, simple generalizations invalid. The degree of strength and hardness attained by the body is influenced by degree of porosity and by the bonding action of fluxes.

Color changes are variable and subtle, as might be expected from the number of factors affecting color. A carbonaceous clay that is not fully oxidized will be gray or a grayish tone of brown or buff. Most of the iron minerals can be fully oxidized at 800°C, and the iron-bearing clay will attain its clearest color in the oxidation range. Ferric oxide begins to lose oxygen at 1000°C, forming the magnetic iron oxide, and ferric oxide cannot exist at 1300°C, even in an oxidizing atmosphere. The latter temperature is well above the range of primitive firing. But clays also begin to lose the clearer colors of ferric oxide when vitrification commences, which may be within the range of primitive firing temperatures if the clay is nonrefractory. In general, colors become darker and less pure as the iron oxide is taken into solution in the glass formed in the body. The iron oxide may also react with other constituents of the body during this stage of firing, or it may be reduced to the ferrous state in which it is an active flux. As a result of these reactions, the clearer buffs and reds change to yellow brown, dark red or brown, chocolate brown, and even black, the particular color depending on the form and amount of the iron oxide, the composition of the body and firing atmosphere.

The color imparted by iron oxide is sometimes affected by other constituents of the clay. Excess alumina under certain conditions contributes to the formation of a buff or yellow color. Lime also lightens the color of ferric oxide. When the lime begins to have a fluxing effect on an iron-bearing clay, the color changes from red to buff as it becomes well oxidized and then sintered. Vitrified, calcareous clays usually have a distinctive olive or greenish buff color. Magnesia has an effect similar to that of lime.

There are other impurities that can affect the color of clay during firing, but they are far less common than the iron oxides, the discussion of which will have served to indicate the many variable conditions in firing that will affect a colorant. The difficulty of judging either clay composition or firing conditions from the color of the fired body alone should be readily appreciated.

The temperatures attained in primitive firing were mainly in the oxidation range but were sometimes high enough to cause incipient vitrification, as is shown by the presence of glass in the paste of some of the harder ware. In consequence of short firing time, oxidation of these wares was often incomplete.

. . . .

I have not attempted to make the subject of clay seem simple. To do so would be grossly misleading. Our concept of pottery would be vague if we failed to realize that clay is intriguingly complex, that it is in fact one of the most complex and variable materials that nature affords. We need more than a nodding acquaintance with clay to recognize how man has matched its variability by his versatility in using it.

NONPLASTIC MATERIAL

Nonplastic material plays the essential role of counteracting excessive shrinkage of ceramic bodies in drying and firing. The modern ceramist, as well as the prehistoric potter, mixes it with all clays that do not contain it in sufficient amount in their natural state. It is readily identified microscopically and is one of the technologist's best means of distinguishing wares and studying the sources of pottery types since the primitive potter drew upon a wide variety of rocks, minerals, and other materials. But before we discuss this subject a word of explanation regarding terminology is necessary.

American archaeologists have used the word *temper* to designate nonplastic material; generally the term is limited to the substance added by the potter, but it is sometimes extended to all nonplastic material in the paste. *To temper* means to add this material to clay. In modern ceramic usage *tempering* is the process of mixing the ingredients with water to a paste of proper consistency. The ceramic engineer does not have a general term for added nonplastics, possibly because he uses fewer kinds than does the primitive potter. The word *grog* (ground brick, tile, or other fired products) is occasionally given a general meaning, although the extension has not found favor with ceramists. Searle (1929–30, article *Grog*) recommended that grog be applied only to materials heated to a high temperature before use, such as fired clay, broken brick or tile, preheated bauxite and sillimanite, etc. A few students have objected to the American archaeologists' definition of temper, believing that adherence to ceramic nomenclature would facilitate exchange of information, but the word *temper* is now firmly established in the literature. March (1934, pp. 14–16) proposed aplastic; however, during the 16 years since his suggestion was made, it has not gained general acceptance. As long as a word conveys a definite meaning and has become established by long usage, it need not be dropped merely because it is peculiar to a field of study. In the present discussion *temper* will be defined as added inclusions, and *nonplastic* will be used in a general sense and for material of indeterminate source.

FUNCTION OF NONPLASTICS

Temper has sometimes been referred to in archaeological literature as a binder which has the effect of strengthening the body. Actually, the plastic clay is the binder and nonplastics weaken the body. Temper is used despite this disadvantage because it counteracts shrinkage and facilitates uniform drying, thus reducing strain and lessening the risk of cracking. The effect is easily understood. Each of the fine particles of a plastic clay is surrounded by a water film. As water at the surface is drawn off by evaporation, it is replaced by water from the interior, but the movement is slow because of the fineness of capillary spaces between particles. Consequently the outer zone may become much dryer than the inner zone, and strains are set up because of differences in rates of shrinkage. The nonplastic matter, being coarser than the clay, opens the texture and allows water to escape more readily. It also reduces the amount of water required to bring the paste to a workable state. When a clay is highly plastic, temper renders it less sticky and easier to work, but an excess will reduce plasticity to the point at which the clay is lean or short and lacks the cohesiveness necessary for shaping. Firing shrinkage occurs when clay particles draw together as they soften and sinter. Nonplastics, being coarser, decrease the effect.

Clays differ in fineness and shape of particles and hence with respect to density of packing. As they vary in texture and in the amount of nonplastics they contain in their original state, so the amount of temper they require varies. Some clays will dry satisfactorily without the addition of temper; others cannot be dried without cracking even when the greatest care is exercised to prevent rapid or uneven drying. But since temper weakens the body, an excess is to be avoided. Potters learn from accident that the heavily tempered body breaks more easily than the untempered one, just as they note the effect of texture on drying and cracking. The relative amount of temper in a body should give some idea of the original plasticity of the clay and its drying characteristics, but deductions must be made with caution because there is considerable latitude in the amount that can be added and primitive potters' estimates and measurements were rough.

TYPES OF TEMPERING MATERIAL

A wide range of materials was used for temper by primitive potters. Sand seems the most obvious material for them to choose, but it is less common than might be supposed. On the other hand, many kinds of rock and various materials of organic orgin were used and there is also the equivalent of grog in ground potsherd. Among the rocks, all three of the major classes are represented. Many are of igneous origin, andesites, diorites, trachytes, and basalts being especially common, as are also unconsolidated volcanic ash, and indurated ash or tuff. The sedimentaries include sandstone, limestone, and dolomite; and the metamorphics, various types of schist and gneiss. The materials of organic origin include such diverse things as shell, diatomaceous earth, sponge spicules, silica obtained by burning bark, plant fibers, and feathers. This list is by no means exhaustive, but it will suggest the range of materials.

These materials differ with respect to the labor required for their preparation, in their effect on the strength and texture of pottery, and in their reactions on heating. Some are consolidated and must be ground, others are unconsolidated. Of the latter some, being fine and uniform in grain size, can be used in their original state; others require sorting or separation. Many of the compact materials such as the softer tuffs and sandstones are easily pulverized, and even some of the igneous rocks are not as difficult to grind as one might suppose because weathering weakens the bond between crystals and the rock becomes friable. Many materials required no sorting or grading. Sands are sorted naturally by water and wind, and some rocks tend to break down to grains of uniform size. This is true of sandstones with a weak cement, fine crystalline limestones, and even some igneous rocks. The more compact and homogeneous rocks and potsherds, which lack lines of weakness, crush to assorted sizes and require grading.

The potter was concerned with the effect of temper on ease of finishing the vessel surface as well as with the effect on strength. In fact, the selection of temper may have been made most often on the basis of texture. Comparison of the effects of various classes of nonplastics on texture of paste and strength of body affords some basis for judging whether or not the materials most frequently used were superior. Structure, hardness, and grain size of inclusions condition, in large measure, the ease with which a plastic, leather-hard, or dry surface can be worked. Hard, coarse grains catch on a scraping tool and drag in the moist clay, making grooves, or they pop out, leaving pits if the body is dry; whereas frothy particles of pumice splinter, leaving the surface unmarred. Fine volcanic ash and siliceous materials such as diatomaceous or infusorial earth are probably the most satisfactory tempers from the standpoint of the finishing process. Silt and other materials as fine in texture likewise cause no difficulty, but primitive potters did not often attempt to reduce their tempering material to this degree.

The bonding of clay and temper has a direct effect on the strength of the body. Clay forms a poorer bond with smooth than with rough surfaces; thus grains of windblown sand will weaken a paste more than rough fragments of rock or sherd in the same grade size. Also rounded grains weaken a body more than sharp, irregular ones. Volcanic ash has the advantage of irregularity of form but the disadvantage of extreme brittleness. The effect of different types of temper on strength can be compared by testing briquettes that are uniform in texture, clay, and methods of drying and firing, and vary only in type of temper. Results of tests with four classes of material (sand, sherd, igneous rock, and volcanic ash) show that of these, sand gives the weakest body, sherd the strongest, and rock and ash, though intermediate, are distinctly stronger than sand (see p. 132).

Temper that is platy like mica or acicular like sponge spicules affects the structure of paste because flat or elongated fragments are in part forced into parallel position in the forming and finishing processes. In low-fired pottery they may then have a reinforcing effect against cross fracture but they cause weakness in their own plane.

The general relationships that have been mentioned furnish a basis for interpreting the choice of temper. The effect of temper on paste texture, and particularly on the ease with which a surface can be scraped, could be recognized more readily by the potter than could effects on strength. Undoubtedly the superiority of volcanic ash with respect to paste texture largely explains its extensive use where available. When sherd or rock was selected instead of sand, which would have required less labor in preparation, it would seem that the relation to strength was being recognized also, although we cannot be certain.

EFFECTS OF HEAT ON NONPLASTICS

Another important factor influencing the choice of temper is the effect of heat on materials. Many materials are stable at the temperatures obtained in primitive firing; others undergo changes that weaken the pottery or cause defects.

Potters had to avoid them or keep the firing temperature below the point at which the change takes place. Finally, a few materials undergo changes which are advantageous; they may strengthen the pottery or produce interesting color effects. We will consider only those changes which occur within the temperature range obtainable with primitive firing methods, generally temperatures below 1000°C. Materials that have a detrimental effect in the upper limits of this range can be and were used at lower temperatures, but defects caused by them are not uncommon because firing was not closely controlled.

The changes that occur in minerals on heating are of many kinds, both physical and chemical. They include dehydration, oxidation, reduction, inversion, decomposition, and fusion. Dehydration occurs in the lower temperature ranges and may be accompanied by swelling as water of crystallization is converted to steam. Oxidation and reduction are controlled by firing atmosphere and occur over a considerable temperature range. These are changes that may have an important effect on color. Inversion is a physical change in atomic structure that takes place at different temperatures with different minerals. Decomposition takes place over a wide temperature range, depending on composition. Fusion or melting of substances occurs in the higher temperature range. We will review the evidence of these changes, grouping them with respect to their effect on the pottery, attempting to cover the major kinds of temper and to consider the nature of the changes.

Feldspars are the most common minerals that are stable at the temperatures employed by primitive potters. Two varieties undergo an inversion at 900°C, but its effect has not been observed in pottery. Parenthetically, it may be noted that the feldspars have played an important role in the advanced stages of ceramic development because they have high fusion points and long softening ranges, which make them valuable fluxing agents. They are an important ingredient of porcelains and most high-grade wares. Potsherds furnish another temper that is generally inert within the range of primitive firing temperatures, but their pastes vary greatly in refractoriness and they may be oxidized, vitrified or otherwise altered if their original firing temperatures are exceeded or if firing atmosphere is markedly different. Not infrequently, sherd temper will be more fully oxidized on refiring, and a higher temperature may increase hardness and occasionally even cause vitrification. In cases of exceptionally high firing, the fragments of fusible sherd are converted to slaggy blobs of black glass. Their identity is established by the fact that sherd particles can be seen in all stages of vitrification. Examples of this condition have been observed in some types of Pueblo pottery (Mesa Verde).

Quartz, a major constituent of common tempers, does not appear to change under low firing. As a matter of fact, however, quartz has three reversible inversion points, two of which are well within the temperature range of primitive firing. The lowest (the inversion from alpha to beta quartz) is sharp and occurs at 572° ± 5°C. The crystal form of the two types differs, and there is a volume change of 2 per cent, which may cause shattering when quartz formed at the higher temperature reverts to the low temperature form on cooling. Quartz or quartz rock has sometimes been heated and cooled to simplify pulverization by first shattering it. The Egyptians are reported to have prepared quartz for faïence in this way. The effect in these instances is doubtless due in part at least to the volume change, but decrepitation or force of steam from liquid inclusion may also be a factor. In thin sections, I have never observed fractured quartz grains that I could attribute to the effect of firing. Possibly inversion would not occur with the very rapid heating of primitive firing, or the grains would be less likely to break in the soft porous matrix of the clay.

A second inversion point of quartz at which it is transformed to the mineral tridymite occurs at 870°C, but this change is sluggish and occurs only under favorable conditions. I have never observed tridymite which was formed in the firing of the pottery. The third inversion point of quartz, 1470°C, is far above the range of primitive firing. In general, quartz was an inert temper, although the technologist should be alert to evidences of the alpha-beta inversion. This inversion would, of course, have a weakening effect on the body.

Another tempering material that ordinarily undergoes no change in the firing of prewheel pottery is volcanic glass. The stability of these glasses is variable. Those which contain water are easily converted to frothy masses as is shown by pitchstone implements that have been in crematory fires. But glasses of this type would be avoided by the potter, and I have seen no evidence of softening or fusion of the vitric ash among the many hundreds of thin sections from the Maya and Pueblo areas that I have examined. Also, when samples of these pastes are refired to 1000°C, most flakes do not lose their form, and the evidence of softening is negligible although occasionally a particle will blister.

Changes in temper that have a favorable effect on the body in the low temperature range are not numerous. The discussion of volcanic ash indicates one possibility—fluxing—which would strengthen the bond. Fusion might take place in opaline silica of organic origin—for example, sponge spicules and diatomaceous or infusorial earth. These materials, being fine and well disseminated in the paste, could have some fluxing effect, but chips of a paste containing sponge spicules showed no evidence of softening of the spicules when refired to 950°C, and I have not noted evidences of softening in thin sections of pottery with this class of temper.

The second favorable effect that temper can have is on color. Either the color as a whole is modified or contrasting spots are formed. It is difficult to estimate the effect that temper has had on the color of prehistoric wares because we usually lack the untempered clay necessary for comparison, but obviously fine, opaque material such as a white limestone will dilute the color of a clay more than will coarse translucent or transparent grains. Mottling or spotting is produced in modern brick by reducing particles of iron compounds on the surface and subsequently oxidizing the clay. Comparable effects have not been reported for prehistoric pottery although they could have been obtained. Mica is probably the most conspicuous nonplastic inclusion in low-fired pottery since the plates tend to become oriented parallel with the surface in the finishing process. When they are abundant they give a golden or silvery cast depending on their variety.

Thermal changes in temper that cause defects include oxidation, decomposition, and dehydration. A simple case of oxidation is the burning out of vegetal temper which leaves the body porous.

The principal tempering materials that decompose on firing are the carbonates. Since shell, limestone, and calcite were used extensively by various primitive potters, it is important to understand the effect of heat on them. As we have previously noted (p. 22), calcium carbonate decomposes at temperatures between 650° and 898°C. Carbon dioxide is driven off, leaving calcium oxide, which readily takes up moisture to form calcium hydroxide, a process we are familiar with in the burning and slaking of lime. Hydration increases the volume of the material; the particles, which after calcination are soft and white, often exert enough pressure to crumble the vessel. Very fine particles that do not have sufficient force to disintegrate the pottery reunite in time with carbon dioxide from the atmosphere, returning to their original chemical composition of calcium carbonate. The mineral structure in this case is very fine (cryptocrystalline); often it bears no resemblance to the original form, which may have been coarsely crystalline. Calcination proceeds very slowly at the lower temperatures and consequently, if the firing is short and rapid, there may be no noticeable change before a temperature of 750° or 800°C is reached. A high percentage of carbon dioxide in the firing atmosphere also raises the temperature of calcination. In the limestone-tempered pottery of the Maya lowlands, it is not unusual to find clear grains of calcite that have an opaque white surface film, or surface grains completely calcined and interior grains clear and unaffected. Again, spots where a hot flame has struck the surface may show calcination. Often the expansion of particles causes fine spalling, leaving the surface pitted. How often calcination was complete, and the pottery disintegrated, we have no way of knowing since all failures of this kind have disappeared.

The carbonate tempers set stringent limits on firing temperatures, and even when potters had been using a material of this class for generations, there were accidents and some loss. This is true not only of the calcium carbonates such as limestone, calcite, shell, but also of the calcareous tempers in which magnesium replaces some of the calcium—dolomite and magnesium limestone. They are subject to similar changes on heating and cause the same defects.

The dehydration of certain minerals is accompanied by swelling. Muscovite mica is one of the most common minerals of this class that occurs in pottery. Anyone who can remember the isinglass windows of old-fashioned wood stoves is familiar with the opaque, pearly appearance of muscovite that has been dehydrated. The change occurs well within the range of primitive firing. Ordinarily the flakes are not large enough or numerous enough to weaken the body, but when they lie near the surface and parallel to it, they cause pitting by forcing off bits of paste.

These examples will serve to indicate various secondary effects of substances used to reduce the shrinkage of clay. How well these effects were recognized by prehistoric potters can only be inferred from indirect evidence. In order to make sound inferences, we should know how the materials that occur in pottery behave when heated. The information that is needed has not all been published. We can obtain some of it by studying the pottery itself, and some of it calls for experiment.

MATTE PIGMENTS

A pigment must meet two conditions to be suitable for the decoration of unglazed pottery: it must retain a desirable color after firing and it must adhere to the vessel surface. These conditions limit stringently the number of available pigments. Many substances are altered and lose their color when fired. All organic compounds, such as the dyes, are normally burned to an ash. There is a special exception to this generalization. Carbon black can be obtained from an organic extract under certain conditions. Not only are the dyes excluded from the potter's palette but also many mineral pigments. They may be oxidized, reduced, or decomposed. Familiar examples are the blue and green basic carbonates of copper—the minerals malachite and azurite—which on firing are decomposed to powdery black oxide of copper. Another example is the rich vermilion sulfide of mercury—cinnabar—which is oxidized, the mercury passing off as vapor. Many times different potters must have painted their vessels with these minerals only to find that, when the firing was finished, the color had vanished. One can easily imagine their amazement and disappointment, and it is no wonder that they sometimes applied these mineral colors after firing.

A check of the pigments listed in *Trial Data on Painting Material* (1939) will illustrate how few of those from the artist's palette are suitable for pottery. The *Trial Data* includes natural dyes and manufactured paints, as well as native minerals. Thirty-one native ores are listed and of these only 13 can be fired: five clays, four iron oxide pigments, manganese, iron-manganese ores, volcanic ash, and diatomaceous earth. The last two cannot be used without a binder, and I know of no evidence of their use by the American Indian. The others nearly cover the range for unglazed pottery. The *Trial Data* lists only artist's pigments. There are, of course, many metal oxides that produce color with glazes. The underglaze colors of hard porcelain are the most limited because of the high temperatures at which they are fired, yet they include oxides of cobalt, iridium, uranium, titanium, chromium, copper, nickel, and manganese. Iron and potassium chromate, platinum, zinc, and alumina are also used in mixtures. Blue, green, yellow, rose, gray, brown, and black are obtained. But all of this was a sealed book to primitive potters, whose materials and methods were crude. Their principal colors, aside from black, brown, and white, were derived from the iron oxides, which produce their clearest colors when the temperature is not too high. The reds and oranges of ferric oxide in clay change to brown at the higher temperatures because they begin to fuse with the silicates. Firing atmosphere also affects color, especially that of the iron oxides, but this subject will be dealt with later in the discussion of each class of pigment.

The difficulty of obtaining a permanent pigment on unglazed, low-fired ware is not always appreciated because we rarely use paints in a comparable way. Unfired paints of all kinds have a medium or vehicle that gives them the proper spreading quality and acts as a binder. Mediums include various oils, gums, and albumin. All these materials are organic. They would burn out on firing and their binding power would then be lost. They serve a purpose in pottery paint, however, both as a vehicle and as a binder before firing. A vehicle is desirable especially if the paint is not finely ground because, when the brush is applied to the dry porous surface, water is drawn out, causing a heavy daub to be left at the beginning of the stroke and leaving the paint on the brush too dry to flow well. Uniformity of line width and evenness of the coat give indication of the spreading quality.

With respect to the problem of binding a pigment, modern glazed ceramics and primitive unglazed pottery are not comparable. The pigments of modern wares are either painted on the body before glazing (underglaze), mixed with the glaze, or painted on it so that, in each case, the pigment fuses with the glaze, which solves the problem of permanence. When a ground mineral, such as iron oxide or an iron-manganese ore, is fired on pottery it will remain soft and powdery unless some change takes place to render it adherent. The impermanent paint is familiar to us through some of the poorly fired wares that present-day Pueblo potters make for the tourist trade.

There are various ways in which a powdered mineral paint can be rendered permanent in firing, chief of which are sintering and reaction with impurities. Fine grinding of the pigment facilitates these reactions. Certain pigments are also rendered more permanent by polishing before firing. This mechanical action compacts and rubs granules into the clay surface. Again, some native pigments contain a natural binder. The most familiar examples are the argillaceous paints —clays colored with iron oxide. The problem of securing permanence and the nature of the bond will be considered in more detail in the description of the firing properties of the various kinds of paint.

The color range of common pigments of prewheel pottery includes black and brown-black obtained from iron oxide, iron-manganese ores, graphite, and carbon (charred plant extract); dark brown from iron-manganese ores; reds, oranges, purplish gray, yellow, and buff from iron oxides and from ferruginous clays; and white from clay or calcium carbonate. In addition, vitreous paints were obtained from ores of lead and of copper combined with various oxides, principally those of iron and manganese. These will be discussed under glazes. The pigments applied after firing will also be discussed in a separate section. For simplicity of discussion, paints will be grouped by composition into four main classes: iron oxides, iron-manganese ores, carbon, and clays. Each of these classes includes paints from different sources and each produces a range of colors depending on composition, degree of oxidation, and presence of impurities. Some are adapted to particular kinds of clay or require special methods of firing for good results.

CARBON PAINTS

Plant extracts. The use of an organic substance, such as the juice of a plant, for pottery paint seems anomalous because in firing it chars, forming carbon which should be burned out, leaving only a trace of white ash. Yet carbon paint is common on the black-on-white pottery of certain parts of the Pueblo area from Basket Maker III times to the present; it also occurs on trickle-slate ware of the Maya of Yucatan and on resist-decorated ware of Mesoamerica and eastern United States. The technique of present-day Pueblo potters of the Rio Grande Valley who use organic paint is well known. An extract obtained by boiling the young, tender growth of the Rocky Mountain bee plant (*Periloma serrulatum*) is concentrated and dried in cakes. When needed, it is mixed with water to the desired consistency. Before firing, the paint, which is called *guaco*, is a dark olive-green. By proper choice of slip and short firing, the paint is charred without burning out, resulting in a uniform, satiny black.

The Rocky Mountain bee plant does not possess exceptional or peculiar properties that make it suitable for a ceramic paint. Any plant extract or other organic substance that will char will produce the same effect. For experimental purposes such diverse substances as concentrated plant extracts—including a species of chenopodium, mock orange, and dandelion—licorice, sugar, glucose, honey, glue, starch, and gum tragacanth have been used. In fact, some Indians learned through their own experience that a sugar solution would serve the purpose and save them the labor of preparing the plant extract. They add just enough *guaco* to the sugar solution to give the paint proper consistency and enough color to make the pattern visible while they paint.

The attempt to explain the permanence of these organic paints has resulted in considerable theorizing and experimentation, which is worth reviewing briefly because of both the importance of carbon paints and our need to understand the place of experimentation in the study of paints. Hawley (1929) was the first to identify and direct attention to the organic paints of Pueblo pottery. She observed that the carbon paints are often difficult to burn out with a blowpipe unless they are treated with hydrofluoric acid. Since this acid attacks silicates, Hawley reasoned that the paint must be protected by a thin coat of alkali glass formed by the reaction of ash in the extract with silica in the clay. This is a logical conclusion; however, there is no direct evidence of this coat. Glass cannot be detected microscopically; moreover, when a vessel that has been decorated with *guaco* is first drawn from the fire, the paint is covered with a powdery white ash left from combustion of part of the carbon.

The theory of a protective coat of an alkali glass has been tested by comparing *guaco* and ash-free organic paints (Shepard in Kidder and Shepard, 1936, pp. 414–20). Sugar, used as the ash-free substance, was prepared in the same strength as *guaco*, applied on various types of clay, and fired under uniform conditions. The color obtained with both paints varied greatly on different clays, whereas the sugar and *guaco* differed but slightly when applied on the same clay. It was also found that the addition of alkali to ash-free substances did not improve their permanence; nor did the removal of part of the ash from *guaco* result in a lighter paint. The possible fire-proofing effect of salts in the paint was also tested with negative results.

None of these experiments gave any evidence of the effectiveness of ash in protecting the surface, and the comparison of *guaco* and sugar showed conclusively that the relative permanence of the paint is not due to the postulated silicate film. Minor variations in depth of black obtained from sugar and *guaco* may be explained by the physical state of the carbon. As an example of this effect, Mellor (1916, p. 722) reports that combustion is spontaneous for very fine carbon but does not begin until a temperature of 660°C is reached for carbon approaching the density of graphite.

The most striking fact brought out by these tests is the effect of the type of clay on the permanence of the carbon. Bentonitic and other highly adsorptive clays retained a good black under firing conditions that completey oxidized the carbon on nonadsorptive, sedimentary clays. All of the clays that held the paint well required a high percentage of water to bring them to the plastic state and they had high shrinkage. These clays take up much more of the paint solution than the less adsorptive clays, and on drying, the clay plates are drawn tightly together, protecting the film of paint that surrounds them. The effectiveness of hydrofluoric acid in facilitating oxidation of carbon paints is explained by the fact that it attacks the clay, opening the surface and loosening the bond and thus exposing the carbon to air.

The importance of penetration was demonstrated by tests in which concentration of paint was varied. The proportion of *guaco* and water used in most of these experiments was the same as that of a modern Pueblo potter. Paint of double strength was too thick to penetrate well and burned out much more readily. Half-strength gave a lighter gray than normal strength because the solution did not carry enough organic matter, but when a line was painted a second time with the weak solution, the color was superior to that obtained with the normal paint, because of more effective penetration.

The relation of temperature, duration of firing, and firing atmosphere to the burning of carbon is so obvious it requires no elaboration. If the organic paint could be fired in an atmosphere free of oxygen, carbon black could be obtained on any clay, but this condition never exists in primitive firing. Even when reducing gases are present during the greater part of the firing period, oxygen must also be present for the fuel to burn; consequently, with shifting air currents, some of it reaches the thin film of carbon paint, which requires relatively little oxygen for conversion to carbon dioxide.

The relation of the type of clay to the depth of color of carbon paint from a plant extract is not a matter of merely theoretic interest to the technologist. It has a bearing on the distribution of this class of paint because it could not be produced in regions lacking adsorptive clays unless such clays could be obtained in trade. The use of plant extracts is not open to free choice or established merely by custom; it is limited by ceramic resources.

There is a second class of carbon paints obtained by applying a plant extract after firing and reheating just enough to char the paint or applying on the vessel that is still hot from the fire. This carbon paint resembles the fired paint superficially but it is much more readily burned out on refiring. A postfiring carbon paint can be produced on any type of body.

Graphite.   The mineral form of carbon appears sporadically as a paint or slip on pottery from many regions. In America it has been reported from Mexico and Guatemala. Graphite is formed principally by the metamorphism of carbonaceous deposits and is found in metamorphic rocks or contact metamorphic zones. Coal beds are sometimes converted to graphite by intense metamorphism. Graphite is not always organic in origin, however, for it occurs in meteorites, and also as scales in granite, gneiss, mica schist, quartzite, and crystalline limestone. It is found in foliated masses, is often scaly or platy and also granular to compact or earthy. Its physical properties vary with the form. The color is iron black to steel gray; the surface has either metallic luster or is dull and earthy. It is soft (1 to 2 in Mohs' scale) and has a greasy feel.

Graphite rubbed on pottery either before or after firing is soft and easily abraded. Some bonding with the clay may occur when it is applied on the unfired clay but it is subject to oxidation on firing. The temperature of combustion varies with grain size and compactness. Samples of graphite-painted ware from Oaxaca and the highlands of Guatemala refired in air showed no appreciable oxidation when carried rapidly to 700°C. It is practicable to use, therefore, on low-fired ware.

IRON OXIDE PAINTS

It is no wonder that potters were attracted from early times by the rich array of colors the iron oxides afford. Their range is wide, their variations are subtle, and they do not disappoint the potters when they are fired. Yellow limonite changed to red is still a bright and attractive color, and when red hematite is reduced in firing, it gives a strong black that throws a design into sharp contrast with a light clay. Nature has supplied the iron oxides freely, for they occur in all types of rock and are widely distributed. Magnetite is common in igneous rocks. The iron-bearing silicates of these rocks are also a source of iron for the oxides. Through the weathering of igneous rocks, the iron is released as oxides, hydroxides, sulfate, or carbonate. It is taken into solution, usually as ferrous bicarbonate, and deposited as oxides in all types of sedimentary rock. These oxides form the "cement" of red sandstones and collect in nodules and concretions; they color limestone, clays, and soils and are deposited in bogs and marshes as bog iron. Magnetite and hematite are widespread in metamorphic rocks, and limonite and hematite are formed around volcanoes and constitute the capping, called gossan or "iron hat," of many mineral and ore veins.

We need only to consider the varied modes of occurrence of the iron oxides and the wide range of their colors to sense their complexity. Limonite, which is amorphous and contains an indefinite amount of water, is one of the commonest forms of ferric oxide. It is an alteration product of other iron-bearing ores and minerals, which are decomposed through exposure to air, moisture, carbonic and organic acids. Iron carried in solution in water forms limonite in bogs and marshes partly through loss of carbonic acid that holds it in solution, partly through the action of "iron bacteria" which absorb the iron and deposit it as ferric oxide. Other oxides of iron are associated with limonite in bog iron ore which carries as impurities more or less sand, clay, and organic matter that were deposited along with the iron oxides.

Although limonite is always an alteration product, its modes of origin are various and its forms are correspondingly diverse. In addition to constituting the principal oxide of bog ores, which are generally dark, loose, and porous in texture, limonite occurs as yellow or brownish, earthy ocher, which contains sand and clay as impurities, as clay-ironstone, brown concretionary masses in sedimentary rock, and in compact, stalactitic, and botryoidal forms which have a submetallic luster. It is also common in gossan as well as in sedimentary formations.

The term limonite is used loosely for all yellowish or brownish hydrous iron oxides. Some so-called limonite is a minutely crystalline variety of hydrous ferric oxide named goethite after Goethe. This mineral, unlike limonite, contains a definite amount of water. Some limonites show a transition to goethite, and when the latter mineral is finely crystalline it closely resembles limonite. When more coarsely crystalline, it occurs as prisms and tablets and as fibrous or foliated masses.

Hematite, the anhydrous ferric oxide mineral, is a common alteration product and in turn alters to magnetite, siderite, limonite, pyrite, and other iron minerals, depending on conditions. It is one of the most widely distributed minerals, for it is abundant in some sedimentary rocks, occurs as a product of metamorphism in crystalline schists, colors many rocks and minerals red, occurs in large crystals around volcanoes, and is common in ore veins. Red ocher is an earthy form of hematite mixed with clay. Clay-ironstone, in which hematite predominates, is hard, reddish to brownish black, and often submetallic in luster. Massive forms of hematite which are finely crystalline or amorphous, are brown to iron black, columnar, fibrous, and reniform (kidney ore). Coarse crystals (specular hematite) have a metallic luster. This form is familiar to American archaeologists, as it was widely used in paints by both Mexican and Mayan Indians. On pottery it appears as small sharp-angled, steel-colored plates in a maroon-red, earthy hematite and is detected by its sparkle. Fine, platy hematite, called micaceous, is soft and unctuous.

The occurrences of iron oxide minerals suggest how readily the potter could obtain them. Hematite and limonite are more widely distributed in convenient form than magnetite. Bog ore, ochers, and ironstone are all likely sources of paint. The softer, earthy forms of these minerals could be used without preparation. Hard ironstone or bog ore had to be ground.

The modes of occurrence of the iron oxides will suggest the frequency with which they carry impurities. These are of interest because they affect the properties of the paint and aid in differentiating paints from different sources. Clay, sand, and organic matter have been mentioned. Other impurities are calcium and magnesium carbonates, aluminum hydroxide, manganese compounds, and phosphates. Ochers formed as spring deposits often carry traces of copper, arsenic, nickel, and cobalt. Some of the rarer metals also occur as traces.

The color range of the powders of the iron oxide minerals can be compared when they are rubbed across a porcelain streak plate—a common field test for ores.

The streak of the hydrous oxides is yellowish brown; of hematite, red; and of magnetite, black. The color of the hydrous oxides is of little interest to the potter because on firing they are dehydrated and transformed to red ferric oxide. Yellow colors in pottery cannot therefore be attributed to limonite. Particle size is one explanation—ferric oxide in the colloidal state is rendered stable by alumina. Hematite exhibits a surprising range of colors, depending on particle size and crystalline state. The amorphous and minutely crystalline forms are red, the coarser crystals black. It is thought that a yellow modification in pottery owes its color to the colloidal state. It would indeed be a task to explain all the subtle color variations of the ferric oxides.

When iron oxides are fired, temperature, duration of heating, and atmosphere affect their color. Amorphous forms of ferric oxide become crystalline between 400° and 600°C. This transformation is referred to as "glowing" because of the appearance of specimens as they emit heat. There is also a well-defined reversible inversion at 678°C called the Curie point, at which heat is absorbed and the crystal form is changed. The temperature of this inversion is lowered by the presence of alumina and also by magnetite. Still another change, referred to as "sintering," takes place when smaller crystals are transformed to larger ones. Sintering occurs at temperatures between 920° and 950°C and is accompanied by shrinkage. It is not comparable to the sintering of clay, which is distinguished by softening and fusion of particles. The changes in state of ferric oxide are of interest to the student of pottery because they may have some effect on the permanence of paints. The temperatures recorded are for laboratory conditions under which the sample is heated long enough to establish equilibrium. The changes may not always take place at these temperatures with the rapid heating of direct firing.

The conditions under which ferric oxide is reduced are of especial interest to the student of primitive pottery. The lower oxides are formed by the action of hydrogen or carbon monoxide on ferric oxide when it is heated to temperatures above 300°C. The lowest temperature at which reduction occurs depends on the form of the oxide. The massive and amorphous oxides are more reactive than the crystalline ones. Magnetite is formed in the first stage of reduction, but mixtures of magnetite and hematite and of magnetite and ferrous oxide are perhaps more common than is generally supposed.

Magnetite also undergoes transformations when heated, but these have been less fully investigated than those of hematite. The oxidation of magnetite begins at about 400°C in air but proceeds to completion very slowly because the ferric oxide that is formed acts as a protective coating and prevents further oxidation. The Curie point of magnetite is between 530° and 593°C. Above this point magnetite is paramagnetic (shows only slight magnetic effect).

Red iron oxide paints. These paints are highly variable in color, texture, luster, hardness, and bonding. It is important to recognize that the fired ferric oxide paint is sometimes granular and powdery, showing no apparent effects of firing. In other words, one cannot tell directly from the appearance of a soft, impermanent ferric oxide paint whether it was fired on the vessel or applied after firing. Occasionally, however, the color of the pottery shows that the paint must be a postfiring application. A clear red could not be retained if the pottery were smudged. Black Teotihuacan cylinders with red-filled, incised design are an example of postfiring application, as is also the so-called fugitive red coat of early gray pottery from the Pueblo area.

Although some fired paints are fugitive, many are well bonded and various factors can contribute to permanence. The clay that occurs as an impurity acts as a binder. Mechanical effects resulting from polishing, particularly compacting and rubbing the pigment into the pores, also increase their resistance to abrasion. Whether or not the inversion of ferric oxide brings about interlocking of particles that improves permanence has not been determined.

Black iron oxide paints. Black iron oxide paint can be produced in two ways, by using magnetite and preventing it from oxidizing in firing or by reducing hematite. In either case it is necessary to control firing atmosphere. This circumstance may well account for the fact that black iron oxide paints are much less common than reds. The paint of certain types of Pueblo black-on-white ware affords the best-known example from American Indian pottery. The ware is unoxidized and grayish white. The paint at its best is a near black and is well bonded, but there are many unsuccessfully fired specimens that are soft and brown or even reddish. There is no direct way of determining whether the original pigment was magnetite or a ferric oxide, but paints that represent failures in firing offer clues. These have the color of ferric oxide, and are therefore hematites that were not reduced in firing or a magnetite that was oxidized. The color of the pottery itself gives some indication of the firing atmosphere. If there had been sufficient oxygen to convert magnetite to ferric oxide, the clay would also have been oxidized. One cannot argue contrariwise that presence of hematite indicates an oxidizing atmosphere because hematite could be fired in a neutral atmosphere without undergoing reduction. If the firing were neither strongly oxidizing nor strongly reducing, a carbonaceous clay would not be oxidized nor would a ferric oxide be reduced. The fact that these red, unsuccessfully fired paints are on gray, unoxidized pottery therefore indicates that they are derived from ferric oxide rather than from magnetite.

The texture and bonding of these paints gives some indication of the changes that have taken place in firing. The reds and browns are soft and powdery. In some cases they have rubbed off completely, leaving only a trace of oxide in the pores of the pottery. The blacks differ in hardness but at their best are adherent and well bonded. The hardest paint frequently shows fine crazing, as from shrinkage, which fact suggests that it has been sintered. Occasionally a paint will have a thin, hard surface crust beneath which the oxide is powdery. This is further indication that these paints are reduced ferric oxides rather than unoxidized magnetites. Polished sections cut through a coat show a reticulated structure which may be explained by sintering.

The impurities of the Pueblo iron oxide paints also affected their permanence. Spectrographic analyses of a few specimens (see Shepard in Morris, 1939, pp. 254–56) show only traces of alumina and alkali, but silica appears as a major constituent. With only a trace of alumina there could not be enough clay to have binding action. The silica, on the other hand, was effective when there was sufficiently strong reduction to convert some of the iron oxide to the ferrous state in which it fluxes with silica to form a glass. The glass can be detected microscopically in some specimens, and the paint of the most effectively fired pieces has a vitreous luster.

It is apparent that a number of independent factors affected the appearance and permanence of black iron oxide paints. This description of Pueblo paints may suggest the kind of questions that must be answered to explain the properties of unglazed pottery paint.

MANGANESE AND IRON-MANGANESE PAINTS

Manganese ores were widely used by prewheel potters for blackish paint, and they are still being used by some Indian potters today. Extensive data for the distribution of this type of pigment are not available, but in the Pueblo and Maya areas, for which we have the fullest information, the black or brownish black paint of the oxidized wares is principally manganese or manganese and iron ore. It has also been identified on the Inca polychromes of Pachacamac and on a number of Mexican polychromes. Manganese ores were probably more generally used for black than was either carbon or iron oxide, for both of the latter require special conditions.

Manganese has certain chemical resemblances to iron and, like it, forms more than one oxide. The mineral hausmannite is the equivalent in its metal-oxygen ratio of magnetite, and manganite corresponds to goethite; but the common oxide of manganese—the dioxide, represented by the mineral pyrolusite—is higher in oxygen than any of the iron oxides. Also the lowest oxide, manganous, occurs in a natural state as the mineral manganosite, whereas ferrous oxide does not occur in nature. The point of interest to the potter, however, is the fact that the common oxides and hydroxides of manganese are black or brownish black and retain their color when fired. There are different shades of dark brown and brownish black but no color changes comparable to those which accompany the reduction of ferric oxide.

The geologic history of manganese deposits parallels that of iron. Manganese is widely distributed in crystalline rocks but is much less abundant than iron. Both elements are released with the weathering of rock, go into solution in soil waters, and are carried by streams and rivers to lakes and oceans, where they are redeposited under much the same conditions. Yet the two elements are more or less separated on redeposition because of differences in solubility. Manganese remains in solution longer than iron.

Nearly all workable manganese deposits are of secondary origin. The ores are widely distributed in sheets or lenses in sedimentary rock, sandstones and limestones. On the ocean floor, manganese coats shells and pebbles, and concretions often form around particles of tuff, the source of the ore being in many instances red muds. The chief fresh-water deposits are bog ores or wad. The manner in which the ore is collected and redeposited is a chemical and physical one which is not yet fully explained, but it is likely that much of the manganese ore was deposited in a colloidal state, which would explain the configuration and also the frequent association of certain other elements which would have been adsorbed by the colloid. Among the common impurities are nickel, cobalt, zinc, lead, barium, and potassium. The presence of certain of these impurities may sometimes serve to identify the manganese from a particular source, or at least to differentiate paints.

Manganese ores were available to potters in many forms. Nodules, concretions, and bog ores were probably their chief sources. Potters of the Pueblo of Zia gather concretions that weather out from a sandstone cliff to collect at its base. Bog ores were known to Zuni and Hopi potters. These may well be typical of the sources of manganese paints in prehistoric times.

The manganese paints from the Southwest and the Maya area that have been studied show no evidence of physical or chemical changes during firing that would make them permanent. None of them have the hardness attained by the reduced iron oxide paints and there is no evidence of sintering or fluxing. Most of them are relatively soft, and a brown powder can be scraped from their surfaces with slight pressure. Much of the manganese in the ores used was present in its highest state of oxidation as manganese dioxide. Consequently, if the final effect of firing is oxidizing, there is no change in state of oxidation and no change in color. When sherds are refired in strong reducing atmosphere in the laboratory, the paint becomes somewhat more brown, probably as a result of the reduction of the dioxide to the oxide, Mn_3O_4. Hausmannite, the mineral of this composition, is browner than pyrolusite (MnO_2). If manganese concretions, bog ore or wad, were used for paint, the manganese would be present largely in its highest state of oxidation, and hence the color would not be changed in firing unless there were reduction.

When iron oxide occurs with manganese dioxide, it does not have a marked effect on color of the paint. Some 40 paints from Maya and Pueblo pottery having iron-manganese ratios between 0.06 and 2.0 showed no color variations that could be correlated with the relative amount of iron oxide. Paints with the equivalent of 22 per cent ferric oxide, refired in air to insure complete oxidation, do not become browner.

Manganese paints do not ordinarily contain sufficient fluxing material to sinter or vitrify. They are soft and easily scraped from the surface, but on prehistoric wares they have been relatively permanent. One cause of adherence in the absence of a binder in the paint is the mechanical one previously mentioned in the case of iron oxides; that is, polishing which compacts the powder and presses it into the clay. Many of the manganese paints of Pueblo pottery have been polished. Frequently they have no appreciable relief, and when they are scraped from the surface a depression is left. These characteristics suggest that the vessel was polished while still moist and the pigment pressed firmly into the clay. Imbedding would be no less effective than compacting.

Some of the Maya paints also show evidence of polishing, but many evidently owe their permanence to another cause. They are protected by some coat of clear material. This is often not detected by visual inspection alone. It is most plainly seen when the surface is scraped. A clear or slightly reddish material is removed before the paint is cut into. Lacquer-like substances or resins of various plants are used at the present time by Indians of many parts of South America. Such a coat applied after firing would prevent soft colors from rubbing.

Still a third factor which may prevent these colors from rubbing is the binding effect of impurities, especially clay. Analyzed samples of manganese paints contained from 12 to 22 per cent alumina, indicating the presence of clay which is not uncommon in bog ore.

CLAY PAINTS

When one considers the array of clay colors and the richness of their contrasts, it is little wonder that they were used decoratively by potters. There is no need to discuss the sources and properties of these paints, for that has already been covered in the general discussion of clay. It will suffice to bring out a few facts relative to their use as paint.

The spreading quality of a clay paint is determined largely by its particle size and dispersion; the finer the texture the more smoothly the paint will flow. Coarse or flocculated clays are unsatisfactory for paint because they settle too quickly. Many clays are not fine enough for delicate linework, and the clay paint often has considerable relief because it was applied as a thick suspension. The texture and luster of clay paints differ depending on properties of the clay and whether or not they were smoothed or polished. Not all clays polish well (see p. 123). The permanence of clay paint depends on its bonding power and temperature of sintering. The purer, more refractory clays do not harden sufficiently at low temperatures to be permanent.

The majority of white paints were relatively pure kaolins or white marls—a mixture of clay and calcite. The kaolins are usually powdery after firing because they are much more refractory than the body.

The red and yellow clays that owe their color to iron oxide or hydrated iron oxide are less refractory and form a good bond. They grade into earthy hematites.

POSTFIRING PAINTS

To the functionalist, the practice of painting a vessel after firing hardly deserves to be classed as ceramic art, but as long as the custom was followed, it is part of the student's task to understand it. Potters can choose any pigment if it is not to be fired, and by drawing on common minerals that would be decomposed by heat, they can add blues and greens to their palette. These colors that cannot be obtained on unglazed fired ware were used most frequently in postfiring decoration. The potter was also free to choose any medium, hence delicate linework was possible and the paint could be made adherent after it was dry. But at best the coating, being soft, could be washed or brushed off easily; consequently, the technique could not be used for domestic vessels.

In the New World, postfiring decoration is best known among the Maya, and both technique and range of colors are comparable to those of mural painting (Kidder, Jennings, and Shook, 1946, pp. 269–77). Moreover, vessels were given a coating of lime plaster or white clay before painting. To indicate the nature of the pigments, it will suffice to mention those that were used most frequently. Goethite and limonite furnished a range of yellows and yellow-browns. Hematite was used for red, and in addition—and certainly more prized—there was cinnabar, the brilliant sulfide of mercury. Cinnabar is found chiefly in veins and fissures of sedimentary rock near igneous outcrops. It is also found about hot springs where it is a product of solfataric action. The hydrated copper carbonates, malachite and azurite, were the chief sources of blues and greens. These minerals are common in the oxidation zones of copper veins and also occur as secondary deposits in sediments. A blue found on Maya murals which has the properties of a clay of the montmorillonite group and a chromiferous clay has not yet been identified on pottery, but these paints have not been extensively tested. Pigments were often mixed with lime plaster or cryptocrystalline calcite, which gave various tints. Pulverized charcoal was used for black. In the study of pigments that are applied in a calcareous coat, the possibility that a true fresco technique of painting on fresh lime plaster was used should be kept in mind, although no evidence of this technique has yet been found.

GLAZES

Much of the fascination of ceramics lies in the possibilities of creating beautiful effects with glazes. Even with the limitations imposed by the necessity of choosing colorants that are not decomposed by heat, the ceramist can produce brilliant colors in many hues by varying firing temperature and atmosphere, and he can obtain entirely different colors with the same glaze. When European chemists first studied the rare and beautiful glazes of Chinese porcelains, they were unable to reproduce them by following their analytical data because they did not realize the importance of reduction in obtaining some of the most prized effects. The ceramist has considerable latitude in glaze composition and in technique of application and can influence texture, luster, transparency, and brilliance by controlling composition and firing. Aesthetic interests lead to experiments with crazing, matte effects, and crystallization; technical requirements demand control of "fit," hardness, and resistance to acids.

Many of the most interesting developments in glazing belong to the historic period, but glazes are not outside the archaeologist's field, for their origin goes back to prehistoric times and the beginnings are marked by accidents and chance trials with slips and paints. In order to appreciate the significance of these, the basic characteristics of a glaze should be understood.

PROPERTIES OF A GLAZE

Technically, a glaze is a glass, which means that it lacks regular atomic arrangement. Glass is familiar enough in everyday experience and yet it represents a special and uncommon state of matter. When a substance changes from the liquid to the solid state, as when molten matter cools, the atoms, which were moving freely in the liquid, have a strong tendency to assume regular positions with relation to each other because of the forces acting between them. The time required for them to take the places they occupy in a crystalline solid depends partly on the shape of the atomic groups or units which make up the solid and partly on the relative strength of forces exerted by the different atoms of a cluster. Sudden chilling checks the process, but most substances cannot be cooled quickly enough to prevent crystallization. This is something that candy makers can understand. They cannot prevent "sugariness" by rapid cooling alone. Glasses are formed when for some reason atoms are prevented from assuming a normal orderly arrangement. There are comparatively few elements that have the characteristics necessary to form a random arrangement in the solid state.

X-ray diffraction studies have given a picture of the structure of the glassy state. In place of the orderly pattern of repetition of units of atoms that characterize a crystal, a glass has a random three-dimensional network of atoms. The word "network" does not imply regularity; the strands are uneven and the spaces unequal. Of the few compounds that form in this way, silica is the most important. It is the network former of all familiar glazes and glasses. Silica alone forms a glass which has a high melting point, low coefficient of expansion, and high chemical resistance but is very brittle. Other atoms can fill the holes of the glass network. These are referred to as network modifiers because they loosen the bond and lower the melting point of the glass. They are the compounds the ceramist calls fluxes, the principal ones in glazes being oxides of lead, the alkalis, the alkaline earths, zinc, and borax. Finally there are ions, referred to as intermediate glass formers, that can partially substitute for the network former. Alumina is the principal intermediate glass former of glazes.

The ceramist calculates the composition of a glaze in terms of the proportions of basic, intermediate, and acidic oxides. These correspond respectively to network modifiers, intermediate glass formers, and network formers. Since the spaces of the network in a glass need not all be filled, a glass does not have the single fixed proportion of components which characterize a crystalline compound. As the proportion of constituents is varied, the properties of the glass are modified. Glazes can be produced over a wide range of temperatures because of the differences in fluxes and also because of the effect of varying proportions. There is always one set of proportions for a mixture (called the eutectic) that has a minimum fusing point for the given constituents. For example, lead oxide fuses at 888°C, but when 12 per cent of silica (melting point 1713°C) is added, the melting point of the mixture is 532°C (lead-silica eutectic). The low melting glazes are of especial interest to the archaeologist because they must have been the first to be discovered. Commercial raw lead and alkaline glazes require a temperature in the neighborhood of 900°C, whereas the feldspathic glazes for porcelain require 1300°C and over.

The oxides of the heavy metals, which are the chief colorants of glazes, play a varied role. Some go into solution in the glass, imparting color through their ions, and others form minute insoluble crystals or colloidal suspensions. Color is influenced by the state of the oxide, its position in the network, and the kind of atoms surrounding it; consequently, the same element can have more than one effect.

It is little wonder that glazes are subject to many defects. Perhaps the first question is how well a glaze "fits" the body, whether it will craze or peel. The problem of avoiding the unequal shrinkage is not entirely one of matching coefficients of expansions. A glaze can have a degree of elasticity that will compensate for a certain amount of strain. The ceramist must know how the various components of a glaze affect its shrinkage and elasticity.

Other defects that must be controlled are blistering from the formation of gases or trapped air, incomplete solution of constituents, recrystallization (devitrification of the glass), and extremes of viscosity.

This bare outline may give a hint of the modern concept of glazes. The successful production of glasses and glazes antedates by centuries the scientific study of them, but even so present-day knowledge can help clarify questions regarding their origin.

EARLY TYPES OF GLAZES

In view of the fact that glazes can be produced with a number of different fluxes, it is not surprising to find that they have been discovered in different ways and at more than one time and place. There is conjecture regarding many particulars in the early history of glazes, but the broad outlines of the story have emerged. The origin of the alkali glaze of the Near East has been discussed by Debevoise (1934) and Lucas (1935–36, 1948), research on the glaze of classic Greek Black-figured ware and Roman Terra Sigillata has been summarized and evaluated by de Jong and Rijken (1946), and the beginnings of porcelain in China have been reviewed by Laufer (1917). American Indian pottery will serve to illustrate my points regarding the origin of glazes, and since my experience has been in the American field my remarks will be confined to the pottery of this area.

American Indian glazes are of two types: the glaze paints of the Pueblo area which have a lead oxide flux, and the vitrified or semivitrified slip of Plumbate ware from Mesoamerica. It is reasonably clear from the composition, properties, and occurrences of these glazes that they were discovered not only independently but also in three different ways: (1) in the course of trying out ores that might be suitable for paint, (2) by the use for matte paint of an ore that contained a flux, and (3) by the use of a slip clay that carried sufficient fluxing material to vitrify under certain firing conditions. It may be interesting to consider how far the nature and occurrence of these glazes support these hypotheses of origin.

It is surprising to find a lead glaze paint in the first pottery-making period of the Pueblo area, Basket Maker III. It appears to have been a localized development of short duration, for it is best known from the Durango district of Colorado which is highly mineralized and has numerous lead veins. There is little doubt that it originated from the potters' curiosity regarding the suitability for pottery paint of certain unusual, interesting-looking minerals because the glaze, a lead-silica glass, lacks pigments, such as iron or manganese oxides, that might attract potters to a flux-bearing ore. The common lead ores, galena (lead sulfide) and cerussite (lead carbonate), being distinctive in appearance, would attract attention, and the steel-colored cubes of galena have been found in prehistoric caches. It is clear that the lead ore, when ground for paint, was mixed with an organic medium, for a dark gray streak underlies the lines; and where the glaze is patchy, the design is carried out in full by carbon formed from the medium. The fact that this carbon stain, presumably from an organic vehicle, did not burn out is explained by the type of clay (see p. 34). If ground lead sulfide or carbonate were painted on the pottery, it would be converted to the oxide in firing and would unite with silica from the clay, but a glaze forms more readily when some silica is mixed with the lead ore. The lead-silica ratio of this glaze is variable, but since these potters did not mix pigment with the ore, it is unlikely that they discovered the effect of adding silica. The pale greenish yellow glass over the grayish body of the ware was neither conspicuous nor particularly attractive, which fact probably accounts, in part at least, for its short history.

An independent discovery of a lead glaze paint came some 600 years later in the Rio Puerco of the West or perhaps on the northern fringe of the White Mountains. This time it evidently happened through the use of an iron-manganese ore which carried enough lead to form a glass. The potters were interested in a black paint, but nature threw in something more. The glaze is not clear, and pottery of the region shows an unbroken transition from a matte iron-manganese paint to a vitreous paint which is opaque with pigment. Some of these glazes have a high percentage of copper, which also promoted fusion. Pottery with this vitreous decoration appears as trade ware in the Rio Grande Valley just prior to the development of the glaze-paint technique in that area, and raw glaze-paint material may have been imported at the start from the West because the earliest glazes on indigenous Rio Grande pottery are similar in copper content to those of the West, whereas copper is absent or occurs only as a trace after the technique becomes well established in the Rio Grande area. Rio Grande glaze-paint technique was followed for a period of over 300 years, during which time there were consistent changes in the characteristics of the glaze. It began as an opaque black mineral paint with a lead-silica binder and became a vitreous, lead-silica glass with low viscosity (Kidder and Shepard, 1936). The association of manganese, iron, and lead minerals in mines of the region in which this glaze was produced lends further support to the theory of its origin.

Before we leave the glaze paints, a case of accidental vitrification may be mentioned. It occurs rarely and sporadically on black-on-white ware having a reduced iron oxide paint. At best it is a thin, well-vitrified, and lustrous black. Analysis has shown that it is an iron-silica glass (Shepard in Morris, 1939, pp. 255–57.) Its formation is doubtless explained by the use of a siliceous iron oxide paint together with firing conditions that reduced the iron oxide to the ferrous state in which it acts as a strong flux. The Indians apparently never recognized the cause of the glaze and were unable to produce it at will. It doubtless required stronger reduction and higher temperature than they usually obtained, which would account for its rarity and the potter's failure to produce it consistently.

These Pueblo glazes originated in painting. The potters never made the transition from a vitreous paint used for design to a surface coating. This fact can be attributed to their lack of interest rather than to properties of the glaze paint.

In contrast to the Southwestern development, Plumbate glaze was derived from a slip. I have designated the coating a glaze because of the extent of glass formation in the best specimens, although the classification might be debated on the ground that vitrification is far from complete in most cases, and even the most fully vitrified coats contain some undissolved material. In fact the relation of this unique surface finish to a slip is perfectly clear. All stages between a soft orange or red clay slip and the distinctive, very hard, lustrous gray surface can be found. Even though constituents of the clay were never taken into complete solution to form a clear glass, yet at its best the coat has the essential charac teristics of a glaze. The wide distribution in trade of the vitrified pieces and the quantity in which they were produced leave little doubt that the potters had some understanding of what was required to produce the desired effect.

The use of a slip—a coat of fine-textured clay of desirable color—is common practice in the Southwest and Mesoamerica. Why did only Plumbate slip vitrify? Did the potters add a flux or did the clay have a very low fusion point, owing to a natural flux, or was the method of firing unusual? Analysis of the clay slip gives no indication of the addition of a flux. The distinguishing feature of the slip is the high iron oxide and alumina content. Iron oxide when reduced to the ferrous state is a strong flux. The characteristic gray colors of the vitreous specimens show that they were reduced. Both composition of the clay and method of firing were there-fore essential for vitrification. One other factor, fineness of particle size, doubtless promoted vitrification. As the fusion point of a material is approached the edges of particles begin to soften first and the smaller the particles in a given amount of material the more edges there are.

Plumbate slip is unique in the New World but it has interesting analogies in the Old. The black glaze of Greek Black-figured ware and the surface coat of Terra Sigillata both owe their vitrification in part to the fluxing action of iron oxide and fine particle size. There are indications, however, that some alkali was added to these glazes. Albany slip, a well-known clay in use at the present time, is suitable for glaze in consequence of fine particle size and iron oxide content.

Accidental discoveries such as these of the American Indian were doubtless made independently many times, but only with favorable circumstances was a glaze developed. All early trials have a place in the history of ceramics and of glazing, and one must understand the nature of glazes to recognize them and under-stand their significance.

II. Ceramic Processes and the Techniques of Prewheel Potters

FAMILIARITY WITH the methods of prewheel pottery making gives the archaeologist an appreciation of potters' skills and of their ability to learn from trial
and error that he could hardly gain in any other way. Recognition of this skill and
cleverness will often enable him to explain features of prehistoric pottery that are
otherwise baffling. Moreover, one picks up many useful clues by observing methods
and noting their results. If these methods are studied in the light of modern knowledge of clay and of basic principles of clay working, they will be much more meaningful. Furthermore, background in ceramic principles enables one to judge
potters' methods and to distinguish the sound practices that have grown out of
experience and intelligent observation from the quirks that spring from lack of
understanding of natural causes and that cling to a craft from generation to
generation.

It is not my intention in this discussion to give a general or systematic review
of the methods of prewheel potters. I have merely drawn on them to illustrate
practices and principles and to indicate where we need fuller information. Many
of our early ethnological records of pottery making are sketchy and incomplete.
The ethnologist trained in ceramics will recognize the significance of the potter's
procedures. For example, when he knows that it is common practice to age clay
in order to improve its plasticity, he will not simply note that it is stored in a
moist place until needed, but will inquire whether this is done as a matter of
convenience or with the intent of improving its working quality.

The relation of the ceramic technologist and the student of primitive pottery
making should be one of mutual aid; so I shall attempt to suggest the important
observations that should be made in a study of pottery making and shall note
wherein our records are inadequate.

PREPARATION OF THE PASTE

CLAY TESTING

One of the first steps in pottery making is to test the clay. The practical potter has simple, direct means of judging working quality; the ceramist has standardized test methods and equipment. It will suffice here to mention the principal criteria and indicate the range of properties that concern the ceramist.

An experienced potter judges texture by the feel of a clay, distinguishing a "fat" or fine-textured clay from a "lean" or silty one. Various methods of measuring particle size have been developed, but a sedimentation test in which the finer fractions are thrown down by centrifuging has proved most satisfactory. Plasticity is another property that is judged by feel and by such simple tests as forming a ball of clay that is worked to its best consistency and flattening it to note how soon cracks appear on the edge of the disc that is formed. Plasticity is one of the most difficult properties to measure accurately, and no completely satisfactory test has yet been developed, although yield point and extensibility afford a convenient basis for comparing clays. Drying shrinkage is measured by either linear or volume change, and a breaking test is used for dry strength. The principal firing properties that concern the ceramist are porosity, strength, hardness, color, maturing temperature, and vitrification range. The firing schedule that will most effectively remove carbonaceous matter is determined, and the clay is tested for impurities that might cause flaws.

In view of the wide variation in the properties of clays, their plasticity, texture, drying shrinkage, thermal behavior, and defects, it is surprising that records of the potter's method of judging the quality of clay are so rare. A partial explanation may be found in the fact that, generally, when observations are made, clay from a deposit that has been drawn on for some time is used, and its properties are well known. Yet there is no doubt that primitive potters have very definite ideas about the suitability of clays, because they are sometimes quite positive in the rejection of new clays offered them.

Among the few records of potters' tests is Tschopik's (1950) report that the Aymara of Peru roll out a ball and flatten it to observe how soon cracks appear. It would be interesting to know whether the Aymara adopted this test independently or learned it from Europeans. Hill (1937) states that the Navajo moisten the clay and "test it for cohesiveness." The potters of Guatajiagua, Salvador, are said to be particularly careful to obtain the proper consistency when they mix clay, and the working condition is of such interest to them that native visitors who come during the process of clay preparation will test and comment upon the consistency of the paste, which is considered right when the paste sticks to the fingers unless they are wet (Lothrop, 1927).

A near blank in the ethnological record is data on the actual properties of the potters' clay. Samples, if collected, are not often tested, and hence we have only general references—descriptions of color and comments on texture and impurities.

The records do report the use of both residual and sedimentary clays. Rogers (1936) notes that Yuman tribes of Southern California use a disintegrated granite that contains 85 per cent of nonplastic material—quartz, mica, and partially altered feldspar. The Indians of Picuris and other Pueblo Indians of the upper Rio Grande valley use a highly micaceous residual clay for cook pots. Fewkes (1944) thought that the pipe clay used by the Catawbas was residual. Sedimentary clays are more generally used, however, than are primary or residual clays. They are widely distributed and have the advantage of being relatively free of coarse inclusions, though they may be more or less silty.

Hand-modeling enables the potter to utilize clays having a greater range in plasticity than can be used for wheel throwing. A clay of low plasticity can be teased into shape with the hands when it would not stand the strain of throwing. This advantage is offset by the restriction imposed by a low range of firing temperatures. Many clays will not harden sufficiently to make serviceable pottery at the maximum temperatures that can be obtained in direct open firing.

METHODS OF REFINING CLAY AND INCREASING PLASTICITY

Clay as it is mined often requires grinding and separation of inclusions and the coarser fractions. In modern commercial ceramic practice many types of crushers and mills are used, and sizing is accomplished by screening and by use of air or water currents. Impurities are removed by magnetic separation, flotation, filtering, and washing.

The primitive potters' methods of preparing clay differ widely, but care is almost always exercised to remove coarse particles. These potters, having learned from experience, explain correctly that if large particles are allowed to remain they may cause the vessel to crack in drying. Hand-picking of the freshly mined clay and of the wet paste is common practice. Grinding clay in a mortar or on a metate is also common. Temper and clay are sometimes ground together, sometimes separately. Soaking the clay is also frequent, and it is sometimes worked by treading with the bare feet before kneading (Coyotepec, Mexico; see Van de Velde and Van de Velde, 1939). It may also be ground after soaking. Sifting through metal screens is reported for the Yuma (Rogers, 1936) and Catawba (Fewkes, 1944). Whether metal screens are substitutes for an aboriginal screen or the potters have simply adopted a modern convenience we do not know, but wicker or similar screens may well have been used in prehistoric times. San Ildefonso potters winnow the ground clay in a light breeze by letting it fall through the fingers held at a height of 3–5 ft. depending upon the strength of the wind (Guthe, 1925). Yuman potters used winnowing trays with a tossing, a to-and-fro, and a rotary motion to separate the coarse from the fine particles.

Although potters take great care and spend much time removing coarse particles of clay, and although their methods are varied, I have found no record of an American Indian potter levigating clay, that is, mixing clay and water to a sufficiently thin consistency to permit the coarser particles to settle and leave the fine material in a suspension that can be poured off and concentrated by longer settling with subsequent decantation of the water. This method is easily practiced, and it may yet be found.

The working quality of clay can be improved by very thorough working with water in order to wet all particles completely. In modern pottery making, for example, the preparation of a batch may require that the clay be soaked 12 hours, turned in a ball mill 15 hours, and wedged half an hour to secure a homogeneous mass. Wedging is the practice of cutting slabs of the plastic clay and throwing them together. It has also been a common custom to age or store moist clay for weeks or months. This allows more complete wetting of minute particles and favors bacterial action. The custom has been replaced in modern commercial practice by vacuum treatment of clay. Another factor that is recognized is the flocculation of clay, which is controlled by the nature of adsorbed ions. A deflocculated clay has too low a yield point for good working quality. Finally, it is common practice to mix a plastic clay with a nonplastic one that has other desirable properties in order to obtain a workable paste.

An ethnological record of the length of time a clay is soaked and worked has little meaning unless the properties of the clay are defined, because the treatment required to develop the best working state will depend on characteristics of the clay, which, as I have emphasized, are highly variable. It is of interest to know whether or not prewheel potters recognized the advantages of aging. There are a few reports of storing clay several days to "sour" it (Aymara, Tschopik, 1950; Navajo, Hill, 1937), but one cannot be certain in these cases that the custom was not learned from Europeans.

Another noteworthy practice is that of adding a gumlike plant extract to the water with which the paste is mixed with the intention of increasing plasticity. Rogers (1936) notes the use of two substances by Yuman potters, the water extract of an herb and the juice of the roasted leaves of the prickly pear cactus. Rogers compares this process with so-called Egyptianizing of clay—the addition of an organic extract which functions as a protective colloid and serves to disperse the clay particles. The use of straw in bricks served a similar function. This is entering a theoretical field that the Indians knew nothing of, but they could notice an improvement in working quality, and it is not surprising that they should think of trying to improve plasticity and cohesiveness by adding a gummy substance. Another instance of the addition of foreign material is the mixing of blood with the paste by the Catawba to "lighten the pottery" (Fewkes, 1944). The use of blood and grease is also reported for Plains tribes (Griffin, 1935).

Evidence of mixture of clays has rarely been recognized in petrographic analysis of prehistoric pottery, but the practice is mentioned in a number of ethnological reports. Fewkes (1944) notes that the Catawba mixed pan and pipe clay, Tschopik (1950) mentions admixture of red and purple clays by the Aymara, and Foster (1948) records mixing of red and white clays by Tarascan potters. It would be interesting to know the Indian's explanations of the practices. A number of properties can be modified by mixing two clays, and the product may be superior to either one alone; also, a common clay of inferior quality may be improved by the addition of a superior but less accessible one.

USE OF NONPLASTICS

It is common practice among both primitive and modern potters to add nonplastic material to plastic clay in order to reduce excessive shrinkage. The variety of materials that has been used by primitive potters and some of the reasons for their choices have been discussed (see p. 26). The method of preparation of nonplastics is dictated largely by the nature of the material, and there is no uniformity in the manner of making the addition. Clay and temper may be ground separately and mixed dry or the temper may be added after the clay is wet. The proportions of temper and clay are measured roughly, or the proportion is judged by stickiness, color, and texture of the paste. Measurements may be made of dry temper and of dry clay or clay mixed to the plastic state. These measurements are, of course, not commensurable. When the potter judges proportions on the basis of plastic clay, it is necessary to calculate the ratio on a dry basis by securing a sample of the plastic clay and determining the percentage of water, since this will vary considerably with different clays.

The amount of temper required depends on the drying shrinkage of the clay, which is quite variable. It would be interesting to know how closely the potter adjusted the proportion of temper to requirements of the clay. The ethnologist can also question the potters about their reasons for adding temper and for choosing a particular material. It is interesting to note that when the potter's explanation is given, it is generally ceramically sound, that is, temper counteracts excessive shrinkage in drying. Correct judgment in this instance is doubtless due to experience. Residual or sandy clays were not tempered, and some clays of fine texture but low shrinkage were also untempered.

The variety of materials used for temper was not recognized until petrographic analyses were made; in fact, when this technique was first considered, we were uncertain of its value because it seemed likely that potters would use common materials that are not distinctive. At that time even the volcanic ash temper of San Ildefonso potters was called "white sand." The great number of rock types that have since been recognized in prehistoric pottery show that potters did not always choose the most obvious materials, and ease of preparation was not their only concern. The advantages of certain materials are fairly obvious; for example, the fine texture that can be obtained with vitric ash and the ease with which it is crushed. Then there is the difference between sharp, rough rock or potsherd and smooth, waterworn sand in their effect on bonding and strength. It would be interesting to know when potters recognized the advantages and disadvantages of various materials and to what extent choices were due solely to custom or to misconceptions. Textural qualities and the labor of preparation are obvious to them; the relative effect on strength is not so easily appreciated. The ideas of living potters cannot explain prehistoric practices but they may be suggestive.

Another question in this connection is whether or not potters understand the cause of defects produced by inclusions which expand in firing. The most common of these are limestone, calcite, and shell, which will cause spalling or pitting of the surface. Some micas will have the same effect on a fine scale. Potters who used these materials and normally kept their temperatures below the point at which defects occurred, occasionally over-fired. We should know how they explained the resulting defects.

FORMING AND SHAPING THE VESSEL

Since the potsherd rarely preserved evidence of the way the vessel was built and shaped, the methods of living prewheel potters are particularly illuminating to the archaeologist. We have to look beyond familiar examples to realize how many methods were employed and how often curious practices were incorporated into custom. Many pottery-making methods remind us how often procedures which seem illogical or impracticable are followed, and we realize anew the danger of reasoning from the "self-evident" when human nature is concerned.

There are a number of fundamentally different ways of shaping a pot. The most direct procedure is modeling from a solid lump. Surprisingly, some potters make fairly large vessels by this method. Coil building is perhaps the most general method, with many variations of the technique, in mode of supporting the vessel while it is being built, of starting the base, of laying the coils (in rings or as a spiral, with interior or exterior lap), and of giving the vessel its final shape. Molding the pot on a form is less familiar but is definitely a prehistoric technique on the American continent. Slip casting is apparently a relatively late technique of the historic period, but the possibility of its use in prehistoric times, even though slight, should not be overlooked. Throwing on the wheel is an Old World process, but archaeologists have been interested in the *kabal* of Yucatan as a possible precursor of the wheel (see p. 61).

The size of the vessel influences the way it is built. Even with a long tradition of coil construction, potters model small vessels by pressing them out from a ball of clay by hand (e.g., San Ildefonso, Guthe, 1925).

MODELING

Direct shaping was the standard method among some potters. Gilmore (1925) reports that the Arikara work a mass of clay with the hands into a rough approximation of the vessel. A smooth stone is then held on the inside and a wooden club is used to beat the clay against the shaping stone. A similar process has been reported for the Mandan (Maximilian, 1843).

Modeling the lower half or even the major part of a vessel and completing it by coil building is not uncommon. Tschopik (1950) describes briefly the Aymara method of forming a nearly hemispherical section which serves as the lower part of jars and other restricted forms or is in itself a complete bowl. A lump of clay is patted into a disc with the hands and then held in the potter's left hand while he beats it with his right fist, turning it constantly with a tossing motion. The hemispherical shape thus produced is set on a pottery plate which is turned constantly while the walls are being thinned. The piece is then set aside to stiffen before coils are added.

According to Van de Velde and Van de Velde (1939), the Coyotepec of Oaxaca form a hollow in a clay lump by striking it with the right fist; then as it is slowly turned with the left hand, the potter "thumps, pulls, and manipulates it" with the right to form the vessel wall. When it can no longer be handled this way it is inverted over the left fist and further stretched by patting until it attains a cylindrical form. It is then transferred to a shallow bowl (base of a broken jar). The shaping and scraping take place while this support or *molde* is "spun" on the rounding base of an inverted broken jar. The final shape of a *cantaro* body is an "almost perfect hollow sphere with a small opening at the top" to which the neck is added with a ring of clay after the vessel stiffens overnight. The question of "spinning" is discussed below (p. 60 ff.).

Vessel modeling among the Darfur of the Sudan (Arkell, 1939) is also unusual. A piece of palm fiber matting about 2 ft. square is spread over a slight depression in the ground. A ball of clay, of a size determined by that of the pot to be made, is shaped by pounding it with a stone pestle while it is turned in the depression. As the walls become thinner, the potter substitutes a mushroom-shaped pestle of unfired clay for the stone pestle. Powdered donkey manure is used to prevent the clay from sticking. The vessel is steadied with the right foot as it is turned with the left hand. The lower half is quickly formed in this way; the piece then is set aside to harden before the upper half is completed by coil building.

A method of modeling practiced in the village of Guatajiagua, Salvador, and described by Lothrop (1927) has seemed almost incredible because the vessel is finished at the bottom. The entire vessel is made from a "cylinder of clay" with the exception of a small coil to close the hole in the base and sometimes a coil for the rim. The potter starts by punching a depression in the cylinder with her fist and then works with the incipient vessel placed on leaves spread on the ground. First a crude form with flat base and thick vertical wall is modeled; then the upper part of the vessel is shaped by drawing up the sides with diagonal strokes of the hands, one on each side of the wall as the potter circles backward around the vessel. The potter's position and motions are hardly less unusual than the upside-down method of building the vessel. She stands before the vessel which is being formed on the ground and with her heels together and knees straight shuffles backward in a circle around it. The natives say that the symmetry of the vessel is determined by the trueness of the circle in which she moves. Pottery making is a young woman's craft among these people because of the taxing position in which they work. After the upper part of the vessel is shaped by drawing up the clay from the initial ring, the surface is evened with a corncob and smoothed. This first stage of the process is completed with the shaping of the rim and the piece is set aside to become firm. When it is ready to be completed it is inverted and set on its rim. The part now uppermost is still moist and plastic. Lothrop describes the next step as pressing out the soft clay of the base "to form a rough cornice on the walls of the inverted vessel." This clay, which is to become the lower part of the vessel, is drawn up and given shape by the same manipulations that were employed in the first stage of forming. Shaping and smoothing are done while the opening in the base is still large enough to admit the hand. When the walls are further drawn in and only a finger can be inserted, the hole is closed by laying a soft coil around the finger, which is then withdrawn, allowing the clay to sink into place. The operation of sealing the base is delicate and requires clay of the right consistency as well as very careful manipulation.

Lothrop states that this method is more rapid than the coiling technique employed elsewhere in Salvador and also that it produces stronger vessels. It has a distinct advantage for large vessels, which must be made in two stages, because it eliminates the union of separate parts. When a normal order of building is followed and the basal section is formed first and upright, its edge will become dry unless precautions are taken, and particular care must be exercised, to obtain a good union since this line encircling the vessel near its mid-point is a zone of potential flaws resulting from trapped air and imperfect joining of plastic and partially dry clay.

For many years the Guatajiagua method seemed to be an isolated technique of interest only because of its curious nature, but essentially the same method with minor variations has now been observed at Santa Apolonia in the highlands of Guatemala by Arrot (1953) and among the Totonac of Mexico by Kelly and Palerm (1952). Nor are the processes involved limited to the Americas. Especially interesting is the practice of Melanesian potters of the Amphlett Islands, who finish by paddling vessels modeled upside down (Malinowski, 1922). The spotty distribution of the technique in Mesoamerica raises questions regarding possible routes and causes of diffusions. It would appear to be a "fossil" practice that marks ancient contacts. Occurrences in other parts of the world, however, can be interpreted as indicating that the advantages of the method were sufficiently plain to be recognized independently at different times and in different places.

COIL CONSTRUCTION

The familiar method of vessel forming commonly referred to as coiling is essentially a process of building up the vessel wall with superimposed rolls of clay. This broad definition has been criticized because the word "coiling" suggests spiral placement of the rolls, whereas they are laid as a succession of rings by many pottery-making peoples (Fewkes, 1944, pp. 110–22). I have chosen the inclusive definition because it is now established by common usage and in the literature; moreover, Webster gives authority for it.

The technique as practiced in the Rio Grande pueblo of San Ildefonso has been fully described by Guthe (1925) and is well known, but within the wide geographic areas of the Americas, Africa, and peripheral Asia where coil building is practiced variations are found in almost every stage of the process. Many of the differences are of secondary importance, but some are specialized and have significant distributions. Methods of supporting and turning the vessel during construction and of bonding the coils are especially interesting. Although coiling may be employed from the beginning when there is spiral placement, the vessel is usually started with a basal disc of clay formed by various punching and patting manipulations. This disc is frequently placed in a shallow piece of pottery or a basket to give the growing vessel support and to facilitate turning while coils are added. An unusual support used by potters of Yucatan has raised fundamental questions that are considered in another section (p. 60). Still another method of starting the vessel is that of using the exterior base of an inverted pot, a process which necessitates different manipulation since only the outside of the piece can be worked while it is on the support. Manipulative skill and judgment are displayed by the ease with which a "rope" of uniform diameter is formed by rolling clay between the hands or, less frequently, against a flat surface. Both length and diameter of the coil vary, depending on size of the vessel, desired wall thickness, plasticity of the clay, and the potter's skill. The more plastic the clay, the more slender the coil that can be formed, but it is not practicable to use small coils for large vessels. The placing of coils in rings has the advantage of maintaining a level edge, whereas spiralling results in a sloping edge and leaves an abrupt end where the spiral is completed. These effects are more pronounced, the larger the coil. It might seem simpler to even the rim than to lay complete rings for each circuit because this often results in pieces of left-over coil and necessitates closing the rings, but these are evidently minor considerations to the potter. Present-day Pueblo potters follow the ring method although spiral coiling for decorative effects was at one time highly developed among prehistoric pueblos. Butel-Dumont (1753, p. 271) refers to spiral coil construction by Indians of Louisiana.

The position of coils in relation to each other is a point of technical interest since it affects the extent of the area of bonding. There is considerably less contact when coils are superimposed vertically than when they are overlapped, forming an oblique plane of juncture. No less important is the fact that, when overlapped, the plane of juncture is subject to more direct pressure in the bonding process than when coils are superimposed; that is, they can be pinched together instead of merely pressed upon one another. Differences in technique of laying coils are of interest because of the importance of complete union. The method of pinching is described by Guthe for San Ildefonso. The coil is given a liberal overlap on the interior, one-half to three-quarters of it being placed below the edge against which it is applied. The coil is held in both hands, the end in the right hand being first tacked in place by pressing with the first two fingers on the inside, the thumb on the outside. As the support is rotated counterclockwise, the remainder of the coil is pressed in place in the same manner. After the circuit is completed, both hands are used to complete the bonding, fingers on the inside, thumbs close together on the outside. Bonding is thus established by careful pressing of the entire circuit. In sharp contrast is the method of Yucatan potters, who hold a thick roll of clay in the right hand to be applied on the inside edge while the left hand is used for support on the exterior. The clay roll is fed onto the interior with repeated, short rotations of the wrist, spreading it as it is applied with the extended index finger. The clay is highly plastic and the effect is almost that of smearing it along the edge of the growing vessel. An even more specialized method of bonding coils is that employing a paddle and anvil, a process discussed below.

The degree of shaping accomplished during the laying of coils varies. A simple procedure is that of maintaining circuits of uniform diameter, which results in a cylindrical form that is given the desired shape by working on the interior with tools of requisite curvature. Often spoon-shaped, gourd-rind tools are used. In the process of pressing out the side of the cylinder the walls are stretched and thinned; they may be further thinned by scraping. The paste should be firm before the exterior is scraped, however, in order to avoid distorting the vessel. When partial shaping accompanies the building process, it may be accomplished by varying the diameter of circuits, the relative position of coils, and by use of the shaping spoon as the building progresses. Control of shape by varying position of coils and diameter of circuits is probably most commonly employed to draw in the upper walls of restricted-orifice vessels. If the vessel is large and must be built in two sections, the first section will be shaped before it is set aside for partial drying.

An essential precaution for satisfactory bonding in coil building is to keep edges moist and plastic. When a large jar is built in two stages, particular attention must be given to the edge of the first section. It will be kept moist while the main body of the piece is drying and may be crimped to secure better union when a fresh coil is added to it.

As a building process, coil construction offers two general advantages: it insures a certain degree of uniformity of wall thickness from the start and, perhaps more important, it permits the utilization of a less plastic clay than is required when the vessel is drawn out from a solid lump because the clay is not subject to the same degree of stretching and pulling. In a sense, coil construction has come to be regarded as a classic method of hand-building. It suggests a nicety of construction lacking in the direct modeling processes. Consequently it is well to recall that it has certain disadvantages. It is probably slower than the most efficient modeling processes, and it involves a great deal of bonding, a potential source of flaws, of which the modeled vessel is free.

PADDLING TECHNIQUES

The use of a tool to beat the clay during the process of bonding, to thin the walls, and to assist in shaping is a specialized method of accomplishing these purposes but is associated with various building processes. It is not comparable to and should not be confused with the building process itself. In broad outline, the method is characterized by the use of a paddle to beat the vessel exterior while a supporting tool, the anvil, is held on the interior. The latter is frequently a smooth, rounded stone, but a mushroom-shaped pottery anvil that is grasped by the stem is used by a number of people. I have referred to the paddle-and-anvil technique of the Arikara and Mandan. The Darfur use of a stone pestle to beat a lump of clay into shape represents a distinct process since in this case force is applied on the interior; also this is a building method, but it is interesting to find that, at one stage, the Darfur replace the stone pestle with a pottery beater which is mushroom-shaped.

When the paddle-and-anvil technique is employed with coil construction, it is a specialized substitute for hard pressure in the bonding of coils and also serves to thin the walls and may replace the use of the gourd-rind scraper on the interior. Rogers (1936) has recorded the details of Yuman practice. These people shape the basal pat on the exterior of an inverted cook pot by paddling. It is therefore necessary to overlap the coils on the exterior. The coil is first joined at intervals by pressure of the thumb and is then beaten with a downward motion of the wooden paddle to flatten and bond it. The vessel must be removed from the support to bond and wipe smooth the juncture for each additional coil until the sides approach the vertical, when it is held in the lap for completion and is paddled against a stone anvil. The Cocopa technique as described by Gifford (1928) illustrates minor variations. These people start the basal pat on a pottery anvil and thereafter hold the vessel in the lap to add coils, using the anvil as the coils are welded by paddling. In both instances the paddle and anvil supplement finger-bonding and function as a substitute for the spoon scraper to thin the wall and shape the vessel.

METHODS OF TURNING THE VESSEL FOR MODELING OR COIL CONSTRUCTION

Methods of turning the vessel during the building process raise interesting technical questions because of suggestions that some of them may contain the germ of the idea of the potter's wheel, or that the final stage of the building process is comparable to that of throwing. When an open bowl or basket is used to support the vessel under construction and is turned with the hand, it serves to keep the side on which the potter is working in convenient position. Obviously these supports have no analogy to a wheel, for, aside from the fact that they are unpivoted, they are turned intermittently and far too slowly to give any effect of rotational or centrifugal force in shaping. It is interesting to note, however, that simple devices are sometimes used to prevent sidewise shifting of the vessel when it is turned. For example, the base may be placed in a depression. I have observed this practice in the village of Chinautla, Guatemala, employed with a large jar that was constructed in two stages. When the lower section was partially dried and ready for the forming of the upper part, it was removed from the dish in which it was started and placed on a board with its rounded base in a small, circular, gouged depression. The lower part of the vessel was sufficiently firm to be turned on its base, and the depression prevented it from swinging out of line during the forming of its upper section.

The critical question in regard to rotation of the vessel during construction is whether or not sufficient speed is attained for rotary and centrifugal forces to play a part in the shaping process. This question does not arise in the case of techniques such as that of Pueblo potters, who depend entirely on the force of their hands and turn the vessel only to shift its position. But there are two pottery-making peoples in Mexico, the Coyotepec of Oaxaca and the Maya of Yucatan, who have simple devices that have led observers to consider their analogy to the wheel because of the speed obtained.

The Coyotepec, in making a *cantaro*, do the preliminary modeling by hand from a ball of clay. The rude cylinder thus formed is placed in a shallow bowl which is set on the upturned convex base of another piece of pottery. The supporting saucer is turned with the left hand, leaving the right hand free for shaping. The two vessels used in rotating the piece under construction must be matched in size, according to the Van de Veldes. These observers state (1939, p. 30) that, "The spinning of the bottoms of the two vessels against each other is the only semblance of a wheel." Judging from an excellent moving picture taken by Dr. George Foster, I am inclined to say that the semblance is to a top rather than to a wheel, because the partially shaped vessel careens and gyrates as the supporting saucer turns upon its convex rest. It is noteworthy that the arrangement for rotation reduces friction to a minimum since the area of contact of the moving part is that formed by two convex surfaces. I am not justified in basing judgment of effects of rate of rotation from viewing a film and can therefore only mention impressions. In the shaping of the body of the vessel, the rate of turning was relatively slow and it seemed apparent that the hands supplied the effective shaping force. In forming the neck, however, the speed was increased considerably and the force of rotation appeared to play a definite role; that is, the hands were briefly motionless as the clay was turned against them and the neck took form. Coyotepec has one outstanding potter whom visitors to the village observe. It would be interesting to know if her methods are representative and if her technique has been influenced by her familiarity with the potter's wheel.

Yucatecan potters form and shape the vessel on a device known as a *kabal*, which is generally a cylindrical block of wood, 4–6 in. high, having a diameter suitable for the size of the vessel under construction. The working surface is a smooth board placed on the ground, before which the potter sits on a low bench. Friction is reduced by waxing or soaping the board, and the *kabal* is turned with the feet, thus freeing both hands for building and shaping. An early observer, Mercer (1897), refers to this device as a potter's wheel, and E. H. Thompson (n.d.) speaks of it as the germ of the potter's wheel or a "primitive potter's wheel." Since the disc is not pivoted, these expressions might be dismissed had not the suggestion of wheel analogies been advanced again in recent years by Brainerd (1946). Brainerd and R. H. Thompson both have papers in preparation, and I shall therefore confine myself to a few comments based on observations of four women and one man (a native of Ticul) in the village of Mama and one man in Maxcanu. The methods of the Ticul potter were not typical since he had got the idea of pivoting and placed his *kabal* on a spike driven through the supporting board. Despite this advantage, he used his hand instead of his feet for turning, and the rate of rotation was less than that attained by the Maxcanu man who skillfully used his feet with an unpivoted *kabal*. Although I have observed in the field only one man employing the typical method, Brainerd has given me the opportunity to view his moving picture of a potter whom he considered outstanding for his skill.

There are different methods of turning the *kabal* and constructing the vessel. Both modeling from a solid cylinder of paste and coil construction are employed, and just as paddle-and-anvil technique is independent of construction method, so is the employment of the *kabal*. The manner of rotating the *kabal* varies with the potter's sex. Women turn it with the big toe of one foot while bracing it with the other foot. Men use the soles of both feet, pushing with one and pulling with the other, thus exerting much more force than the women. The rate of revolution is a question of primary importance since speed is necessary for the forces resulting from rotation to be effective in shaping. The speed and continuity of motion vary with the manner of turning, the potter's skill, and the stage of vessel construction. Watching an experienced woman of Mama, I counted 10 revolutions per minute, whereas I estimated 30 revolutions per minute as the maximum speed obtained by the man in Maxcanu. During the building stage, the motion of the *kabal* is slow and intermittent; it serves primarily to keep the vessel under construction in convenient position. While the vessel is being scraped on the interior in the shaping process, the speed of rotation may be increased somewhat and the potters observed attained maximum speed when finishing the rim. The force of rotation enters into the shaping process when the plastic clay is moved against or across the hand or a tool, but this force alone does not define throwing. The extent to which centrifugal force enters into the throwing process and the speed required for it to be effective have not to my knowledge been determined, and these factors, rather than appearance, should be considered in judging and comparing processes.

Markings on the neck and rim of Yucatecan vessels which are similar in appearance to the striations of wheel-thrown vessels have often attracted attention. These marks are formed when the rim is smoothed with a strip of wet leather, which is folded over the edge and held firmly against it. Grooves formed by the dragging of granules are parallel to the lip because the strip is held against it (cf. fig. 13*f*). This feature is a reminder that fundamentally different processes may produce effects that appear identical.

The effects of the use of the *kabal* and its origin are matters of interest to the archaeologist because some prehistoric Yucatecan vessels, aside from having the parallel striations on the rim, are remarkably symmetrical. Use of the *kabal* by no means insures symmetry of form, however. Among the potters I observed, for example, the one attaining the highest speed produced a rim that was noticeably unsymmetric. Nevertheless, a symmetric form should be more easily attained with this device than with a simple hand-turned support. In any case, whether or not the *kabal* has come down from prehistoric times, the extent to which present-day potters have been influenced by their familiarity with wheel techniques and the reason for the curious lack of standardization of methods are questions that should be considered in further field studies.

MOLDING

Molding may seem to be a more advanced process than modeling or coil construction, yet pressing clay into a form is a simple thing to do. The complication comes when restricted shapes are made, since they cannot be withdrawn from a single complete mold. Speed of production is an advantage of molding, especially when plastic decoration is employed. It is interesting to note that in two areas of the New World where vessels have been molded, Peru and Mexico, the process was also used for decorative effects.

The various methods of molding pottery employed in Mexico have been discussed by Foster (1948a). He distinguishes two main techniques, one employing concave, the other convex molds. The concave mold has two parts with vertical juncture and resembles a pot split in two from rim to base. Its use is apparently restricted at the present time to certain villages in Michoacan, and Foster has described the technique employed at Tzintzuntzan (1948). Potters line each half of the mold with a sheet of paste which has been pounded on a rock to flatten it and give it proper thickness. This "tortilla" of paste is pressed into the mold with a damp cloth, and the excess at the edge is trimmed with a horsehair or a maguey fiber. The two halves of the mold are joined immediately, and the juncture on the inside is then smoothed with a wet cloth. The molds are removed after a short drying period; when the vessel is nearly dry, the outside is evened with a rock scraper and rubbed with a wet cloth. This process removes all traces of the weld on the exterior. Vessels with a capacity up to 50 liters are molded in this way.

Foster (1948a) reports a variant of this technique in Coyotepec, Oaxaca. A single mold is used so that half the body is molded and removed before the other half can be formed. The two parts are joined after the second is removed from the mold, and a narrow neck is modeled by hand.

Convex molds are more widely distributed than the concave in Mexico, and the technique is more variable. The mold is like a plate or shallow bowl and sometimes has a handle on the inside giving it a mushroom-like appearance. It is used to form open vessels such as comales and bowls, which are molded on it completely, and also to form the lower part of vessels with restricted orifice or neck. The upper part of the restricted vessels is finished in one of three ways: by hand-modeling, by adding a duplicate section made from the same mold and hand-modeling the neck, or by adding a part made on a special mold including upper body and neck. In all cases junctures are necessarily completed after the parts are removed from the mold. Foster (1948a) reports that hand-modeling of the upper section on a molded base seems to have been the common technique in much of Jalisco and

Colima until fairly recent years. When the upper part is made on the same mold as the lower part, the neck opening is formed by removing a circle cookie-cutter fashion. The neck is then modeled by hand or made with still another mold consisting of concave, vertically joined halves. This technique is used at Metapec near Toluca, in Texcoco, and in many other villages of central Mexico. Foster believes it is the most common and widespread of all mold techniques used in Mexico today.

With respect to molded decoration, Foster points out that the concave mold is adapted to effigy ware in which decoration is on the exterior; whereas the convex mold is used to produce patterns in the bottom of *molcajetes* ("chili grinders").

The important variables in these techniques are: the extent of molding, whether partial or complete; the number of parts of the mold, whether single or two- or multiple-part; the form of the mold, whether concave or convex; when the parts are joined, while still in the mold or after removal from it; and in two-part molding, the position of the juncture, whether vertical or horizontal. These variables are not all independent. Obviously, with two-part, convex molding, the juncture can be made only after removal from the mold when the form has a restricted orifice. Foster (1948a) notes that the technique of concave molding is much less variable than that of convex molding, but the only concave mold he describes has a vertical juncture, which in itself limits the technique if the vessel is to be symmetric because there must be two identical molds or the same mold must be used for the two parts. The only possibility of combining hand-modeling with this technique is by the addition of supplementary parts, such as neck or pedestal. With this type of molding, the two parts can be joined either while the sections are in the molds or after removal, but the choice is likely to be decided by the advantage of making the joint first. The more plastic the paste, the better the union, and when the parts are still in the mold, the juncture can be worked from the inside without risk of pressing the wall out of line since it is still supported by the mold. If the sections are first removed from the mold, they must be left until the paste is sufficiently firm to maintain its shape, which will necessitate wetting or roughing the edge to obtain a good weld when they are joined. Another factor to consider is which side of the vessel is in contact with the mold as this side will require a minimum of evening by hand. Since the exterior is in contact with the concave mold, it is especially suitable for jars; conversely, the convex mold is suitable for open forms in which the interior is the better-finished side.

Although some of the limitations of molding technique in Mexico can be explained by the dependence of variables, it is noteworthy that the Mexicans are not exploiting all possibilities. Foster mentions no convex mold with vertical joints and no horizontal concave molds. There would be no particular advantage in vertical convex molds, but the apparent absence of the horizontal concave form is surprising because it would have the latitude for variation of the horizontal convex mold and would permit use of exterior decoration. Moreover, a concave mold for at least the upper bodies of jars is known archaeologically.

OTHER FORMING PROCESSES

Modeling from a lump, building with coils, and molding apparently exhaust the prewheel techniques of pottery making. The introduction of the wheel represented an advance in speed of production and in the degree of symmetry obtainable. Now the wheel has come to hold the place of a hand process for art ware; for rapid mass production, pressing and slip casting have largely replaced it. I know of no analogies for the process of using a dye box or of slip casting among prewheel potters. Each method is characterized by techniques that rest on a knowledge of the physics and chemistry of clay. In slip casting, the vessel is made by pouring slip in a plaster mold that absorbs the water. After standing a sufficient time, the excess slip is poured off, and the piece then remains in the mold until dry. The amount of water required and the viscosity of the slip are controlled by the use of electrolytes. There are a number of advantages in the method, for there are no joints, there is no need to add parts such as handles and spouts, little skill is required, and the body is more uniform and dense than that of thrown ware. It is improbable that a technique comparable to slip casting was ever used by prewheel potters, but the possibility cannot be ruled out, and ethnologist and archaeologist should ever be alert to evidence of new methods.

FINISHING THE SURFACE

The method of surface finishing and the stage during which it is accomplished depend on the purpose of the vessel and whether or not it is to be decorated. The finishing may be completed in one process immediately after shaping and while the clay is still plastic, or it may not be completed until the vessel has become leather-hard or dry. Finishing serves first to remove irregularities left in forming and shaping the vessel—finger depressions made when welding coils, marks left by the edge of the support, or weld-marks of joined sections. Simultaneously, contour is evened. Generally texture is improved, luster may be imparted or, if the vessel is slipped, color may be modified. The removal of surface irregularities often proceeds with building and shaping—as a coil is applied and welded, the line of juncture is wiped over with the wet fingers. The use of shaping tools, such as a piece of gourd-rind having suitable curvature, also has the effect of removing high spots and filling in depressions. Techniques that are applied after the vessel has become leather-hard or dry are intended primarily to improve surface quality.

EVENING AND SMOOTHING

Technically the simplest finish is that produced by hand alone as soon as the vessel is formed and while the paste is still plastic and easily redistributed. Rogers (1936) reports that Yuman potters smooth the surface immediately after modeling, using a rotary motion of the wet palm. No scraping tool or mop is used, and the polishing stone is unknown to them.

Corncob, gourd-rind, and waterworn pebbles are all common tools for finishing in the plastic state. Lothrop (1927) reports that the Guatajiagua smooth and polish with much water and a corncob while the bottom of the vessel is still soft enough to quiver. The word "polish" in this connection must refer to smoothing because permanent luster cannot be produced by polishing very wet clay that will undergo considerable drying shrinkage. These Indians polish with a stone when the vessel is dry, presumably by moistening the surface, though the process is not described. The Navajo, according to Hill (1937), work over their pottery with a corncob, gourd-rind, and waterworn pebble as soon as the last coil is laid and smoothed. After decoration—appliquéd fillets or simple incising on the neck— is applied, the pot is again polished with a pebble. The finishing technique employed by potters of Tzintzuntzan (described by Foster, 1948) differs in several respects. Mold-marks are first scraped off with a knife. The potter then takes a handful of very damp, pliable paste, douses it in water and goes over the entire surface of the pot, filling in cracks and depressions. Next a "polishing" stone of coarse volcanic rock is dipped in water and rubbed over the outside to level ridges and smooth the surface. The finishing process is finally completed by rubbing the surface with a wet rag.

POLISHING

Among prewheel potters who do not use glaze, polishing or rubbing the vessel surface to give it luster is an important means of obtaining fine finish. The technique can be applied to either a slipped or an unslipped surface. In either case it is essential that the surface be even and smooth at the start because the polishing tool will not touch pits, grooves, or small depressions, which therefore remain dull, marring the appearance. A fine-textured paste is desirable because its surface can be scraped when leather-hard without dragging or tearing out grains. A fine paste is required, if the vessel is evened with a piece of sandstone when the body is dry. This technique is used by the Hopi with an untempered clay (M. R. F. Colton, 1931). The principal difference between polishing a slipped and an unslipped surface is that the polishing stone picks up slip more readily than paste when the condition of moisture is not correct. The optimum moisture for polishing varies somewhat with different clays. Tschopik (1950) reports that the Aymara polish with a smooth pebble after the slipped vessel has dried in the sun for an hour. This is unusual, for ordinarily high luster cannot be attained after the surface has dried. The slip is described as "hematite-stained clay."

Polishing while the clay is still moist is mentioned by Fewkes (1944) in describing Catawba technique. Vessels are prepared for polishing by wiping with a piece of an old sack that removes excess paste, obliterates cracks and defects, and evens the wall. Smooth pebbles, bone tools made of rib or shank, or pieces of hard wood are used for polishing. Fewkes reports that a piece of cloth or a soft skin vigorously applied will produce a polish comparable in compactness and luster to a stone polish, but that the process leaves identification marks easily distinguished from the facet left by a stone. This would seem to be an exceptional case in which the clay retained a gloss given it in the moist state, although ordinarily drying shrinkage destroys the regular arrangement of surface particles on which luster depends. The exceptions to this general rule that I have noted are certain ball clays, which are easily given a high luster by simply rubbing with the fingers while still damp, a luster largely retained after firing.

Guthe (1925), in his report on San Ildefonso pottery making, has given one of the most detailed descriptions of polishing technique that has been published. The finishing of highly polished black ware illustrates the care that must be taken to even the surface that is to be slipped and polished. The gourd-rind scraper used to shape the vessel also serves to smooth the surface immediately after the last coil is laid. After the vessel has dried, the surface is dampened and scraped to remove marks of the support and to thin the walls. Wall thinness is judged by weighing the vessel in the hand. After scraping, the surface is again dampened with a wet cloth and rubbed vigorously. Guthe says the thin surface film is redistributed in this way. Formerly fingers were used instead of a wet cloth, and a corncob or piece of sandstone served for smoothing. Some potters sun-dry the vessel again after scraping, others commence slipping at once. Before the slip dries, the surface is polished with a smooth stone. Considerable pressure is exerted and the surface is worked over several times. Potters say that poor polish is due to lack of persistence of the potters. Guthe remarks that the secret of good polish seems to lie in the potter's ability to go over the surface as many times as possible before it dries, and my own experience with this slip is in agreement.

SLIPPING

Surface color and texture can often be improved by a coat of superior clay prepared as a slip—a suspension of clay in water. There are several technical requirements of a slip. First, it should adhere well to the body, neither peeling nor crazing. Both these defects result from difference in coefficient of expansion of slip and body. Second, the slip should harden within the same temperature range as the body. A highly refractory clay is unsatisfactory because it remains soft at the temperatures attained in primitive firing. Finally, the slip should have sufficient covering power to conceal the body. The consistency of the slip mixture depends on type of clay mineral, particle-size range, adsorbed ions, and degree of dispersion of the clay.

The slips employed for different wares by San Ildefonso potters will give a hint of the diverse types of clay suitable for slip. A ferruginous clay is used for polished black ware. This slip has been described as a "saturated solution" of clay in water, but the term refers properly to the concentration of a substance that is soluble. Since clay slips are in suspension, the term "saturated" can be understood to refer to the maximum amount of clay that will be held in suspension. The actual proportion of clay thus held will vary greatly depending on the properties of the clay, particularly on particle size and adsorbed ions. It is doubtful if a slip is ever made with less clay than will be held in suspension; generally the coarser fraction of the clay settles immediately and the potter often stirs it with each application. The red clay used by San Ildefonso potters is not distinctly fine-grained, and much of it settles after a few minutes, leaving a thin suspension. The slip is applied with a cloth mop, and the surface is coated several times until it attains the desired color.

A dark red slip composed of a mixture of red slip clay, native white slip, and temper has been used by these potters for black-on-red ware. This was applied and polished in the same manner as the red slip but does not attain as high luster. The potters, according to Guthe (1925), say the luster is not as high if the work is completed when the vessel is very damp, an observation that shows they recognize the effect of drying shrinkage on luster.

These potters also use a very fine-textured white slip obtained in trade from Santo Domingo Indians. It is mixed to a thin consistency with water and applied with a cloth mop. The motion is free, backward and forward. Five or six separate applications are made and the pot is allowed to dry after each. The surface may not be smoothed between applications but is always rubbed with a cloth after the last application and before the slip has dried completely. A polishing stone is never used because this slip does not take a high luster. The number of applications is probably explained by the fact that Santo Domingo slip has high shrinkage and only moderately good covering power. If a single thick coat were applied, it would craze badly. Thin applications reduce the tendency to craze, but more than one coat is necessary to cover the body color.

It is evident from the practices of this one group of potters that slipping technique is determined in part by the properties of the clay. A slip can be applied and smoothed without polishing, especially if it is used primarily for its color, or if the ware is to be fired high enough to destroy luster through firing shrinkage. It is usually rubbed to make it more compact. There are many variations in methods of preparation and application; for example, Stevenson (1904) reported that the Zuni prepared slip by "dissolving" white clay in water and then making it into cones which were dried in the sun. This was doubtless done to remove some of the coarser constituents and might be compared to levigation. When required for use, the cones were rubbed to a powder on a stone, again mixed with water, and the slip was applied with a rabbit-skin mop.

These illustrations will serve to indicate the importance of identifying materials and describing properties of the clays used by potters, because a technique can be fully understood only in relation to the material with which it is employed.

DECORATIVE TECHNIQUES

Pottery affords great latitude in decoration, a fact of which prewheel potters have not failed to take advantage. The yielding paste of the freshly shaped vessel lends itself to a variety of manipulative techniques such as gouging, scoring, stamping, modeling, molding, appliqué, and incising. These produce decorative effects through texturing and relief. The leather-hard or dry paste or even the fired vessel with a soft body can be scraped, grooved, and carved with a strong, sharp tool. The surface of a vessel gives the potter a free hand in painting. Color patterns can be obtained by painting with various substances that withstand the heat of firing, by cutting through a slip to expose the contrasting color of paste, by filling grooves or cut-away background with pigment, and by localized reducing or smudging.

It would be fortunate if we had more present-day survivals in areas which were characterized in prehistoric times by specialized decorative methods; if, for example, the potters of the eastern United States were demonstrating the details of stamping and impressing; and if we could find among the people of Mesoamerica and Peru, polychrome and resist painting, incising, modeling, and molding at its best. But the ethnological record of decorative techniques is scant and contains many gaps.

Probably techniques of decoration reflect decadence more sharply than any other part of the pottery-making process because, when modern utensils come into the primitive household, the handmade vessel declines in value and the potter no longer has the same incentive to refine and elaborate. And when there is a revival of the potter's art, we are as likely to find development of a new style or technique as a return to the old. For example, the matte-paint decoration of lustrous black ware of San Ildefonso Pueblo is an innovation which has no prehistoric prototype in the region. The European technique of glazing has spread even beyond the wheel; and where molding is practiced, it is often difficult to determine which elements of the practice are native and which European. But even though the evidence is disappointing, it is still suggestive and well worth reviewing.

PLASTIC TECHNIQUES

There has been a revival of pottery making in the eastern United States among the Catawba. Fewkes (1944) reports that decoration is by simple incising, grooving, fluting, and impressing. Impressed designs are obtained by rolling or rocking a corncob over the surface. Rubbing with a corncob produces a different texture. The looped end of a hairpin is the principal tool used for impressed decoration. Other modern artifacts—the milled edge of a coin, a shoe buttonhook, pieces of wire—are also used, along with native tools such as mussel shell, gourd-rind, and cane knife. The edge of a sharp knife, a piece of wire, or a hairpin are preferred in executing the more delicate designs of pipes, and it is not rare to find juxtaposition of differently produced decorations on the same specimen. Although modern objects are prominent among the impressing tools of these people, the potters do not seem to differ from their ancestors in the readiness with which they take up anything that might make an interesting pattern. An impressed decoration can be executed most effectively immediately after the vessel is shaped and smoothed. Fewkes notes that all decoration is executed while the vessel is in the plastic state.

Stamped and molded decoration is represented in Mexico. Rendon (1950) describes bar-shaped clay stamps from Cuauhtitlan that are incised with a motif or a sentiment to form a figure in relief. Small molds are also used for making decorative elements, which are appliquéd to the vessel.

The Tarascan technique of polishing described by Foster (1948) suggests the prehistoric decoration characterized by lustrous lines on a matte surface. The polishing tool is a pyrite or quartz crystal mounted on a stick for a handle. An angle of the crystal is used for narrow lines, a broader surface for wide ones. Foster mentions the importance of the condition of the slip in this process. It will peel if it is too moist; if too dry, streaks will be left.

PAINTING

Ethnological data on painting are somewhat less sketchy than those on plastic techniques of decoration. From the technical point of view, it is of interest to know how the potter prepares mineral pigments—what, if anything, is done to improve their consistency and spreading quality, and whether or not the problem of making them permanent is solved. The ethnologist's observations often have a direct or indirect bearing on these questions.

Particle size is an important factor in the quality of mineral paint because a coarse paint will settle quickly in water and will have a grainy texture when applied to the vessel. A bare statement that a paint is ground does not tell whether the potter merely crushed lumps and coarser particles to obtain uniform texture or actually attempted to reduce the particle size of the mass.

The use of an organic vehicle or medium to improve spreading quality and bind the paint before firing is a very general practice. Even potters who do not make highly finished ware know the advantages of a medium. Thus Rogers (1936) reports that the Yuma grind their mineral pigment (hematite) dry in a pottery cup or large sherd and then mix it with water containing the juice of baked mescal. When mescal cannot be obtained, cane sugar is substituted for it. The method of grinding would suffice to crush lumps in the paint but could not have reduced the particle size appreciably. The syrup from the mescal would improve spreading quality and bind the pigment before firing, but could have no further effect because it would be burned out during firing. Rogers reports that the Indians believed the pigment to be set during firing by the mescal syrup, but he notes that the paint rubs off after firing, a defect that is to be expected of paint of this type.

Other examples of use of a medium with mineral pigment are found among the Pueblos. The Hopi prepare tansy mustard by boiling the plants, pouring off the water, and squeezing the remaining pulp through a cloth (M. R. F. Colton, 1931). The thick, black liquid is allowed to cool and thicken and is then used immediately or poured on boards to dry. This organic substance is mixed with a black mineral paint, which Colton describes as a finely ground black clay, perhaps a manganiferous clay containing organic matter. There is little doubt that the coloring agent is a manganese-bearing material because organic matter would burn out in the method of firing used by these potters. The tansy mustard extract is also used as a fixative for ferruginous clay paint.

Practices of Zuni potters are similar. Stevenson (1904, p. 376) states that they grind pigment in stone mortars and mix them to a paste with water to which syrup of the yucca fruit is added. Water in which the Rocky Mountain bee plant has been boiled is mixed with the black pigment which Stevenson identified as a manganiferous clay containing organic matter.

These descriptions give no indication of the cause of permanence of mineral paint. Various factors which may affect permanence have been discussed under pigments (see p. 32).

Despite the obvious advantages of using an organic vehicle with mineral paint, the practice is not universal with prewheel potters. Tschopik (1950) mentions a dark red hematite and a white pigment that the Aymara prepare by grinding on a stone slab or in a small stone mortar, but he does not mention a medium. He notes that the white paint (identified as calcium carbonate) smudges or rubs off but he does not comment on the quality of the red. There is a considerable difference between a hematite and a ferruginous clay in both spreading quality and permanence. The clay gives a better suspension and also acts as a binder. The term "hematite" is often applied to any red, earthy material, but unless a material is specifically identified, we cannot judge how well the potter's technique is adapted to his materials.

The Indians in several pueblos of New Mexico are using an organic paint, the boiled extract of the Rocky Mountain bee plant (see Guthe, 1925, p. 66, for a description of preparation), a survival of prehistoric practice. Here the question is not with regard to spreading quality, because this paint is sometimes employed as a medium, but how a thin coat of organic substance can be fired without being oxidized completely. The role of the adsorptive properties of the clay has been discussed under pigments (p. 34), and it is interesting to note that the Pueblos use this type of clay to slip vessels decorated with organic paint.

In this discussion of painting, I have emphasized the problems arising from the properties of the paint because these are frequently overlooked. No less important are the painter's techniques—the kind of brush that is used and means of steadying the hand. Guthe (1925) and Chapman (1936), in describing methods of Pueblo potters, bring out the advantages of a brush that retains the paint effectively. They point out the relation of evenness of line to the way the brush is held, because the greater the contact of bristles with the surface, the less tendency to waver. If the side of the brush rather than its tip is used, friction or drag will have a steadying effect. The Pueblo brush, which is made by separating fibers of a yucca leaf, has long bristles and is held under the hand at a low angle to the vessel, as in lining. Style of painting doubtless has some influence on brush technique. Small scattered elements will require a different technique than long sweeping lines. Painting technique should therefore be considered in relation to design style. Methods of design composition are considered under style (pp. 264–66).

DRYING

Certain precautions are necessary in drying pottery because strains result from too rapid drying and there is danger of cracking. In commercial practice, where efficiency demands that drying time be reduced to a minimum, the factors affecting the rate of drying have been investigated extensively. These studies show that the rate of drying is uniform and comparable to evaporation from a free water surface up to a certain point; beyond this point the rate is much slower. The obvious explanation is that in a plastic clay the particles are surrounded by water which evaporates freely (fig. 2, A). At the point of decrease in drying rate, the water envelope has been removed and the particles drawn into contact (fig. 2, B;

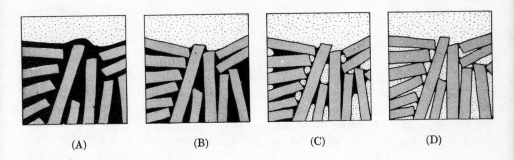

(A)   (B)   (C)   (D)

FIG. 2—STAGES IN DRYING MOIST CLAY

Diagrammatic cross section at the surface. The letters correspond to those in the curves of fig. 3. (From F. H. Norton, *Elements of Ceramics*, 1952, Addison-Wesley Publishing Co., Inc., Cambridge, Mass.)

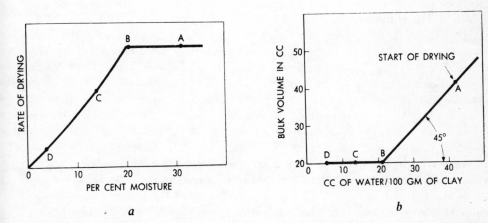

a   *b*

FIG. 3—MECHANISM OF DRYING IN RELATION TO RATE AT WHICH MOISTURE IS LOST AND TO SHRINKAGE

a: Rate of loss in drying moist clay. Compare lettered points on curve with those in corresponding diagrams (fig. 2). Rate of drying is constant while there is a film of water on the surface (between points A and B). Below B the rate decreases more and more as the remaining water shrinks farther and farther into the pores. *b:* Drying shrinkage curve of a moist clay. From A to B the water lost comes from between the particles which are gradually drawn together until they touch (point B, cf. fig. 2). There is then no further change in bulk volume and the water removed comes from the pores. (From F. H. Norton, *Elements of Ceramics*, 1952, Addison-Wesley Publishing Co., Inc., Cambridge, Mass.)

fig. 3a, point B). The water that remains in the clay is held in capillary spaces from which it escapes slowly. Measurements of drying shrinkage are consistent with this explanation because shrinkage stops at the point of decrease in drying rate when the particles are considered to be in contact (fig. 3b, point B). It is also at this point that the color of the paste becomes lighter.

The effect of paste texture on drying rate has been mentioned in the discussion of temper (p. 25). Other factors are temperature, humidity, and velocity of the air. Since rate of evaporation increases with rise in temperature, heating will speed drying, but this cannot be done under ordinary atmospheric conditions without danger of cracking the ware. In commercial practice this difficulty is overcome by heating the pieces thoroughly in a saturated atmosphere in which they lose no moisture, and then reducing the humidity as fast as it can safely be done. Aside from the factors of atmospheric conditions and paste texture, size and form of the pieces have an influence on rate and evenness of drying.

In view of these variables, it is not surprising that time and rate of drying varies greatly among different pottery-making people. We might expect potters to discover from experience how fast the pottery can be dried safely, although reports on pottery making rarely mention the potter's ideas of the causes of loss in drying. The difference in time allowed is very great. Thus Tschopik (1950) reports that the Aymara allow the vessel to dry a few hours; Fewkes (1944) says that the Catawba left their vessels from several days to a week, depending on conditions. Rogers (1936) reports a short drying period for the Yuma, four hours between finishing and firing, and suggests that the properties of the local clays may accelerate drying. In view of the large percentage of coarse nonplastic material (85 per cent by Rogers' calculation) this would be true for two reasons: first, the surface area of particles would be greatly reduced and the paste would hold much less water than the average; second, the texture would be more open. The Yuma dry pottery in the sun unless the day is very hot, in which case vessels are placed in the shade. The potters explain that too intense heat causes crazing.

It is plain that, in order to give an idea of how well the potter judged conditions and requirements, it is necessary to have a report of the time allowed for drying with reference to atmospheric conditions and characteristics of the paste.

FIRING

Firing is the inevitable and relentless test to which the potter must subject the product of her skill and patience. Up to this point the clay yields to her will; she shapes it as she pleases and derives the enjoyment of creative activity in decorating it; but to keep and use it, she must trust it to the fire where she cannot decide whether it will be a thing of pride or a handful of potsherds for the scrap heap. It is understandable that the task of firing is approached with misgiving and anxiety, and it is no wonder that superstitions grow up about it. Yuman potters, according to Rogers (1936), considered it bad luck to watch or go near the "kiln" until the fire was entirely out. Cushing (1920, p. 314) tells of the Zuni's concern for the effect of noise. When the vessel was being finished and decorated, there was no laughter or singing, and conversation was carried on in whispers or by signs because it was feared that the "voice" might enter the vessel and then, during firing, escape with a loud noise and such violence that the vessel would be shattered. In contrast to such beliefs is the apparent absence of any superstitious practice among some present-day potters; for example, Guthe (1925), in his detailed account of San Ildefonso pottery making, states that he observed nothing during firing that suggested superstition.

The techniques of a craft can be relearned, but what we call superstition springs from a people's attitudes and beliefs. Irrespective of the attitude toward supernatural influences, potters learn some lessons by experience, and their procedures generally conform with sound ceramic theory whether they explain it by natural causes or otherwise.

PROVISIONS FOR FIRING

The first consideration in firing is the provision that will be made to retain heat. The long history of ceramics is marked by repeated advances in kiln design from the simple updraft beehive to the continuous tunnel kiln. The kiln not only retains heat but also permits control of draft and of firing atmosphere. In view of the simplicity of building an updraft kiln, it is surprising that crude improvised methods of firing were so widespread among prewheel potters and permanent kilns so rare. In the absence of a permanent kiln, the potter either fired in a pit or surrounded the pottery with fuel above ground, raising the vessel on rocks or a grate. When the pit was used, fuel was either stacked around the pottery, as was the custom of the Yuma, or a large fire was built first, the fuel allowed to burn to coals, the pottery then placed in the hot "oven" and coals raked around and over it. Rogers (1936) gives an example from the Yuma. These potters dig a pit on the lee side of a hill for shelter from wind. The bottom is lined with small stones spaced so that twigs can be put between them. Vessels are inverted and surrounded by the fuel—slabs of oak bark gathered from dead trees. A second tier of pots is set on the first and the heap covered with large slabs of bark. Hill (1937) describes the practice of preheating the pit by the western Navajo, who left vessels in the pit from four to seven hours. When firing is above ground, it is more difficult to retain the heat. Fuel placed around the pottery forms, at best, a loose open cover and soon burns out. When dung fuel is used, as among present-day Rio Grande potters, it forms a more satisfactory covering than wood because of the more suitable shape of chips and slabs. An additional advantage of dung is that it retains its form as it burns. In some instances, the larger part of the fuel is laid beneath the pottery. At Chinautla, Guatemala, for example, dung chips are laid to form a circular platform on which the pottery is set; only bundles of grass are placed around the sides of the stack. The Aymara also fire on a circular platform of dung, using grass and tinder between the vessels and scattering manure hunks lightly over the pottery without attempting to fill in all spaces with dung (Tschopik, 1950). Adobe kilns and deep, stone-lined pits with connecting fire boxes are used in Mexico, but it is difficult to trace their origin and determine what elements are native.

Descriptions of pottery making indicate that all primitive potters do not have the same concern for the effect of uneven draft in firing. Rogers is specific in his explanation of the precautions taken by the Yuma. He says they recognize the advantage of updraft in obtaining even heating and avoiding sooting, for they fire in the evening when the air is most likely to be still. Obviously a strong cross draft will result in higher temperature on one side of the "kiln" than the other, and the difference will be greater in an open heap of fuel above ground than in a pit. Nevertheless, Guthe (1925) reports that San Ildefonso potters paid no attention to the direction of the prevailing wind, and Tschopik (1950) says that the Aymara fired on a rise of ground to take advantage of the wind.

The custom of heaping fuel around the pottery presents the problem of protecting it from discoloration by deposition of soot or local reduction, defects that go under the general term of fire-clouding. These defects are especially likely to occur when the oxidation period is short. It is then necessary to protect the pottery from direct contact with the fuel if a clear, uniform color is desired. Large sherds (or, in modern times, pieces of sheet metal or flattened cans) are sometimes set around the pottery or between pottery and pieces of fuel. This precaution is unnecessary when the ware is not oxidized, that is, if it is to be gray or blackish. Likewise, protection may be neglected if the ware is to be well oxidized at the completion of firing. The Diegueno, for example, set slabs of bark against the pottery; after the fuel has burned down, the coals are sufficient to maintain a temperature that will burn off sooted spots. Potters I observed at Chinautla, Guatemala, remarked that the last armloads of grass laid over the heap of pottery must burn white (to ash) before the pots could be removed, or they would be discolored.

The type of fuel influences the provisions that are made for retaining heat. An interesting example of change in firing practice that occurred with the use of dung, following the introduction of livestock, is recorded for the pueblo Zuni. Cushing (1920, p. 312) describes methods observed between 1879 and 1884, making no reference to dung, but he says pottery was fired in a "little underground kiln" or else above ground, the pottery being surrounded top and sides with a "dome of turf and greaseweed or other light fuel." During firing, blankets were held up to intercept drafts. Some 20 years later, when Stevenson was at Zuni, potters were using dung from the sheep pens. She says (1904) that they chose a quiet day and built an "oven" of the dung. Of particular interest, from the technological standpoint, is her observation that the fire was carefully managed to produce gradual heating and then the "mass was subjected to intense heat." The firing process took from one to two hours.

FUEL

The modern ceramist compared fuels with respect to their heat value and the length of time they burn. Primitive potters have no way of comparing heat values of different fuels, but they can note whether or not a particular fuel has a clean or a sooty flame, burns quietly or snaps, falls to pieces or holds its form and retains heat after the flame has burned out.

A variety of fuels has been used by primitive potters. A particular kind of wood may be chosen because it does not burn with a smoky flame. Thus, the Pueblos choose juniper rather than piñon to kindle their fire. Gilmore (1925) explains that the Arikara prefer elm wood because it burns quietly without snapping. Dung, a fuel widely used by potters who had domestic animals, has both advantages and disadvantages. It burns easily and rapidly because it is open in texture and composed of fine material. It also retains its form after the more combustible material has been burned out and thus maintains a warm blanket around the pottery, but it gives a short firing because it burns out quickly.

The length of time a fuel will burn depends on the proportion of volatile material it contains, the density of the carbon, and the kind of ash it forms. The ash of certain kinds of wood acts as an insulating blanket over the charcoal, and thus serves to slow the rate of combustion and prolong burning. There is a great difference in the rate of combustion of fuels used by primitive potters. Fine fuel, such as coarse grass (Chinautla, Guatemala; Aymara, Peru), is consumed rapidly, giving quick heat and requiring frequent renewal; other fuels, such as oak wood, burn more slowly and are frequently not replenished. Long-burning fuel, such as coal, used in prehistoric times by Pueblo Indians of the Hopi country and at times by present-day Hopi to supplement dung (M. R. F. Colton, 1931), burns slowly and therefore affords a distinct advantage in the oxidation of ware because temperature is maintained after volatile matter, which is reducing in effect, has been expelled from the fuel. Long firing without refueling is especially advantageous for carbonaceous clays that require oxidation, and it is not improbable that the use of coal was a factor in the development of fully oxidized wares in the Hopi country.

An idea of differences in rate of temperature increase and length of burning of dung, wood, and coal can be gained from the results of experimental firings (fig. 4). Simple methods which a primitive potter might follow were employed; consequently, weight of fuel in the different firings was not constant and the data do not give an absolute comparison of the fuels but rather an idea of the results that might be expected when they were employed by prehistoric potters. An exception was made in the case of dung, in order to learn how much maximum temperature is raised when the amount of fuel is increased by varying methods of stacking chips. In this experiment, pottery, placed on an improvised grate, was surrounded by a wall of cow chips laid flat and then capped by chips across the top. No fuel was added after the fire was started with juniper wood kindling under the grate. The rise in temperature was abrupt at the start, and the entire heap burned with a flame for 20 minutes to a temperature of 900°C, but the rate of heat increase had begun to level off 10 minutes before. After volatile matter was burned out, as shown by the cessation of flame, the temperature continued to rise to a peak of 940°C and then fell rapidly because the dung chips do not leave charcoal that maintains heat. The abrupt drop in temperature occurred before the chips were raked off at the points marked by transverse lines. In this firing, the increased amount of fuel gave a higher temperature than was attained in any Pueblo firing except the Zia (cf. curve for dung in fig. 4 with curves for dung firings at Cochiti and San Ildefonso pueblos, fig. 5) and also maintained heat considerably longer.

The firings with coal and juniper wood (fig. 4) illustrate the relative effectiveness of these two fuels in oxidizing carbonaceous clays. The experiments were made at Awatovi in the Hopi country, where potters had used coal in prehistoric times. The wood was set around the pottery tepee-fashion in a circle 0.8 m. in diameter and extending 0.7 m. high. Wood was added when the temperature had reached its peak and shortly afterwards but was ineffective. Nine minutes after the peak was reached (transverse line on curve), the three large pieces of wood which had served as a tripod support for the balance of the fuel burned through and fell, covering the pottery with partially burned wood, ashes, and charcoal. Flame persisted 20 minutes longer, but the temperature had dropped from its peak of 905° to 825°C. There was sufficient burning charcoal to hold the temperature above 800° for three-quarters of an hour longer, but there was little circulation of air through the heap of ashes and charcoal, and the pottery was not oxidized. The form of the firing curve after the peak is passed depends largely on the charcoal and the effectiveness with which the pottery is blanketed.

In firing with coal, large chunks were laid in a circle of the same diameter as that of the wood. Small pieces of coal were placed in courses until the test specimens were surrounded and enclosed. No fuel was added except for a few

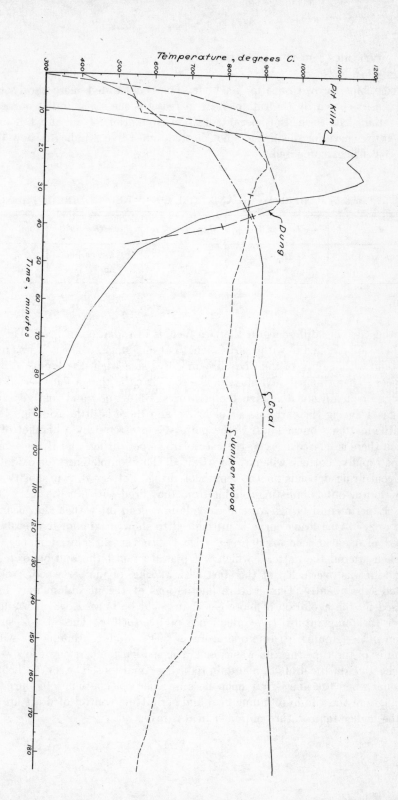

FIG. 4—TEMPERATURE CURVES FOR EXPERIMENTAL FIRINGS WITH VARIOUS FUELS

juniper chips thrown on after an hour. The coal ignited more slowly than the wood, as is shown by the rate of heat increase at the start; but it burned longer and retained its form, thus permitting free circulation of air and full oxidation. The entire curve for this firing is not plotted, but Table 2 indicates how the wood and coal firings compared.

TABLE 2—JUNIPER WOOD AND COAL COMPARED IN DIRECT FIRING

Fuel	Time to Max. Temp.	Max. Temp. C	Time Over 750°C	Total Firing Time
Juniper wood	21 min.	905°	1 hr., 40 min.	3 hr., 27 min.
Coal	3 hr.	970°	7 hr.	10 hr., 10 min.

Another striking difference in the two fuels is in radiation of heat. The coal fire could be approached to within arm's length at any stage, whereas it was impossible to stand within 10 ft. of the wood fire on its lee side when the temperature was at its peak. The principal advantage of the coal firing is that a long period of oxidation can be maintained at high temperatures. Both wood and coal give off reducing gases during the early stages of firing, and there is little oxidation before the volatile matter is burned out. If the pottery is protected by a blanket of ashes in which there is charcoal, as in the case of the wood firing, and if the temperature drops rapidly, pottery will not be oxidized. The completeness of oxidation with the coal firing depends on the length of firing. Pottery drawn shortly after the flame burns out is indistinguishable from that fired with wood.

Experimental firings were also made in a deep pit with a flue near its base (see p. 217). One firing curve is introduced to show maximum temperatures compared in open and enclosed firings (fig. 4). In the pit kiln, juniper wood was stacked around the pottery, which was placed against the wall opposite the flue. The kiln was overfueled at the start with 31.5 kg. of juniper wood. No fuel was added subsequently. Temperature fluctuations at the maximum may have been caused by the evolution of more gas than could be burned, which would tend to lower the temperature. In consequence of overfueling, dense black smoke was given off, beginning at a temperature of 500°C and continuing to within four minutes of the time the kiln was closed. The sudden temperature drop was caused by shutting off the draft to maintain reducing conditions. The loss of heat is more gradual when the flue is left open because charcoal continues to burn. The advantages of the kiln in retaining heat and permitting control of draft are reflected in the higher temperature obtained in this firing.

FIRING SCHEDULE

In general ceramic practice, as we have noted, there are three distinct phases in firing: the dehydration period, when water is driven off at low heat to avoid too rapid formation of steam; the oxidation period, when carbonaceous matter is burned out from the clay, and iron and other compounds are fully oxidized; and the vitrification period, when the constituents of the pottery begin to soften and cement. Even though potters had no concept of these changes, they learned by experience some of the precautions that should be taken during these stages of firing.

Water smoking.   Part of the water that is driven off during dehydration is the last remnant of capillary water and the interlayer water held between plates of the clay mineral. Although held too tenaciously to be lost in air drying, such water goes off at a lower temperature than water of crystallization. This first stage of dehydration is referred to as *water smoking* in commercial ceramic practice because of the white steam that issues from the stacks. Shattering of pottery from steam trapped by too rapid firing is probably what the Zuni referred to when they spoke of the "voice escaping." The rate of heat increase can not be controlled in direct firing as in a kiln; hence pottery is sometimes warmed before the firing, which effects at least a partial water smoking. The Yuma place their jars around a brush fire for about 15 minutes, and many Pueblo potters follow a similar practice, taking care to turn the vessels in order to heat them evenly.

The time required for water smoking differs, depending on the texture and structure of the body. Ethnologists describing pottery making should recognize the importance of this step in firing because, in the absence of reference to it, there is no way of knowing whether it was omitted from the record or actually neglected by the potter. Even though potters did not make a preliminary fire, they may still have taken some measures to maintain a slow heat at the start. Ethnologists, with this question in mind, will observe closely how the fire is fueled, and consider the requirements of the clay.

Oxidation.   As we have noted in the discussion of the effects of heat on clay, oxidation requires a good draft and a temperature sufficiently high to burn off carbonaceous matter. The process should be completed before vitrification commences; otherwise some organic matter will be trapped in the clay, and expansion of gas will cause bloating. The most effective temperature for oxidation depends partly on the particular properties of a clay because it must be below the vitrification point, which varies greatly for different clays. The variability of clays also affects requirements for oxidation. Some highly carbonaceous and dense clays require a long oxidation period; those which are open in texture or contain little organic matter are easily oxidized. In commercial ceramic practice, the firing schedule is adjusted to the requirements of the clay, and oxidation is carried out at the most efficient temperature. But complete oxidation of the body has not been a serious concern of primitive potters since their temperatures have rarely been high enough to cause vitrification, and consequently unburned carbon causes no harm. I have found no indication in the literature that present-day prewheel potters attempt to oxidize their ware fully, but conclusions can not be based on absence of reference.

Although low-fired ware did not have to be fully oxidized, it does not follow that potters gave no attention to oxidation. They were directly interested in it in so far as it affects surface color. The precautions taken by Chinautla potters to burn fuel to a white ash have been mentioned. Rogers notes that the Yuma sometimes put use-blackened cook pots in the pit when pottery was fired in order to burn off the carbon.

Length of firing and method of fueling, as well as temperature, affect oxidation. Primitive potters either follow a simple routine, fueling once and giving no further attention to the fire until it has burned out and the vessels can be removed, or they watch the fire, adding fuel from time to time and judging when the temperature is adequate. The size of fuel influences firing method because refueling is necessary if small wood or grass is used. Rogers' description (1936) of Yuman firing serves as an example of a method that requires no refueling. After the pottery is stacked in the pit with oak bark placed around it, the kindling of twigs is lighted, and the potter does not return to remove the vessels until the following morning. In the firing Rogers observed, it took 45 minutes for the fuel to be reduced to coals, during which time all the vessels were subject to the same conditions. For two hours longer, vessels in the lower tier were subject to the heat given off by the coals. The heat from the burning fuel was sufficient to keep the vessels adjacent to it dull red. Sooted areas were formed where fuel rested against vessels, but these were later burned off. With this method, the potter decides at the start how much fuel is needed and lets it burn out. If the firing is done in a pit, there is little choice because fuel cannot be added conveniently except at the top, where its heat would be largely lost.

There is no uniformity in the conditions that prevail when fuel is added during the course of firing because this practice may follow from the use of fine fuel that necessitates frequent replenishment, or from standards that require maintenance of high temperatures for a longer period than average. In any case, the proportion of oxygen in the atmosphere fluctuates as volatile matter is released with each additon of fuel. Fine fuel that burns out quickly shortens the oxidation period, which fact may explain the Chinautla potters' awareness of the importance of allowing grass to burn to white ash before removing the pottery. When additions are made of coarse fuel, in order to maintain temperature longer, the length of time during which conditions favor oxidation may be comparable to that obtained with a single fueling, or this period may be prolonged if fuel is added gradually to avoid the release of a large volume of reducing gases at any one time. In other words, the temporary checking of oxidation with the release of reducing gases upon the addition of fresh fuel is more than counterbalanced.

Vitrification. The final stage in standard firing practice, during which constituents of the body soften and melt, so that particles first adhere to each other and are then cemented by the glass that is formed, causing the body to become increasingly dense and less pervious, occurs within a temperature range that was often not attained in open firing. Since the composition of a clay may lower this range considerably, and since fluxing impurities are common in the low grade of clay that primitive potters often used, the incipient stages of vitrification could at least be reached. The essential factor is a maximum temperature, adequate for the given clay and maintained long enough for thorough heating. A measurement of porosity affords a means of judging the progress of vitrification.

Temperature of firing. A report of firing is incomplete without a temperature record, and such data should be considered in terms of the type of clay that is used. Unfortunately, ethnologists are rarely equipped with a pyrometer, and consequently we have relatively few records. Fewkes used an optical pyrometer to measure temperatures of Catawba firings; H. S. Colton (1951) has reported on 14 Hopi firings in which he used a thermoelectric pyrometer, weighed the fuel, and recorded pottery loss; and I have recorded firing temperatures in the Rio Grande Pueblos of Santa Clara, San Ildefonso, and Zia, also using a thermoelectric pyrometer (Kidder and Shepard, 1936). This is the most satisfactory and reliable instrument for the purpose. Unfortunately, pyrometric cones, which are inexpensive and simple to use, are not reliable because they bloat with reducing gases, and their softening point depends on rate of heating as well as on temperature.

Excessive loss of heat by radiation and lack of forced draft limit the temperature that can be obtained in firing without a kiln. The maximum temperature that I have recorded in firing with wood stacked around pottery was 962°C. The day was windy, which increased draft and caused extreme unevenness of heating. Dung chips laid horizontally to form a thick wall gave a maximum temperature of 940°C. It is safe to say that 1000°C was rarely attained in direct firing in the open. It could have been exceeded easily, however, by firing in a pit with a flue (see fig. 4). There is no definite lower limit to the potter's range because some clays harden at much lower temperatures than others, and some potters were content to produce soft ware. Among my records of Rio Grande Pueblo firings, which have included four wares (San Ildefonso and Santa Clara polished black, San Ildefonso red, Cochiti black-on-cream, and Zia polychrome), the lowest temperature was 625°C. This was for Santa Clara black ware made by a potter who was careless in her management of the fire. The maximum temperature recorded was

940°C in firing Zia polychrome. The Zia potter was eager to show how well she fired and consequently may have used more fuel than was customary.

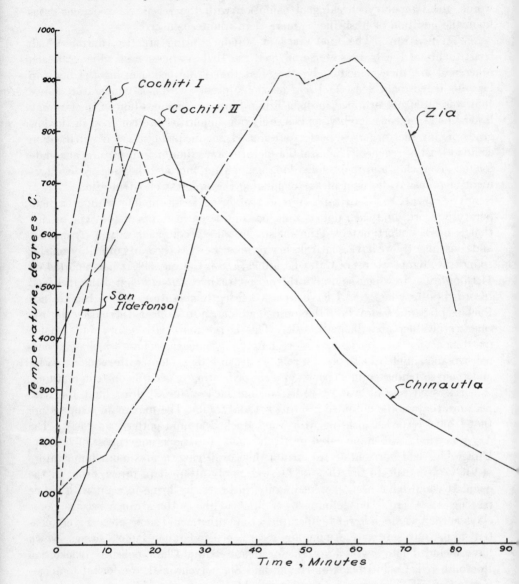

FIG. 5—TEMPERATURE CURVES FOR FIRING OF OXIDIZED WARE

A series of time-temperature curves for Rio Grande Pueblo firings and for one in Chinautla, Guatemala, will illustrate variations in rate of heating and firing time, as well as maximum temperature for oxidized wares (fig. 5). The temperature at which the curve starts is variable because a bed of coals often remains from the preliminary fire built to dry the vessels. In firing red ware (fig. 5), the San Ildefonso potter stacked the vessels on an improvised grate and covered the heap with dung chips placed on edge and leaned against the pottery to form a loose covering the thickness of a single chip. The fire was started with juniper wood under the grate. The method of the two Cochiti potters differed only in the substitution of cottonwood kindling for juniper. In each case the rate of temperature increase was rapid, and the fuel burned out quickly. The Zia potter also stacked her pottery on a grate and enclosed the heap with dung, but she used thick slabs from the sheep corral instead of chips. By the time she had laid the fuel, a temperature of 415°C was reached. The slabs burned more slowly than chips; consequently the rate of heat increase to the first peak was less than half that of the other three Pueblo firings, and since there was more fuel, a high temperature was maintained much longer. The second temperature peak was reached after the potter stuck corncobs into openings between dung slabs. The difference in temperatures of the Zia and the San Ildefonso and Cochiti firings is due largely to difference in amount of fuel used; slabs of dung taken from the sheep corral are much thicker than cow dung chips. If fuel is added as fast as it is burned, temperature can be maintained, but these Pueblo potters did not attempt to keep up the fire in this way.

Variation in cooling time was probably affected less by the type of dung used than by the size of the bed of coals under the grate and the relative extent to which the partially burned dung enclosed the pottery. After volatile matter is burned out from the dung and the temperature peak is passed, the remaining carbon and ash retain the shape of the chips, which form a hot blanket around the pottery; hence the importance of placing the chips carefully. The three potters using chips did not wait for the pottery to cool but began raking them off soon after the temperature had passed its peak, and drew the pottery at temperatures ranging between 670° and 715°C. The Zia potter started to remove the covering of burned dung while the temperature was still high, but the pottery had cooled to 450°C before it was taken from the grate.

In the firing at Chinautla, Guatemala (fig. 5), dung was used under the pottery but not around it. Kindling was first laid on the ground and a circular platform of dung chips built over it. The dung ignited before the pottery was all placed on the platform. Coarse grass, laid in bundles around and over the pottery, afforded the only means of retaining heat. The grass was quickly consumed, and armfuls were added from time to time, but the heat was not retained effectively.

The rate of heat increase was slow compared with that of the Pueblo firing, and the maximum temperature was low.

The clays of all these wares are red-firing and have a relatively low vitrification range. Data on these firings, together with others for smudged ware, are summarized in Table 3. The Rio Grande record can be compared with H. S. Colton's report (1951) of 17 Hopi firings. These are for a single ware, and the temperature range is narrower, from 720° to 885°C. Temperatures ranging from 760° to 960°C, reported by Fewkes (1944) for the Catawba, are not comparable to those of the Pueblos because his measurements were made with an optical, rather than a thermoelectric, pyrometer.

Potters have different bases for judging when firing is completed. They may burn a predetermined amount of fuel, or judge by the appearance of the fire or of the pottery, or be guided by time. Maria Martinez of San Ildefonso, famous for her lustrous black ware, follows a careful routine and times the different stages. On the other hand, a Santa Clara potter explained that she knew when the pottery was hot enough by its color. On two different occasions, her firing temperatures were measured with a thermoelectric pyrometer, and in each case her maximum was 750°C. It is not uncommon to judge temperature roughly by color. This can be done because light emitted by a black body is proportional to the fourth power of its absolute temperature. Pottery is near enough to a theoretical black body for rough temperature estimates to be made from color.

Fewkes (1944) mentions changing color and resonance of the vessels as the guiding criteria of the Catawba, but it appears that the colors considered are due to the progress of oxidation rather than to the temperature of the hot pottery. He mentioned the difficulty of obtaining an explanation of the basis for judging when the vessels are fully fired. This is understandable since potters are guided by experience and tradition rather than theory, but the conclusions drawn from experience and the extent to which craft tradition holds are important parts of the record.

In general, the firing schedule is significant in relation to the requirements of a clay and the precautions that must be observed in firing—maintenance of low temperatures until water smoking is completed, maintenance of the temperature and draft that will secure the desired degree of oxidation, the attainment of the temperature necessary to harden the clay, and avoidance of thermal shock on completion of firing. In view of the variability of both clay and firing methods employed by prewheel potters, it is important to record the firing schedule.

Control of firing atmosphere. Since archaeologists sometimes classify pottery with respect to the kind of atmosphere in which it is believed to have been fired, it is important to know to what extent potters who did not have kilns could control firing atmosphere. In considering this question, the general char-

TABLE 3—FIRING DATA FROM PUEBLO AND GUATEMALAN POTTERS

Pueblo	Ware	Amount of Pottery	Rate of Heating °C/Min.	Max. Temp. °C	Min. Above 700°C	Rate of Cooling °C/Min.	Drawing Temp. °C	Firing Time in Min.
Santa Clara (curve I)	Polished Black	3 jars 20–25 cm. ht., 7 small pieces	80.7	750	7	12.9	570	34
Santa Clara (curve II)	Polished Black	3 jars 30 cm. ht., 1 bowl 15 cm. diam., 4 small pieces	31.6	750	8	14.7	545	39
Santa Clara	Polished Black	1 jar 50 cm. ht.	22.4	625	0	21.8	440	27
San Ildefonso	Polished Black	33 bowls, 4 small pieces	28.4	670	0	4.3	400	114
San Ildefonso	Light Red and White on Polished Red	2 covered boxes, 3 bowls 10–18 cm. diam., 3 small pieces	59.5	770	8.5	...	700	20
Cochiti (curve I)	Black-on-Cream (organic paint)	1 pot 20 cm. ht., 2 bowls 12–15 cm. diam., 2 small pieces	62.6	890	9	62.5	715	18
Cochiti (curve II)	Black-on-Cream	2 bowls, 1 jar 20 cm. ht.	57.5	830	12	15.7	670	23
Cochiti	Black-on-Cream	1 bowl 36 cm. diam.	66.6	825	5.5	15	810	17
Zia	Black and Red on Tan (mineral paint)	40 bowls 14 cm. diam. av.	22.6	940	42	10	450	80
Chinautla, Guatemala	Plain Red and White-on-Red	275–300 small vessels	17.6	715	8	10.4	125	95

acteristics of direct, open firing must be borne in mind. The composition of gases given off by the fuel and formed during combustion varies during the course of firing and, at the same time, draft changes with shifting air currents. It is not possible, therefore, to control firing atmosphere fully. The degree of oxidation that is attained will depend on clay composition, temperature and duration of firing, method of fueling, and draft. Short firing or repeated refueling, which releases a supply of the reducing gases formed in the early stages of combustion, will prevent oxidation or actually reduce if the temperature is high enough. Consequently, the potter could produce oxidized, reduced or smudged ware even though firing atmosphere was not uniform. In the firings that have been described, surface oxidation was obtained because draft was adequate and smokeless fuel was used in the final state of firing. I know of no record of present-day Indian firing in which the ware is reduced without smudging, a special technique in firing, which should not be confused with smudging alone. In experimental firing, colors comparable to Pueblo black-on-white ware have been obtained by checking the fire as soon as volatile matter is burned out. In order to avoid sooting or formation of fire-clouds, it is important to have fuel that burns with a smokeless flame. This general subject of firing atmosphere and its effect on the color of pottery is discussed more fully on pages 217–22.

Smudging is a means of blackening pottery by causing carbon and tarry products of combustion to be deposited on it. There are various ways of securing the effect. The method used by present-day Pueblo potters of the Rio Grande valley is perhaps best known. The first part of the firing, up to the point of maximum temperature, is the same as that which has been described for oxidized ware. The heap of burning fuel is then smothered with very fine, loose manure. As the draft is shut off, the temperature begins to drop. After a few minutes the scraps of sheet metal, which protect the pottery from contact with the dung, are forked out, and the dung pushed close to the vessels. The sooty smoke from the smoldering dung settles on the pottery, turning it a permanent black since the carbon penetrates the pores. Details of technique vary with individual potters. The time of smudging varies from 15 minutes to over an hour. Some potters spread ashes over the fine manure, others do not, but all potters are careful to prevent flames from shooting through the protective blanket of fine dung because vessels near these points are not smudged, and mottling of the ware would result. It is particularly interesting that the potters recognize that luster will be impaired if the temperature is too high. They smother the fire before shrinkage commences and, if a vessel comes from the fire with dull or semilustrous spots where flame has played on it, they explain that it got too hot.

Time-temperature curves for three firings (fig. 6) will indicate the variation in rate of heating and length of smudging period, and also the rate of cooling as compared with that of oxidized ware (fig. 5). The two Santa Clara firings, made by the same potter in different years, are the ones in which temperature was judged by the color of the hot pottery (see p. 86). Fine manure was thrown on the heap before the temperature reached its peak and smothering was completed either at or slightly before this point; 15–20 minutes were allowed for smudging.

The San Ildefonso firing was made by Julian and Maria Martinez, potters well known for their skill. They worked methodically and with easy confidence.

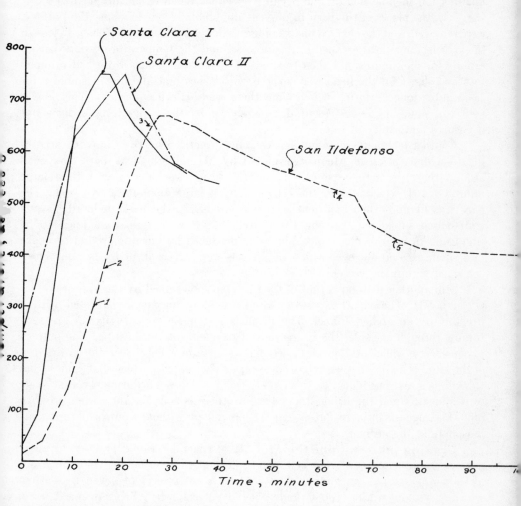

FIG. 6—TEMPERATURE CURVES FOR FIRING OF PUEBLO SMUDGED WARE

Everything that would be required was assembled near-by at the start, and the stages of firing were timed by clock. A small amount of fuel, dung and juniper chips, was added when the temperature had reached 300°C (fig. 6:1–2), but a constant rate of heat increase was maintained. The ware was intentionally fired at low temperature to avoid the risk of impairing high luster. After 25.5 minutes, at 650°C (fig. 6:3), two washtubs of manure dust, used to smother the fire, were thrown on all at once. The temperature continued to rise for one and a half minutes and then leveled off and began to decline. When it had dropped to 525°C (fig. 6:4), the pieces of tin, used to prevent dung chips from touching the pottery, were removed, and the charred and smoldering dung and ashes were pushed close to the vessels. Some heat escaped in this process, and the temperature dropped more rapidly for six minutes and then tapered off. When the temperature had dropped to 426°C (fig. 6:5), the heap was covered with ashes and allowed to smolder for 25 minutes longer, during which time there was little loss of heat. This longer period of smudging is not essential, as is shown by the Santa Clara firings, but it ensures uniformity of results.

Another technique of smudging was once practiced by the Catawba, according to a description of Mooney's, quoted by Myer (1928). Oak bark was piled around the objects to be smudged and the heap closely covered with a large unfired vessel, which was in turn covered by a large amount of oak bark. The bark was lit and when sufficient heat was produced, the bark under the vessel ignited and smoldered, causing the objects which were tightly confined to be smudged. An inferior black was said to be produced by burning ground corncobs in a small excavation, over which the vessels were inverted, or by burning corncob meal within the vessel.

Still another method is that of the Coyotepec described by the Van de Veldes (1939, p. 34). These potters use a cylindrical stone-lined pit connected with a fire box by an arched tunnel. The firing is watched closely; if flames are seen coming through one side, the fire is moved to avoid uneven heating. The pottery is considered sufficiently fired "when flames emerge evenly over the entire top of the kiln." The fuel is then removed at once. The sooted pottery that comes from the kiln is a lustrous black. In this case the soot is deposited during the first stage of combustion and the firing stopped before there is time for the carbon to burn off. This suggests how oxidation can be prevented without control of firing atmosphere in the ordinary sense.

Drawing pottery from the fire. It is general ceramic practice to allow pottery to cool slowly before it is drawn from the kiln, in order to avoid the strain of sudden, excessive contraction. This caution is not always observed by potters who fire without a kiln. Rio Grande Pueblo potters, when firing oxidized ware, draw it soon after the temperature has passed its peak. In three instances, the temperature at which the first vessels were removed ranged from 700° to 810°C (see Table 3). The wares are low-fired, and their softness and porosity save them from cracking. Pueblo polished black ware is drawn at lower temperatures, 400°–570°C in the firings recorded, not as a matter of caution but in consequence of the time required for smudging and the fact that temperature is dropping during this process. Unlike the Rio Grande potters, the Hopi, according to H. S. Colton (1939), "do not remove the pottery until it is cool enough to handle easily." Likewise, when pottery is fired in a pit and left overnight before drawing, as among the Yuma and Navajo (reported on by Rogers, 1936, and Hill, 1937, respectively), it has ample time for cooling. It would be interesting to know what reasons potters give for a long cooling period and if there is any relation between temperature of drawing and brittleness of the pottery.

ACCIDENTS OF FIRING

Accidents that occur during firing may be caused by either flaws in the vessel or careless firing. Faulty workmanship in any stage of pottery making can result in firing loss. If the clay is not well cleaned, pebbles or other coarse inclusions that differ in rate of expansion can cause cracking or spalling. Inclusions of material that undergo changes accompanied by volume increase when heated sufficiently, such as limestone or mica, will cause spalling or pocking, depending on the size of particles. In building a vessel, coils or parts that are formed separately or at different times may be imperfectly joined or air may be trapped in the clay. Trapped air expands on heating and causes cracking. Abrupt changes in wall thickness produce lines of weakness because the sections will differ in rate of drying and contraction and will set up strains. Guthe (1925) remarks of San Ildefonso pottery that the entire base often breaks off in firing. Either a poor juncture between the first coil and the hand-modeled base or a difference in thickness of base and sides could be responsible. Strains are also caused by uneven or too rapid drying. Thorough drying is essential; otherwise expansion of steam on firing will shatter a vessel.

The first precaution in firing is to dry the ground on which the firing is to take place, and to have dry fuel because steam can cause deformation of vessels. The importance of gradual heating until dehydration of the ware is complete has been discussed under water smoking. Uniform heating should be maintained to avoid underfiring or overfiring of some pieces. Either strong wind or careless fueling can result in uneven heating. Underfired ware will be soft and may have a grayish color from incomplete oxidation. The clearest mark of overfiring is deformation from softening of the body by too rapid vitrification. This is not a common defect with open firing because maximum temperatures are generally below the vitrification range. The defect may have occurred in firing or subsequently in the burning of a building. When warped vessels are found in an excavation, it is important to note whether or not there are evidences of a conflagration. Indian potters today are not unaware of the possibility of warping. According to Hill (1937), for example, the Navajo set their vessels upside down and explain that they would "come out of the fire crooked" if laid on their sides. If a vessel were placed on its side, deformation would be conspicuous; whereas if it is set upright or inverted, deformation will be symmetrical and not so noticeable unless it is pronounced. This circumstance is not the main reason why vessels were usually inverted in firing; they are usually most stable in this position.

Another effect of firing to the point of incipient vitrification is increased brittleness, which makes a vessel more subject to rupture on sudden chilling. Van de Velde and Van de Velde (1939) note that Coyotepec vessels became brittle and gray when "overfired." Guthe (1925) describes the effect of overfiring on Santo Domingo slip, a cream-colored bentonitic clay. It has higher firing shrinkage than the body and it crazes. Guthe reports that it also becomes gray and in extreme cases even black, but temperature increase alone does not produce this color change. It is probable that some sooting occurs early in firing, and Santo Domingo slip—being highly adsorbent—takes up more carbon and holds it more tenaciously than other clays. Another special, conspicuous defect that occurs either with prolonged firing or in the higher temperature ranges is the burning out of organic paint.

One of the most common defects caused by careless firing is localized discoloration or fire-clouding, which occurs where fuel comes in contact with the ware or where a jet of gas from a smoky flame strikes it. Poor draft or too close packing of one vessel upon another may prevent the oxidation of carbon deposited on the vessels in the early stages of firing. Some clays will absorb and hold carbon much more readily than others. Still another cause of discoloration is careless handling of certain light-colored clays that adsorb oil from the hands. On firing, the oil is charred, leaving a black mark.

It is not surprising that potters should sometimes attribute accidents to supernatural causes and should have a variety of taboos with regard to firing, since the causes of some of the many accidents that can occur in firing are obscure to them. Nevertheless, experience and good observation often taught them to recognize the true cause of a defect. I well remember the first time I put the long thermocouple tube of a pyrometer in a Pueblo dung "kiln." I expected the Indian to blame any accident that might occur on this new, strange contraption. Unfortunately there was a loud snap just as the fire was beginning to burn briskly. When the firing was completed and the "kiln" was opened, we found that a beautiful black jar had a large spall on the side. Without a remark, the potter examined it carefully; then after a moment she exclaimed, "Oh, I left a grain of corn in the clay."

Sometimes the potter may attribute a firing accident to a natural but incorrect cause. It is important that the ethnologist who is making a record of firing understand the causes of defects in order to judge whether or not the potter is giving the correct explanation. This means knowing the working and firing properties of the clay.

POSTFIRING TREATMENT OF POTTERY

After firing, vessels may be either coated on the interior with some substance that renders them less pervious or painted on the exterior with a lacquer-like substance that improves their luster or protects a fugitive paint. Cushing (1920, p. 312) describes the Zuni method of treating cook pots. They were placed on a bed of coals when removed from the fire and coated on the interior with the mucilaginous juice of cactus leaves and with piñon gum. The pots were then reheated under a dome of "coarse" fuel to carbonize the coating. Other substances such as tallow are sometimes rubbed into a vessel to fill the pores.

The use of gums and resinous substances on the exterior is a widespread practice, especially among South American potters.

These methods are of interest primarily because the archaeologist should bear them in mind when judging the utility of prehistoric wares.

THE ETHNOLOGICAL RECORD

Occasionally I have received requests for an outline of points to be observed in studying pottery making. After complying with several of these, I am of the opinion that they may do more harm than good. No matter how long and detailed a list of questions might be prepared, some things would always be omitted because the potter's practices are influenced by experience with particular materials and conditions, by tradition, and by superstition. These cannot be anticipated. If the observer is burdened with a long list of things to look for, his attention may be distracted from new and significant methods.

It does not follow from this circumstance that anyone can go out without preparation and make a fully satisfactory record. In this review of ceramic processes, I have referred to omissions in the record in order to emphasize the importance of understanding basic principles and of judging potters' methods in relation to the properties of their material. The customs and methods of different potters cannot be compared unless the records have been made by observers with sufficient background in ceramics to recognize the significance of what is done and to make their questions pertinent. If the student has first-hand experience in pottery making, so much the better; but in any case, if he is to be alert to the meaning of methods, he should have an understanding of the properties of clay, the ways in which its working quality can be improved, the effect of nonplastics on clay, the principles of sound construction, the theory of drying, the importance of gradual removal of water, the nature of combustion, and the effects of heat on clay. Samples of the potter's material should be collected for identification and the working quality and firing behavior of the clays tested.

III. Ceramic Analysis and Description

THE PURPOSE of this section is to review and evaluate current methods of pottery analysis. It is necessary to consider the distinctiveness and usefulness of various aspects of pottery for purposes of classification and to judge methods by their reliability and practicability. It is no less important to evaluate methods with respect to the information they may afford regarding the potter's techniques, the place of origin of pottery, the relationship of types as indicated by source and technique, and the stage of development of the potter's craft.

The subject of analysis and description is treated under four heads: physical properties, composition of materials, technique, and style. These are obvious divisions but they do not represent independent or unrelated aspects of pottery. The physical properties are directly affected by materials and by the potter's techniques, also the nature of the material often limits the choice of technique, and both material and technique in turn influence style. It is part of the analyst's job to recognize these relationships. Evidence obtained from one aspect of pottery will suggest observations that should be made with respect to another. Interpretation of the meaning of technique and style serve to cross-check one another, and each feature is best understood in its relation to the whole. Consequently the subject of pottery description and analysis should be considered in its entirety, and emphasis should be given to those aspects that reflect most directly the potter's knowledge, skills, standards, and tastes. This circumstance is sufficient to explain the inclusion of style in this review.

The significance and reliability of ceramic data depend in no small measure on proper balance of methods and full correlation of results. Much time will be saved if all aspects of analysis are conducted concurrently. To take a simple illustration, paste affords a simpler approach to classification than does style because every sherd has adequate evidence for identification, and the principles of mineralogical and petrographic identification are well established. But the implications of the results of this basis of classification should be tested before it is carried out extensively or in detail because differences in composition do not necessarily indicate different sources. Potters turning out the same shapes and decorating in the same style may use different materials, or change in style may be unaccompanied by change in technique. On the other hand, a primary stylistic breakdown is often difficult because of the complexity of stylistic features, and when sole dependence is placed on style, important intrusives and local variants may be missed without the clues to origin that paste composition offers.

This section on pottery analysis is written for the archaeologist, not for the specialist in ceramic technology. I have attempted to explain the work of the specialist in order to give the archaeologist a better idea of the kind of questions that can be answered, of the extent of sampling that is desirable, and of what to expect by way of results. Detailed descriptions of technological methods would be out of place. The technologist must depend for his preparation on special training in optical crystallography and petrography, chemistry, particularly microchemistry, and in ceramics. There are, however, many observations, tests, and interpretations that the archaeologist himself can make, some of which have not been exploited fully to date. These are described in this section.

An outline for pottery description has not been included. One reason for this omission is that the various features of pottery do not bear fixed positions of importance in relation to each other. Their value to the student and the attention he will give them depend on the extent to which they were developed. In general, the greater the elaboration and the higher the development of a particular feature, the greater the need for detailed study. The turns that potters' interests take are many, and they are not necessarily closely correlated. A sophisticated style of design can find expression through simple decorative techniques, or complicated decorative techniques can be employed for simple patterns. Potters sometimes become interested in experimenting with the effects obtained with different pigments, but again techniques are often stabilized whereas function and form of vessel change; elaborate shapes and decorations may be produced in technically poor ware, or technically superior ware may lack commensurate finish and decoration. Consequently, in any given case, the nature of the analyst's job will depend on the direction that ceramic development took, and the analyst's methods must remain flexible at all times in order to deal with unexpected features.

A fixed procedure is likewise undesirable from the standpoint of method because analytical techniques are constantly being refined and new methods introduced. Still another reason for omitting a standard outline is to avoid the impression that pottery analysis is a matter of cut and dried recording. It should be primarily a means of answering questions.

"POTTERY SENSE" AND OBJECTIVE METHODS

There is a deeply rooted, popular idea that the expert recognizes subtle characteristics that are significant but indefinable. This conviction is not infrequently shared by archaeologists whose experience in pottery classification seems to support it. Most of us know what it is to identify potsherds with complete confidence and then find ourselves at a loss if we must explain the basis of our judgments. The inadequacy of verbal descriptions of pottery is generally granted. Even the most laborious attempts often fail to serve the individual who would depend on them for identification. To the archaeologist, the immediate, unreasoned recognition of likenesses and differences, frequently called "pottery sense," seems to be a special gift without which he would be unable to get meaning from the bushels upon bushels of potsherds that pass under his scrutiny. The analyst who is trained to use instruments, make measurements, and eliminate subjective evaluation is expected to be critical of immediate, untested personal judgments, but the expert's faith in his judgment is based on experience and not easily shaken.

It seems to me we must recognize the value of the ability called "pottery sense" and at the same time acknowledge its limitations. I do not for a moment depreciate the ability; on the contrary, I believe that without it, the ceramic student would be seriously if not hopelessly handicapped, because identification and classification are thereby greatly facilitated. Pottery sense is characterized by a sensitive and receptive state of mind, and fortunately it is developed by experience. Its most conspicuous limitation is that it places pottery analysis on an individual, and therefore unscientific, basis. Often it does not aid in transmission of information. Moreover, the idea that there are important likenesses and differences that can be perceived but not described, tends to restrict in some measure the student's efforts. It is worthwhile, therefore, to consider pottery sense from the psychological point of view and to ask: (1) to what degree it is innate and to what extent it can be developed by training; (2) how reliable it is; and (3) what basis there is for the belief that indefinable features are recognized.

Unquestionably one of the principal factors in pottery sense is keen perception. This implies much more than keen vision because as Cattell (1941, p. 468) has said, "Our minds are constantly at work thrusting organization into sense data even onto the most uncompromising sensory material, for one thing we cannot abide is chaos of sensations in the perceptual field." In perception we integrate the evidence of different senses and interpret stimuli in terms of past experience and knowledge. This is clearly indicated by the constancy with which we perceive objects. We are not confused when things are seen in different positions or under different illuminations; just as long as the accompanying circumstances register, we perceive them as constant in size and shape. For example, when we view a plate sidewise, we do not mistake it for an elliptical object.

Perception is further distinguished by selection. Boring (1939, p. 417) states that perception is always abstractive, that is, we never perceive all that we can at a glance, even of a single object. From a crowding multitude of stimuli, we unconsciously choose according to our interest or purpose. Attention, a state of receptivity, is aroused either by the nature of the stimulus—by increase in its intensity, by its movement, repetition, novelty or change—or by the priming of the observer, that is, his interest and preparation. Observations may be incidental or deliberate, informed or uninformed. Coupled with perception is imperception, the ability to ignore stimuli, which is a protection against the complete confusion which we would experience were we equally aware of all the sensations that we are constantly receiving. But imperception may be carried to the embarrassing extreme of mental abstraction. Particularly striking are the results of psychological experiments on the effects of suggestion on perception. When a person is told what to look for, his perception of a figure may be grossly inaccurate; he may distort the shape of an object or fail completely to see parts of it.

These observations suggest the extent to which pottery sense can be developed by handling pottery and by gaining an understanding of its characteristics. The first recognition of a pottery type is an example of the organization of experience. The archaeologist, confronted with a mass of potsherds varying in color, surface finish, texture, thickness, hardness, shape, and decoration, selects certain features which he thinks will serve his purpose in classification. He is not dealing with identities; in fact each feature varies, in some instances through a wide range. But the archaeologist can learn to understand the significance of these variations. He notes the range of color through which a finishing technique remains constant, and sees the variation of color in a single sherd. He recognizes the association of a textural range with a color range and these he relates in turn to wall thickness; he sees the shape of a sherd and the fragment of design in terms of what he knows of vessel form and of design plans, elements, and motifs. The examination of large lots of potsherds trains him in ways we may not fully appreciate. It is not simply a matter of familiarization through repetition. It is seeing continuous variations and their limits, and recognizing associations and discontinuities. Only large lots of sherds can give one this experience. The curious thing is that the process of organization of impressions is in large measure unconscious, which means that one fumbles for reasons when asked to explain the basis of his judgment, or, at best, he gives a partial answer.

The question of the reliability of pottery sense can be broken down in several ways. First, are results reproducible—will the individual always come out with the same classification of a sherd lot? Second, what will be the agreement between individuals with comparable experience? One might go further and consider the significance of the likenesses and differences that are recognized intuitively. Are they individual, arbitrary distinctions, or do they arise from differences in materials, techniques or styles, on which there can be general agreement? The fact that pottery sense rests on individual experience and aptitude precludes simple answers. The archaeologist knows that his reliability, consistency, and agreement with others vary with different classes of pottery. Nevertheless, the general usefulness of pottery types clearly reflects a large area of agreement. The question of the significance of intuitively recognized likenesses is a matter that I shall refer to throughout the discussion of pottery analysis.

In general it seems to me there is something artificial in the way we set pottery sense apart. When we classify sherds by visual inspection, we are not relying on a faculty entirely distinct from that on which we depend in making a series of color readings. In both cases we are exercising perception because the color readings require the selection of representative samples and for this we are dependent on experience. Intuitive responses will serve us more fully and reliably if they go hand in hand with conscious analysis and reasoning. In fact, a critical examination of classifications or identifications based on simple visual inspection is desirable from time to time because of the possibilities of error arising from the effect of suggestion on perception. Susceptibility to suggestion is probably one of the principal sources of error in results dependent on pottery sense, and its control calls for constant vigilance.

The disparity between ease of recognizing that sherds are different and the difficulty of describing wherein the differences lie is really not surprising. The difficulties of pottery description lie partly in the complexity of pottery, partly in the inadequacy of our methods of identification and standards of description, and partly in the nature of the observer. The number of features that must be judged, the wide and continuous variations in them, and the fact that slight or subtle differences may be significant combine to test severely the archaeologist's perceptions. Consider a relatively simple property, color. There are transitions, peculiar blends, shadings and undertones, the effects of wear and of absorption of stains, and faint but effective changes due to differences in texture. How can color readings convey the image? Even if all the subtle color variations of a vessel were matched and recorded, could the reader visualize them?

There is no question of the inadequacy of our methods of description. We have no standards to describe such features as texture and luster, and the standards we have for other properties do not enable us to make fine distinctions. Color charts, for example, do not begin to include the number of colors the eye can perceive. Furthermore, terminology is not refined. Aside from imprecision and lack of standardization, it often reflects limitations of individual experience, as when terms for paste texture are defined in relation to a regional range.

We have learned to live with the shortcomings of the observer and we take a genuine satisfaction in the exercise of perceptions acquired in handling thousands of sherds. But to recognize the criteria upon which judgment is based, to put one's finger on those which are significant, and to weigh one against the other, require a different kind of ability from that of recognizing differences, and we may not be called on to analyze often enough to do it without effort. This may be partly because we rely too largely on routine methods of description. When a group of observations is accepted as adequate, they tend to encourage mechanical treatment.

The difficulties of description due to the nature of pottery, we cannot change. Some of the limitations due to the inadequacy of our standards and terminology can be removed by refinement of methods, by the introduction of new ones, and by more precise definition. If the observer's difficulties arise in part from insufficient knowledge of pottery, failure to think in terms of processes and composition, and inexperience in examining the bases of his impressions, these handicaps can be removed. When one thinks in terms of the nature of ceramic materials and processes, what were confusing masses of detail become meaningful.

Objective methods which are often contrasted with pottery sense have been subject to more or less criticism. Aside from the charge that they are inadequate and mechanical, it is sometimes argued that they are not actually objective, that true objectivity is an impossibility. These arguments often take a philosophic turn, but no matter how impressive they may be, they do not alter the fact that the possibilities of agreement and of meaningful reporting are enhanced by establishment of common standards and the use of instrumental methods. Two people taking a measurement with a meter stick will agree more closely than if they estimate the distance by eye. Descriptive standards are tools that can be used in different ways; carefully or carelessly, wisely or foolishly. Most criticisms of objective standards are not criticisms of the standards but of the way they are used. It is well that we examine our standards critically, judging their applicability, considering the kinds of questions they can reasonably be expected to answer, and remembering that the significance of results depends on the formulation of appropriate problems together with sound interpretation of results. Our recognition of the limitations of objective methods must not blind us to the fact that they afford data that cannot be obtained otherwise and they approach a common language more nearly than any other methods of description.

PHYSICAL PROPERTIES OF POTTERY

The field archaeologist is largely dependent on the physical properties of pottery for his judgment and description of technological features. He can use a color standard, make a scratch test of hardness, observe texture and the manner in which the sherd fractures much more easily than he can identify the chemical composition of the paint, or even the mineralogical classification of the temper, and more easily than he can learn to what temperature and under what conditions the vessel was fired. In consequence, it has become customary in pottery description to record such properties as color, hardness, and texture. In many instances, description is a relatively simple matter of matching or measuring. Moreover, a number of methods of description have been standardized in modern ceramic practice, and despite the fact that the ceramist is interested primarily in testing the value of clay for commercial purposes and not at all concerned with the particular problems of classification and interpretation which occupy the archaeologist, many ceramic standards are entirely applicable and adequate for archaeological purposes. Our primary problem, therefore, is to evaluate the properties and decide how much time we are justified in devoting to them.

The physical properties of pottery can be viewed from several angles. The potter may think of them as determining durability or affecting attractiveness. For example, hardness, porosity, and strength indicate how well a vessel will stand usage, whereas color and luster appeal to the eye. For purposes of identification and description, properties that can be judged visually are considered, irrespective of their relation to the quality of the ware. The student of technique is interested in the evidence physical properties afford of composition and of the potter's methods. This is a challenging approach because each property is conditioned in varying degree by a number of aspects of technique and never by one alone. Consequently it is important to understand how each property can be affected by paste composition and method of forming, finishing, and firing; in other words, the description of physical properties requires analysis, interpretation, and correlation, as well as measurement. This may be considered a technological approach, but it has advantages even when the only objective is identification, because such analysis increases the precision with which a criterion can be judged.

Ease of definition, rather than significance as a measure of durability or as an indication of technique, has largely dictated the choice of properties reported in standard outlines for the description of pottery types. Unfortunately, properties related to durability, aside from hardness, are difficult to measure and hence are omitted from description. But even though it is impracticable to include these properties in routine description, we should know what evidence they record and understand how they can be measured, in order to be prepared to judge when their significance justifies the time required to measure them.

I do not argue, as some have done, that all possible data should be recorded because it may be of use to future students even though we can see no significance in it now. This contention raises the question, How can one make an intelligent record when he does not know how data are to be used? The fact remains that our descriptions are far from complete. Considerations of convenience or time result in omission of evidence that could be interpreted.

The turn that pottery analysis takes reflects in large measure the archaeologist's use of, or interest in, ceramic data. As long as pottery is used primarily as a means of establishing relative chronology or setting up sequences, attention will be centered on means of type identification. If we are interested in pottery as a means of establishing trade and cultural contacts, we will very likely concentrate on composition and source of materials. If we are interested in tracing the history of technological development, we will give special attention to physical properties. In any event, it is necessary to know what can be done with various methods of analysis in order to avoid falling back on vague impressions and groundless guesses when new problems arise. Generalizations regarding technological development occasionally appear in archaeological literature. To be convincing, such generalizations should be accompanied by specific data. Direct, unaided observation does not suffice to establish stability or change in technological features. Systematic analyses and comparisons are necessary.

The principal surface properties are generally included in field description, but unfortunately there is not a great deal that can be said about the basic properties of the paste from visual inspection alone, with the exception of color. Texture certainly influences judgment, but standards for description have not yet been adopted. Fracture is often mentioned but it is a characteristic conditioned by a number of distinct properties (texture, homogeneity, density, hardness, and soundness of paste), which in themselves are more significant than their combined effect on breaking. Moreover, fracture is affected by method of breaking, which has not been standardized. Two properties, porosity and strength, are important from the technical point of view, but their determination is time-consuming and they are of little value for identification and therefore have rarely been reported.

In this section, physical properties are considered with respect to their relationship to technique, their value for identification, and the practicability of field tests.

COLOR

The importance of color in pottery description is attested to by the frequency with which color adjectives are used in naming types. Nevertheless, the question is often asked, Is it necessary to describe color specifically? When the colors that a single clay will acquire on firing are so subtle and varied that they defy full and exact description, what is the point of attempting to record them in detail? This is a legitimate and important question. It should be answered to our satisfaction before we submit to the tedium of preparing lengthy records of color readings.

The answer depends on the significance of color, its causes, its meaning in terms of technique, and its value in analysis and identification. The taxonomist may ask how reliable color is as a criterion of classification. But a physical property should be considered in relation to the materials and process that determine it; hence, the basic question is, What does color tell about the clay and method of firing? If this question can be answered, color will become a more meaningful criterion of classification.

Causes of pottery color.   The primary causes are the composition of clay and the atmosphere, temperature, and duration of firing. Secondary modifications are produced by postfiring conditions, such as absorption of stains during use, deposition of carbon in cooking over the fire, wear, deposition of substances from the soil after discard, leaching by soil waters, and accidental reheating as in the burning of a building. The effects of these fortuitous factors should be recognized in order to discount them in color description.

Let us review briefly the primary causes. Clay is colored principally by impurities, the chief classes of which are iron compounds and carbonaceous matter. The common iron compounds are converted to oxides in firing if they are not already in that state and they become a permanent colorant of the pottery. The amount, particle size, and distribution of iron oxide, together with characteristics of the clay, determine primarily whether a clay will be white, buff, or red when it is fired to a condition of full oxidation. Carbonaceous matter colors pottery only when there is lack of or insufficient oxidation. When there is adequate oxygen in firing, carbonaceous matter is decomposed and driven off as carbon dioxide gas. Thus clays differ widely, not only in the amount of permanent colorant they contain in the form of iron oxide, but also in the relative volume of oxygen they require to burn out carbonaceous matter and bring them to a full state of oxidation.

Although color is sometimes taken as a basis for judging the percentage of ferric oxide in a clay, it is at best a rough and at times a misleading indicator because particle size and distribution of the iron oxide and particle size of the clay have a considerable influence on color. A further variable is introduced when the iron oxide reacts with other constituents of the clay at higher temperatures or when components of the clay suppress the iron oxide color. This effect is especially noticeable in calcareous clays. Irrespective of the fact that color does not afford an accurate key to the chemical composition of clay, it serves as a simple, direct criterion for classification when firing conditions are standardized, and, for comparative purposes, pottery samples can be refired under standard conditions.

The most striking effect of firing conditions in the low to moderate temperature range (700°–900°C) is in brightness of color. Full oxidation produces clear colors; reduction results in grays. It is customary to speak of firing atmosphere as oxidizing (containing free oxygen) or reducing (containing gases that take oxygen from constituents of the clay), but in either case the effect can be strong or weak, and at times during a firing it may be nearly neutral. Furthermore, neither oxidation nor reduction can take place until the temperature is high enough to promote reaction.

Proportion of oxygen in the atmosphere, the length of firing, and temperature all affect the rate at which carbonaceous matter burns. When draft is poor, firing time short, or temperature low, carbon may be burned only from the surface of pottery, the core of the vessel wall remaining dark gray. If firing atmosphere is neutral or reducing, carbonaceous matter may be charred, intensifying gray color, but carbon and its color effect are unchanged. This is not reduction, properly speaking, because oxygen has not been taken from the carbon.

The effect of firing conditions on the iron-bearing minerals is somewhat more complex. Hematite or any form of ferric oxide is unchanged if the firing atmosphere is oxidizing. Yellow or brownish limonite and related hydrous ferric oxides are converted to red ferric oxide when the water they contain is driven off at low temperatures. The color of some pottery is similar to that of limonite or yellow ocher but it is never due to these minerals because they are decomposed early in firing. The ferro-ferric oxide (magnetite) and other nonsilicate, iron-bearing minerals, such as pyrite and siderite, will also be converted to ferric oxide when fully oxidized, although oxidation of these minerals commences only after carbonaceous matter has been burned out. Ferric oxide is therefore the normal form of iron in fully oxidized, low-fired pottery.

These are effects that occur when firing promotes oxidation. If reducing gases are present and firing temperatures are high enough, ferric oxide will be reduced to ferro-ferric oxide, coloring the clay gray. Magnetite originally present in the clay will be unaffected or further reduced. If reduction is sufficiently intense, ferrous oxide, which acts as a strong flux, will be formed. The lower oxides of iron all impart a gray color regardless of their mode of formation. Deposition of carbon from a smoky fire also grays the color of pottery and, when intense, blackens it.

To summarize, fired clays attain their clearest colors when fully oxidized. They are grayed by carbon and by the lower oxides of iron. Carbon may be derived from carbonaceous matter in the clay or be deposited from the smoke of smoldering fuel, and the iron oxide may occur originally in its lower state of oxidation or ferric oxide may be reduced in firing.

Inferences drawn from color. When color is studied in relation to clay composition and firing method, it affords several criteria of classification instead of one, and the interests of taxonomist and technologist converge. This is not a new proposal. It has become customary to classify pottery as "fired in oxidizing (or reducing) atmosphere." This is a step in the direction of considering properties in terms of technique and hence of interpreting them meaningfully. But a warning regarding misleading over-simplification is necessary. Since pottery color is conditioned primarily by two independent variables, sound inferences cannot be drawn regarding one alone unless the other is controlled. In order to recognize the possibilities and limitations of interpretation, it is essential to understand the basic facts regarding firing (see p. 213 ff.) and the range of variability of clays in their oxidation requirements. A firing that will oxidize one clay will only partially oxidize another. Only when sherds are identical in paste can variations in firing be inferred from color.

These interrelationships do not present as serious an obstacle as at first appears, for technique can be analyzed in relation to clay. Moreover, the adaptation of material to method is in itself significant. If pottery from two regions with different resources is being compared, the question is not if firing methods were identical. There is no reason why they should be as long as the clays differed. The important point is whether, with the clays they had, potters obtained full or partial oxidation or fired for a special effect such as reduction or smudging.

With experience it is usually possible to judge directly by color whether or not pottery was fully oxidized. The most satisfactory training for such color interpretation is obtained by refiring chips of sherds at temperatures between 750° and 850°C and studying the changes. One can be confident of clear creams, yellows, oranges, and reds. Brown pottery, on the other hand, may owe its lack of clarity to incomplete oxidation or light smoking, or the color of the fully oxidized clay may be brown. Refiring chips under controlled conditions will settle the point. The interpretation of grays also requires firing tests since the color may be caused by firing method, condition of the clay, or a combination of the two. Black usually indicates smudging. Pure white clay, theoretically at least, does not reveal the nature of the firing atmosphere, since such a clay is free of constituents that can be either oxidized or reduced; however, in an open firing it is unlikely that there would be no smoke if the atmosphere were reducing, and absence of carbon in the pottery therefore suggests that oxidizing conditions prevailed at least in the final stage of firing.

When composition of clay is judged by color, one can consider evidence of original state with respect to oxidation and of color class of the oxidized clay, i.e., if the clay is red-, buff- or white-firing. Direct evidence of original oxidation state is at best meager, and if pottery is fully oxidized in firing, all evidence is destroyed. If oxidation is incomplete, a gray core usually marks a carbonaceous clay, but there is always the possibility that a paste was smudged at some stage of firing. It is advisable therefore to determine the ease of oxidation, since the lightly held carbon from a smoky fire burns out at a lower temperature than most carbonaceous matter (see p. 217). The limitation of these interpretations points up the importance of studying ceramic resources and locating sources of clay. Color of fully oxidized paste affords a useful criterion of classification, which has as yet been little exploited. If pottery was oxidized in the original firing, it is possible to judge paste color approximately, but a more reliable estimate can be made after refiring chips under standard conditions. If oxidation was originally incomplete or if the pottery was reduced or smudged, refiring is necessary (see p. 217 for specific suggestions).

Interpretations of pottery colors can be summarized in outline.

COLORS CLEAR THROUGHOUT CROSS-SECTION OF WALL.

Fully oxidized.
Color caused primarily by ferric oxide; varies in hue and value with amount, particle size, and distribution of the oxide and with texture and composition of the clay. Gives no evidence of original state. Classification of fired color estimated without refiring.

COLORS CLEAR ON SURFACE, GRAY IN WALL INTERIOR

Incompletely oxidized. Combination of temperature, time, and draft was inadequate for full oxidation.
Probabilities are that the clay was carbonaceous, unless a uniform oxidation is obtained by refiring at low temperature (500°–550°C). Clay classed as red-, buff- or white-firing by color of refired chips.

LIGHT GRAY SURFACE, DARK GRAY WALL INTERIOR

Partially oxidized. Firing conditions inadequate for full oxidation.
Some carbon burned from surface zone but unburned from interior. Clay probably carbonaceous and iron oxide in lower state. Tested by refiring as above.

BROWN, LIGHT TO DARK

Incompletely or fully oxidized.
Iron oxide may be incompletely or fully converted to ferric state; paste may be lightly smoked. Condition differentiated by refiring. Color may be uniform or section through vessel wall may show less fully oxidized central zone.

LIGHT GRAY, UNIFORM

Unoxidized or reduced; condition distinguished by refiring.
Refiring necessary to determine class of clay.

DARK GRAY, UNIFORM

Unoxidized or smudged; may also be reduced.
Highly carbonaceous clay distinguished from smudged paste by refiring. Firing color determined by reoxidation.

BLACK

Generally smudged.
Black surfaces and clear central zone show short smudging of an oxidized paste. Black surface and paste show complete smudging or surface smudge of highly carbonaceous paste unoxidized in firing. Condition distinguished as above.

PALE GRAY TO WHITISH

Incompletely oxidized.

Clay with low iron oxide content reduced or white clay lightly smoked. Distinguished by temperature required for oxidation.

WHITE

Method of firing indeterminate.

Clay free from iron oxide (rare).

In considering the effects of firing and the class of clay, we refer to color ranges rather than to particular colors. This fact brings us back to the question of color reporting, Is it necessary to describe colors specifically and by reference to a standard? Subtle differences in color may be more useful in identifying pottery types than in studying evidences of firing technique, but even in this case the value of detailed reporting is questioned and variability of color within a pottery type is advanced as an argument against a specific record. This position is most often taken when color is thought of in general terms without considering its causes and meaning. I would argue that the use of standards is desirable for both classification and interpretation because the boundaries of a range, colors of the most fully oxidized examples of a type, preponderant color, and degree of graying of unoxidized samples should all be defined in common terms. The very looseness and independence with which we use familiar color names calls for the adoption of a standard.

Description of color. Many systems of color arrangement have been devised, and at least three color standards have been used by archaeologists for the description of pottery: Ridgway (1912), Maerz and Paul (1930), and Munsell (1942). The advantages of the Munsell system are so great that it is hardly necessary to argue its superiority. It is the only one of the three which has equal visual spacing of color. As a standard for color matching, it covers the range most uniformly in consequence of the fact that it is based on the way we see color rather than on the way colorants are mixed or color is calculated by laboratory or instrumental methods. One of the reasons why it has been widely adopted in scientific work is that is has been subject to the most exacting measurements, and optical constants have been determined with a degree of accuracy which ensures exact reproduction even though every copy were to be destroyed. Equal visual spacing and a convenient system of symbols facilitate interpolation in color reading. A practical advantage to the archaeologist using a limited color range is the fact that separate hue charts for any part of the scale can be purchased. The range of color of unglazed pottery is covered by the Munsell Soil Color Charts which are well suited for rapid matching, as they have a spiral binding and are provided with an aperture beside each chip so that the sample can be held adjacent to the color.

In order to use this chart efficiently, it is important to understand the relation of the three visual variables of color: *hue*, the position of the color in the spectrum; *value*, lightness or darkness; and *chroma* or *brightness*, the purity of the color. This relationship can be demonstrated by reference to a solid figure with a central axis representing neutral grays which grade from black at the bottom to white at the top (fig. 7). The purest colors arranged in spectral order occupy

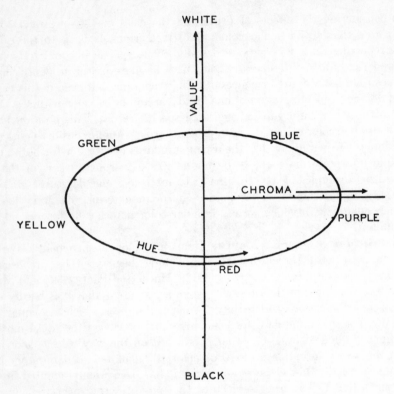

FIG. 7—RELATION OF THE THREE COLOR VARIABLES
Arrangement of hues, chromas, and values in the color solid.

FIG. 8—MUNSELL SOIL COLOR CHARTS IN THE POSITIONS THEY WOULD OCCUPY
IN A COLOR SOLID
Charts for the median hues of Yellow and Yellow Red are numbered. The highest chromas for the various hues are not included because the diagram was drawn with relation to the soil charts. Also the highest values of other hues are drawn only to complete the arrangement and without respect to availability. The charts are planes cut into a solid which is unsymmetric, owing to the fact that some hues attain their highest chromas in light, others in dark values.

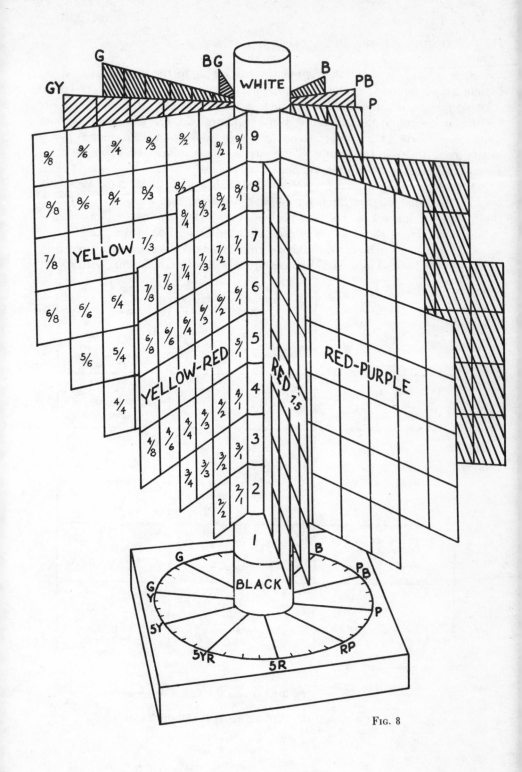

FIG. 8

the outer circumference of the figure. On moving in to the central axis, colors become grayer; on moving upward, lighter; and downward, darker. Every known color occupies a definite position in such a solid, and the Munsell charts are vertical planes cut to the central axis of the figure (fig. 8). The complete color solid does not have a regular surface because some hues attain their greatest purity in the tints, others in the shades. There are no clear yellows that are dark, for example; whereas blues of greatest purity are shades.

Colors are designated by symbols that define the three color variables: hues by the initial letter of the hue name and a number indicating the position of the color in the hue range. The hues in the soil color chart are red, yellow-red, and yellow. Positions in each hue range are numbered to 10. Four within each hue—2.5, 5, 7.5, and 10—are included in the soil color charts. Values are numbered from 0 for black to 10 for white, and decimals are used for interpolation. Neutral gray

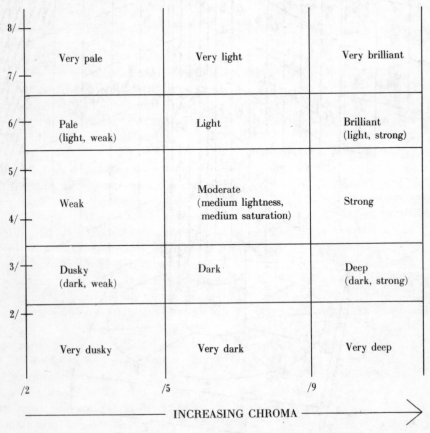

A SYSTEM OF MODIFIERS FOR COLOR NAMES

is zero in chroma, and the chromas of colors illustrated are designated by even numbers. Value and chroma readings are recorded as a fraction, with value as the numerator and chroma as the denominator. The symbol is therefore a more specific and meaningful designation than a name can be. For example, 5R 5/8 is a red of medium hue, medium in value and high in purity; 7R 8/5 is more orange, lighter, and grayer. How could one make such comparisons between two colors from names alone, say Dragon's Blood Red and Japan Rose?

There is need, nevertheless, for names for general color designation, and a committee of soil scientists has standardized the names for the colors of the soil chart, a copy of which is supplied with the chart. This chart uses the adjectives for chroma and value originally recommended by the Inter-Society Color Council and the National Bureau of Standards. The simplicity of these adjectives is illustrated in the preceding diagram. Ideally, names for color blocks would employ basic hue names in combination with these adjectives, but names such as brown, pink, and olive are so firmly established in usage that it is impracticable to follow the system fully.

Before using a color standard it is important to establish the reliability of one's color matching by taking one of the tests that have been devised for the purpose. In matching, the surface of the specimen should be held in the same plane as the color chip, and held in a position such that the light striking the specimen makes the same angle with the surface as does the light reflected to the eye. Reading should be made in a uniform light, preferably from a north window. Direct sunlight should be avoided.

The tendency in color reading is to report the closest match, but this is an unnecessary makeshift. A color can be designated more closely by observing its deviations from the nearest match in value, chroma, and hue, an order which many people find easiest for interpolation. For example, if the nearest match is 5YR 6/4, but the sample is darker, clearer, and redder, its position between values 6/ and 5/ on the 5YR chart is judged. An estimate of chroma is then made on the same chart comparing the sample with /4 and /6. Lastly, comparison of 5YR 6/4 and 2.5YR 6/4 is made for hue. If the sample is closer to the nearest match in all three variables, a notation such as 4YR 5.7/4.5 may be obtained. There will, of course, be individual variation in the number of steps between chips that can be estimated with confidence.

The final question is how to sort and select sherds for color description. Limited or even extensive random sampling is unsatisfactory. Degree of color variability, typical color, and extremes of the range should all be defined. This does not necessarily mean taking a greater number of color readings, but rather making a preliminary color sort and considering the significance of color characteristics. The degree of uniformity of surface color is significant in relation to the extent to which potters controlled firing atmosphere, and color zoning of the paste through a section of the wall should be considered in terms of progress of oxidation and original oxidation state of the clay. It is also important to consider the extent of deviation of the characteristic color of a type from that of the fully oxidized paste and from the clearest color in the sample. Ordinarily we have no proof that a pottery type includes examples of only one body clay, although a certain similarity of color may give the impression of homogeneity. Yet we know that a single clay may exhibit a great range of firing colors; consequently, unevenly fired sherds are especially useful in color analysis because they serve as keys to the range of color variation that one paste will attain.

If a large lot of sherds is to be sorted by color, it is advisable to start by separating the extremes in the range, the exceptionally clear sherds at one end of the scale and the dull ones at the other. The size of the group that is left (which, for purposes of color description, may be considered representative of the type) and its comparative uniformity will be conditioned in part by the extent to which firing was controlled. When potters fired carefully to obtain a particular effect, the extremes in the color range will represent accidents of firing; hence there will not necessarily be uniform gradation from one end of the range to the other. If, however, potters were indifferent to color—did not avoid a smoky fire or attempt to oxidize fully or burn out soot—color will be more variable, and the limit of what might be called the typical color will be less narrowly defined.

In any case, the characteristic color of a type can best be described from the relatively homogeneous group which excludes extremes and in terms of the range of each of the three color variables (hue, value, and chroma) rather than by color readings for individual sherds. The most carefully chosen "representative" sherd will only approximate the color of the majority of sherds and will deviate slightly from most of them. Moreover, readings for one sherd or for a handful do not delimit the color block within which the typical sherds fall. This will appear to be an unstandardized method of reporting since the proportion of sherds in the representative group will vary not only from type to type but also with each archaeologist's judgment of what constitutes the exceptional. Procedures might be standardized by setting limits of variability for the representative group, but this would be unjustifiably arbitrary. It is necessary to have flexible limits and to exercise judgment in recognizing discontinuities in the color range. In any case, as long as the Munsell system is used and limits of the characteristic color range and the exceptional colors are defined, individual differences in judgment can be recognized and discounted.

This method of reporting does not necessarily require a greater number of color readings than selection of a few "representative" sherds for complete color readings, but it does require an analytical approach and also more care in cleaning the sample as a whole and eliminating sherds exhibiting variations caused by post-firing conditions. To read paste color, fresh breaks are necessary, but this is not an added chore because a fresh paste surface is also necessary for the study of texture and composition. When lots are large, a random sample of a hundred or more sherds can be taken, depending on the variability of the sample.

Color reporting with the Munsell system is a means of translating to common symbols the color perceptions on which we rely in pottery classification. At the same time, the system is an effective means of developing color perception. A standard of this kind aids in making reliable comparisons and meaningful interpretations.

HARDNESS

Hardness is one of the specifications by which we judge the serviceableness of pottery, the likelihood of its being broken or marred. Yet the term "hardness" does not designate a well-defined property. This fact is illustrated by our usage of the word. A hard bed is one we do not sink into; hard flooring resists wear; a hard varnish does not scratch easily; a hard nut is one we cannot crack; and a hard ball has a good rebound. It is plain that by hardness we may mean resistance to penetration, abrasion, scratching, crushing, and resilience or elasticity. And then there is the softness of a baby's cheek, which is smoothness or texture. It is not surprising, therefore, to find that the various devices for testing "hardness" actually test different properties, and data from one test cannot be correlated with those of another. In ceramic description, hardness is usually recorded by reference to a simple scratch test.

Hardness has concerned engineers more often than it has interested physicists; hence its theoretical aspects have not been fully explored. Furthermore, ceramic engineers have given hardness a minor place among the physical properties of pottery, as is illustrated by the brevity of the recommendations made by the Committee on Standards of the American Ceramic Society (1928, p. 457): "Changes in the hardness are determined by cutting the trials with a knife blade or noting the relative hardness of the trials as compared with steel." It is one thing to standardize a manufactured product and quite another to use a physical property for identification, description, and interpretation. Consequently, the value of a hardness test in the study of archaeological ceramics should be judged independently by the evidence it affords and its usefulness as a criterion of classification.

The hardening of clay when it is subject to heat and the increase in hardness with rise in firing temperature are such familiar and fundamental properties that we must guard against the error of thinking of hardness as an indicator of firing temperature. There could be direct, uniform relation between hardness and firing temperature only if all clays were identical. Unless the great variability of clays is borne in mind the significance of hardness will be misinterpreted. Hardness is affected not only by firing temperature but also by impurities that render the clay more fusible; fineness of grain and density of clay that promote sintering; amount and kind of nonplastic material as it affects closeness of contact of particles and ease of sintering; and firing atmosphere, to the extent that it acts on constituents of the paste and converts them to stronger fluxes. Consequently, both composition of paste and firing conditions are primary determinants of hardness.

As a result of differences in composition, clays become hard at widely different temperatures, and the rate at which they harden varies also. It would be possible, for example, to find two sherds differing markedly in hardness, the softer of which had been fired 500°C higher than the harder. Extreme effects are uncommon, however, because primitive potters have not ordinarily used the highly refractory clays that remain soft within their temperature range. Nevertheless, there is need of caution in interpreting hardness data; one factor must be checked against another.

If pottery is hard, it may have been made from a low-fusing, dense-firing clay, or it may have been fired at a relatively high temperature or in an atmosphere that promoted vitrification. Often several or all of these conditions prevailed in varying degrees. There are different ways of checking the possibilities. The condition of mineral inclusions will sometimes give evidence of firing temperature (see p. 222), a fragment of a sherd can be refired to determine the vitrification point of the paste, and color will give some indication of firing atmosphere (see p. 217 ff.). If identity of paste can be established for a series of sherds, then variations in hardness will reflect differences in firing conditions, but uniformity of hardness does not prove identical firing temperature when pastes differ in composition.

A simple scratch test of hardness gives an indication of how well a surface will stand abrasion. Wares that are 2-1/2 to 3 in Mohs' scale not infrequently have high luster and bright colors, but, from the standpoint of the technologist, they are cheap bric-a-brac for the whatnot. Pottery that is 5 to 6 in hardness will be good service ware, and when it attains a hardness of 7, it will really command the respect of the technologist.

As a criterion of classification, hardness is of limited value, because of lack of uniformity within types and similarity of the ranges of many types. The 18 types and subtypes from the pueblo of Pecos in the Southwest may be mentioned as an illustration (Kidder and Shepard, 1936). All of these fall within the range of 3 to 5 in hardness (measured in Mohs' scale). Two types include examples covering the entire range; however, the majority of sherds of most types are sufficiently uniform to be designated by a single value. Eight types are soft; ten, medium or hard. Refiring sherds to 1200°C shows that 13 pastes are nonrefractory, the remainder relatively refractory. In this instance, hardness gives a basis for comparison of types with respect to serviceability, and aids in differentiating pastes but has little value as a criterion for identification.

Devices for measuring hardness test penetration, abrasion, elasticity, and magnetic and electric properties. The majority of tests employing mechanical procedures are of the penetration or scratch type. A scratch test may measure either penetration or abrasion, depending on the properties of the material tested. If the material is ductile or plastic, like a metal, the point will penetrate by causing plastic flow and displacing rather than removing material. On the other hand, if the substance is brittle like glass, the point will tear particles from the surface. Scratch tests are of many kinds. The simple field test employing a set of graded minerals that is commonly used by mineralogists and often by archaeologists was first proposed by Friedrich Mohs in 1882. It is an exceedingly rough test, for there is no uniformity in the shape of the point or in the pressure applied in making the scratch. The test has the further disadvantage of unevenness of scale, as is shown in Table 4, which records measurements made with a delicate instrument for testing scratch hardness.

TABLE 4—RELATIONS BETWEEN MOHS' SCALE AND MICROHARDNESS NUMBERS
(From Table II, Williams, 1942)

Minerals	Mohs' Scale	Range of Microhardness	Average*	Differences
Talc	1	0.8– 21.5	1	
				10
Selenite	2	10.2– 56.6	11	
				118
Calcite	3	126.0– 135.0	129	
				14
Fluorite	4	138.0– 145.0	143	
				434
Apatite	5	870.0–1740.0	577	
				398
Orthoclase	6	2100.0–2500.0	975	
				1725
Quartz	7	2066.0–3906.0	2700	
				720
Topaz	8	2770.0–4444.0	3420	
				1880
Corundum	9	3906.0–8264.0	5300	

* Estimated by H. C. Hodge and J. H. McKay.

The range in hardness of each mineral is due to variations in texture, impurities, and normal differences in different crystallographic directions. The series from calcite to quartz is used most frequently for pottery. From the last column of the table it will be seen that the difference between calcite and fluorite is very slight compared with that between succeeding pairs and the difference between ortho-clase and quartz is very great.

Despite these limitations, Mohs' method has continued in use because of its simplicity, economy, and quickness. It is adequate when exactness is not required and the range of hardness is wide.

In the more refined scratch tests, of which there are a number, a hard, weighted point, often a diamond of standard shape, is moved across the specimen at a uniform rate, and the dimensions of the scratch are measured microscopically. The microcharacter, one of the most recent instruments of this type, is an exact and delicate instrument, but since it requires a very smooth surface, it cannot be used on primitive pottery.

The Knoop Indenter, one of the most sensitive instruments for testing hard-ness devised in recent times, is based on penetration. The indentation is made by a pyramidal-shaped diamond point, and its dimensions are measured microscopically. The method is so perfectly controlled and delicate that the hardness of a glaze can be tested in cross-section. Hardness of the surface coat of Plumbate pottery, which has an exceptional, vitrified slip, was measured in this way, the cross-section being polished in order to obtain a surface smooth enough to test (Shepard, 1948, p. 169).

In general, primitive pottery is not suitable for exact hardness measurement since it is porous and heterogeneous—a mixture of clay and other minerals. Scratch-ing tears particles apart, testing the bond between constituents instead of the interatomic forces of a homogeneous material. Surface roughness is another con-dition that prevents exact measurement. When a point drops into a depression, it has a shearing effect and tears material, giving a different value than when it is pressed against a smooth surface. Consequently, accurate hardness tests cannot be made except on perfectly smooth surfaces of homogeneous materials.

In view of these conditions, Mohs' standard has served as a quick, prac-ticable field test. With care and experience, reproducible results can be obtained. It is important to maintain a sharp point, and unnecessary abrasion of the point is avoided by first testing the unknown with a hard mineral followed by suc-cessively softer ones until one matching hardness is found. The unevenness of the scale led March (1934) to propose intermediate minerals, but he introduced them between minerals closely spaced in hardness as well as between those that are widely spaced. Furthermore, the minerals introduced have been less fully stand-ardized than the original ones and are subject to the same disadvantages.

The archaeologists should be prepared to adopt a more even, reliable standard than Mohs' when one becomes available. In commercial ceramics, a set of steel rods of graded hardness has been used for scratch tests of glazes (Koenig, 1939). These are recommended for the simplicity of maintenance of cutting edge. The rod is ground off squarely at both ends and is held at 45° when it is drawn across the surface. The circumference of both ends can be used, and the rods are easily dressed to maintain sharpness. In Koenig's work on glazes the test was further roughly standardized by performing it on a torsion balance. A suitable weight was placed on one pan and the test plaque on the other pan was pressed just hard enough in making the scratch to maintain balance. It would be an advantage if a standard of this kind could be extended to cover the range of pottery, but the demand is slight and until a more uniform hardness scale is introduced, Mohs' method can be applied to smooth surfaces to obtain an approximate comparative measure of resistance to scratching and abrasion.

TEXTURE

Paste texture is influenced primarily by nonplastic inclusions: their amount, grain size, grading, and shape. Grain size and porosity of the clay also affect texture. Variability of texture is limited by the requirements of a sound vessel, by the potter's standards, and by the characteristics of certain tempering materials. In preparing a paste, sufficient nonplastic material should be added to counteract excessive shrinkage and insure uniform drying but not enough to weaken the body seriously. Clays differ markedly in the proportion of nonplastics they require and in the latitude of variation they will allow.

Variability of grain size depends on the nature of the tempering material and on the potter's method of preparation. Some materials are used in their original condition; others are ground, crushed, or pulverized. Certain materials, such as disintegrated sandstone, have uniform grain size in their natural state; others, like sand from a stream bed with variable current, are heterogeneous. Some solid materials break into particles of relatively uniform size when they are ground, as, for example, a weathered, equigranular, igneous rock that parts on crystal boundaries. Other materials, like potsherd or massive limestone, have no natural planes of cleavage nor regular pattern of structural weakness to determine the size of particles that will be formed. When these materials are used as temper, grain size depends on the potter's method of preparation. Various means of sorting were doubtless used in some cases, just as they are being used by prewheel potters today. It follows, therefore, that the significance of texture bears a direct relation to the kind of temper used and to technique. Uniformity in one kind of temper will reflect technique, whereas in another it may be predetermined by the material itself. When these relationships are disregarded, texture classification is an unevaluated procedure.

The adoption of standard terms for description of texture is essential. Otherwise, each person's usage is dependent on the range of pastes with which he is familiar, and one man's "fine" may be another's "coarse." Geologists have given considerable attention to grade scales for sediments, and since these apply to the same classes of material that were used for tempers, they meet our requirements perfectly. Sedimentary petrologists recommend the Wentworth scale, which has a geometric ratio (Krumbein and Pettijohn, 1938, p. 80). The section of this scale which would be used in description of paste texture is shown in Table 5.

TABLE 5—WENTWORTH'S SIZE CLASSIFICATION

Name	Grade Limits (Diam. in mm.)
Pebble	64–4
Granule	4–2
Very coarse	2–1
Coarse	1–1/2
Medium	1/2–1/4
Fine	1/4–1/8
Very fine	1/8–1/16
Silt	1/16–1/256

The grade "pebble" is included to cover the exceptional inclusions in crude wares that exceed the grade limits of granules. The importance of the fine grades is appreciated when a paste is examined microscopically.

The limits of a grade scale would appear to be purely arbitrary. It is interesting to note, therefore, that Wentworth has studied the limits of these grades in relation to the physical properties involved in transportation, and has found that they agree well with certain distinctions between suspension and traction loads (Wentworth, 1933).

Paste texture can be judged by visual inspection or measured microscopically. One gives a relative estimate, the other an absolute measure. The visual estimate is relative for two reasons: first, very fine grains cannot be seen with the unaided eye; second, the appearance of texture is unfluenced by color contrasts of inclusions and clay. For example, black particles of basalt temper will stand out conspicuously in a white clay, but will blend into a dark brown one, and be almost indistinguishable in a black one; opaque white feldspar, which is scarcely discernible in a white paste, is clearly visible in a reddish one; translucent or transparent grains are much less conspicuous than opaque ones; and finally, all inclusions may be masked if the paste is smudged. Fortunately this variable factor of color contrast, which is actually irrelevant to texture, does not completely invalidate, although it influences, judgment based on direct inspection because the texture of a fractured surface is conditioned by the grade size and amount of inclusions. Textural differences can therefore be recognized even when individual grains cannot be seen. At best, however, direct observation gives only an approximation, which might be designated "apparent texture" to distinguish it from definitions based on measurement.

The most practical method for field description is by comparison with standards. A large number of standards would have to be prepared to cover the range of apparent texture as it is influenced by grain size, shape, grading and percentage of inclusions, color relation of clay and inclusions, and texture of clay; but by judicious selection, a series of standards can be brought within the bounds of the practicable, and such standards would not only introduce the consistency in description that we lack, but would also lead to more specific designations than we now have. A simplified set might consist of high and low proportions of tempers of preponderantly fine, medium, and coarse grain and of mixed grain size in clays of contrasting and similar color. This would make a set of 16 chips. In addition there should be examples of extremes in clay texture (dense and open) and of the effects on paste texture of particle shape (smooth, rounded; rough, angular; platy; and needle-like). These would bring the set up to 22 chips. Standards could be mounted on a stick for convenient handling in the field. The simplest procedure in preparation of samples would be to measure proportion of temper by dry weight and grain size by standard sieves. The specifications regarding ingredients and method of preparation should be exact in order to permit duplication at any time. Standards of this kind have been prepared to test their practicability for the field archaeologist. They can be supplied in quantity for general use when the demand arises.

Microscopic techniques offer direct quantitative means of describing texture. Various devices are available for measuring particles in thin section—oculars with scales calibrated for measurement, and micrometer stages provided with spindles that record the distance the stage is moved in bringing first one edge of a constituent and then the other in line with a cross-hair. These give an absolute figure for amount of granular temper and a relative figure for grain size. With either the micrometer eyepiece or the stage, the volume of a granular temper or the percentage of various constituents can be computed with comparative ease, provided grains are equidimensional. The method is not applicable to platy or needle-like inclusions. Occasionally it is difficult to apply even with granular temper because outlines of grains are indistinct, as for example a fine temper of marly limestone in a calcareous clay of similar color. The method is satisfactory for most sand, sherd, crushed igneous rock, and limestone tempers, but is not applicable to volcanic ash.

The proportion of calcareous tempering materials such as limestone, dolomite, and shell can be determined by solution in acid, but the method is inapplicable if the clay is calcareous and it is not a highly accurate one.

Measurement of grain size can be made in thin sections. A relative value is obtained because the slice does not cut through the maximum diameter of all grains, but instead grazes some and cuts only part way into most of them. Consequently, measurement of either maximum grain size or average grain size gives values less than the true ones. Nevertheless this method is very useful because the same error is introduced in all specimens and the figures obtained are therefore comparable. Also it is possible to correct for the error by calculation if the grain size is uniform. There are strict specifications regarding the number and distribution of grains to be measured when the micrometric method is used.

The principal disadvantage of micrometric analysis is in the time required. The method is justified when the proportion of constituents is an important diagnostic feature, but, for general description, estimates based on comparison with prepared standards should be adequate. If these comparisons are made with a binocular microscope, using a magnification in the neighborhood of 50×, fine grains can be seen and the effects of color contrast can be discounted. True rather than apparent texture can then be estimated.

Surface texture refers to the minute arrangement of the particles of the paste. It does not include such features as general contour or sweeping-marks of a finishing tool. These are characteristics of finish. Surface texture is determined primarily by two conditions: texture of the paste and method of finishing. These can be broken down into four sets of factors: (a) temper or nonplastic inclusions —their texture, shape, and amount as they affect graininess and limit the finishing technique; (b) the quality of clay—its homogeneity and its stickiness or adhesiveness; (c) the condition of the clay at the time of finishing—whether plastic, leather-hard, or dry; and (d) method of finishing—whether one of wiping, patting, scraping or rubbing, and whether the finishing tool is soft and yielding as the hand, a piece of leather, or a bunch of grass; hard and smooth as a waterworn pebble; or a sharp edge, as a flake of obsidian or flint. Many of these conditions leave distinctive marks, and consequently the terms "rough" and "smooth," as now used, cover a multitude of textures. How are we to know whether rough describes a quality of workmanship, condition of the paste, or a characteristic due to the finishing technique? The qualities of roughness caused by coarse, protruding temper, by hand-smoothing in the plastic state, and by scraping in the leather-hard state are not comparable. The differences are not differences of degree but of kind, and since they are produced by texture and working condition of the paste in combination with finishing technique, the effect of each must be recognized.

The effect of paste texture is most pronounced when the surface is finished in the plastic state with a yielding tool because under these conditions the non-plastic particles protrude. If the nonplastics are coarse, the surface is usually described as granular. This is not a fortunate choice of terms because granular refers to a material composed entirely of granules. The term grainy is preferable for the description of a heterogeneous material. It can be used specifically as "grainy surface of a medium-textured, heavily tempered paste" or "grainy surface of a very coarse textured, sparsely tempered paste." The term "grainy" would cover a wider textural range than that to which the term granular is now applied. It is the protrusion of grains, not their size, that make a texture grainy. Only when inclusions are too fine to be distinguished by the unaided eye does the texture cease to be grainy and the surface appear smooth.

Surfaces that are not grainy either have a fine-grained paste or contain non-plastic particles that have been leveled in the finishing process. The difference between the surface that is made smooth by rubbing with a hard, smooth tool, and one that is smooth by virtue of the texture of the paste is basic and should always be recognized. It is customary to describe the surface that has been rendered smooth and compact by rubbing as polished. This is a misleading use of a term that generally implies the presence of luster. Many clay surfaces that have been rubbed with a hard, smooth tool lack luster in consequence of peculiarities of the clay or of shrinkage after rubbing, but all surfaces that have been rubbed while they are sufficiently moist to allow the rearrangement and packing of particles can be recognized unmistakably by feel. Texture is a property that is best sensed tactually, and definitions based on visual impression do not necessarily agree with those based on feel. It would simplify description if the word "smooth" were limited to the texture obtained by compacting the surface, but a term that has long been used loosely cannot suddenly be confined to the strait jacket of precise and restricted definition. The expressions "tactually smooth" or "smooth and compact" would avoid the ambiguity of the word "polished" when applied to surfaces that have been finished by rubbing with a hard tool. If one is uncertain of this quality, he should experiment with pastes and methods of finishing until he has satisfied himself regarding it. Surfaces that have only been wiped with a yielding tool will appear smooth if the paste is fine-textured and if they have been carefully evened, but they are readily distinguished by touch from the compact surface. The term "fine-textured" is less ambiguous than "smooth" for this class.

Only basic distinctions in surface texture have been mentioned. Many kinds of roughness are due to particular finishing techniques, and are therefore discussed under technique (p. 187 ff.).

LUSTER

Luster is a property that results from the way a surface reflects light. The word has no implication of technique; it does not define the manner in which the property was produced.

The light that falls on a body is transmitted, absorbed, or reflected, depending on the characteristics of the body. A transparent body transmits light, an opaque one absorbs and reflects it. Reflected light may be diffused or reflected specularly as from a mirror. Only specular reflection produces a lustrous or glossy appearance. A surface must be even, perfectly smooth, and compact to reflect specularly, that is, at a uniform angle. A surface that is porous or finely granular will diffuse light, sending the rays off in all directions so that only a small part of them reach the eye, and the surface then appears matte or dull.

The characteristics that produce specular reflection can be obtained in various ways and with many substances. Lacquered wood, burnished metal, polished stone, and glazed pottery are all lustrous bodies. Pottery can be made lustrous by entirely different means: by rubbing the slightly moistened surface with a smooth tool before firing, by applying a fusible material which will melt and flow in firing to form a smooth, compact coat, and by coating with a varnish-like substance after firing. Also certain clays become glossy on drying from suspension without any special treatment. We are familiar with this phenomenon in the sheen of a dry mud flat.

A lustrous surface is not sufficiently described by reference to its degree of gloss. The cause of luster should be ascertained whenever possible, and simple observations and tests are often sufficient for identification. Of the four classes of lustrous surfaces mentioned above, the polished one is distinguished by the fact that pits, grooves, and all depressions not reached by a tool are matte. The other types of lustrous surface are obtained by applying a liquid—glaze, lacquer, or clay slip—that flows into depressions. Tool-marks are another distinguishing feature of the polished surface. They may show through a lacquer but will be covered by a glaze and will be absent from a naturally lustrous clay coat.

The lacquered surface is identified by the fact that it will blacken on heating in an oxidizing flame, since the coating is organic. The reducing part of the flame must be avoided in making the test because it may soot the surface. Also, it is essential to ascertain whether or not the sherd has been impregnated with organic matter after discard. This possibility can be checked by heating an unslipped surface or an original broken edge. If the presence of organic matter is indicated by darkening, allowance must be made in interpreting the change in color of the slip. Even when heating darkens the slip more than other surfaces, the presence of a secondary coat is not established because the amount of organic matter a clay will take up depends on properties such as adsorptive capacity and particle size, and clays differ greatly in these properties. Experience with these variables affords a basis for judgment when quantitative tests cannot be made.

The glazed surface is recognized as a vitreous coat. Its identity may be thrown in doubt by various defects such as incomplete vitrification, opacity caused by undissolved inclusions, and decomposition. In case of uncertainty, microscopic examination of a powdered sample in oil mount will show whether or not glass is present.

The luster of clays that dry naturally with a gloss is identified tentatively by eliminating the other possible causes of luster. It is present in depressions and consequently could not have been produced by stone polish; it does not blacken on heating and therefore is not organic; and finally, microscopic examination shows that it is a clay, not a glass.

Various factors influence the degree of luster obtained with each class of surface. A consideration of these limiting conditions may elucidate technique and serve as a more useful diagnostic than measurement of degree of luster.

Polished surfaces.   There is a good deal more involved in producing a high luster by polishing than diligence in applying the polishing stone. The mechanical factors are obvious. The surface must be even because the polishing tool will not reach into pits, grooves, and small depressions. The degree of moisture is also important. If the surface is too wet, the clay picks up on the polishing stone; if it is too dry, clay particles will not pack, and, no matter how long the surface is rubbed, it will remain matte.

More fundamental are the effects of properties of the clay on the luster produced by polishing. Clays differ-greatly with respect to the kind of surface they will attain when rubbed. Some acquire an almost mirror-like gloss, whereas others remain matte, or acquire only a slight sheen even with the most assiduous rubbing. There are doubtless several causes for this difference. Packing of particles, which is determined by shape and grading of grain sizes, is a primary factor since porosity causes diffusion of light. In laboratory tests, we have observed that clays that do not attain high luster are bentonitic types or types in which the clay mineral montmorillonite preponderates. Although the relative importance of the various properties of clay that affect gloss has not been fully investigated, the fact of marked differences in clays with respect to this property is well established and should be borne in mind in judging pottery because it shows that the production of lustrous ware cannot be regarded as a simple matter of choice or custom. Whether or not a people made polished pottery depended in part on the kinds of clay their environment afforded, not alone on their taste and skill.

Shrinkage is a primary concern in the production of a polished surface. The effect of contraction after polishing is obvious. Even though the accompanying buckling or wrinkling is on such a minute scale that it cannot be detected visually, it will have the effect of diffusing light and destroying specular reflection. Ordinarily the effect of drying shrinkage is eliminated by air-drying the vessel before polishing. Only the surface is then moistened for polishing or a thin mixture of clay and water is applied as slip. During the polishing process this thin layer of wet clay is drying out so that there is very little, if any, drying shrinkage after polishing is completed. But during firing, if the temperature is carried high enough, there will be sufficient shrinkage to reduce luster or render the surface dull. A number of changes take place in firing that cause shrinkage. Sintering and fusing are the principal causes. Since clays differ widely in their firing properties, the temperatures at which they shrink sufficiently to destroy luster will also vary within wide limits, but, for a great many clays, that temperature is relatively low. The glossy wares are therefore generally low-fired and soft. The potter had to choose between strength or durability and a pleasing finish of no utilitarian value.

Recognition of these factors increases exactness of description. One no longer need fall back on such expressions as "poorly polished," which does not indicate whether luster is low because of the quality of the clay or firing shrinkage or because of careless workmanship, which in itself may be resolved into such diverse factors as failure to even the surface before polishing, permitting the clay to become too dry during the polishing process, and failure to cover the surface uniformly and completely with polishing strokes. Even though the work of the careless potter may be marked by all of these defects, one does not need to use a vague expression. Degree of luster and perfection of technique are distinct and should not be confused. Even when the potter hit only the high spots, carelessness may not have been the primary factor that determined the luster attained by the portions of the surface that were rubbed. Degree of luster can be described by such adjectives as matte, low, medium, high. The mechanical condition of the surface, which directly reflects the potter's technique, can be described with specific reference to evenness of surface as uneven, pitted, grooved, scored, and so forth; to the completeness with which strokes cover the surface—whether it is streaked or uniform; to presence or absence of faint troughs left by the polishing tool; and finally with respect to the direction of polishing strokes.

To summarize, there are three main factors affecting the luster of polished pottery, the properties of the clay, the mechanics of polishing, and shrinkage after polishing. Although a lustrous surface suggests manipulative skill and a certain standard of excellence, it also marks the sacrifice of hardness to appearance.

Glazed surfaces.   The perfect smoothness of a glaze is impaired by various defects, such as blistering, incomplete solution of constituents, incomplete fusion, and recrystallization. The composition of the glaze also has an effect on luster. The higher the optical density of the glass, the higher the refractive index and the greater the brilliance of the glass. Thus lead glazes have a brilliance not attained by alkaline glazes, but the effect of the refractive index of the glaze may be masked by defects.

Lacquer-like coats.   The application of a lacquer-like substance to a vessel after firing is not a ceramic practice in the strict sense. It is a secondary treatment with a substance that will not stand firing, but we have examples of its use by present-day potters and there are evidences of it on some prehistoric wares, particularly certain Classic Mayan types (Thompson, 1939, pp. 264–65). Vessels that have received such a coat may have a luster similar to that of an exceptionally well polished slip, but tool-marks will be absent, unless the slip was polished. Aside from mechanical imperfections, the composition of these lacquers affects their luster. We have, however, no comparative data on those used by prewheel potters.

Natural luster of clays.   The luster which some clay suspensions attain on settling and drying is developed only under certain conditions and is rarely high. It is a colloidal phenomenon that is dependent on dispersion of the clay particles and certain limits of concentration. Because of these requirements, it is unlikely that the phenomenon occurred often in clay slips, but one example of luster which seems to have been caused in this way has been recorded (Shepard, 1948, p. 97). The luster of such specimens is variable, probably because the requirements of dispersion and concentration were not always met. As in the case of polish, this type of luster would be destroyed by firing shrinkage.

Description of luster.   There is no simple, quantitative means of defining the luster of curved pottery surfaces. Many types of optical instruments have been introduced to measure the luster of various materials such as paper, paints, and enamels. But they are adapted to plane surfaces and they do not all measure the same property. Instruments and their uses have been discussed by Hunter (1937), who shows that the problem of measurement is complicated by the fact that there are a number of kinds or qualities of gloss. Certain instruments might be adapted for our purposes, but exact measurements are rarely required. A simple method dependent on distinctness of image obtained from the filament of a flashlight was proposed by March (1934, p. 31), but it was intended primarily for glazes and does not have sufficient differentiation in the lower range of lusters obtained with clays. However, some standardization of terms would be desirable. Greater uniformity in terminology could be established if reference standards were adopted. The range of gradations could be obtained by preparing briquettes from a series of clays attaining different degrees of luster and by firing them to different temperatures. Such standards would be inexpensive and simple to use.

POROSITY

The porosity of pottery is defined as the ratio of the volume of pore space to the total volume of the piece. A closely related property is permeability, the condition that permits gases and liquids to pass through a porous body. It depends on connecting channel pores and capillaries that extend from one surface to the other and is measured in terms of volume of fluid that will pass through a unit area, of unit thickness, in unit time, under specified head pressure. If one were comparing water storage jars, he would consider permeability rather than porosity because water is kept cool by seepage and evaporation. In general, however, porosity gives the more useful measure of body structure. True porosity, which measures the total pore space, is distinguished from apparent porosity, which expresses the relative volume of the open pores. True porosity is one-and-a-half to two-and-a-half times greater than apparent porosity in well-vitrified wares that contain sealed pores, but there is little difference in the two values in low-fired pottery that lacks sealed pores. Apparent porosity is therefore a satisfactory measure for prewheel pottery.

Porosity is one of the basic properties of pottery. Volume of pore space and the size and shape of pores affect density, strength, permeability, degree of resistance to weathering and abrasion, extent of discoloration by fluids, destructive action and rate of efflorescence of soluble salts, and resistance to thermal shock.

Porosity increases the resistance of fired pottery to thermal shock because the grains in a porous mass have more freedom of movement than those in a dense one; also the stresses produced by sudden changes in temperatures are relieved when there are numerous air pockets, and porous clay vessels can withstand sudden changes in temperature that would shatter dense ones. This explains why present-day Indian potters can open their "kilns" when the temperature is 700°C or more and expose the pottery to cold air. Another relation of interest to the student of primitive pottery is the fact that porosity increases absorption of carbon and thus influences the depth of black that is obtained in smudging.

Clays differ greatly in the porosity they attain on firing. The refractory clays (kaolins, flint clays and siliceous clays containing little fluxing material) remain porous in the ordinary temperature range of kiln firing. They may have 45–50 per cent apparent porosity after firing at 945°C and 30–40 per cent even at 1300°C. Other clays attain sound vitrification at much lower temperatures, and the progress of vitrification is sufficiently gradual to avoid the development of vesicular structure. Such clays may have 20–40 per cent porosity at 945°C and only 1–5 per cent at 1200°C. Still other clays fuse rapidly at low temperatures and develop a vesicular texture that makes them unsuitable for commercial products (Parmelee, 1946, pp. XVII-5-9).

A clay undergoes changes in porosity throughout the course of firing. During early stages, when water is driven off, porosity increases, often as much as 10 per cent. The clay continues to become more porous with the oxidation of carbonaceous matter but begins to shrink when sintering or incipient vitrification starts. As vitrification proceeds, interstices are filled with liquid matter, the body shrinks, and porosity decreases. The vitrification point of a clay and firing temperature are the primary determinants of porosity, but texture also has an effect. In the raw state, fine materials with large·surface area adsorb more water than coarser materials, but this difference is offset in firing because fineness increases area of contact, thus promoting vitrification and lowering porosity. Uniformity of grain size gives higher porosity than mixed grading because fine grains pack between coarse ones. In commercial practice, pressure applied in molding and shaping reduces porosity by compacting particles, but in hand-modeling this factor is negligible.

Porosity must be determined in the laboratory, but only a good balance and an overflow-type volumeter are required. The dry test pieces are weighed, and saturated by boiling in water for two hours. They should not be in contact with the bottom of the container because of the risk of abrasion in bumping. After cooling in water, the saturated sherd is wiped with a damp sponge and weighed rapidly to avoid evaporation. Finally, volume is determined by displacement. Porosity is then calculated from the formula:

$$P = \frac{Sf-Wf}{Vf} \times 100$$

P = per cent apparent porosity
Sf = weight of saturated test piece in gm.
Wf = weight of dry test piece in gm.
Vf = volume of fired test piece in cu. cm.

The principal source of error in this determination is in obtaining complete saturation of the open pores. The procedure outlined is that recommended by the Committee on Standards of the American Ceramic Society (1928).

As an illustration of the variability of low-fired pottery in porosity and its possible significance, I have plotted results of tests of a series of types from Pecos, New Mexico (fig. 9). This graph shows the difference in apparent porosity of types which represent the ceramic output of a village during the course of approximately four centuries, together with the types which are identified as trade pottery from other parts of the upper Rio Grande region, on the basis of paste composition. Three main classes—Black-on-white, Glaze paint, and Modern—represent a chronologic sequence. The two Biscuit types introduced between the Black-on-white and the Glaze-paint series are trade ware contemporaneous with the Glaze-paint series. The Black-on-white ware is unoxidized and decorated with organic paint. Rowe is the only type in the series which is certainly indigenous. Santa Fe may be partially intrusive and partly local in origin. Galisto and Wiyo are intrusive. Glaze-paint ware represents a sharp break in ceramic tradition, being oxidized and decorated with lead glaze. All the Glaze-paint types are indigenous except the first two and the last. The Modern series, which includes monochrome smudged and oxidized types and a matte paint polychrome, belongs to the post-Spanish period. The vitric ash-tempered types of this group are unquestionably trade ware. The source of the sand-tempered ones is uncertain.

This series of pottery types therefore represents striking changes in decorative technique, paste composition, and firing method, and also covers a sufficiently long span of time to reflect any basic changes that were taking place in the quality of pottery. Yet the solid lines on the graph representing the range in original porosity show no trends. The averages for all except the unusually porous Biscuit types fall between 20 and 30 per cent in porosity and there is no significant grouping within this range either by time, source, or composition. It is plain that porosity would have no value for identification. Only the Biscuit types stand out, and there is no need to refer to porosity for their identification.

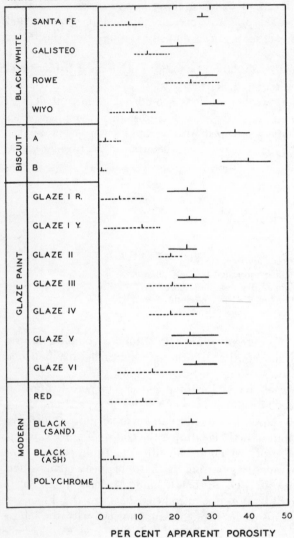

FIG. 9—POROSITY DATA, POTTERY TYPES FROM PECOS, NEW MEXICO

TABLE 6—THE RELATION OF POROSITY TO PASTE COMPOSITION

POROSITY RANGE	POTTERY TYPE	Av. % APPARENT POROSITY		Av. % DECREASE	TEMPER	SOURCE
		Original	Refired to 1200°C			
Low	Biscuit A	36.4	1.8	94.5	Vitric ash	Intrusive
	Biscuit B	39.8	0.8	98.1	Vitric ash	Intrusive
	Polished Black (ash)	27.4	3.4	86.4	Vitric ash	Intrusive
	Polychrome	28.6	2.0	92.5	Vitric ash	Intrusive
Medium	Santa Fe	27.9	8.1	70.5	Silt	?
	Wiyo	31.4	8.9	68.4	Vitric ash	Intrusive
	Galisteo	21.2	13.3	36.8	Sherd	Intrusive
	Glaze I Red	23.6	5.6	76.0	Igneous rock	Intrusive
	Glaze I Yellow	24.1	11.5	52.4	Igneous rock	Intrusive
	Glaze VI	25.8	14.3	46.5	Igneous rock	Intrusive
	Red	25.7	11.3	55.9	Sand	?
	Polished Black (sand)	24.1	13.9	41.5	Sand	?
High	Rowe	27.2	24.9	8.7	Sand	Indigenous
	Glaze II	23.5	19.1	17.3	Sand	Indigenous
	Glaze III	25.2	19.7	22.2	Sand	Indigenous
	Glaze IV	26.6	19.1	26.6	Sand	Indigenous
	Glaze V	24.2	23.7	−2.3	Sand	Indigenous

A different picture is obtained when these types are refired to 1200°C. Some pastes show little change in porosity or actually increase slightly, whereas, at the other extreme, there are types that become very dense. The group with high porosity is set off more plainly than that with low, but for purposes of summary and comparison, I have taken 5 per cent as the upper limit of low porosity, 5–15 per cent for moderate, and over 15 per cent for high.

Types classed as intrusive are distinguished by tempering material which does not occur at Pecos. This applied even to Galisteo black-on-white since the sherd temper it contains is marked by inclusions of igneous rock that is not found in the vicinity of Pecos. Differences in clay and geographic distribution of this series of types support the evidence of temper. Table 6 suggests a relation between class of temper and porosity, but the basic factor is the vitrification point of the clay. The various intrusive types are from different sources, and therefore the different classes of temper are associated with different kinds of clay. Temper is a secondary factor which retards vitrification, an effect which increases as texture becomes coarser. Vitric ash and silt are the only fine-textured, nonplastic inclusions in this group, and it is noteworthy that the low-porosity types are all ash-tempered intrusives. The other paste of this class, Wiyo, is low in the medium range and approaches the silty paste, Santa Fe black-on-white, which it overlaps in geographic distribution. Although the intrusive Glaze-paint types are all tempered with igneous rock, they are from different localities and distinguished by different classes of clay. The red-firing clay of Glaze I Red has a distinctly lower vitrification point than the buff-firing clay of Glaze I Yellow, and despite its coarser texture, it becomes more dense on refiring than the two fine-textured pastes in the medium group (Wiyo and Santa Fe), being on the border line of the low-porosity class. All pastes in the high-porosity range (Rowe black-on-white and the sand-tempered Glazes II to V) are indigenous. It is interesting to note how closely Rowe conforms to Glaze V, the most characteristic of the native Glaze-paint types. The sand-tempered modern types, on the contrary, fall in the medium range, indicating a less refractory clay and suggesting that they are intrusive.

In general it may be said that the porosity of refired pastes brings out differences and relationships that are often unrecognized in the original sherds, but it is necessary to make allowance for the effect of temper when interpreting results.

STRENGTH

Resistance to breakage affords a practicable means of judging the serviceability of a vessel, and strength is a significant property that would be useful in comparative studies if it could be measured satisfactorily. In the study of a ceramic sequence it is pertinent to ask if there was consistent improvement in the technical quality of pottery. General impressions are gained through handling sherds. The force required to break an edge with pliers or the ring of sherds as they are tossed on a table often convinces us that there are consistent differences between types. But these simple tests are of little value for comparison since they are unstandardized and insensitive as well. Experience in breaking sherds does not enable one to correct reliably for variations in wall thickness and length of break, and ring is affected by density which is not identical to strength.

Strength is not a simple property, for it is influenced by many conditions: texture of the paste, particle size and composition of the clay, method of preparing the paste, technique of building the vessel, rate of drying, temperature and atmosphere of firing, size and shape of the vessel, and alteration after discard. The finer the clay particles, the more readily they soften and adhere to one another in firing. Fluxes determine the nature of the bond formed between particles and the temperature at which bonding occurs. Texture, as conditioned by the amount, size, and shape of nonplastic inclusions, is a primary cause of the variability in strength of low-fired pottery. The range of grades and shapes is wide. In general, the greater the amount of temper, the weaker the body, but there is considerable difference in the effect of different kinds of temper depending on shape and surface characteristics of the particles. Rough-surfaced grains form a better bond with the clay than smooth ones. Thus potsherd, crushed rock, and volcanic ash weaken a paste less than waterworn sand. These effects are illustrated by tests of transverse breaking strength of prepared briquettes (fig. 10). The three clays used in these tests cannot be compared with each other because they were not fired at the same temperature, but the samples within each group are comparable among themselves because grain size of sherd, sand, and rock are constant for the Santa Fe red and Zuni series. It is noteworthy that in both groups all tempered pieces are weaker than the clay alone; also the same relative order is maintained by the different classes of temper, and increase in volume of temper from 15 to 25 per cent reduces strength. The spread between values for various classes of temper is increased with increase in volume of temper. The fact that the range of variation within each paste (shown by the length of bars) is reduced by the higher percentage of temper may be explained by the fact that temper permits more uniform drying and therefore reduces flaws.

There are differences in strength of modern commercial ware that are conditioned by method of forming; but the methods of hand-preparation and building do not produce as great differences in compactions of paste, and it is probable that individual differences in care and skill introduce greater variation than difference in method. Thoroughness of kneading is essential to develop the homogeneity of paste necessary to obtain uniform shrinkage and avoid strain. Flaws or areas of weakness are caused by air pockets left in forming the vessel and by imperfect

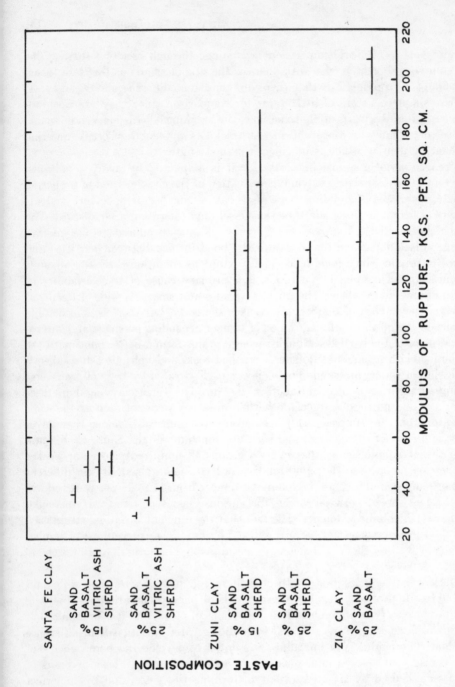

FIG. 10 THE EFFECT OF VARIOUS CLASSES OF TEMPER ON TRANSVERSE
BREAKING STRENGTH

joining of parts, but the actual manipulative processes are more comparable in their effect on strength. Either uneven or too rapid drying causes small flaws as well as actual cracking. The flaws of forming and drying increase the difficulty of obtaining consistent results from strength tests.

Firing method affects strength because it determines the degree of sintering or vitrification that is attained with a given paste. Firing atmosphere, as well as temperature, must be taken into consideration because reduction affects some fluxes that promote vitrification; in particular it reduces ferric oxide to ferrous. Sudden chilling of the vessel on removal from the fire may cause strains and flaws, but the risk is reduced by the high porosity of low-fired wares.

It is important to recognize the possible effect of weathering on sherds when judging the strength of a ware and to select well-preserved specimens for tests. Exposure to leaching by acid soil waters and repeated freezing and thawing may weaken a body considerably. The solution of a carbonate temper is a special case of alteration that is recognized easily unless the carbonate is very fine. These many factors show that tests of strength do not measure a simple property but they do afford a means of comparing the serviceability of wares.

Various methods of testing strength are employed in commercial ceramic practice for special purposes, but they all require some apparatus. A compression test is suitable for structural products such as brick and drain tile, and impact tests are designed to subject china ware to the kind of stresses it receives in usage. One method employs a pendulum which is swung against the test piece, another uses a ball that is repeatedly dropped from increasing heights until the specimen cracks. The specifications for these tests differ for different products, but they have not, to my knowledge, been applied to prehistoric pottery. A widely used method that measures transverse breaking strength seems best adapted to archaeological purposes. The test is made on briquettes, the ends of which rest on knife edges while force is applied through a knife edge that is lowered midway between the ends. The breaking knife edge is moved by a dynamometer which measures the weight applied. Transverse breaking strength or modulus of rupture is calculated by the formula:

$$M = \frac{3Pl}{2bd^2}$$

M = modulus of rupture in kg. per sq. cm.
P = breaking load in kg. (read to the nearest 0.1 kg.)
l = distance between knife edges in cm.
b = breadth of bar in cm.
d = depth of bar in cm.

Standard specifications for this test require a span of 15.5 cm. between the supporting knife edges (Jour. Amer. Ceram. Soc., 1928, p. 472). There are few sherds from which a nearly flat piece 15.5 cm. long can be cut. It is therefore necessary to reduce the span of the knife edges, in applying this test to prehistoric pottery.

As an illustration of possible interpretations of strength data, the modulus of rupture of a series of Pecos types has been plotted (fig. 11). This is the same series that was used in the evaluation of porosity data (p. 128). Nearly flat pieces were selected for the tests, and the knife edges were set 2.5 cm. apart. Results are not comparable to those reported in commercial work but can be compared among themselves. In standard ceramic practice all results that differ more than 15 per cent from the average are discarded, and the test is repeated if more than two out of 10 samples are eliminated. This procedure, intended to eliminate errors caused by invisible flaws, applies to test pieces made from a homogeneous clay with standardized preparation and firing. Sherds of even the most uniform pottery type will have much greater normal variation because they differ in composition, texture, workmanship, or firing. All these variables affect strength and may well introduce a normal variation greater than 15 per cent of the average value. Any limit of variability which might be set for a pottery type would be arbitrary, and the same limit would not fit all types equally well because of differences in composition and technique. In view of these circumstances, it seems advisable to plot all data. In figure 11, each test is represented by a point. An exceptionally low modulus of rupture (points far to the left) may have been caused by flaws or may show exceptional weakness that would result from lower firing or paste texture that was coarser than average. The unusually strong pieces (points far to the right) may represent the results of occasional high firing. All samples plotted were included in calculating the average value for each type (indicated on the graph by a short transverse line). Twenty-one sherds that showed marked deviation from the average were retested with results that reflect multiple causes of divergence. Six gave the same values as originally; eleven, values nearer the average; and four, values that deviated from the average more than the original. This result might be anticipated because flaws and nonhomogeneity may be sporadic or characterize the sample as a whole. In the plotting of this series, values nearest the average were used.

Despite the wide scattering of values for each type, there is a difference in the massing of points, and the Glaze-paint group stands out as distinctly stronger than either the Black-on-white or Modern. Here the controlling factor is probably firing temperature because the glaze had to be relatively well fired to vitrify, and the porosity tests have shown that these pastes are not low-fusing as compared with others in the series. There are interesting variations in average strength within the Glaze-paint series. The first two types, rock-tempered intrusives, are

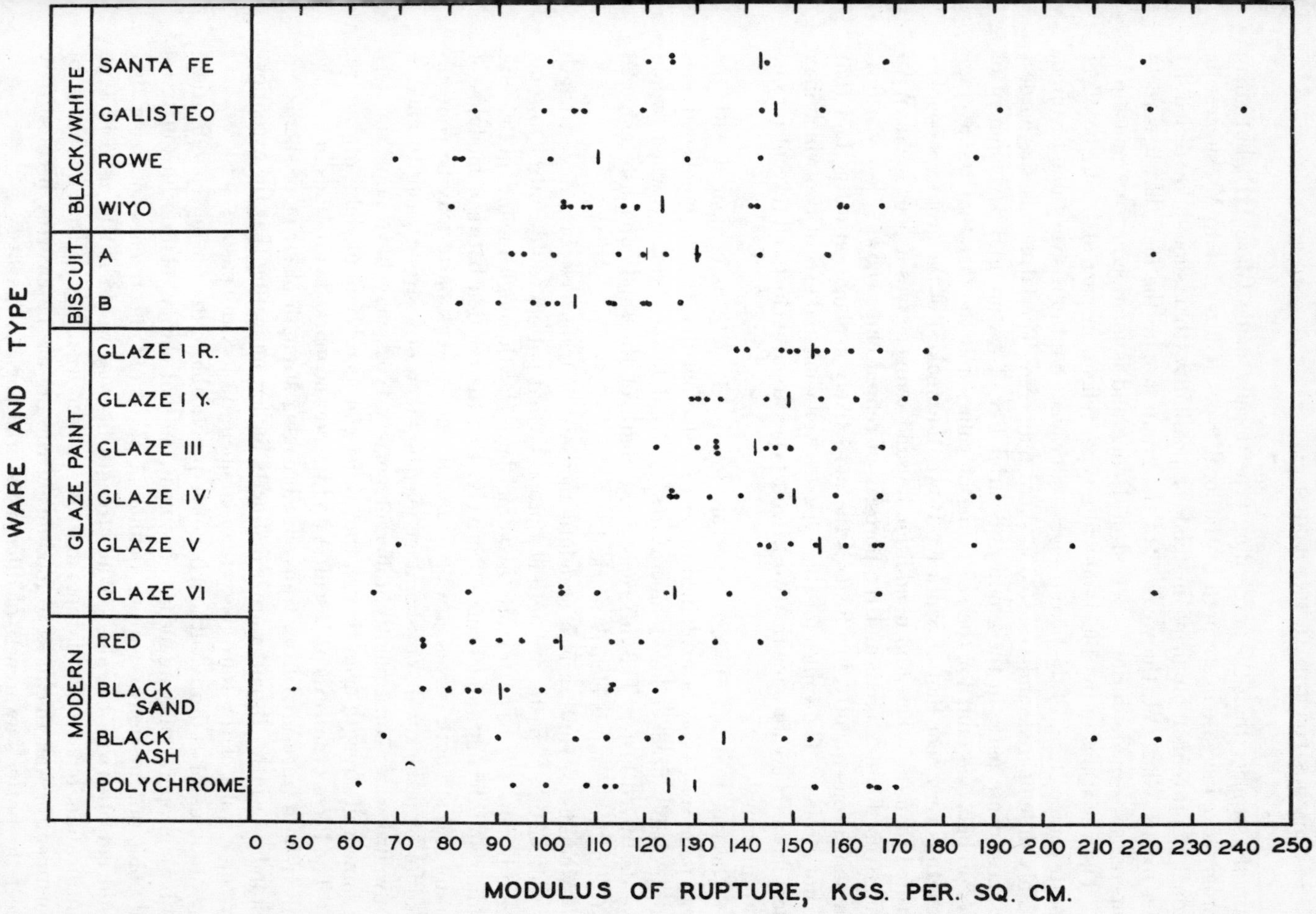

FIG. 11—DATA ON TRANSVERSE BREAKING STRENGTH OF POTTERY TYPES FROM PECOS, NEW MEXICO

distinctly stronger than the succeeding type (locally made Glaze III), but there is progressive increase in strength of the local types (Glazes III to V), suggesting gradual improvement in firing method—a possibility that should be tested by other means. Glaze VI, the weakest of the group despite the fact that it is rock-tempered, was made during a period of decline and is inferior in workmanship.

The variations in the Black-on-white types reflect, in part at least, the effect of paste composition. Of the two strongest, silty paste Santa Fe is very fine-textured, possibly untempered, and Galisteo is sherd-tempered. The latter has the hardest and most dense paste in the group but variability of texture and development of flaws probably account for the scattering of values and the fact that the average strength is very near that of Santa Fe. Rowe, the weakest of the group, is coarser-textured than the others and in addition its sand temper gives a poor bond. Wiyo is relatively fine-textured, and the porosity of refired chips shows a low vitrification point; consequently, low firing is the most likely explanation of the fact that it is not stronger. The values for this type are well clustered except two which may reflect flaws. The values for the two Biscuit types are also clustered (except for one aberrant sample).

The fact that the Modern types are low in strength as compared with the Glaze-paint series may be explained in part by the fact that the three polished ones were probably fired at low temperatures to avoid firing shrinkage which would have destroyed luster. The difference in strength of the sand- and ash-tempered pastes in this group is clearly marked.

Modulus of rupture is a standard measure of transverse breaking strength per unit section of paste. Strength is a property that potters could control to some degree by altering paste texture, avoiding flaws (by thorough mixing and careful welding and drying), and firing effectively. But the relation between modulus of rupture and strength of vessel walls is not direct. A weak paste may be compensated for by a thick wall, or advantage may be taken of a strong paste to make a thin-walled ware; consequently, different pottery types may have approximately the same wall strength even though they differ considerably in modulus of rupture.

The Pecos types, except Biscuit A and B, show no marked variations in average wall strength (measured from transverse breaking strength of strips of sherds cut to standard width). Biscuit ware is distinctly higher, indicating that the exceptionally thick walls of the ware more than compensate for soft paste.

Modulus of rupture, although not a practicable criterion for classification, is a basic property offering means of comparison that clarify relationships of types and point up questions regarding quality of paste and effectiveness of firing that would not otherwise be raised. Wall strength likewise would not be used in type identification but it affords one measure of serviceability. Clear instances of adjustment of wall thickness to modulus of rupture are noteworthy because they reflect the potter's awareness of differences in strength of pastes.

OTHER PROPERTIES

The properties discussed so far affect the quality of pottery; hence they throw some light on potters' standards and, in so far as causes can be ascertained, on methods also. In consequence, these properties assume greater interest and significance in ceramic studies. A few other properties, either less easily tested or interpreted, may be mentioned since they are sometimes reported.

Fracture is a feature that catches the archaeologist's eye, but it does not interest the person who has just broken a good vessel. It has become an item of description because it is occasionally distinct. A very fine, homogeneous paste of medium hardness often has a square, even break; a fine, dense, very hard paste may fracture conchoidally; and very coarse-textured pastes have an irregular, ragged break. But the common paste classes in the medium-texture, medium-hardness range are undifferentiated with respect to fracture, and this fact limits the value of the property in pottery description. From the point of view of the analyst, fracture is a secondary feature because it is conditioned by a number of other properties that can be defined more precisely.

Specific gravity (the ratio between the weights of equal volumes of a material and water) of clay or pottery has to be differentiated with relation to porosity. The commercial ceramist may be interested in bulk specific gravity (calculated from a sample including both open and closed pores) or apparent specific gravity (only closed pores included), but in basic scientific work true specific gravity (all air spaces eliminated) is of interest. The clay minerals vary in true specific gravity (kaolinite 2.667, montmorillonite 2.348) and the impurities in common clays extend over a considerable density range (gypsum 2.3, hematite and magnetite 5.2). The iron oxides therefore increase the specific gravity of clay but carbonaceous matter reduces it. On firing, true specific gravity of pottery changes with inversion of mineral inclusions, decomposition and change of state of constituents, fusion, chemical reactions, and crystallization. Apparent specific gravity is further affected by change in pore space and formation of blebs. These many factors render specific gravity data difficult to interpret and they have rarely been used in the study of prehistoric pottery (see Matson, 1945, for an example).

*   *   *   *   *

By way of summary it may be said that all physical properties are influenced in some measure by both composition of materials and technique of manufacture. In order to understand and interpret them it is necessary to distinguish the role of each factor—to recognize the effect of various techniques on different classes of paste.

Not all physical properties are useful criteria for the identification of pottery types, nor are they equally significant in the study of ceramic standards and practices. Simplicity of recording has in some instances influenced the choice of properties that are customarily reported but they are not recorded with comparable reliability. Only color is satisfactorily standardized. A more uniform and easily maintained standard than Mohs' scale should be found for hardness, and reference standards should be adopted for texture and luster. Porosity and strength, although they require laboratory determination and would not be used in classification, are basic and afford evidence of the progressive effects of firing; hence they may be expected to find a place in any comprehensive study of pottery.

ANALYTICAL METHODS FOR IDENTIFICATION OF CERAMIC MATERIALS

The identification of ceramic materials often involves the performance of tests requiring special equipment, but it does not follow from this circumstance that the methods of analysis need be a mystery to the archaeologist, that he must depend entirely on the technologist to decide what tests shall be made. Furthermore, he should not have to take the results of technological analysis entirely on faith or without inquiry into their meaning. Even though the archaeologist may never use a piece of laboratory equipment, it is desirable that he understand the underlying principles of the important analytical methods, and that he have some idea of the applications and limitations of each. He will then know in general what to expect from them and what their use involves in terms of time and expense.

To the popular mind analysis suggests chemistry—breaking a substance down into the elements of which it is composed and determining their proportions—but there are other facts about matter that aid in understanding it, and certain methods of the physical sciences have become very important in analysis. Often it is the way in which elements are combined that tells what we want to know. The regular patterns of arrangement of atoms in all crystalline substances afford a powerful means of investigation and identification. Chemical analysis does not give this information directly, whereas there are various refined and highly accurate means of studying the properties which result from atomic arrangement, most important of which for our work is the technique of optical crystallography. The actual pattern of atomic arrangement can be studied by X-ray diffraction analysis. Other physical methods of interest to the ceramist are differential thermal analysis and spectroscopy.

The nature of ceramic materials and what we need to know about them determine our selection of analytical methods. Before considering the analytical problems presented by different classes of material we will review the methods that have proved most useful.

PETROGRAPHIC MICROSCOPE

In the study of prehistoric pottery, the most widely applicable and useful analytical tool has been the petrographic microscope. We think of a microscope as an instrument that magnifies, but the distinctive feature of the petrographic microscope is that it reveals how a transparent substance affects the light that passes through it. In chemical analysis we identify an unknown substance by observing how it reacts with known substances that are chemically pure. In optical crystallography we identify an unknown substance by observing how it affects light with known characteristics of vibration. Polarized, monochromatic light (light vibrating in one direction and having defined wave length) plays a part in analysis analogous to the chemically pure reagent. The petrographic microscope, therefore, is a very specialized type of microscope. It is provided with a polarizing prism below the stage that transmits light vibrating in one direction only. A second polarizing prism, mounted to slide in and out of the microscope tube, is oriented to transmit only those light rays which are vibrating at right angles to the ones that enter the specimen. The microscope stage revolves and is laid off in degrees so that the specimen can be turned at any angle to the direction of vibration of the entering light, and the angle of rotation measured. There are wedges and plates of minerals that can be inserted in the tube to determine the relative velocity of light traveling in different directions in a mineral and to make other observations. The various optical properties that can be measured with the petrographic microscope afford precise criteria for the identification of transparent minerals.

To use the petrographic microscope analytically requires training in optical crystallography. It also requires special preparation of materials. Light must pass through the substance. The vast majority of rock forming minerals are transparent when examined in sufficiently thin fragments. Specimens can be prepared for analysis in two ways, by making a thin section and by powdering and immersing them in refractive liquids. The thin section is permanent and can be kept indefinitely as a record. It must be ground to standard thickness (0.03 mm.) because the effect of a mineral slice on light depends not only on its identity but also on its crystallographic direction and its thickness. Thickness can be controlled, whereas orientation in a random aggregate cannot. Since primitive pottery is soft and friable, special preparation is required to grind a section thin enough for light to pass through it. To counteract friability a thin slice of the pottery to be sectioned is impregnated with bakelite. Without this or some similar treatment it would be impossible to section most prehistoric pottery. Grinding and mounting take approximately an hour, but two days should be allowed to complete a section because of the time required to impregnate with bakelite and to harden it by gradual heating. Time and material are saved by preparing a large number of thin sections at once.

The method of immersion is quick and simple compared with thin-sectioning. A bit of the powdered sample is transferred to a slide and covered with a drop of liquid of known refractive index. By manipulation of the cover glass, the grains can be rolled about in the liquid and viewed from different sides to facilitate measurement of optical properties. Refractive index, a measure of the optical density of a substance dependent on the speed with which light travels through it, is an especially important criterion of identification. A series of refractive liquids that cover the range of values for the majority of minerals is used, and the sample is examined in successive liquids until its index or one of its indices is matched. With this technique either a sample of paste or particular mineral grains dissected from it can be examined. For the identification of individual minerals the immersion mount is just as satisfactory as the thin section. The obvious limitation of the powdered sample is that it does not show the texture or structure of paste or the association of minerals. This is a serious limitation, particularly in the study of rock temper because rocks are classified not alone by the mineral species present but also by the proportion and relation of constituents and by texture, evidence of which is lost when the specimen is powdered. Therefore, the immersion mount is not a substitute for the thin section, but an important supplement to it. The immersion mount is sufficient when a paste is known to belong to one of two types distinguished by mineral composition or when mineralogical composition alone is significant. Permanent mounts of powders can be made by using Canada balsam or some of the synthetic materials. There is also a series of compounds with high refractive index that are particularly useful in making permanent mounts of samples of glazes or materials of high refractive index.

BINOCULAR MICROSCOPE

The wide field binocular microscope is an instrument that is indispensable in technological work. It functions as a magnifier, and has the advantage of stereoscopic vision and correction by prisms for reversal of the image. It is, therefore, adapted for manipulating the specimen while examining it. One can, for example, test the hardness or the magnetism of mineral grains with a needle point, pry particles of temper out from the paste for examination in refractive liquids and scrape samples of paint, glaze, or slip without cutting into the paste. This microscope is also very convenient in microchemical work in which drops and particles of reagents are used to obtain reactions marked by the formation of microscopic crystals.

The binocular microscope is particularly useful for making preliminary or broad paste classifications. For this purpose experience is needed but technical background is not. Mineral inclusions in the paste are identified by the same properties that are relied on in examining a hand specimen—crystal form, color, hardness, luster, cleavage, and magnetism. If there are fragments of igneous rock, differences in texture as well as in color can be recognized, and under favorable circumstances some of the principal minerals identified. Various textures of volcanic ash and the structure of metamorphic rock are often clearly seen.

Ease of identification with the binocular microscope depends, of course, on the texture of inclusions. Fine grains (under 0.25 mm. in diameter) are identified with difficulty (magnification up to 50×), and pastes with textures as fine as or finer than this should be analyzed petrographically. In general, the more specific identifications must be made with the petrographic microscope. The binocular microscope is perfectly satisfactory for distinguishing the principal classes of temper: sherd, sand, igneous and metamorphic rocks, volcanic ash, sandstone, limestone, shell, and fiber in medium or coarser grades. Varieties within these classes can also be distinguished, as for example igneous rocks by colors and textures, sandstones by their types of cement, and so on. But to identify the igneous rock specifically, to recognize the particular features that distinguish a volcanic glass, to pick out the rarer minerals that define a sand, it is necessary to use the petrographic microscope.

It is always advantageous to use both instruments; or, if the binocular microscope is used by an archaeologist, he should work in co-operation with a petrographer, because identifications are precise and can be more meaningful after the paste has been analyzed in thin section. Petrographic analysis shows the significance of relatively inconspicuous diagnostics that are easily overlooked when one does not know their importance and is not prepared to search for them. On the other hand, there is the element of time; the sherds that one can classify by paste with the binocular microscope in the time it takes to make and analyze a thin section can easily run over a hundred. Because of the quickness of this method—a glance is often sufficient if one is experienced—it is practicable to classify the paste of sherds from stratigraphic tests, and one can obtain sufficient data for statistical work which will enable him to follow changes in composition over a period of time. One can also spot the foreign pastes in entire lots of sherds. This is a great advantage in studying trade relations because a considerable proportion of sherds with foreign paste, being small, lack the diagnostic features of form or decoration by which they can be identified.

MICROCHEMICAL ANALYSIS

As compared with microscopic and particularly petrographic methods, chemical analysis has played a limited and secondary role in technological studies. Yet chemical data have a definite place and there is no substitute for them. They have been used principally for the analysis of paints and glazes. One of the chief difficulties encountered in chemical analysis of archaeological ceramic material is the small size of available samples. An hour spent in scraping pigment from a sherd may yield a sample only a hundredth the size of that used for ordinary methods of chemical analysis. Fortunately great strides have been made within recent years in the development of techniques, instruments, and reagents for microchemical analysis, and a large proportion of our work has been on a micro scale.

The principal advance in qualitative microanalysis has been the introduction of new organic reagents that give very sensitive reactions. Many of the reactions are accompanied by a characteristic color change, and the tests are referred to as spot reactions. These can be performed in the depression of a porcelain plate, on a slide, or, in many cases, on filter paper. If filter paper is stamped with paraffin rings to confine the area of reaction, a rough quantitative estimation can be made in some instances. Certain colors are permanent, and the results of tests made on filter paper can be filed for reference. When crystals are formed in microchemical reactions, their shapes and colors are often distinctive, and their growth and change can be watched microscopically. The disadvantage of qualitative tests performed without preliminary separation of constituents of the sample is that certain associated elements may interfere with the reaction; either the characteristic reaction is inhibited or suppressed by a stronger reaction. It is therefore necessary to know the limitations of various reagents and to have some idea of possible interfering substances in the unknown. Fortunately there is a wide range of reagents from which to choose, and many tests can be performed with reagents that are specific for particular elements. For some of the newer reagents, it may be necessary to make preliminary tests of their sensitivity to the range of elements with which one is dealing.

Quantitative microchemical analysis requires a number of special instruments for separating, weighing, and measuring small quantities. Microchemical balances will weigh a sample a thousandth the size of that ordinarily taken for analysis. Apparatus is reduced to dollhouse size, and methods are used that eliminate transfers of material, an important consideration because losses that would not be noticed with a 5-gram sample may introduce serious error when one has only five thousandths of a gram. Sensitive color reactions make practicable colorimetric determination that can be carried out with a photoelectric instrument, and equipment for electrolytic separation has been reduced to micro scale.

The simplest qualitative tests require little equipment and few reagents, and they can be performed by anyone with experience. They include tests for manganese and iron that may occur in black pigments, lead and copper in glazes, mercury and copper in postfired paints, and magnesium in limestones and dolomite. Quantitative determinations, on the other hand, require delicate and expensive equipment, manipulative skill, and a background in chemistry that will enable one to judge the relative advantages of different procedures. It may be necessary to know the proportions of constituents no less than their identity in order to explain the nature of a material or its properties, and consequently even though quantitative microchemical analysis is slow and expensive, its use may be justified more often than we realize.

SPECTROGRAPHIC ANALYSIS

Spectrographic analysis is a physical method for investigating the chemical composition of materials. It is based on the fact that atoms emit light when they are subject to certain kinds of excitation—a strong electric field, violent collision with other atoms under high temperature, bombardment by electrons. This phenomenon is well understood. Within the atom, the electrons occupy orbits at fixed distances from the nucleus. Under excitation the electrons are knocked from inner to outer orbits, thus acquiring potential energy which they release as light when they drop back to their original orbits. Their movements are always from one orbit to another, never to random positions between orbits, and the atoms of each element emit light of certain wave lengths which are characteristic of it. Everyone is familiar with the yellow color of a flame when salt is thrown into it. The flame test is one of the simple, quick methods that mineralogists have long used in blowpipe analysis. The color is due to the dominant wave length of the light, but when this light is resolved into its component wave lengths, a characteristic spectrum is formed. Some elements have very simple spectra consisting of only a few lines, whereas others have complex spectra consisting of thousands of lines. Fortunately it is not necessary to measure the wave length of all the lines in a spectrum, for there is always a series that is diagnostic.

The spectroscope is designed for viewing the spectrum obtained from a substance under excitation. The spectrograph, developed to photograph the spectrum, makes possible measurement on the plate of wave length and intensity of lines. There are many types of spectrographs, each with its particular advantages and disadvantages, their primary difference being in the manner of forming the spectrum. Either a prism or a grating—a plate ruled so finely that it breaks light into its separate wave lengths—is used. When the prism is of glass, light of the visible spectrum and the infra-red region is transmitted. A quartz prism will transmit ultra-violet rays as well as those of the visible spectrum but not the infra-red. The grating will reflect the entire range, and it has the additional advantage over the prism of giving uniform dispersion of lines, thus simplifying measurement. The delicacy of the ruling of the grating is a disadvantage especially in industrial work where it is subject to dust and fumes. In analytical work, the spectrograph must be chosen with reference to the nature of the materials under investigation. There is no standard instrument for all types of work. The complexity of the spectra encountered in analysis determines the size of the instrument that should be employed. The elements occurring in ceramic materials, especially iron, have complex spectra, and it is therefore desirable to use instruments having high dispersion.

Spectrographic analysis has certain distinct advantages over the long established and standard procedures of chemical analysis. From the mechanical standpoint, it is relatively quick and easy. A small powdered sample can be placed in the cup of an electrode and arced very simply, eliminating the slow, exacting, tedious procedures of taking difficultly soluble substances into solution and separating the constituent elements. Taking a spectrogram requires little training compared with chemical analysis; this part of the procedure is often left to a laboratory assistant, and the analyst has only to read the plate. Even this is not too difficult. The hundreds of lines on a plate suggest innumerable measurements, but an experienced spectroscopist identifies an element from certain of its most characteristic lines. Analysis is simplified in some instances by exposing the spectra of elements sought in the unknown against its spectrum. But the simplicity of the method can be overstressed. Even the exposure of the plate requires judgment and some knowledge of the nature of the unknown, for there is risk of losing volatile elements before the exposure is made, and refractory elements may not be volatilized in the time allowed for the exposure. This difficulty can be overcome by making successive exposures or using a moving plate. These are technical details that can make the difference between a reliable and an unreliable analysis, and which may be overlooked if a simple routine procedure is followed.

Aside from advantages in mechanics of operation, spectrography has the considerable advantage of sensitivity to elements occurring in traces that would be missed in ordinary chemical analysis. These trace elements may have little influence on the properties of the material, but they often serve to distinguish it from similar material from a different source. Unsuspected elements that would not be sought in chemical analysis often show up in the spectrogram. Another advantage of the method is that small samples are sufficient. This is especially important in the analysis of paints and glazes since the quantity of these substances that can be scraped from the surface of a sherd is stringently limited.

Coupled with the advantages of spectrography are certain disadvantages. It is not satisfactory for the analysis of the majority of nonmetallic elements, and in general cannot be used for quantitative determination of elements that occur in concentrations greater than 10 per cent.

Spectrography is employed most frequently for qualitative analysis and the lines for all elements in the unknown that can be detected by this method are present on a single plate. In reading such a plate, a rough estimate of the concentration of elements is made by judging width and density of lines; the particular lines of the characteristic spectrum that are present are also significant because certain lines persist longer than others as the concentration of an element in the sample is reduced. Proportions are designated by the terms major, minor, and trace. The sensitivity of the spectrograph is such that all elements occurring in concentration over 1 per cent are classed as major elements, and some of the minor elements would not ordinarily be detected in chemical analysis.

Quantitative or semiquantitative determinations can be made spectrographically for elements in low concentration from the intensities of lines. Various techniques have been used in commercial work, but in undertaking the analysis of a new material, the method must be adapted to its requirements and the limits of accuracy determined.

Spectroscopy, both qualitative and quantitative, is finding increasing applications in commercial ceramics (Harrison and Bassett, 1941; Zander and Terry, 1947), but we cannot assume that it will be equally useful in the analysis of archaeological materials: first, because a wider range of materials is dealt with in commercial ceramics, among which glazes and enamels are important; and second, because the ceramic engineer has problems of routine control of purity or specifications of materials which do not enter in archaeological work. Our concern is more often with the identification of the rare or unusual material.

The applications of spectroscopy in pottery analysis are the same as those of chemical analysis. It is of minor importance in the study of clays because mineralogical composition, physical properties, and thermal behavior are of greater interest than chemical composition. Spectroscopy has also had very little use in the study of nonplastic inclusions because mineralogical composition, structure, and texture are of primary interest, and these are most satisfactorily determined by petrographic methods. There may be instances in which the impurities or trace elements in either clays or minerals would afford a reliable means of identifying source or of distinguishing samples from different sources, but it is principally in the study of the chemical composition of paints and glazes that spectroscopy is useful.

DIFFERENTIAL THERMAL ANALYSIS

Many substances undergo changes when they are heated. They may lose water of crystallization, they may be decomposed or oxidized, their crystalline structure may be destroyed, or new crystalline phases may be formed. In some of these changes (endothermic reactions) heat is absorbed, in others (exothermic reactions) heat is given off. The number of such reactions, the temperature at which they occur, and their intensity are characteristic of a mineral and can be used for its identification. In the analytical procedure, the unknown is heated at a uniform rate. This is referred to as dynamic heating in contrast to static heating in which successive temperatures are held until the test material comes to equilibrium. In the dynamic method the temperature of the unknown is compared with that of an inert reference material, and their temperature difference is plotted, hence the name differential thermal analysis. When there is no temperature difference, the heating curve is horizontal; but if the unknown undergoes an endothermic reaction, there is a dip in the curve because the temperature of the sample drops. When an exothermic reaction occurs, a peak is plotted because the unknown is hotter than the reference material.

This is not a new method of investigating materials. The French chemist, Le Chatelier, famous for his studies of chemical equilibrium, used it in 1887. But the technique was not perfected at that time and reproducible curves could not be obtained. It is only within the period of modern clay research that apparatus has been improved and the method has been rendered practicable and used extensively. Its special advantage is in the analysis of very fine-grained materials that are difficult to identify by petrographic methods.

Differential thermal analysis has been used extensively in clay mineral research, and it affords a useful means of identifying types of clay. Since each mineral has a characteristic set of peaks, the components of a mixture can often be recognized, and under favorable circumstances semiquantitative estimates can be made; but the more complex the material becomes, the greater the likelihood that peaks of different constituents will overlap, and the greater the difficulty of analysis. The method can be effectively used in conjunction with X-ray diffraction studies and petrographic analysis.

Unfortunately, differential thermal analysis is not satisfactory for the identification of the clay minerals in pottery because the temperatures at which the most useful and diagnostic changes occur are usually passed in the original firing, and this part of the heating curve is lost. The value of this method in archaeological technology will depend largely on the importance of the analysis of raw clay in our work.

X-RAY DIFFRACTION STUDIES

X-ray diffraction patterns afford means of studying the atomic structure of materials. Von Laue first proved in 1912 that a crystal forms a three-dimensional grating for X-rays and that the pattern can be interpreted in terms of the atomic arrangement of the crystal. Later it was found that a powder or fine, random aggregate of crystalline particles produces a diffraction pattern of sharp lines— a crystal spectrum. The position of the lines corresponds to planes of atoms in the crystal. In a powder pattern many sets of such planes are registered simultaneously. The crystal X-ray spectrum of any pure chemical element or compound is characteristic, and the standard reference data that have now been amassed make this a highly useful method for identification.

X-ray diffraction analysis has been used extensively in the study of the clay minerals and also in the investigation of the effect of heat on these minerals and on synthetic ceramic materials. It has rarely been used in the analysis of prehistoric pottery because of the mixed composition of the paste and the fact that crystalline structure of the clay is generally destroyed in firing. In one instance it was used to study the anomalous birefringence of a clay slip (Shepard, 1948, pp. 96, 170). The method would have much more extensive use if the technologist were called on to study raw clay more frequently.

IDENTIFICATION OF CERAMIC MATERIALS

CLAY

The analysis of clay has generally held a secondary place in technological studies of prehistoric pottery. There are two reasons for this seeming neglect of the potter's basic material: first, the difficulty of analyzing clays because of extreme fineness of grain, impure state, and alteration in firing; and second, the fact that clay is generally less useful as a criterion for pottery identification than nonplastic inclusions. For example, to describe a paste as having a red-firing, nonrefractory clay identifies it less specifically than to say it has a ground diabase temper. Even a fuller description of clay, including mineral and chemical composition, which could be arrived at only by lengthy laboratory analysis, would define a material that is far more common and widely distributed than many types of temper that can be identified quickly and easily. This is not to imply that tempering materials or nonplastics are always distinctive, although many are. The important point is that they include a great range of minerals and rocks, and the ease of their identification permits rapid preliminary classification whereas the characteristics of the clay give confirmatory evidence or indicate subdivisions.

As long as the technologist's chief objectives are to determine the relationship of pottery types, to identify intrusives, and to trace interregional trade in pottery, clay is likely to play a secondary role to temper identification. The fact remains that clay is the essential constituent of pottery, and its properties are of primary concern to the potter; whereas tempering material modifies the clay in much the same manner whatever its composition. When our primary interest is the history of the potter's craft and evidences of the stage of technological advancement represented by pottery, it is imperative to learn as much about the composition and properties of clay as possible in order to learn how well the potter's techniques were adapted to it. In any case the available methods for clay analysis and testing should be understood and applied whenever practicable. How fully clay is analyzed will depend on our objectives, the nature of our problems, and the facilities at our disposal.

Analyzing raw clay and testing its working and firing properties is a very different matter from studying the clay of fired pottery. It is no exaggeration to say that in firing, the clay becomes a different class of material, and many tests that can be applied to the raw clay are inapplicable to the fired body. The fired clay has been dehydrated, its plasticity destroyed, and all direct evidence of its working properties lost. Even indirect evidence of these properties is slim. If vessel walls are exceptionally thin, we may surmise that the clay has good plasticity and dry strength. In extreme cases this is a reasonably safe guess. If the wall is unusually thick, however, there is no way of knowing whether poor quality of clay or crude workmanship is responsible, and the great majority of specimens with medium wall thickness give no basis for a guess. Firing also destroys the crystalline structure of the clay minerals, unless the temperature is very low; when crystalline structure is lost, identification of the clay minerals is difficult. Finally, the nonplastic material with which clay is usually mixed alters its firing behavior.

If one has ethnological samples and data, one can test the raw clay and study how well the potter's methods were adapted to its peculiarities. But samples of prehistoric pottery generally come to the laboratory without raw clay. It is always desirable to reconnoiter the locality of a site for clay; sometimes the archaeologist is fortunate enough to discover caches of potter's material or unfired pottery in the course of excavations. But caches are not common, and surveying a region for clay has its limitations. In some cases clay deposits are not found near a site and the question arises whether clay was brought in from a distance or obtained in trade, or if pottery was not made locally. In other instances there may be considerable variety in the clays of a region; to test them and determine which ones exhibit firing properties comparable to those of the principal pottery types becomes a time-consuming task. If the geological formations of an area are uniform and if the clays are of the same general class, their common properties may be more significant than the location of the exact bed from which clay was obtained. When there are many clay deposits of similar type in a locality, it is rarely, if ever, possible to prove by analysis which deposits were used; furthermore, such information is not of sufficient value to justify the expense of detailed and extensive comparisons. It will simplify our discussion to consider separately methods for the study of raw and of fired clay.

Analysis and testing of raw clay.   There are several different approaches that can be made in the study of clay. Its composition can be identified mineralogically or determined chemically; certain of its properties, such as particle size and base exchange capacity, can be measured; and its working and firing properties can be tested. The mineralogical composition of clay and its particle size have a direct effect on working and firing properties, but the latter are more simply and quickly determined directly and the principal value of the mineralogical study is in classification and in explanation of properties.

Identification of the clay minerals requires technical methods of analysis and expensive equipment. Differential thermal analysis and X-ray diffraction patterns are generally the most satisfactory methods. Under favorable circumstances—if the clay is not too fine-grained or impure—optical properties are sufficient for identification. They can be determined from a small powdered sample in an immersion mount with the petrographic microscope. In any case this technique is important for the identification of the foreign inclusions or accessory minerals in clay. These minerals can be very useful in distinguishing clays and they have some effect on properties. They are most easily determined when the clay is first centrifuged in a series of heavy liquids to separate them in groups according to specific gravity.

One comparatively simple method, a staining test, has been used for clay mineral identification. It is not always reliable, however, and is best used as a preliminary test in conjunction with other methods. This test rests on the fact that certain types of clay will adsorb organic dyes or other substances and produce a color change in consequence of their mineral composition and structure. The adsorptive clays which produce the color change are of the montmorillonite type, whereas the kaolinitic types do not have this effect. Two types of reactions are used in these tests, an acid-base reaction in which the treated clay acts like an acid, and an oxidation-reduction reaction in which certain ions in the space lattice of the clay mineral oxidize the reagent. The acid treatment of clay should be carried out in the laboratory because it requires thorough washing which is impracticable without a centrifuge. The oxidation-reduction test can be made in the field, for it does not require treatment of the clay. The reaction is sometimes inhibited by impurities in the clay. These methods have been tested by a number of workers, and the reactions for a series of reference clays have been published by Mielenz, King, and Schieltz (1950), together with a description of technique.

Chemical analysis has been essential in clay research, but it has played a secondary role in commercial clay testing because it is easier to make direct tests of the suitability of clays for particular products than to predict firing behavior from chemical composition. In the archaeological field, chemical analysis has been employed only in special cases, particularly to explain properties of slips. Admixture of tempering material in the body increases the difficulty of determining clay composition.

Chemical analysis is slow and expensive because clay, a silicate, requires fusion to bring it into solution, and it carries a number of impurities that must be determined in addition to its essential constituents. A complete chemical analysis is referred to as an ultimate analysis. A short method, referred to as rational analysis, has sometimes been used, especially in Germany. It serves as a rough method for relatively pure kaolin but can be misleading for highly impure clay. Rational analysis therefore can be dismissed from consideration as a method of analysis in archaeological work.

Various deductions can be drawn from the results of ultimate analysis, especially when it is used in conjunction with physical tests. For example, a high percentage of silica may decrease workability, reduce shrinkage, and increase refractoriness. The clay minerals are characterized by different silica-alumina ratios, but the total silica content of a clay is almost always in excess of the theoretical amount in kaolinite, 46 per cent. Clays with the approximate composition of theoretical kaolins are refractory and as the alumina increases, refractoriness is increased. Certain impurities, particularly carbon and sulphur, cause difficulties in firing. A knowledge of the occurrence, percentage, and form of these can be used in planning the firing schedule. The percentage of iron oxide gives some indication of the probable color of the body after firing. As a rough generalization it may be said that if alumina, lime, and magnesia are not present in excess, a clay containing less than 1–1.5 per cent of the iron oxide will fire white or cream; from 1.5 to 3 per cent, buff; and more than 3 per cent, red. Chemical analysis alone affords a very rough means of predicting color, however, because particle size and distribution of the iron oxide and particle size of the clay influence coloring power.

In the analysis of archaeological materials, chemical data on slip clays which are free from tempering material are most easily interpreted. As an example of the kind of deductions that can be drawn, the study of Plumbate slip may be cited. This slip has an interesting range of colors extending from buffs, oranges, and reds to light and dark grays. Slips that indicate full oxidation by their reddish color are soft; the grays are hard and frequently vitrified. The question of principal interest when the Plumbate investigation was undertaken was whether the unusual characteristics of the slip were due to properties of the clay or to method of firing. Spectrographic analyses were first made to learn whether or not elements that would act as fluxes in the range of primitive firing were present. When such elements were not found, quantitative determinations of the major constituents were made. Microchemical methods were required because of the thinness of the slip and the difficulty of securing a large sample free of paste. Silica, alumina, and iron were determined on samples weighing 5–10 milligrams. The results showed that the clay was high in both alumina and iron. Since the gray color of the pottery indicated reducing conditions in firing, the fluxing effect of iron in the ferrous state offered an explanation of vitrification. The high alumina would influence the hardness of the fused slip. This explanation indicated that the unusual properties of the slip were dependent on both composition and technique. When questions regarding the source of clay arise, spectrographic analyses, which show diagnostic trace elements, may be valuable.

Methods and theories of particle-size determination have been extensively investigated because this property affects plasticity and other characteristics (see summary in Norton and Speil, 1938). The method most widely used is based on rate of settling of particles in water. Particle size is calculated from settling rate by Stokes' law. The assumption is made that the settling rate of clay particles is comparable to that of spheres, the diameters of which correspond to the maximum dimensions of the particles. The clay must be separated into its individual particles without breaking them, a process which requires long soaking in an electrolyte and working with a rubber-tipped pestle or a stiff brush. Prolonged treatment is required for some clays; a few do not yield to it and cannot be measured. Norton and Speil have recommended measurement in a centrifugal field of force for particles under one micron in size because below this point static settling becomes so slow that thermal currents and Brownian movement may introduce serious errors. Analyses which fail to report the finer fractions omit essential data because these fractions have a marked influence on working and firing properties.

Plasticity is a property of primary concern to the clay worker and his experience enables him to judge it with confidence, but it is a complex property, and the ceramic engineer has not yet developed a thoroughly satisfactory direct test of it. It is sometimes judged from related properties such as viscosity and water of plasticity (the percentage of water required to bring the clay to its best working condition), but they have limitations. Norton (1952, chap. 8) has recommended that yield point and extensibility be reported. Since these properties influence plasticity and can be measured precisely, they should offer a satisfactory means of comparing clays with respect to workability.

Drying shrinkage and dry strength are also considered in judging clay. The percentage volume shrinkage is calculated from the difference between plastic volume and dry volume taken in terms of dry volume. Dry strength, which determines the care required in handling unfired pottery, is reported as modulus of rupture of test briquettes. The drying schedule is important in this test (see Jour. Amer. Ceram. Soc., 11:460, for procedures).

Plasticity, drying shrinkage, and dry strength are fundamental properties that have concerned clay workers of all times. A property of special interest to students of low-fired pottery is the luster a clay will acquire when rubbed (see p. 123). In testing a clay, a briquette or plaque is formed, and the surface is well smoothed when it is in the leather-hard state. Since drying shrinkage reduces luster, and clays differ in shrinkage, plaques should be thoroughly air-dried before they are polished. If the surface is moistened with a wet cloth just before polishing, the clay will yield to the polishing tool but will dry during the process of polishing, and shrinkage will be negligible. Any hard smooth tool, such as a waterworn pebble, is suitable for polishing. This is essentially the technique of present-day Pueblo potters who make highly lustrous ware. In this test, the fact that certain clays do not become lustrous is more significant than the degree of luster that others attain.

The amount of carbon from an organic extract that a clay will retain on firing is of interest whenever organic paints were used. Base exchange capacity influences this property, but the relation has not yet been studied. A direct, non-technical test can be made by painting the clay test piece with a standard solution (25 per cent sugar), firing in air to fixed temperatures and recording the depth of gray that is obtained. Rate of heating, as well as the temperature of drawing, should be standardized, and since the test is to determine how well the clay is adapted to a primitive technique, a very rapid rate, 35°C per minute, is taken. Test pieces are drawn immediately on reaching temperature in general accord with primitive practice. The lowest temperature chosen for the test will depend on the firing temperature of the pottery types with which the clay is being compared. It would seldom be under 600°C, and 700°C may be low enough. Some clays do not retain a trace of carbon after firing to 700° and many show only a faint gray, but some retain a good black. The latter can be tested further by firing at successively higher temperatures taken at 50° or 100° intervals.

The firing properties of clay are determined on molded briquettes of standard size and shape, dried and fired according to a standard schedule. Progressive changes in color, hardness, strength, and porosity are determined. It is important to burn out all carbonaceous matter and bring the clay to a state of full oxidation before recording color. Oxidation must be carried out at a low temperature if the properties of the clay are being compared with those of low-fired pottery. If the record is started at 650°C, for example, the clay must be oxidized at or below this temperature. The conditions required for oxidation are an important consideration in judging a clay. If oxidation is slow, it is probable that direct-fired pottery made from it would have a gray core. The measurement of porosity is important because it indicates the maturing of the clay and the progress of vitrification. Methods of recording color, strength, hardness, and porosity have been described under physical properties. For the firing schedule, intervals of 100°C within the 600°–1000°C range can be taken. For comparison with exceptionally low-fired ware, lower minimums may be necessary. Even though the pottery with which a clay is being compared is not vitrified, the refractoriness of clays, as indicated by vitrification points, should be determined, because this is a basic property. Briquettes should be fired in air for the standard tests, but if the clay is compared with pottery that was not oxidized, it should also be fired in a reducing atmosphere, obtained most simply by placing charcoal in the tube of an electric resistance furnace, provided with an air-tight tube. For standardized firing atmosphere, tank gases should be used to control composition.

Tests of the properties of clay, as well as determinations of its firing behavior, require laboratory equipment. There are, however, some simple tests and observations that can be made in the field to judge the suitability of clay for pottery. Color will often indicate whether or not a clay is highly carbonaceous; if it is not, the possible color range within which it will fall when fired can be predicted in some cases (p. 17). Bentonitic clays can be recognized by their swelling on adding water dropwise to a small lump. A montmorillonitic type of clay turns blue when allowed to stand five minutes in a saturated aqueous solution of benzidine. This is a preliminary test that should be confirmed by more exact methods, because certain impurities, especially manganese dioxide, also cause the color change. Texture of clays can be judged by feel. Very fine clays having a waxy or soapy feel are often described as fat, and granular or silty clays as lean. To judge plasticity, a lump of clay is worked up with water, formed into a ball, and flattened between the palms to note how thin the disc becomes before cracks develop. A drop of hydrochloric acid will show by effervescence if a clay is calcareous. These tests are not substitutes for laboratory analysis, but they indicate whether or not a clay is suitable for pottery, and they afford some basis for predicting whether or not it may correspond to that of pottery types under investigation. It is therefore advisable to make them before collecting clay for analysis.

Classification of fired clay.   In the study of the clay base of pottery, it would be desirable to identify the clay minerals as a criterion for primary classification, and to account more fully for the properties of the ware, but this is difficult to do. Differential thermal analysis is of limited value after the clay has been dehydrated, and the method of X-ray diffraction does not give direct information after the crystalline structure has been destroyed. Effects observed in polarized light show that the clay of some low-fired pottery is still crystalline, however, and it is possible that characteristic X-ray diffraction patterns could be obtained from these samples although the potentialities of the method for our work have not yet been extensively tested.

The optical constants of the clay minerals are well established, and some work has been done on the changes in these constants on heating. Under favorable circumstances, therefore, significant differences can be recognized with the petrographic microscope, especially for refractive indices which are quickly determined on small, powdered sample. The thin section gives especially clear evidence of the condition of the clay. When crystalline structure of the clay mineral has not been destroyed, the paste has a distinctive stranded appearance in polarized light owing to the parallel orientation of platelike particles, and a slip that has been thoroughly compacted by polishing acts optically like a unit. Differences in birefringence of the clay minerals are also clearly shown in thin section in consequence of uniform orientation. In the study of Pecos pottery, optical properties indicating a distinct montmorillonitic clay supported the evidence which volcanic ash temper gave of the source of Biscuit ware. In general it may be said that data on optical properties and the basic constitution of clay can be useful when considered in relation to pottery types defined by temper or when studied in reference to specific questions, but that they do not afford a practicable, primary basis for classification of pastes.

Accessory minerals of the fired, as of the raw, clay may aid in differentiating material from different sources. In the case of pottery, however, we have the additional problem of distinguishing the accessory minerals from those that may have been added as temper, except when there is reasonable certainty that the clay was not tempered. Ordinarily the accessory minerals occur in a smaller size range than temper, but size is not a reliable criterion for differentiation because a fraction of the temper may be ground to flourlike fineness. The only reliable basis for differentiation is by natural association of minerals; for example, the temper may be derived from a type of rock in which some of the accessory minerals would not occur.

A simple, ceramic classification of pastes that serves to distinguish major types by their firing properties is useful for making broad comparisons. In commercial practice, color and refractoriness have been used as primary criteria because they determine the kind of product for which a clay is suited. Three broad color ranges have generally been recognized: white, buff, and red, including brown. White clays are subdivided as noncalcareous and calcareous because they differ greatly in commercial value. The buff and red clays are subdivided with reference to plasticity and refractoriness. This color grouping has been found convenient for comparison of pastes of prehistoric pottery, provided the pastes are fully oxidized and fired to the same temperature. It is therefore necessary to refire chips from sherds, in order to bring them to comparable condition. Ceramists have not adopted a standard definition of these color classes; furthermore, ranges should be independently defined for archaeological purposes, especially as we are less interested than the commercial ceramist in distinguishing pure whites. Divisions defined by the Munsell system, shown in Table 7, have been found convenient for work with Pueblo and Maya pottery. In the higher chromas the 7/ values have more color than we associate with a light clay, but these very clear colors are seldom attained by unglazed pottery. Chroma is not included in these definitions because it is influenced more by degree of oxidation than by composition of the oxidized clay.

A few examples will illustrate the usefulness of these broad color classifications. In the study of Rio Grande Glaze-paint wares, it was found that an andesite-tempered type usually had a buff-firing paste, whereas basalt-, sherd-, and sand-tempered pastes were red-firing. The andesite temper was traced to a locality where most of the clays were buff-firing. In this instance the general classification of the clay reinforced evidence of the place of manufacture of a pottery type which was too widely distributed to indicate its source. In other cases the relationship

TABLE 7—PROPOSED COLOR CLASSES OF OXIDIZED POTTERY

Color Class	Hue	Value
Light-firing	Entire range	Over 7/
Buff-firing	Yellower than 2.5YR	7/ and under
Red-firing	2.5YR and redder	7/ and under

of types may be clarified by clay classification; for example, among the common types of Monte Alban are cream, yellow, and gray wares. Oxidizing the gray paste brings out the colors that characterize the yellow types. Paste composition supports this grouping because both the yellow and gray wares have sand temper, whereas the cream ware has a feldspathic temper. Thermal tests will also help explain the changes that take place in pottery types over a period of time; for example, the painted pottery of Awatovi in north-central Arizona starts with black-on-white, goes through black-on-orange to black-on-yellow. Thermal tests showed that the pastes are, respectively, buff-, red-, and buff-firing, which means that black-on-orange introduced a different class of clay along with a different method of firing, and black-on-yellow represented a return to the first class of clay while retaining the new method of firing.

·The reliability of distinctions based on firing behavior of paste is increased if progressive changes in color and density are followed. To interpret the results of such tests the effects of tempering material must be borne in mind. The vitrification point of the clay will be raised by most, but not all, types of temper; color will also be affected by temper, not only through dilution but also by change in density, and by effect on sintering. It is therefore important to determine how pastes compare in texture and type of temper before drawing conclusions regarding the clays from their thermal behavior.

Comparison of a raw clay and a fired body. When an attempt is made to locate the clays used by potters of a prehistoric community, comparison of the clay and the body of the pottery must be made. Under favorable conditions strong circumstantial evidence may be found but direct proof cannot be given. Both mineralogical composition and firing properties should be considered. Each approach holds particular difficulties and sources of error, hence the need of drawing on all lines of evidence. Comparison of the basic mineralogical composition of the clay is limited by the difficulties of identification that have been discussed. Comparison of accessory minerals is simpler and more direct, but it necessitates differentiation of temper and accessory minerals in the pottery. Thermal behavior may seem to afford a simpler approach, but it must be remembered that all the firing properties of a clay are modified by temper, and unless one has data on the kind, amount, and texture of temper in the pottery, he is working blindly. With such data, the raw clay can be similarly tempered, and progressive changes in color, hardness, and density on firing to successive temperatures can be compared with those of the pottery. Matson's study (1945) of unglazed pottery from Seleucia on the Tigris affords an example of a detailed investigation undertaken in order to identify the clays used for given pottery types.

To attempt to identify the particular clay that ancient potters used is, of course, quite a different matter from studying the general characteristics of the clay of a region in relation to the basic characteristics of pottery or from comparing the pastes of different pottery types. Identification means establishing exact identity, and there is always the possibility that other clays may have the same properties as those we have tested. On the other hand, broad comparisons, such as those that have been cited, easily establish differences that may be quite as significant as similarities, and the differences afford a positive answer rather than circumstantial evidence.

The analysis of clay is time-consuming and beset with uncertainties. It should not be undertaken without well-defined objectives and full recognition of the sources of error as well as of the many tempting methods at our disposal. When a realistic approach is made, the data can add materially to our understanding of pottery.

TEMPER AND OTHER NONPLASTIC INCLUSIONS

Temper has proved to be one of the most useful technical features by which to identify pottery. More than that, it often affords clues to the source of trade wares and indicates the relationships between types. There are several reasons for the fruitfulness of paste analysis. One is the great variety of things used for temper. Potters had the curiosity to try out a great many different materials—they ground rocks, sherd, and shell; used volcanic ash; found deposits of diatomaceous or infusorial earth; and burned bark for the silica in it—and it is reasonably clear that they recognized the superiority of certain kinds of materials over others. Innumerable varieties of igneous, sedimentary, and metamorphic rocks were used;

consequently, the identity of minerals and rocks affords a wealth of detail that serves to set one kind of pottery apart from another. A second fortunate circumstance is that we have the means of identifying temper with exactitude by processes that are practicable for extensive application. We can give detailed descriptions because we can spot minute grains of rare minerals and note the particulars of rock texture. We can also make statistical calculations of the temper classes in entire sherd lots from stratigraphic tests because such identifications require hardly more time than it takes to look at the sherds. A third advantage in the analysis of temper is that sherds are just as satisfactory for the purpose as entire vessels. The distinctiveness of temper and its usefulness in classification can be appreciated when differences within plain-surfaced pottery of simple form must be defined. Examples of such pottery made in widely separate places and in different periods may be indistinguishable in outward appearance, but the diverse resources of different localities and the changes in custom of tempering adopted at various times show up plainly in the paste. Moreover, these differences are qualitative and clear-cut.

Methods of temper identification.   The methods of temper identification are primarily microscopic, although supplementary microchemical tests are sometimes employed. Whether a hand lens, a binocular microscope, or a petrographic microscope will be used depends on the coarseness and nature of the material, the exactness of identification required, the quantity of sherds to be analyzed, and, by no means least important, the questions we are attempting to answer. A hand lens is satisfactory only for coarse, easily identifiable material. If exact mineralogical description is required, the petrographic microscope should be used along with the binocular microscope. The latter serves for the preliminary examination that should be made before selecting a sample for detailed petrographic analysis, and for determining the class of temper in lots large enough for statistical summary. The binocular microscope is also essential for techniques requiring manipulation, such as scratch tests of the hardness of individual grains, microchemical tests of constituents, and the separation of grains of particular minerals for petrographic identification in refractive liquids.

As previously noted, pottery can be examined with the petrographic microscope either in thin section or in powdered form. The thin section has many advantages over a powdered sample. It shows the texture of paste, the proportions of inclusions, the size and shape of grains, the relationship and proportions of different constituents, the texture and mineral components of rocks, and the structure and texture of the clay (fig. 12). The thin section can be used for quantitative, as well as qualitative, determinations. With a micrometer eyepiece or a recording micrometer stage, the proportion of temper or the percentage of the different minerals can be measured and the texture of pastes compared (see p. 119).

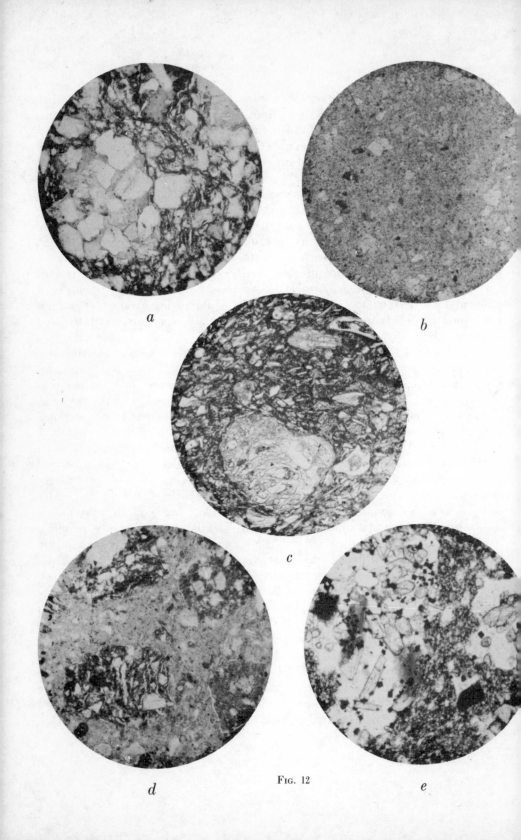

c

d　　　　　　　　　　Fig. 12　　　　　　　　　　e

This technique is applicable only to equidimensional inclusions. Estimates can be made for platy or needle-like temper by comparison with prepared standards of similar materials. Finally the thin section constitutes a record that can be kept permanently for reference and comparison.

Sherds submitted for petrographic analysis should be selected carefully, in view of the expense of preparing thin sections. Although it is true that a distinct paste may in itself be sufficient to mark a sherd as intrusive or to assign it to a known type, ordinarily it is important to relate a paste to the exterior features of the vessel, its finish, shape, and decoration if present. When the sherds submitted for analysis are small, featureless, and of undefined type, the petrographic analysis, no matter how accurate and detailed, can give only a loose tag end of datum. There should be no hesitancy in submitting rare sherds or ones that show design and form exceptionally well, because petrographic analysis is not a destructive procedure. Much can be learned from powder scraped from a broken edge, and if the chip for a thin section itself is cut with a diamond saw, a quarter-inch wide sliver from a nearly straight edge is adequate. It is also possible to sample many entire vessels without destroying their exhibit value, by cutting a small disc from the base with a circular saw. If a vessel is to be restored from sherds, a chip can be held out from an inconspicuous part.

In connection with a permanent file of thin sections, the importance of keeping sherds that are sampled as "controls" should be recognized. There are two reasons why this is important. First, we need a record of the pottery that has been analyzed, and neither verbal descriptions nor illustrations are as satisfactory as the actual sherds. Second, when distinctive inclusions are found in the petrographic section, we need to examine the paste with the binocular microscope to ascertain whether or not these inclusions can be recognized, thus permitting a finer and more significant identification to be made by the quick method. This process of checking back and forth from specimen to petrographic section is important and can be facilitated by mounting small chips from control sherds for quick reference and easy handling.

The second basic technique used with the petrographic microscope is the examination of powdered samples immersed in refractive liquids, for which a set of 40 or more stable liquids graded and accurately calibrated with respect to

---

FIG. 12—TEMPERING MATERIALS

Photomicrographs of thin sections taken in ordinary light, magnification 45×. *a:* Medium-textured paste with sandstone temper. *b:* Fine-textured paste with nonplastic inclusions such as occur naturally in silty clays. *c:* Vitric ash temper. A common texture showing vesicular particles and irregular splinters. *d:* Sherd temper. The sherd fragments have a sharp, irregular outline, vary in texture and color, and contain grains of sand temper. *e:* Igneous rock temper. Sanidine basalt with augite and magnetite crystals enclosed in sanidine.

refractive index is required. The powdered sample can be prepared by grinding a flake of pottery or by locating grains of particular inclusions, prying them out with a needle, and powdering them. The preparation of a mount requires only a few minutes, and the method is entirely satisfactory for the identification of minerals; but since it does not show their associations, it often fails to indicate their source. For example, it alone would not show whether minerals were derived from rock or sand. The binocular microscope does enable us to make this distinction; we can pick out rock fragments and determine their mineral components in oil mounts, which leaves us in doubt only of the details of rock texture. Refractive liquids, therefore, afford a relatively quick and flexible method for petrographic identification, but they fail to give the complete picture of the paste that the thin section does, and the mounts are not permanent.

Special methods of separation of minerals might be mentioned in connection with the examination of powders. If a paste is very soft and contains a hard temper, such as sand, it can be powdered without crushing the sand grains. A more effective separation of clay and inclusions can often be obtained by rubbing the sample in water with a hard rubber pestle. The clay can then be washed out and the minerals separated by gravity, using heavy liquids. This method is especially useful for a sand containing minor proportions of small grains of high specific gravity. The method concentrates the minerals of this class from a far larger sample than that included in thin section. An alternative method of separation is by magnetic properties, using an electromagnet. This requires clean separation of minerals and clay for satisfactory results. In general the usefulness of both methods is limited by the difficulty of obtaining complete separation when the pottery has been well fired.

Background in optical theory is not required in order to use the binocular microscope because it only magnifies and gives a stereoscopic image, but more is required than visual acuity, important as that is. Knowledge and experience sharpen perception, and some knowledge of mineralogy, though not essential for the simplest temper identifications, will increase materially both the number of specific identifications that can be made and their reliability. A number of the properties that are observed in identifying a mineral from a hand specimen can also be recognized on the microscopic grain. These include cleavage, crystal form, hardness, color, opacity or translucency, and luster. Cleavage and crystal forms are not observed as frequently in microscopic grains as in a student mineral collection, but they are by no means uncommon and they are important diagnostics. Hardness can always be estimated by scratching the grain with the fine point of a needle, and sometimes characteristic cleavage can be obtained by pressing the point against a grain. For these manipulations the binocular microscope is very convenient. In any case, in order to use the binocular microscope, familiarity with the appearance of the minerals, rocks, and other kinds of temper that occur in pottery is necessary. The archaeologist should first study identified samples thoroughly and systematically; and when he commences to identify unknowns he should have his identifications checked repeatedly until their reliability is well established. Even after he has acquired considerable experience, he will find that knowledge of the characteristics shown in thin section will bring to his attention many distinctive details that would otherwise be overlooked.

The special advantages of the binocular microscope have already been mentioned (p. 140). Once the archaeologist has become accustomed to its use, he will be as lost without it as a nearsighted man without his glasses because a sherd takes on character and meaning when its paste is examined microscopically.

Ideally the petrographic and binocular microscopes should be used to supplement each other. There are chances of error in identifications with the binocular microscope because distinct materials have superficial resemblances; also, there are definite limitations. For example, sherd, limestone, feldspar crystals, and igneous rock can be distinguished, but to identify the igneous rock or judge whether feldspar crystals are from ground rock or from sand often requires the petrographic microscope. When the archaeologist uses the binocular microscope, he can have the benefit of petrographic data by working in co-operation with a technologist. Finally, in reporting paste composition, the method used in identification, as well as the size of the sample examined, should always be reported.

Microchemical tests can supplement microscopic examination in the study of temper, although they are rarely required when the petrographic microscope is used in analysis. To perform microchemical tests, grains can be removed from the paste and treated in any way required, or, for reactions that take place in cold solution, the reagent can be applied to the thin section before the cover glass is mounted or to individual grains in the paste. In the last case the reaction is observed with the binocular microscope. A few tests can be performed in the field. Probably the ones for carbonates would be most frequently used by archaeologists. These are described under the discussion of limestone temper (p. 381).

Distinction between natural inclusions and temper. A fundamental question regarding the mineral inclusions in pottery is how to distinguish temper from the accessory minerals of a clay. In the vast majority of pastes, the characteristics of the inclusions answer this question; that is, they are materials that do not occur naturally in clay—for example, sherd, various igneous, sedimentary, and metamorphic rock fragments; coarse sands; and pumice. Often grain size and relative abundance show whether or not a material is a temper. For instance, quartz as fine silt occurs in some clays, but coarse, waterworn sand does not become mixed with them in the processes of nature; or volcanic dust settling in a lake where clay is being deposited may become incorporated with it, but the ash does not occur in the quantity and particle size in which it is generally found in pottery. Coarse mineral grains do occur in residual clays, but they are not waterworn.

There are two classes of paste with nonplastic inclusions that could be either original or added constituents. One is fine and silty, the other highly micaceous. The principal mineral in the silty paste is quartz. Mica, calcite, shells of foraminifers, volcanic dust, and rare grains of the more stable of the heavy minerals may also occur in these pastes. They may be untempered, coarse sedimentary clays, but fine texture alone does not prove that they are. Silt may have been used as temper. In pottery containing siltlike inclusions, the relative uniformity of texture among sherds may be significant. If a sandy clay were used, the amount and grain size of inclusions would generally be more uniform than if silt were added as temper.

Most of the pottery with silty paste that I have examined has not had the range in texture I would expect had it been tempered. I have referred to these as "pastes having the texture of untempered clay" because the evidence that they are not tempered is at best circumstantial. A less awkward term is needed. A simple textural term, "fine paste," is often applied to them but logically it should be used in a strictly textural sense, and some tempered pastes would then be included in it. A descriptive term, such as "fine silty paste" might be applied. Those pastes in which inclusions of any kind are very sparse, a fact which can be established only by petrographic examination, can be designated untempered. In no case does the adoption of such terms relieve us of the responsibility of weighing and reporting the evidence bearing on the question whether or not the pottery was tempered.

Pastes containing a high percentage of mica are frequently referred to as mica-tempered. This term is misleading because it implies that mica was added by the potter, whereas a micaceous paste may be rock-tempered or untempered. We are accustomed to think of an untempered paste as exceptionally fine-textured, but this is not true of a residual clay because these clays contain the stable minerals of the rock from which they were formed. A residual clay derived from a mica granite contains numerous flakes of mica and grains of quartz, and these may be as coarse and abundant as grains in a tempered clay. Consequently, such residual clays do not require temper and the mica may be quite conspicuous, especially as flakes tend to be forced in a position parallel to the surface in the finishing process. It may be difficult in some instances to distinguish a residual clay paste from one tempered with sand high in mica, or a mica-bearing rock such as gneiss and schist. Petrographic analysis of thin sections is desirable for the identification of micaceous pastes; when an analysis cannot be obtained, the paste should be described as micaceous rather than as mica-tempered.

Nonplastic inclusions as criteria for identification. Microscopic methods for identifying nonplastic inclusions are practicable and reliable. The question is, Of what value are the data that are obtained? We might consider first the usefulness of temper in classification. In any region, the value of temper for purposes of classification will depend in part on the variety of geological formations that potters drew upon, and also on the stability of custom with respect to choice of temper. A region like the upper Rio Grande Valley where there is volcanic ash, basalt, andesite and related igneous rocks, sandstone, schist, sands, and residual and sedimentary clays, and where all of them, in one locality or another, found their way into the pottery, affords the most favorable opportunity for definition of paste types and location of sources of temper. The usefulness of temper data also depends in part on its distinctiveness and the ease with which it can be identified. When one finds a rare type of rock, such as the sanidine basalt that was used by Pueblo potters at the eastern foot of the Chuska range, the pottery is about as clearly labeled as it ever can be. Temper may be so distinctive that the pottery types it characterizes can be recognized even though the surface is destroyed and the sherds are found hundreds of miles from their source. This was done, for example, in the case of the Mexican ware, Thin Orange, when eroded fragments were found at Uaxactun in Guatemala and at Copan in Honduras. But these are the rare rocks. The potters did not always oblige us by choosing unusual kinds. The question is, What can be done with common material of wide distribution? On the whole, the possibilities of finding special varieties among the common materials are greater than is usually realized. However, the more detailed the identifications that are required, the more time-consuming the analyses and the less the likelihood of recognizing the specific variety of material with the binocular microscope. Consequently, temper is necessarily less useful for some types and in some localities than in others. To illustrate the possibilities of differentiation of varieties within a class of tempering material, four classes that are common in American Indian pottery are discussed in Appendix C.

Consistency in selection of temper. A fundamental question with regard to temper is how consistent potters were in their practice of tempering. Did they have individual preferences among the various materials available to them and did they try new materials from time to time, producing at one time and in one place pottery in the same stylistic tradition with a variety of pastes? The value of paste analysis depends in no small measure on the answer to this question because if there were no consistency in practice, temper would have little value either for distinguishing types or tracing their source. The question cannot be answered directly, but the clearest evidence bearing on it is to be found in the uniformity or lack of uniformity of pottery types. This argument appears circular when one recalls that the pottery type is generally defined as being homogeneous in paste; but for the medium to fine pastes here considered, this condition cannot be established without microscopic analysis, and for practical purposes this part of the definition has been ignored by archaeologists. We have a broad basis for judgment in the vast volume of pottery from both the Southwest and Mesoamerica that has been analyzed. Many of the samples sent to the laboratory are classified with respect to exterior appearance. They appear to belong to the same stylistic tradition. These preliminary classifications cannot affect the judgment of the technologist because his identifications are based on entirely independent evidence and are made by methods that free him from personal bias. The paste uniformity of types representing an established ceramic tradition is remarkable. The variations that are usually found are the simple, quantitative ones that would result from individual differences in grading and measuring. Where there is lack of uniformity in the temper of a type, the pottery is re-examined to determine whether or not it is completely homogeneous in surface features and style. Many times diversity of paste within a type calls to our attention differences in style that otherwise pass unnoticed. Whenever a difference in temper can be correlated with a difference in body clay, slip, finishing technique, shape, decoration, or any other feature, the evidence for a difference in source or tradition is strengthened.

Extreme conservatism in the selection of temper is illustrated by the customs of some Pueblo potters. The Rio Grande potters of San Ildefonso, Santa Clara, and San Juan use fine volcanic ash, and the prehistoric pottery of the region shows a continuous use of this temper for certain types back to the earliest times. Zia pottery is tempered with ground basalt, and the same temper occurs in the prehistoric Glaze-paint ware of this area. Again, Acoma and Zuni potters use potsherd, which carries on the tradition of the prehistoric peoples in these localities.

These instances of conservatism in the selection of tempering material are striking but perhaps not surprising. When a satisfactory material is found, there is little reason for change because temper is not like paint or clay with which different colors and effects can be obtained with the introduction of new materials. The fact remains, however, that changes in paste composition are often found when a stratigraphic sequence of pottery types is followed through. In all such instances the cause of change, whether a native development or the result of the influence of people with a different ceramic tradition or change in population, should be sought. Premature generalizations regarding conservatism should not be allowed to limit or discourage such investigations.

Our chief concern in considering the reliability of paste composition as a criterion for classification is the uniformity of temper within groups that are stylistically uniform. The paste uniformity of a great many pottery types, that is, the correlation of paste and style, has been well established. Yet exceptions do occur. The same potters may have used several tempering materials indiscriminately, or potters of the various settlements within a region having the same stylistic tradition may have been dependent on different natural resources for temper. The differences in the significance of these two causes points up the importance of ascertaining whether or not paste variations are correlated with differences in clay or unrecognized differences in style or technique. When a question of this kind arises, a large sample of the type should be sorted by paste and the groups compared systematically with respect to other features. The justification for such studies is to be found in the large number of instances in which paste composition has been a means of establishing a common origin.

Interpretation of petrographic data. The value of temper identification in the recognition of intrusives has been stressed repeatedly. Some of the most striking results of technological studies have given strong circumstantial evidence of trade that was not indicated by superficial features. Since the bases for judgment are considered at length under Interpretation of Ceramic Data (pp. 336–41), it will suffice to review the main points here.

Petrographic analysis aids in identifying intrusives under four circumstances: (1) When there has been extensive exchange within a region in which the same basic styles and techniques were followed. Paste then shows local differences which surface appearance, design, and shape, at least as they are observed in the sherd, do not. (2) When pottery was imported in sufficient quantities to give the appearance of local manufacture. Petrographic analysis can show that the materials are foreign, whereas stylistic data do not because styles can be copied. Clays, tempering, and pigments can be imported, but tempering material is the least likely to be obtained from distant sources, because its specifications are broad and because something that will serve the purpose can be found nearly everywhere. (3) When well-known pottery types with distinctive pastes occur in sherds too poorly preserved for recognition from outward appearance. (4) When there are unidentified or new types that can be recognized as probable intrusives by a distinctive temper. This situation occurs most frequently in little-explored areas. These postulated intrusives have potential significance and should be recorded fully and preserved for reference when knowledge of the area is extended.

In view of the value of temper analysis for the identification of trade ware, it is important to understand the requirements for such identification and the bases for interpretation. There are two general cases. In the first, a specimen is suspected of being an intrusive, and its source and relationships are postulated from surface features. All that is necessary in such instances is to analyze the unknown and a sample of the pottery to which it is thought to belong. The principal caution is with regard to sampling the type with which the unknown is to be compared. The sample should be collected with regard to possible lack of homogeneity and regional variation. A difference noted when only a few sherds are examined from part of the range of the type will be inconclusive; that is, lack of correspondence can be interpreted as indicating lack of relation only when the type chosen is well known. If correspondence is found, the distinctness of the material and the limitations of its use will determine the degree of assurance with which identity can be postulated.

In the second case, a general study is made of a pottery collection from a site, horizon, or region, and the technologist is asked to define the paste types and to distinguish the local from the foreign. In these instances also adequate sampling is obviously of primary importance. One must know what the preponderant pastes are and the range of variation in them in order to be prepared to recognize the strange ones. A handful of representative sherds is not sufficient for this purpose. Simple rules cannot be laid down to define the size of an adequate sample because much depends on the number of pottery types, their elaboration, the variability of their pastes, and on the length of periods of their manufacture. There are many instances in which it is desirable to examine entire lots in order to recognize all possible intrusives. Some of the intrusives in any lot will be recognized from surface appearance, but others will be featureless, or weathered, or undefined, and in order to have full data all sherds of doubtful classification should be analyzed. In this case a quick method of identifying paste class is essential, and it is in these studies that the binocular microscope used in conjunction with the petrographic is most useful.

No less important than sampling is the analytical technique used. The requirements will again depend on circumstances, particularly on the coarseness of the temper and on its class. In the studies made to date, certain unusual kinds of temper have been found only in certain pottery types. Such materials are most often igneous rocks that are either rare or seldom used—for example, in the Southwest the sanidine basalt of Black-on-white pottery from sites along the eastern foot of the Chuska range, the diabase of the Bluff variety of Alma plain, in Mesoamerica the variety of schist in Thin Orange ware, and the vitrophyre of Plumbate.

Some classes of tempering material include a greater number of distinct varieties than others. Of all the materials used for temper, igneous rocks are the most diverse, and their identification is a straightforward matter of petrographic identification based on mineralogical composition and texture. Petrographic analysis is essential for identification, but an igneous rock can be distinguished easily from other classes of temper with the binocular microscope provided paste texture is not too fine. Certain classes of igneous rock temper can also be recognized with the binocular microscope, since differences in texture and color can be observed, but many identifications have to be made with the petrographic microscope. Metamorphic rocks also occur in great variety although they are not so commonly used for temper as igneous rocks. The requirements for their identification are the same as those for igneous rocks. The two main classes of sedimentary rock temper—sandstone and the carbonate rocks—can be distinguished with the binocular microscope and simple chemical tests, although, as in practically all cases, the petrographic microscope must be used to identify varieties. The problem of differentiating varieties of other common materials—such as sand, sherd, and volcanic ash—is more involved, as I have indicated in the discussion of these materials (Appendix C). Whether detailed petrographic identification or mere recognition of classes is required will depend on the nature of the problem under consideration. The class of temper is often sufficient to label a sherd as a probable intrusive, but to postulate its source, petrographic data are generally required. The important circumstance regarding analysis is that when identifications have been made with the petrographic microscope, classes of paste can be distinguished quickly with the binocular microscope and consequently paste analysis is practicable for large samples such as are obtained in stratigraphic testing.

To distinguish possible or probable intrusives by means of distinctive paste composition is quite simple; to determine the source of such sherds is generally more difficult. The technologist cannot always go into the field and search for the material used as temper; even if he does locate a possible source, he may not be able to prove that the temper came from it and not from some other exposure of the same or similar formation. Negative evidence is inconclusive also because we cannot take time to become as thoroughly familiar with the resources of an area as the potters were. Nevertheless a general knowledge of the geology of an area is important because it will show where certain materials could or could not have occurred.

Since location of the source of temper is the obvious means of ascertaining the source of intrusive pottery, it is necessary to stress that there are other more practicable means. Often the clearest evidence is obtained from the geographic distribution of the paste type represented by the intrusive. The relative frequency of a type within a site does not offer a sound basis for distinguishing indigenous from trade ware because pottery can be traded in large volume; but when a study can be based on pottery collected in surface survey from sites throughout an area, the evidence is much clearer because it shows centers of high frequency of occurrence and diminishing percentage with distance from these centers.

There is still another possibility of recognizing the source of pottery when it is widely distributed and has a distinctive paste. This rests on the fact that the same paste was sometimes used for types that were traded and those that were made only for domestic use. In other words, additional circumstantial evidence of source is obtained when associated wares have the same paste as the type in question. The significance of paste similarities depends, of course, on the distinctiveness of the temper and the restriction of its natural distribution.

The pottery type has been used extensively as a tool for establishing the relative chronological position of sites or deposits, and the question is often asked, What contribution does paste composition offer toward this end? It is hardly necessary to point out that paste analysis frequently confirms the identification of a definitive type. Its value as an independent means of establishing time relations has not been demonstrated as often. The usefulness of paste for this purpose depends upon frequency of change in custom of tempering. If clear modifications of style occur more often than changes in temper, then style will be more useful as a chronological indicator than composition. This relation is not invariable. There are instances in which paste changes while the exterior features, as far as they can be judged from the potsherds, are constant.

Another value of paste analysis which could well be exploited more fully than it has been in the past is the study of evidences of a common source of pottery having different style and finish. Plain and decorated types and types having different techniques of decoration, the outward appearance of which gives no indication of a common origin, may be shown to have identical pastes. In some instances distribution will bring out associations that suggest relationship, but the technological data are more direct and more easily obtained. Neglect of evidence of this kind results in an oversimplified picture of pottery production.

The purpose of this discussion has been to point out some of the possibilities of interpretation of petrographic data and to emphasize the importance of adequate sampling and of drawing on independent lines of evidence. In petrographic analysis we possess a keen analytical tool. Whether the information obtained by its use remains an item of description or becomes a means of explaining the sources and relationships of pottery types depends largely on the formulation of problems and adequacy of sampling.

PAINTS AND GLAZES

In the identification of paint composition, chemistry comes to the fore. Microscopic methods are secondary because paints, unlike the rocks and sands so frequently used for nonplastic material, are generally chemically homogeneous. Furthermore, their original form is often destroyed in firing, and therefore petrographic examination cannot reveal the mineral or minerals from which they were derived. Information on their source must be sought by indirect means.

The particular methods of analysis that will be chosen in the study of paints depends on the information required. When the only purpose is classification, a qualitative test that will identify the major constituents is generally sufficient. The tests most frequently used are simple and can even be performed in the field if necessary (see Appendix D). But they are adequate only for routine work. Once one has learned something about the nature of pigments, their sources, the wide range in their properties, the changes they undergo in firing, and the causes of their defects, he will no longer be satisfied to stop with general identification because paints present challenging questions regarding technique. The firing behavior of mineral pigments is modified by the various impurities that most of them carry; these impurities afford means of differentiating varieties within a major paint class and of distinguishing material from different sources. Since impurities are significant, complete qualitative analysis is often desirable, and spectrography affords the most practicable method for this purpose because it identifies all the metallic elements, even in traces, and can be applied quickly and on small samples. For the determination of the major and principal minor constituents, sensitive microchemical tests can be used. Although these do not require expensive equipment, they are time-consuming. Quantitative analysis is required when the proportions of elements have some significance, as, for example, when percentage composition distinguishes classes or explains properties. Since paint samples are generally very much smaller than the samples required for the standard methods of chemical analysis, exacting microchemical procedures must be employed, and it is rarely feasible to make a complete analysis.

Microscopic examination, although a secondary method in the study of fired paints, has its place, which will be illustrated in the discussion of special problems of paint analysis (p. 175). The physical properties of paint give some information also and they can be studied without instrumental aid.

Physical properties.   From the practical standpoint a paint will be judged by its spreading and covering quality and by its color and adherence after firing. The analyst will also ask if it was applied as a solution or a suspension (a fine powder dispersed in a liquid) with or without a medium, if color was modified in firing, and how permanence was obtained. These questions point up the importance of the physical properties of a paint, since they offer clues to many of the answers.

Colors considered in relation to firing conditions afford some clues to composition. Differences due to variable firing conditions, which are judged by the color of the vessel surface, are significant; thus one will note color differences in and adjacent to firing-clouds on oxidized ware and in the accidentally oxidized areas of reduced ware. The distinct effect of the oxidation state on the color of the iron oxide paints—the red of the ferric and black of the ferro-ferric oxide—is familiar. The iron-manganese paints, which are bone black, become more brown on reduction but the change is not distinct. Black carbon paint turns gray and becomes increasingly light when oxidized. Color changes in the argillaceous paints are comparable to those in clays.

There are more or less subtle color differences between pigments within the same color range; for example, the manganese paints have, as a rule, a brownish cast as compared with black iron oxide. But the slightly or partially oxidized iron oxide paints range through a variety of browns, and color alone is not a reliable criterion of composition.

The relief of a paint, together with its luster and texture, indicate the physical state in which it was applied—as a solution or as a suspension. The soluble paints, such as plant extracts, sink into the body without disturbing the arrangement of surface particles. On firing, the thin surface film is oxidized, and color is imparted by the carbon that is held in the clay. As practically no material is left on the surface, these paints lack relief and are similar in texture and luster to the unpainted surface. On the other hand, paints that are suspensions leave a deposit that covers the surface. Their texture and luster are independent of the body on which they are applied. Since the mineral paints are insoluble and therefore form suspensions, they normally have some relief, and the exceptions are easily recognized. Soft mineral paints may become so eroded that only pigment embedded in the pores remains, or a mineral paint may be pressed into the damp surface of the vessel by polishing and thus be made even with it. A polished mineral paint can be recognized by strokes of the polishing tool and by smearing on the edges of lines. Luster is not common in a paint applied as a suspension, but aside from the effect of polishing, it may be produced by vitrification. The two causes of luster are easily distinguished by the relief of the paint and its hardness. Vitrification is uncommon. The carbon paints obtained from plant extracts which are applied as solutions are usually lustrous, not in consequence of any treatment they received after application, but because they were applied on a polished surface which they do not conceal.

The hardness of pigments that are applied as suspensions indicates their degree of bonding and their relative permanence. The paint is easily brushed off if there is no bonding. The extent of bonding can often be judged by scraping the surface while viewing it with a binocular microscope. One can recognize, for example, partial bonding, as when a firm surface film is formed and the paint beneath is powdery, and also the difference in bonding in different areas. The color of the powder obtained in this way is comparable to that of the streak obtained in the common test for ore. In this test the opaque mineral is powdered when rubbed on a porcelain plate.

Uniformity of color and covering power are largely dependent on concentration and body of a pigment. The depth of color of a soluble paint bears a direct relation to its concentration and viscosity because they determine the amount of colorant applied and effect the degree of penetration. Covering power of a pigment in suspension will be affected by fineness of particle size where the coat is thin, and uniformity of color will be influenced by the properties of the medium. If the pigment is to be spread uniformly, it is necessary to have a medium that will not be sucked into the dry paste as soon as the brush touches it. A plant extract such as is used in the Southwest for carbon paint affords a satisfactory medium for mineral paints because of its viscosity. The length of the brush stroke, difference in line width and in intensity of color at the beginning and end of a stroke are indicative of spreading quality.

These remarks are intended to suggest how the physical properties of paint assist in identification, and what they tell about the quality of paint and the technique of painting. Physical properties are useful for identification when the classes of paint that may occur in a given sample are known and their properties have been fully described. The black paints of the Southwest afford an excellent example (see Appendix D).

Identification of the basic constituents of a paint.   We have considered the physical properties by which soluble paints and pigments that are suspensions can be distinguished. These observations are useful in the classification of large lots of sherds when the only purpose is to separate these two fundamentally different classes. To use these properties effectively and reliably, basic composition of the paint should first be established by extensive testing. The identity of the paints of Pueblo Black-on-white ware, for example, was not recognized until they were tested chemically and by oxidation (Hawley, 1929). It is important, therefore, to understand the requirements of qualitative chemical tests for major constituents.

Chemical analyses must be carried out on a micro scale because of the difficulty, or more often the impossibility, of obtaining a sample large enough for macro methods. To collect the sample, it is advisable to observe the process of scraping with a binocular microscope to avoid digging into the clay and contaminating the paint. A diamond point or a carborundum crystal makes a good scraper. The area of painted surface required for a sample varies greatly, depending on the thickness of the coat. A minute pile of powder the size of the head of an ordinary pin is adequate for a single microqualitative test, which can be performed on the corner of a glass slide. The sample is taken into solution in a drop of acid with gentle heating, care being exercised to prevent the drop from spreading. Reagents are then added as drops or grains, and a positive test is marked by the formation of a distinctive color or a crystalline phase. After a paint sample has been taken into solution, the test can also be carried out on filter paper which has been impregnated with the reagent, the drop being confined by a ring of paraffin. Tests for iron and manganese, two of the most common elements in pigments, can easily be performed by the archaeologist, and procedures for them are therefore outlined in Appendix D. Less familiar classes of paint should be identified in the laboratory because it may be necessary to draw on a number of tests and to check for interfering substances.

Methods of chemical analysis have been stressed in this discussion, but the place of microscopic examination in the study of paint should not be overlooked. Aside from the usefulness of the binocular microscope in the study of the physical properties of paints, the petrographic microscope shows whether or not a sample is homogeneous. The mineralogical purity of a paint and mixtures of colorants can be recognized in this way. The paint is powdered and immersed in a drop of a refractive liquid for examination. Certain pigments of classic Maya polychrome pottery illustrate admixtures of minerals. They include pinks and violets in which particles of ferric oxide and white clay can be seen; browns composed of manganese ore and ferric oxide; and grays that are mixtures of manganese ore and white clay. All such mixtures are readily detected microscopically, whereas chemical tests alone would not prove whether different substances had been combined or a highly impure pigment had been used.

Special problems in paint analysis.   The assignment of a paint to a major class such as carbon, black iron oxide, iron-manganese or argillaceous, serves for general description, but it leaves many questions unanswered. One may want to know if the paints of particular types came from the same or different sources, what minerals or ores were used, what makes iron oxide paints adherent, and whether a difference in color of paint was caused by difference in composition or in firing technique.

Either qualitative or quantitative differences in paints of the same class may indicate that they were derived from different sources. Qualitative differences will be found in the minor and trace elements, which are most readily detected spectrographically. An application of this method is illustrated in the discussion of glaze paints. Quantitative differences in the major constituents can be determined either microchemically or by quantitative spectrographic analysis. As a test of the practicability of spectrography the manganese-iron ratios in a series of 40 paint samples from the Pueblo and Maya areas was determined by Dr. Rockwell Kent III at Massachusetts Institute of Technology. As a check of the reliability of the spectrographic data, three samples were analyzed microchemically by use of a photometer for colorimetric determinations of iron with thioglycolic acid and manganese as permanganate (Table 8).

TABLE 8—COMPARISON OF RESULTS OF SPECTROGRAPHIC AND MICROCHEMICAL DETERMINATION OF MANGANESE-IRON RATIO

Source of Sample	Spectrographic	Colorimetric
La Plata Pueblo I Black-on-red	.11	.12
Jeddito Black-on-yellow	.084	.0795
Uaxactun, Tzakol polychrome	.56	.49

The first spectrographic analyses were estimated to have a possible error as great as 25 per cent, later reduced to 10 per cent. The Uaxactun sample was among the earlier. Only the more reliable results are shown in Table 9 to give an idea of regional variation. Although there is considerable range of values within sites and localities, there are nevertheless consistent differences between areas and pottery types.

TABLE 9—RATIO OF MANGANESE TO IRON IN IRON-MANGANESE ORE PAINTS

PUEBLO I BLACK-ON-RED		JEDDITO		CLASSIC MAYA POLYCHROMES	
La Plata	Chuska	Black-on-orange	Black-on-yellow	Uaxactun	San Jose, British Honduras
.09	.95	.08	.31	.56	.25
.13	.48	.13	.21	.71	.25
.11	.35	.14		.48	
.15	.52			.62	
.29	.40			.44	
.29				.58	
.06				.69	
				.60	

These figures give an idea of the range in ratio of the two major constituents in this type of paint. The Pueblo I Black-on-red sample illustrates the possible significance of data of this kind. This is a minor pottery type widely distributed in the San Juan area. The paste of sherds from different parts of the area are alike in having an igneous rock temper that could have been derived from any one of several laccolithic formations. It was not known whether the examples from the La Plata region and those from Chuska some 50 miles to the southwest were each made locally or were obtained in trade from a single source. The quantitative spectrographic analyses, showing average manganese-iron ratios of .16 in the La Plata and .54 in the Chuska sites and no overlapping in the range of the two, indicate that the pigment was from different sources. This pottery type was not brought in to the two regions from the same source. Quantitative determinations, although they give significant evidence of this kind, are more time-consuming than petrographic analysis, and therefore would be employed only when petrographic evidence of source of pottery is inconclusive.

An investigation of the cause of permanence of the black iron oxide paint of Pueblo pottery will illustrate some of the methods that can be brought to bear on questions raised by the properties of paints. These iron oxide paints must have been prepared as a powder. What makes them hard and adherent? Any organic medium would burn out on firing and have no permanent binding effect. In the investigation of this question two possibilities were considered: the presence of an impurity that fluxes with the paint, and physical changes in the iron oxide itself during the process of reduction.

In order to learn whether or not the minor constituents included fluxes, spectrographic analyses were made by Dr. E. G. Zies, of the Carnegie Institution's Geophysical Laboratory, of four samples from the La Plata region. Two of the samples had a matte surface, two were vitrified. The latter had the appearance of a black glaze. The fact that vitrified paints are of sporadic occurrence on pottery that corresponds to the matte-paint type in every other respect suggests that vitrification was accidental.

As the paint is an attractive, thin, smooth, glossy black, free of defects, the potters would almost certainly have used it more frequently had they understood how to produce it. Since alkali is a common fluxing agent, the assumption had been made that these vitreous paints were alkali glazes formed when natural fluxes were accidentally included with the pigment. Contrary to expectation, the spectrograms of these paints gave no evidence that vitrification was caused by an alkali. A small amount of sodium was present in two samples but absent or present only as a trace in the other two, including one of the glazes. Potassium was estimated as present in less than 1 per cent because of the absence of the weaker ultra-violet lines of this element. The alkaline earths, calcium and magnesium, occurred as minor constituents or traces; other impurities—manganese, aluminum, and titanium—were of minor and variable occurrence, but silica showed a well-developed spectrum in all samples. Composition, therefore, indicates that the vitrified paint is an iron-silica glass and that the iron oxide itself, when reduced to the ferrous state, supplies the flux. A sample of an ironstone pebble found in excavations of the region also contained considerable silica; the other impurities corresponded to those of the paint with the exception of barium, which was present in the pebble and absent in the paint analyzed. The fact that vitrified iron oxide paints are not more common is doubtless explained by the variable amount of silica in ironstone pebbles and by the particular firing conditions—strong reduction in the higher temperature range—required to form sufficient ferrous oxide to vitrify the pigment fully. It is clear from microscopic examination, however, that incipient vitrification was not uncommon and undoubtedly was an important cause of permanence of the paint.

Another factor that may affect the permanence of the reduced iron oxide paint is the physical change referred to as sintering—that is, the tendency of the iron oxide particles when heated, and especially if the oxygen content changes, to become more compact and to unite in a more or less coherent mass. In order to learn whether or not sintering was a factor in the permanence of this paint, polished sections such as those used in metallographic studies were prepared and studied with a vertical illuminator (an accessory of the microscope used for the study of opaque specimens). The sections, first impregnated with bakelite to bind the loose material, were cut transversely through the coat of paint. The vertical illuminator affords means of studying difference in reflectance of opaque minerals, and it reveals the structure of opaque paints. Very fine powdery material diffuses light, and large grains or coherent masses reflect it. The soft paints show a granular texture, light being reflected from individual grains, but the harder paint has a distinctive structure distinguished by porous masses showing irregular nets of contiguous or united particles, an indication of sintering. Both soft and hard paints appear homogeneous. The vitrified paint, on the other hand, appears nonhomogeneous; brilliantly illumined grains are scattered through a pale gray matrix. Many of the grains are collected near the outer surface of the paint. The gray white material is the iron-silica glass; the bright grains are particles of iron oxide which were not dissolved in the glass.

It is desirable to test hypothetical explanations that are suggested by analytical data. One means is to apply a postulated technique and compare the effects obtained with the characteristics of the material under consideration. In the investigation of the black iron oxide paint, experiments were made with pigments prepared from ferric oxide, magnetite, and ironstone pebbles fired in oxidizing and reducing atmospheres to different temperatures. As was anticipated, samples remained soft and powdery when fired in oxidizing atmosphere, but when reduced, the reds and brown changed to dark or blackish gray. When reduced above 900°C, they became crusted on the surface, though some brownish powdery material remained underneath. Since this reaction was obtained with commercial iron oxide free of silica, the effect must be attributed to sintering. The appearance was more metallic than that of typical Pueblo black-on-white ware paints although some of the earliest paints have this effect. When commercial ferric oxide was painted on clay and fired in reducing atmosphere to 1100°C, a glass was formed at the contact of paint and clay, the ferrous oxide having reacted with the silica of the body. These tests were conducted in an electric resistance furnace using charcoal to produce a reducing atmosphere. The atmosphere in primitive firing was much more variable. Additional tests were therefore made using wood fuel in a pit kiln. In these tests, vitrified paints were obtained at 1100°C, suggesting that the requirement of very high temperature may have been the limiting factor in the production of an iron-silica glaze with primitive firing methods.

Both causes of permanence that have been suggested are dependent on reduction of ferric oxide in firing, a fact consistent with the observation that hard paints are black and the soft ones are brown or reddish. It is necessary to guard against the supposition that a single factor is operative in instances of this kind. Sintering and incipient vitrification have contributed to permanence of the iron oxide pigments in the La Plata district. Whether or not they are also the principal factors affecting the permanence of this class of paint in other parts of the Pueblo area has not yet been tested. Different sources of iron oxide were used in different regions, and firing techniques may also have differed. The iron oxide paints of the Mimbres area, for example, were accidentally oxidized more often than the paints of the San Juan area. To ascertain whether or not this difference is due to composition would require qualitative analyses for impurities and quantitative determination of proportions of major constituents. If no significant differences were found, the evidences of technique in the two areas would have to be investigated. Extensive analyses, utilizing a number of chemical and physical methods, would be required because the problem involves far more than mere identification. Before undertaking such an investigation, one would wish to consider how significant a difference in technique would be. It is more than a matter of passing curiosity in this instance because the assumption that Mimbres people learned to make black-on-white pottery from northern people has been accepted generally, but the extent of their dependence has never been determined by systematic comparison.

A method of rendering powdery mineral paints less fugitive, which is entirely different from those just discussed, is the application of an organic coat after firing. The identification of these protective coats is discussed under postfiring paints (p. 178).

The method of paint analysis that is recommended in any particular case depends on initial information regarding the paint and on the kind of information desired. If the classes of paint which occur in an area have been well defined by extensive tests and if they exhibit clear-cut differences in physical properties, the trained archaeologist can identify the majority of specimens by direct observation; doubtful ones can be checked by microscopic examination or by rapid qualitative tests that require only the simplest equipment. Under these circumstances large lots of sherds can be rapidly classified with respect to paint composition, which may be a definite criterion of classification. If, on the other hand, the sample is from an area in which paints have not been studied and if the possibilities of composition are not defined, the analyst must be prepared to apply systematically a wide range of tests. If only the major chemical constituents are in question, qualitative microchemical methods and microscopic examination are generally adequate, but when an explanation of properties or information on possible differences in source is desired, a variety of exacting and special methods must often be drawn upon. Since these methods of analysis are expensive and time-consuming, they should be applied only when details regarding composition will have some bearing on significant archaeological questions.

Paints applied after firing.   The same methods of analysis are applicable to both fired and unfired paints, but the latter include additional minerals and sometimes afford evidence of the nature of the binders or mediums; hence they present special problems and demand special techniques. Microscopic examination plays an essential role in the study of unfired pigments because the original mineralogical composition of the unfired pigment can be ascertained. The basic copper carbonate minerals, malachite and azurite, which were commonly used for blues and greens, are readily identified petrographically in refractive liquids; likewise clay and calcite, common white pigments, are quickly distinguished in this way. Many unfired paints owe their light color to admixture of one of these white pigments. The petrographic microscope serves to estimate the proportion of pigments in such mixtures, as well as to identify the constituents. The binocular microscope is used in studying the order of application of paints when there is overlapping and in detecting successive layers.

The simple qualitative tests used for fired paints are, of course, applicable to the unfired paints, and there are also tests for the pigments peculiar to this class. Limonite and goethite, which are commonly used for yellow and yellow-brown, are converted to red ferric oxide when dehydrated by heating. The color change affords a rough preliminary test, but many of these pigments are earthy ochers, and microscopic or chemical methods are necessary to distinguish the oxides from the argillaceous paint colored by oxide. The mineral cinnabar, a favorite pigment because of its brilliant vermilion color, is identified by a micro-chemical test for mercury (Appendix D).

A number of mineral pigments which are well known in the Old World have not yet been identified on American Indian pottery or murals, but since our work has not been extensive, it is possible that some of them may yet be found. These pigments include white lead (native lead carbonate), orpiment (native yellow arsenic), realgar (the orange-red arsenic sulfide), red lead (oxide of lead), chrysocolla (a silicate of copper), and *terre verte* or glauconite (a hydrous silicate of iron and potassium which owes its color to ferrous iron). One of the most interesting pigments of the Old World is rose madder, a dye which is prepared as a lake on aluminum hydroxide. Farnsworth (1951) used a reflectance curve in addition to microchemical, spectrographic, and microscopic methods to identify this pigment on a specimen from Corinth. The dye was confirmed by its characteristic absorption curve.

It is not improbable that many unfired paints were applied with an organic medium. Although some of these would be subject to leaching and decay in exposed locations, they may have been preserved under some conditions. Gettens (1938, 1938a) has identified animal glue as the medium of wall painting in Afghanistan and Chinese Turkestan. When a drop of water is placed on a small particle of the pigment, a glue ring with characteristic crackles is formed as the drop dries. In this connection the problem of identifying an organic coat applied after firing to fired paints may be mentioned. This problem has arisen in the analysis of certain types of Maya polychromes and lustrous monochromes. The presence of such a coat is often suggested by the fact that the surface turns very dark gray or black when heated. Caution must be exercised in interpreting the effect of heating because sherds in the tropics sometimes become impregnated with organic matter. It is therefore important to heat an edge of the sherds as a check against this condition. If it does not turn gray, the discoloration of the surface may indicate the presence of an organic coat. The charring of organic matter is not the only indication we have of such a coat. A colorless film can sometimes be detected microscopically, and organic matter has been extracted from slips with acetone although the samples so far obtained have been insufficient for identification of the substance (Thompson, 1939, pp. 264–66).

Pottery that was painted after firing was generally coated first with a lime plaster or, less frequently, with white clay or gypsum plaster. This technique, referred to as stucco painting, is comparable to that of mural painting; similar pigments were employed in ceramics and architecture (Kidder, Jennings, and Shook, 1946, pp. 269–77; Kidder and Shepard, 1944). Stucco painting was in a sense independent of the making of the vessel. It could have been executed at any time after firing. Vessels from different sources may have been decorated by the same potter; furthermore, style suggests that in some instances the artist was a mural painter. There are different styles and techniques of stucco painting and also different palettes which should aid in establishing periods and centers of the art.

Painting on a stucco coat has been compared with fresco painting. True fresco is defined by technique and by nature of the bond. The pigments, which are mixed with water or lime water, are applied while the plaster is still wet and are partially bound as it sets. As the lime is converted to carbonate, the process of binding is completed. The palette is limited because chemical changes that take place alter the color of many pigments. When a plaster coat is painted after it is dry (fresco secco), a medium must be used to bind the pigments. Among Mesoamerican stucco-paint specimens there are many examples of pigments mixed with calcite and also secondary impregnation of pigment with calcite, but true fresco painting has not been reported.

Analysis of glazes. The basic method for the analysis of glazes, as for paint, is chemical. Glazes are more complex in composition than paints, however, and they are not taken into solution as easily; consequently, they do not lend themselves as readily to simple qualitative tests. Although the microscope holds a secondary place in glaze analysis, it nevertheless has a definite role; a preliminary microscopic examination may well precede chemical analysis since it will show the homogeneity of the glass and the amount of undissolved pigment which is present. The refractive index of the glass serves to distinguish the lead glazes from other types; it has also been used to estimate the lead-silica ratio in glazes of this class (Kidder and Shepard, 1936, pp. 531–33). To judge the homogeneity of the glass and its relation to the surface of the ware a thin section cutting through the glaze and body should be prepared. This will show the distribution of different phases of glass and of inclusions (undissolved constituents, bubbles), the extent of reaction of clay and glaze, and the penetration of the glass into the body. Glazes were sometimes produced from natural mixtures of a flux with a mineral pigment, as for example when cerussite, the lead carbonate, was associated with manganese and iron ores. Many Rio Grande glaze paints contain so much pigment that they are completely opaque and are hardly distinguishable from a matte pigment. Since the microscope shows the relation of pigment to glass, it is a particularly advantageous tool with which to follow this interesting developmental period in the history of a glaze.

The justification of quantitative determinations of pigments or glazes has sometimes been questioned because the materials were impure, and primitive potters had no means of accurate measurement of the components of a mixture. It does not follow from these circumstances, however, that significant quantitative changes did not occur. Such changes are of especial interest in the study of glazes because the ratio of flux to silica and the percentage of alumina affect fusibility and other properties of the glass. In the study of Rio Grande glaze paints, a microchemical method for quantitative determination of eight elements on 5-milligram samples was developed, and a series of 24 glazes were analyzed (Shepard, 1942, pp. 221–25; 255–56). Although the major constituents of these glazes remained the same throughout the period of their production—some 300 years—the analytical results show a distinct and consistent increase in the percentage of lead in the late glazes. This quantitative change accounts for the greater fluidity of the late glaze. Of especial interest is the fact that synthetic tests indicate that a glaze of this composition could not be obtained without the addition of silica.

Qualitative spectrographic analyses were made of these same glazes for evidence of differences in trace elements which might give some clues to the number of sources of the ore, a question of interest in relation to centers of production and extent to which production was controlled by people in the vicinity of deposits. If data of this kind are to be valid, two conditions should be fulfilled. The composition of the ore of each deposit must have a unique pattern of trace elements, and elements which are essential to the recognition of these patterns should not be subject to volatilization during firing. Spectrographic studies of minerals from the sulfide zone of ore bodies have given some encouragement regarding the possibility of distinguishing ore from different deposits by their "fingerprint" of trace elements, especially when these are determined quantitatively and analysis is complete. Volatilization of constituents in firing would cause only minor changes in composition if the atmosphere is oxidizing, since only two elements, molybdenum and venadium, are volatilized under these conditions.

The spectrographic analysis of the Rio Grande glaze paints was not complete, and no quantitative estimates were made. Although 119 samples were analyzed, they were distributed over the entire area; consequently, samples from different regions were not large enough for statistical comparison. Comparison of the data for the northern and southern districts of the Rio Grande area shows no presence-absence differences in the eight trace and minor elements reported. It is possible that intermingling of specimens from different centers of production through trade accounts for this fact, because there are differences in the frequency of a number of elements that suggest the use of distinct ores in various parts of the area (Shepard, 1942, pp. 215–20; 258–60).

In a study of this kind it is not essential to identify the ore deposit from which the paint was obtained. The relation of composition to pottery type and the distribution of pottery types or even the distribution of paints of distinct composition would be sufficient to demonstrate the presence of centers of production drawing on different sources of material. The limitation of the method lies in the large number of samples that must be analyzed and in the expense of analysis as compared with tha of microscopic examination. Such a study would not be undertaken, therefore, unless the data have unusual archaeological interest and the problems involved can not be solved by more direct methods.

Glazes, since they are complex in composition, raise more questions regarding technique than do pigments. As an illustration, the lustrous black paint of Athenian vases may be cited. A number of investigators have studied this paint and attempted to reproduce it. The pigment is well bound by glass and has a vitreous luster, although de Jong and Rijken (1946) have objected to the term glaze on the ground that the material does not become liquid when heated. It does contain glass, however, and is more properly discussed with glazes than with pigments. Experiments of Binns and Fraser (1929) showed that the black color is due to reduced iron oxide. The composition of the paint is similar to that of the clay. From these facts it was concluded that the paint was a clay high in iron oxide and that, in firing, the ware was subject to reduction. The iron oxide would then be converted to ferrous or ferrous-ferric oxide, and the paint would be protected from subsequent oxidation by the coating of glass surrounding the particles. The body of the ware, being porous, could reoxidize to a clear red. Vitrification of the paint is explained by the low fusion point of the clay, due in part at least to fine particle size. The clay may have been prepared as a suspension, and the suggestion has even been made that protective colloids and peptizers were used to prevent flocculation. It has also been suggested that some alkali, possibly derived from wood ashes, was added to promote vitrification. This technique of producing a vitreous paint or slip spread throughout the Mediterranean, and terra sigillata is a well-known example of it. Some interest has been shown recently in its revival (Amberg, 1948), and it is of interest to Americanists because of parallelism with the vitreous slip of Plumbate ware. It well illustrates the intricacy of problems that arise in attempts to explain the properties and techniques of vitreous paint, and it brings out the importance of drawing on a number of independent analytical methods.

STUDY OF THE EVIDENCES OF POTTERY-MAKING TECHNIQUES

Prehistoric pottery presents a challenge to the student who would learn something about the techniques employed in its manufacture. To a considerable extent it has been a challenge too difficult to meet, the evidences have seemed so slim, so uncertain. Also we have not always been aware of the range or significance of techniques that may have been employed for the different processes of pottery making. But now and then someone has made bold deductions and, again, there are the seemingly self-evident conclusions that are accepted without question. I have discussed present-day prewheel pottery making to suggest the techniques that might have been employed by prehistoric potters. The present section is to review the efforts that have been made to identify techniques of prehistoric pottery and to examine the kind of evidence needed to draw conclusions regarding them.

There are questions regarding technique that, for the present at least, we have to set down as unanswerable, others that may be answered with the benefit of special methods of analysis, and still others for which part of our material will give a more or less certain answer. The fundamental requirements are to know the marks of techniques and the limitation of the evidence. It is rarely possible to classify all sherds or even a major portion of a sample with respect to shaping or other manipulative techniques, but the exceptional sherds that do preserve evidence are nonetheless important for this reason. Classification of entire samples of sherds by whatever characteristics they show has become such a well-established procedure in pottery study that there is risk we will place the classification of the sherd above the recognition of evidence in whatever manner it appears, whether on one sherd or on all.

The study of prehistoric pottery techniques can best be approached through a review of the methods of present-day prewheel potters, together with systematic experimentation. Telltale marks of method of manufacture are often overlooked until brought to the archaeologist's attention by ethnological observations; for example, Gifford's study (1928) of the paddle-and-anvil shaping method led to a great deal of interest and theorizing regarding small depressions that previously had not been noticed. Experimentation is necessary because it enables one to control the various factors influencing an effect and to judge when a feature can be attributed to a specific method.

PREPARATION OF MATERIALS

The archaeologist seldom attempts to draw conclusions regarding the preparation of paste aside from an occasional interpretation arrived at from fineness of texture or apparent homogeneity, as, for example, in the description of a paste as made of "well levigated" clay. In the American field this is either a loose usage of words or a misinterpretation of evidence, and fortunately the term is now seldom used. In commercial ceramic practice, to levigate means to separate materials of different particle size by allowing them to settle in water. If this method is used to clean clay, the silt settles and the clay remains in suspension and can be poured off. In the processes of nature, clay is redeposited from water suspension and its fineness will vary, depending on velocity of current and other factors. Under favorable conditions it can be as fine as that obtained by levigation. It is quite impossible, therefore, to judge from texture whether or not a clay has been cleaned by settling.

Differences in uniformity are seldom conspicuous in prehistoric pastes. Evidences of imperfect mixing and insufficient kneading should be seen most clearly in thin section. Uneven distribution of temper would be most noticeable, but lack of homogeneity is rarely noted. This fact doubtless means that potters generally kneaded their clay well enough to obtain uniform distribution of constituents. This observation is not surprising because there would be far greater risk of cracking, in consequence of uneven shrinkage, with a poorly kneaded paste. The differences which are noticeable on megascopic examination, particularly with respect to size and shape of pore spaces and sometimes even lamination, are very often due to characteristics of the clay rather than to preparation. A mixture of two clays, if thorough, will not be recognized by the unaided eye but should be detected in thin section since pulverization would seldom be sufficiently complete to reduce all microscopic particles.

Another question of interest is whether or not organic matter, such as gummy substances, grease, or blood was added to the clay. If the pottery is fired long enough and with sufficient draft, there will be no evidence because organic material will burn out. If oxidation is incomplete, these substances will char, causing the paste to take on a black or gray color. Such a paste would look not unlike a highly carbonaceous or a smudged clay. Relative ease of oxidation on refiring may in some instances distinguish an organic extract added from organic matter of natural occurrence, but little work has been done on the problem.

CLUES TO FORMING AND SHAPING METHODS

Ideally, construction should be included among the criteria for pottery classification, for it is a fundamental part of technique; moreover, basically different methods of vessel forming are employed by prewheel potters, as we have seen in the review of practices of present-day potters. But unfortunately, as the archaeologist is well aware, potsherds are generally quite uncommunicative on this matter. This circumstance follows from the requirements for soundness. The chances that a vessel will withstand the strain of contraction in drying and firing and the shocks of usage depend in no small measure on homogeneity of body, freedom from air pockets, and perfect union of parts. Guthe (1925, p. 36) has described the care San Ildefonso potters exercise to secure thorough bonding of coils and to eliminate trapped air. Consequently, fracture on a coil juncture occurs only when there has been faulty construction. Also, surface marks of the forming process, such as traces of coil junctures, and of the unions in two-stage modeling and two-part molding, are most often found on carelessly or crudely made vessels because these surface indications are normally obliterated in the scraping and smoothing processes.

Since faulty pieces often constitute a small percentage of the sherds in a sample, and since the marks they bear are not always clear, hope has been entertained that laboratory methods could be developed for identifying forming techniques. Differences in density that might be shown by X-ray and possible relations between orientation of particles and direction of forces applied in building have been considered. Titterington (1933) investigated the possibility that difference in density at coil junctures would be revealed by X-ray, with negative results. Radiographic examination has been useful, however, in the study of details of construction, as for example in Digby's study (1948) of Peruvian methods of spout attachment, which gave promise of distinguishing techniques having chronological significance.

Alignment of particles with respect to the forces applied in shaping can be recognized only when particles are not equidimensional. Linné (1925, p. 53) noted the alignment of sponge spicules parallel to surfaces that had been rubbed. Some arrangement of particles may also take place in forming processes. The pressure applied in welding coils may force platy fragments into alignment with the plane of contact of coils, and the process of modeling the vessel from a ring by drawing the clay upward (see p. 56) should also produce some parallelism through dragging action. Although 1 have not sought evidence of this kind and have not cut petrographic thin sections in directions designed to reveal it, a conspicuous example came to my attention in the study of Pecos pottery. Platy fragments of fine vitric ash temper in a black-on-white type were so fully oriented that at first I mistook the material for a needle-like form of ash since by chance the section cut the plates edgewise. A second section cut at right angles to the first showed the faces of plates, the plane of which extended obliquely outward and downward through the vessel wall. Evidently the plates were pressed into a parallel position by the welding of coils which had an exterior overlap. Unless inclusions are very fine, orientation of platy material can be recognized with a binocular microscope, and the edges of plates are seen most plainly in a vertical cross section through the wall.

The evidence of forming methods shown by inclusions is limited by the fact that the majority of inclusions are granular and approximately equidimensional and hence show no preferential orientation. Another possibility that may be considered is the orientation of clay particles themselves, which, though generally platy, are so fine that their position is recognized only in thin section. The orientation of plates in slips has been mentioned (p. 154). In the body, streamers in which clay crystals have the same position can be observed with polarized light, and also the parallelism of faces of clay particles to the surface of hard inclusions is noticeable. A systematic study of such phenomena with respect to the direction of forces they indicate might throw some light on forming method, but this means of study would be applicable only to ware fired below the temperature at which crystalline structure of the clay is destroyed.

In view of the difficulties of studying forming methods—the near obliteration of marks of the processes and the limited nature of microscopic evidence—it is imperative that every source of data be utilized. The observations that can be made in the field are especially important because the handling of thousands of sherds multiplies the chances of finding the discards and imperfectly finished pieces that preserve evidence of construction. Only familiarity with the diagnostic marks of the various techniques is required for identification.

Marks of the coiling process are more easily recognized than those of modeling from a lump because of the many junctures necessitated by coiling. Imperfectly joined coils form a plane of weakness, which a fracture will follow. Often such a break reveals the smooth surfaces of the original coils. The extreme rarity with which such fractures are observed in pottery that is known to have been coiled attests to the thoroughness of welding which was indeed a necessity for sound pottery. When the union of coils is perfect, fracture is no more likely to occur along their plane than in any other direction. More frequently observed than poor junctures are surface marks of coiling, even though these remain only when scraping or smoothing was neglected as on jar interiors. Lines or grooves may mark the juncture of coils and gentle undulations may be formed by their profiles. Distinguishing marks of the technique of modeling from a lump are not as well established as those of coiling, but the possibility that additions of slabs or reinforcing sheets may result in laminations roughly parallel to the surface is being studied by Arnold Withers (personal communication).

The marks of molding on vessels for which the details of construction are known have been studied by Foster (1948a). He reports that the horizontal weld ridges at the juncture of the two parts of a vessel made in a convex mold are easily felt and are unmistakable. He also notes that when the top section is hand-modeled, it is relatively unsymmetric compared with the smooth regularity of the molded lower section. On the other hand, the vessels from Michoacan made in a vertical concave mold, the two parts of which are joined before removing the vessel from the mold, are often so well joined and smoothed that the weld-mark is often entirely obliterated. Foster reported difficulty in finding traces of the weld in some instances, even when he knew its position. When the parts are joined while still in the mold, it is possible to exert more pressure on the line of juncture than if there were no support. It does not follow from this fact that junctures were always fully obliterated in this type of molding. Techniques and standards of finish differ. Joining the parts while they are still in the mold facilitates working over the junctures, but potters did not necessarily always take this care. Also, potters might be expected to reinforce the weld by leaving excess clay on the interior since this is a line of weakness. All factors considered, therefore, it is possible that molding can be recognized in a large proportion of molded vessels and sherds that include the weld.

The use of a paddle and anvil to shape a vessel and thin the wall is a technique brought to the attention of archaeologists by the study of an ethnologist (Gifford, 1928). It is important to recognize that this is a shaping and not a forming technique. It is used in conjunction with the coiling process as among certain Yuman, Piman, and Shoshonean potters and also with direct modeling from a lump as among certain Plains tribes. When interest was first aroused by evidence of it in the Southwest, it was contrasted with coiling, a confusion that should not have occurred, since the process is sometimes employed to complete the union of coils and may replace the use of the gourd-rind scraper in shaping.

The marks of the technique are the rounded depressions of the anvil on vessel interiors. These are more pronounced than the unevenness resulting from hand-finishing, but are obliterated if the surface is scraped after shaping. Vessels with restricted orifice most often show such marks. Wendorf's study (1953) of the distribution of paddle-and-anvil technique in the Southwest is an outstanding example of the value afforded by data on technique for archaeological reconstructions.

The use of classificatory systems that pigeonhole every potsherd has become so habitual that we may not be properly prepared to recognize or appreciate the significance of features that appear only rarely. Foster has suggested that the rarity with which molding has been noted in prehistoric Mexican pottery may be due to the fact that students have not always been alert to the evidence. I can corroborate this statement from personal experience. When my study of Plumbate ware was nearly completed, I saw an early-type jar with molded upper body. The upper body, which bore a raised line decoration, was unquestionably made in a horizontal concave mold, for the welding strokes at shoulder and neck junctures were prominent on the interior. I had previously examined many jars of the fully developed Plumbate (Tohil) without considering the possibility that jar bodies were molded, although molded decorative details such as small appliquéd animal and human heads were not uncommon. The use of a horizontal mold for jar upper bodies might explain the trimming-marks frequently found around jar shoulders and would raise a question regarding the relation of technique to peculiarities of form such as angled and girdled shoulders and pronounced differences in contour of upper and lower body. Even more interesting is the question of similarity of technique of early and late types of Plumbate, since stylistic differences raise doubt that the two were made by the same people.

Data on forming and shaping processes are not necessary for the establishment of taxonomic systems, but the value of such data is evident. There is growing recognition of the fact that pottery need not be abstracted from its cultural matrix to serve for relative dating, and that it has significance beyond this as long as it is viewed in terms of technique, function, and style. Although ethnological studies have awakened us to neglected possibilities, it would be foolish to deceive ourselves regarding the difficulties of establishing definitive criteria, but these difficulties can be regarded as a challenge rather than an obstacle.

SURFACE FINISH

The term "surface finish" is here used to designate all surface characteristics that result from the manner in which the vessel was evened and smoothed during the shaping process and subsequently. The technique of slipping is included, but the various forms of surface patterning (e.g., cord marking, net impressions, grooved paddling, and stamping) that cover the entire vessel exterior I have considered under decorative techniques (p. 194 ff.), although they are referred to as surface finish in eastern United States archaeology.

To interpret surface features in terms of technique, we can draw on the ethnological record of present-day pottery making for suggestions regarding the range of methods used and their specific effects. Such knowledge should be tested and extended by systematic experimentation with different types of clay and various tools. Finally, examination of prehistoric pottery will show the frequency with which various marks of the finishing process are preserved.

The deductions regarding finishing methods that can be drawn from examination of pottery are limited by the fact that the final process usually obliterates all marks of previous treatment; thus, when a vessel is polished, marks of tools employed in evening, scraping, and smoothing are destroyed. Likewise, slips cover the evidences of all previous work; it is possible to judge the care of surface preparation only from evenness, except in the rare cases in which slip has parted from the surface, revealing its texture after the last preparatory treatment. Surface finish is one of the principal means by which general classes of pottery are distinguished, rough or so-called "utility" or "culinary" ware from finely finished ware. Three main surface types are generally distinguished in pottery classification: unslipped and unpolished; polished, unslipped; and slipped. Of the two techniques by which a vessel is given fine finish, polishing is the more basic and slipping the more specialized because a secondary coat used to improve color, texture, and surface density is unnecessary when the body clay meets the desired standards for these properties. It is common procedure in pottery classification to make a preliminary sort by surface finish; slipped sherds are separated and then the unslipped are subdivided with respect to smoothness or polish. Thus the taxonomic approach raises the question of how to identify slip at the start. In this review, however, it will be more convenient to consider first the evidences of the common basic techniques which are found on unslipped and unpolished vessels. Thus we will follow finishing techniques in the order of their original execution.

Unslipped and unpolished surfaces. Surfaces of this class often show evidences of finishing method. Features to observe are: texture of paste, evenness of contour, indications of the condition of the paste when the surface was finished, and tool-marks.

This discussion is based in part on experiments with five types of paste, three textures of ball clay—untempered, tempered with fine sand, and tempered with coarse sand—a micaceous primary clay from the pueblo of Picuris, New Mexico, and a short, sedimentary clay from San Ildefonso Pueblo. These were worked when plastic, partially dry (leather-hard), and dry. The tools used were of four classes: yielding tools for rubbing—the hand, cloth, leather; hard, smooth tools for rubbing—a waterworn pebble, bone, hardwood; sharp-edged scrapers—a gourd-rind, sherd, wood, shell, obsidian blade; abraders—sandstone, vesicular basalt.

Fine-textured paste places no restriction on finishing method, whereas a coarse-textured paste limits finishing techniques. There is little that can be done to smooth the surface when drying shrinkage leaves coarse grains protruding.

Scraping, when the vessel is still moist, drags grains, forming grooves (fig. 13d); rubbing or polishing is ineffective once the body has become too firm to yield and allow the particles to become embedded. Scraping or sanding the dry surface pulls the grains out, leaving pits. Hence there is a definite relation between paste texture and finishing process. Coarse-paste ware is most easily finished in the plastic state. When it is smoothed with the hand or a soft, yielding tool, grains are coated with a film of clay, but they are not pressed level with the surface, and a grainy texture results (fig. 13a). Shrinkage of the body in drying also tends to leave grains elevated. Rubbing with a hard tool while the clay is still yielding will level grains, but subsequent shrinkage may bring them into relief again. Only when the surface is carefully rubbed while it is still yielding but not too plastic can it be well smoothed. Some leveled grains are then bare and unless the vessel is subsequently slipped they can be plainly seen. These effects of texture are stressed because it is important to recognize their relation to technique.

The initial steps in evening occur while the vessel is being shaped and the surface is being worked over with hands and tools to obtain uniformity. The method used and the care exercised in this process have much to do with the success of later stages of finishing. The surface may be scraped or rubbed repeatedly at various later stages and the tool-marks then obscured by polishing or slipping. Yet telltale traces of careless evening—depressions and grooves—will remain. Generally, however, the more careful and skillful the potter, the more difficult it is to recognize any but the final process.

The quality of surface contour differs, depending on whether the vessel was scraped with a sharp-edged tool of proper curvature or was merely wiped over with the hand or something flexible, such as a piece of leather. The scraping tool, if used on the interior while the clay is still plastic, will level elevations and fill depressions with an effectiveness that cannot be equaled by rubbing or wiping with a yielding tool which follows rather than cuts down high parts. Even when a hard tool is used for rubbing, it will leave depressions because it drops into

---

FIG. 13—FEATURES OF FINISHING TECHNIQUES

a: Wiped surface of a coarse, grainy paste. b: Medium-textured, heavily tempered paste scraped while plastic. Note short, horizontal ridges formed by plastic flow of clay. Contour shows surface was scraped rather than wiped. c: Experimental plaque, untempered ball clay. Left side, finished while plastic with downward strokes of the fingers, shows characteristics of plastic flow. Right side, scraped after drying with even-edged obsidian flake. Note sharpness of grooves and small pits where grains have been pulled out. d: Grooves formed by dragging grains in leather-hard paste with scraping tool. e: Troughs left by smoothing tool used on yielding surface. f: Parallel striations produced by dragging of particles when smoothing with a yielding tool while the clay was in a plastic state. Marks are preserved despite subsequent slipping because the surface is unpolished. The parallelism of the striations to the rim, which suggests mark left in throwing, results from folding a piece of leather or cloth over the rim and holding it against the lip while the vessel is turned.

a   *b*

c   *d*

e   *f*

Fig. 13

those that are already present and deepens rather than fills them. Scraping may be done carelessly or carefully but the principal difference is not in relative evenness of the parts scraped but in the uniformity with which the surface is covered with scraping strokes. The characteristic contour of the scraped surface is often evident, even after the vessel has been polished or slipped. To obtain a fine finish, scraping in some stage is necessary. The process is generally recognized by quality of contour rather than by tool-marks.

There are a few marks that distinguish the condition of the surface during the finishing process. It must be remembered, however, that the plastic, leather-hard, or dry states merge into one another; moreover, the surface of the dry vessel may be rewet and some of the effects of plastic clay obtained. The principal mark of finishing in the plastic state is plastic flow, which is most often shown by fine ridges formed in wiping the surface. The ridges have the appearance of striations, but they are elevated and have rounded contours which are plainly visible with a hand lens (fig. 13c). They can be distinguished from striations made by a scraping tool on firm clay because the latter are cut into the surface and the edges are sharp (fig. 13c). The striations of a surface scraped when dry will be ragged if the paste is tempered.

Luster and marks of the rubbing tool give some hint of the stage in which the tactually smooth surface was rubbed. I have called attention to the fact that luster produced by polishing is destroyed by drying shrinkage. Since rubbing in the leather-hard state is only one of the possible causes of absence of luster of a tactually smooth surface, the state of the paste when rubbed cannot be proved by this condition alone. On the other hand, the surface that is lustrous was in all probability polished after body shrinkage was completed. Qualification is necessary here because there are a few clays with low shrinkage that retain the luster produced in the leather-hard state. If the clay is plastic or not fully firm when it is rubbed, the tool leaves shallow troughs (fig. 13e), but once the body has become firm, depressed strokes are not noticeable even though the surface has been rewet or slipped. It is important, therefore, to distinguish streaks caused by difference in elevation from those marked by variation in color and luster. The latter will occur in slipped or rewet surfaces that become nearly dry before polishing is completed.

There are various marks that indicate the type of finishing tool used. Plastic flow occurs when the surface is wiped with something soft and pliant. Anything yielding, drawn across the surface—the hand, cloth, leather—makes the same kind of marks. Scraping tools—gourd-rind, obsidian blade, sherd, bone or cane knife—generally have fine nicks that cause sharp striations. A straight-edged knife cuts a characteristic plane-surfaced stroke on convex parts of a vessel. A firm, smooth tool—a waterworn pebble, bone, horn, large smooth seeds—used to rub and polish produces streaks that are tactually smooth and compact. In general, therefore, finishing marks are indicative of processes executed with a certain class of tool rather than of specific tools. Wiping tools cause plastic flow, scrapers make striations and grooves according to the form of their edges, and rubbing tools leave smooth streaks.

Experimentation with finishing techniques makes many peculiarities of surface meaningful; nevertheless the interpretations that can be made are limited and, consequently, we must distinguish between well-established, general deductions and tentative hypotheses.

Polished, unslipped surfaces. Strictly speaking, a polished surface has luster; however, many matte surfaces are as smooth to the touch and were produced in the same way, i.e., by rubbing with a hard, smooth tool. Any clay that is made thoroughly compact will be smooth, but not all clays acquire luster and those that do can lose it with shrinkage. These relations have been discussed under luster (p. 122 ff.).

It is important to differentiate the smoothness produced by using a hard tool and applying pressure when the clay is partially dry from that resulting from working over a wet, fine-textured clay. One is a process of compaction, the other of redistribution of clay particles. The resemblance between them is superficial and they are easily distinguished by touch. The term "floated" is sometimes applied to the surface that has been worked while wet. At one time I objected to this term because it was being applied to compacted surfaces (Kidder and Shepard, 1936, p. 441). I also thought that the tendency for fine particles to rise to the surface was exaggerated, but there is no doubt that redistribution of particles, with the fine ones coming to the top, takes place when the surface is repeatedly wet and lightly stroked. Minimum particle size and size range will influence the texture that is obtained.

In the description of the compacted surface, it is important to distinguish the effects of the preparation of surface (evenness), of the actual polishing process (coverage), and of the quality of clay (see p. 123).

Slipped surfaces. Slipping represents a definite refinement in ceramic technique. It is an effective means of improving surface color and texture, and it also renders pottery less permeable, particularly when well polished, since it fills the pores with finer material. We have no basis for judging the extent to which the latter advantage was appreciated by prehistoric potters, but there can be no doubt that slips were used to obtain colors lighter and clearer than those of the bodies. Consequently, slips are generally recognized by their color contrast with the paste. When the difference is prominent, as with light or clear red coats on brown pastes, they present no difficulty in identification, but when they approach the paste in color, microscopic examination is often required for their detection. A

10-power hand lens is an aid, but it is often advisable and sometimes necessary to use a binocular microscope. A fresh cross fracture through the vessel wall should be examined. In making the break, it is important to avoid touching with the breaking tool the edge that is to be examined because pressure tends to powder the clay on the angle at the surface, leaving a light line that looks deceptively like slip.

Microscopic thin sections afford distinct advantages for slip identification because they show minute differences in texture of body and slip not otherwise detectable. Furthermore, polarized light reveals orientation of particles, which is often the only means of distinguishing a slip made from the same clay as the body. The effect is often striking because smoothing and rubbing align the platy clay particles of the slip parallel to the surface; hence, a coating that is indistinguishable in ordinary light will stand out as a sharply demarcated layer acting optically as a unit when the polarizing prism is introduced. Surfaces that are smooth, fine-textured, and of identical color to the body are sometimes designated "self-slipped" on the assumption that the slip was prepared from the same clay as the body. However, unless the body exhibits a textural difference owing to temper, such a coat cannot be detected except in thin section. On the other hand, a very fine-textured paste that has been well smoothed or polished may superficially resemble a slipped surface, and the term "self-slip" has sometimes been applied to such surfaces. Confusion can be avoided by stating specifically the basis on which identification rests. Under special circumstances, texture is a useful diagnostic of slip, as for example when the peeling reveals temper particles in the smooth surface beneath.

A misleading color change may be caused by compaction of clay in polishing. The effect varies with different clays, but a dense and particularly a lustrous surface is generally clearer and darker than the porous paste, and in some cases the contrast is sufficient to suggest the presence of a coat of different composition. Streaks on the surface that have been missed by the polishing tool aid judgment of the effects of compaction.

The opposite condition, an unpolished slip, may also be deceptive, perhaps partly because its rarity leaves us unprepared for it. A coat applied without subsequent smoothing or polishing has a texture resembling that of a wiped unslipped surface. Esperanza Flesh-color (Kidder, Jennings, and Shook, 1946, p. 174) is an example.

These remarks refer to oxidized ware. When pottery is smudged, color distinctions are masked, and surface texture alone does not afford adequate basis for judgment of finishing technique. It is necessary, therefore, to oxidize smudged sherds by refiring in order to determine if they are slipped. A small chip is sufficient, and the most satisfactory oxidation is obtained in an electric resistance furnace.

Partial oxidation in the original firing occasionally produces color zones which look strikingly like slip in a cross fracture through the wall. Thinness of the surface zones and sharpness of boundaries caused by short, strong oxidation heighten the effect. Such partial oxidation occurs principally with highly carbonaceous clays. The core is dark gray or blackish and the margins are light. Refiring to complete oxidation shows whether or not a slip of contrasting color is present. Without refiring, it may be very difficult to judge by inspection of a single sherd, but when a number of sherds of a type are available, pronounced difference in width of the light zone will mark the effect of oxidation, since firing atmosphere varies with resultant differences in depth to which carbon is removed. In any case, a dark gray or blackish core serves as a warning of the possibility of color variation due to partial oxidation.

Another phenomenon that may be mistaken for slip is bloom, caused by scumming or migration of soluble salts in the clay to the surface during drying (see p. 21). Examples of this effect that could be confused with slip have not come to my attention. It has been suggested as the explanation of surface color of a Hohokam pottery type by Rogers (1928) but without chemical or microscopic data.

Slips vary greatly in thickness, depending on viscosity of the material (influenced by particle size and dispersion) and on number of applications. Several coats may be used to cover a dark paste, or different clays may be combined to modify color, as when a whitish primary coat is used under a thin red one to lighten it. The secondary slip may be so thin as to pass notice, but ordinarily it is shown by color contrast. Microscopic examination is necessary to identify multiple applications and very thin slips.

The various factors that may influence the appearance of slip would render identification tedious were it not for the fact that they follow directly from basic principles of clay working. It is important that surface finishes be studied and described with reference to technique, and it is equally important that the basis of all inferences regarding technique be plainly stated.

DECORATIVE TECHNIQUES

In the study of decorative techniques, the archaeologist is frequently thrown on his own resources because present-day prewheel potters are not employing the variety of methods once used, and we cannot depend on them for clues to the explanation of all the effects found on prehistoric pottery. To compensate, the archaeologist should allow himself to doodle with plastic clay. Close observation and reasoning regarding the results of various procedures can explain much, but shrewd guessing is needed, too, and that should always be followed by systematic testing.

The technique of many simple types of decoration is self-evident, as, for example, application of fillets or discs, gouging moist clay with the nail, punching with a reed, or impressing with a textile or the edge of a shell. But there are also many decorative techniques that are obscure: a textured or impressed pattern may leave one at a loss to guess the kind of tool that produced it; there may seem to be no way to tell whether a design was incised in the dry or the fired paste; and the relation of colors in a painted pattern may seen to contradict every method of application one can conjure up.

The problem of recognizing the details of a complex technique has the fascination of a puzzle, but to determine their value or significance in ceramic studies, it is necessary to distinguish between chance and well-established practice. Convenience may dictate whether a bunch of stiff grass or the edge of an obsidian flake is used to score a cook pot, or whether a gouge or a bone point is chosen for incising. On the other hand, the employment of a particular tool may reflect a firmly established custom. A specialized technique can be a useful criterion of classification, and it is a significant part of ceramic tradition no less than style of decoration. It is the purpose of this discussion to review a few of the more specialized techniques with relation to methods of identification and description. I shall consider in detail only those techniques with which I have experimented—incising and painting—and refer briefly to others.

Plastic techniques include scoring, stamping, modeling, molding, incising, and carving, and each has certain variations. Although they are distinct as techniques, there are some similarities among them with respect to the effects produced. For example, scoring and some forms of stamping create a surface elaboration without formal plan, which may be described as texturing. Freehand modeling and the mechanical process of molding are both adaptable to representation in the round. The freehand methods of incising and carving are adaptable to simple geometric or advanced representational design.

Stamping is a mechanical method, by which a variety of textures and imprinted patterns can be produced, depending on the kind of stamp or die used. Several special techniques of stamping are widely distributed in eastern North America, and it appears from their association that people who began decorating in this fashion became interested in quick methods of patterning the entire surface or large areas of the vessel and exercised their ingenuity to find new dies. The stamps include cord-wrapped sticks and paddles, wooden paddles bearing carved designs, continuous roulettes, and rocker roulettes. The impressions of the cord- or textile-wrapped stamping tools are distinguished by lack of continuity between successive impressions. The continuous roulette makes an unbroken series of impressions comparable to those left by the cogs of a wheel rolled over plastic clay. In some instances, similar effects were produced by end-to-end repetition of straight, dentate stamps. Rocker rouletting is easily recognized as a zigzag of straight or crescentic impressions. The impression made by "walking" a shell over a surface is an example.

In Mexico, pottery stamps were used extensively. They are of two forms: a flat seal often provided with a handle, and a continuous stamp on a cylinder. Mexican stamped designs differ stylistically, as well as technically, from those of the eastern United States. In classification of technique, however, reliance should not be placed on style unless it is conditioned by technique. Direct criteria should be found.

The techniques of *modeling* or hand manipulation and *molding* or casting from a mold are both used for high-relief decoration and for the representation of human and animal figures. Either the surface of the vessel itself is worked or elements are formed separately and welded to the vessel. The difference between hand-worked paste and that shaped in a mold is usually recognized immediately, without conscious search for criteria, by one familiar with the appearance of each, but it is important to keep in mind the marks of these processes because the evidence has sometimes been missed. A basic characteristic of molded work is lack of undercutting. This is negative evidence; the specimen with undercutting was not molded, the specimen without undercutting could have been but was not necessarily. If the vessel itself was molded, proof can be found in the juncture of parts, but junctures can be obliterated more or less successfully. If the juncture is vertical, the two halves are often made in the same mold and identity is another proof of technique. A series of molded appliqué elements can also be recognized by identity. If the juncture is horizontal, the two parts may be formed in different molds, and only evidence of juncture or quality of impression will reveal the technique. When a one-piece mold was used, as for a *molcajete* or an appliquéd effigy head, identification depends on quality of molding. There is a softness of contour and a uniformity of surface texture that is characteristic. Imperfectly molded pieces sometimes bear secondary tool-marks when details were retouched or lines sharpened.

There are two distinct types of molds: the hand-decorated mold, on which the design is incised or modeled, and the pressed mold, which is the impression of a natural or modeled object. The hand-decorated mold is suitable for geometric design; casts from it frequently have low, relatively uniform relief. An incised mold, for example, will produce a line design in a slightly raised welt. Casts from hand-decorated molds sometimes bear a superficial resemblance to stamp decoration but are distinguished by lack of repetition. The pressed mold often has variable relief and is suitable for casting images of human figures or animals.

Incising or freehand decoration by pressing or cutting lines into the paste is a widespread and important form of pottery decoration. It is essentially a graphic technique and admits of considerable artistic expression. In its simplest form, it appears as series of crude strokes or scratches on a roughly finished surface. At the extreme of refinement is the elaborate and delicate underglaze incising of Chinese porcelains. Basic distinctions in incising are defined by the order of the decorating and finishing processes. If the vessel was slipped, simple inspection is sufficient to determine whether it was incised before or after slipping. Within a style or pottery type there is usually consistency in technique of incising. Postslipping technique emphasizes pattern when there is a distinct color contrast between slip and paste. Slipping over incising leaves a shallow groove without color contrast. This technique, though it has long been familiar, raises a question that has not been investigated. Many slips could not be wiped over an incised line without filling it, yet preslipping-incised wares usually have the same uniformly thin coat in the groove as on the surface. This fact suggests the employment of some means, such as the addition of gummy substances, to control viscosity of slip and dispersion of clay, but, as yet, proof of such technique is lacking.

The combination of polishing and incising also affords a distinction based on order of processes. Most vessels were obviously incised after polishing because the surface is level up to the edge of the trough, which is sharp and free of overhang; also, incised lines cut through straight polishing strokes. Polishing after incising depresses and rounds the edges of the trough and tends to leave a slight overhang where the polishing tool was pressed onto the edge of the groove (fig. 14a).

Order of incising, slipping, and polishing are easily determined by these observations, but there are certain minor relations that raise puzzling questions. For example, a highly lustrous slip and postslipping lines that show the smoothness and compactness of moist-paste work seem to contradict the generalization that luster is destroyed by drying shrinkage, for if the luster of slip resulted from polishing, it must have been produced while the paste was still moist. Exceptionally low drying shrinkage or application of a slip which becomes lustrous on drying without polishing might explain instances of this kind.

Quality of incising is influenced principally by the paste texture, firmness of paste at the time of incising, and kind of tool employed. The effects of these factors can be studied by systematic experimentation.

FIG. 14—INCISING TECHNIQUES

a: Polished after incising. The surface of each diamond slopes off slightly toward its outline. The upper line shows where clay has been pushed into the groove. *b:* Point incising. Compare with gouge incising, *c.* A motif copied from Plumbate ware to reproduce line quality. Note difference in contour and asymmetry of trough, cleanness of line and ends of strokes. In using the gouge (plaque *c*), it was necessary to turn the piece upside down when making the stroke on the right and the upper half of that on the left, in order to maintain the same position of broad, deep ends as in the original. *d:* Postfiring incising on smudged ware. Note color contrast of surface and trough and chipping of line edges.

a

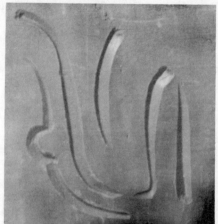

b

c

Fig. 14

d

A fine-textured paste is obviously necessary if the incised lines are to be smooth and even. Coarse, hard grains offer resistance to a tool; they drag if the paste is yielding and cause chipping and pitting if it is dry. Despite these disadvantages, coarse wares were sometimes incised. It is important to consider texture in relation to smoothness of line, otherwise the raggedness caused by coarse temper may be misinterpreted as an indication of postfiring technique.

A vessel can be incised when the paste is plastic, leather-hard, dry, or after it is fired. Each state offers certain advantages. The moist paste is easier to work than the dry, but the fired vessel that is highly polished can be handled without risk of marring the luster. Although it may seem impracticable to incise the fired vessel, many low-fired pastes are relatively soft (2-1/2–3 in Mohs' scale). The condition of the paste at the time of incising can often be inferred from the appearance of line edges and trough, provided the surface was not slipped after incising. If the paste is plastic or yielding, a pointed tool drawn over it displaces material and leaves a slightly raised edge along the line, or a burr, if the trough is deep. If the body is firm or leather-hard, shavings are formed. They part easily from the surface and can be brushed off when dry, leaving a clean margin. Both plastic and leather-hard incising are characterized by a smooth, compact trough. If the paste is dry or if it is fired before incising, it tends to chip, and the surface of the trough shows a porous, grainy structure (fig. 14d). The degree of line irregularity and surface roughness will depend largely on paste texture, but dry- and fired-paste technique can always be distinguished from that of moist paste by the difference in quality of a powdered and a compacted surface. Experiments have shown that texture of the cut and quality of the line edge may be indistinguishable in dry-paste and low-fired-paste incising. When pottery is smudged, however, color contrast of surface and line will distinguish postfiring technique, provided the carbon has not penetrated to the depth to which the line is to be incised. Postfiring lines cut through the blackened surface expose lighter paste, whereas there is uniform blackening when the vessel is incised before firing. In the absence of smudging, I know of no criterion that will invariably differentiate dry paste and postfiring technique. This limitation of evidence should be recognized and the basis for identification stated in description. It would be desirable to adopt an inclusive term for these two incising methods. The word engraving, which has gained some acceptance in recent years for postfiring incising, could be given this broader definition to advantage, especially as the basis for identification of postfiring technique has rarely been stated.

To distinguish incising techniques specifically, it is sometimes desirable to consider the class of tool that was used. The sharpness of line of certain styles of incising suggests gouge or knife work. The effects produced by various tools have been studied to ascertain whether or not they will afford useful criteria for the identification of techniques. In general the profile of the trough and width of line are determined by the shape of the effective part of the tool, rather than by class of tool. The depth of the line depends, of course, on the pressure applied. There are, however, subtle characteristics that distinguish the incisions made by each tool.

The pointed tool allows greater freedom of movement than either the knife or the gouge. It can be held like a pencil with only the tip in contact with the clay or it can be held low under the hand, bringing a part of the tapered end in contact with the surface. The pencil grasp gives greatest facility in drawing strongly curved lines or making sharp turns. Holding the pointed tool under the hand has an advantage in making long straight lines because there is more drag, which counteracts wobble and gives an even stroke. The profile of the trough will be angled or rounded, depending on whether the point is sharp or blunt; it will be symmetric if the point is held in a plane at right angles to the surface, asymmetric when the tool is inclined, extreme if held under the hand (fig. 15a,b). Asymmetry is more conspicuous in an angled than in a curved trough, but is not typical because in the inclined position the edge is employed and becomes an ineffective scraper; moreover, it is difficult to avoid undercutting. If the paste is plastic, the groove is formed partly by compressing the clay but mainly by throwing out a burr; some clay is usually carried along by the point, leaving a heel at the end of the stroke. When the point is pushed, it acts like a plow and leaves a cleaner edge and end than when pulled, but is likely to undercut. A straight or moderately curved stroke can be made by either pushing or pulling, but a circle or closed line made without moving the vessel or lifting the point will combine pushing and pulling. Also the inclination of the point and, therefore, the symmetry of the trough will vary on such a stroke.

A gouge, which can be made from wood or bone, is pushed as it is held at a slight angle from the surface to avoid digging deeply into the paste (fig. 15c,d). It produces a smooth groove by cutting the clay rather than compressing and displacing it. The line formed is free from burr and the end of the stroke has a sharp break instead of a heel. The profile of the trough may be angled or rounded, symmetric or inclined. The directions in which strokes can be made with ease are limited, and closed lines or scrolls must be cut with more than one stroke. On a sharp curve the gouge is turned toward the center of curvature in order to follow it, and the trough will slope to that side.

A knife, such as an obsidian flake, affords a thin, sharp cutting edge. The profile of the trough formed depends on the shape of the knife point. A knife with a squarish end produces an angled and distinctly asymmetric groove. When the knife is used to cut, the plane of the blade is only slightly inclined to the surface (fig. 15e). If the blade is held in a vertical or near-vertical plane, it acts as a scraper and pushes moist paste ahead of it (fig. 15*f*). It is easier to draw a smooth line by cutting than by scraping; the chief advantage of the scraper, as compared with the point or gouge, lies in its sharpness; it is useful for grooving a dry or fired body. The blade used as a cutting tool on moist paste leaves a clean edge, free from burr. At the end of the stroke, the little paring of clay is cut or broken off, and the line is free from the heel which is characteristic of point incising. In using the knife, it is important to avoid undercutting or chisel action, which leaves the upper edge of the trough ragged. The cutting edge may be either drawn toward or pushed from the worker, but when drawn toward him the blade is more easily grasped and the working edge is visible. Since pushing and pulling cannot be combined in a single knife stroke, the directions in which lines can be drawn from one position with ease are limited. A horizontal or near-horizontal line requires an uncomfortable twist of the wrist, whereas the hand is in a natural position in drawing a vertical line or one inclined no more than 45° to the vertical. It will be noted that a horizontal groove can be drawn with the hand either above or below the line, and consequently the end of the stroke may be either on the right or on the left, but both positions are difficult. It follows from this limitation of direction of stroke that straight lines or sweeping, moderate curves can easily be cut with a knife, whereas circles, ellipses, or complete scrolls cannot be made with a single stroke. When a circle is made with two knife cuts, the bevel will be on the inside of the curve on one side and on the outside on the other, unless the position of the vessel is shifted before the second cut is made. As compared with a point, therefore, the knife cuts a groove of equal depth with far less effort or force, leaving a clean edge; but it cannot be turned with the facility of a point, and consequently more strokes and more frequent turning of the vessel are necessary.

To summarize, there are no characteristics by which the work of these three tools can invariably be recognized. Considerable variation in depth, width, profile, and symmetry of the trough can be obtained with each tool. Nevertheless, in some instances there are identifying marks. These distinctions hold for moist-paste incising. Burr, a heel at the end of a stroke, a slight swelling or elevation at the edge of a line, all show that the groove has been formed partly by displacement rather than by complete removal of paste, and therefore they distinguish the work of a point. These features can be observed only when the paste has been somewhat plastic at the time of incising. The trough of a line made with a point is generally symmetric; that is, its axis is at right angles to the surface, although its inclination often varies in different parts of a strong curve. Deep, narrow lines are more easily formed with a point than a gouge or a knife; circles, scrolls, and any lines involving up-and-down and back-and-forth motions that have been drawn with a single stroke must have been made with a point.

A line that is wide, angled, and has a strong inclination is in all probability

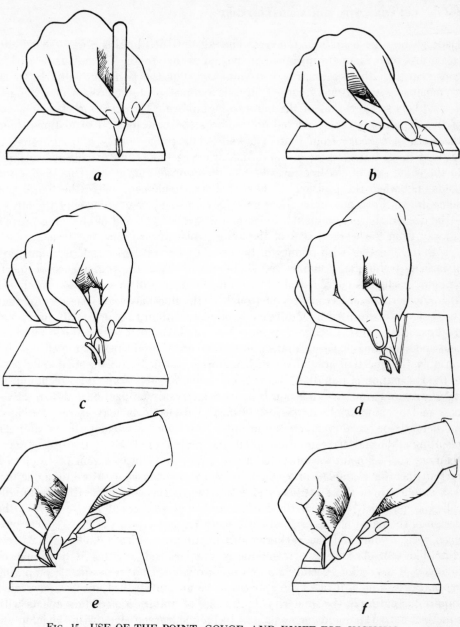

FIG. 15—USE OF THE POINT, GOUGE, AND KNIFE FOR INCISING

The pointed tool. *a:* Held like a pencil in a plane at right angles to the surface and pulled, forms a line with a symmetric trough. *b:* Held under the hand and inclined, forms an unsymmetric trough. **The gouge.** *c:* Held in a plane at right angles to the surface and pushed, cuts a symmetric trough. *d:* Inclined to one side, leaves an unsymmetric trough. **The knife.** *e:* Blade inclined to the surface cuts an unsymmetric groove. *f:* Held at right angles to the surface, scrapes an unsymmetric groove.

made with either a knife or a gouge. The edge of such lines is always sharp and clean, and there is an abrupt break at the end of the stroke. The cut made with a gouge can be either symmetric or asymmetric, but the knife cut is likely to be asymmetric. On a strongly curved line the symmetry of the trough of a gouged line is likely to vary, that of the knife to be uniform. The direction of inclination of the trough on strongly curved lines affords the best method of distinguishing the work of a gouge from that of a knife. The gouge makes a trough that is inclined toward the center of curvature, whereas knife cuts are always inclined to the same side of the line regardless of direction of curvature. This distinction holds only when the position of the vessel was unchanged while the figure was being drawn. Position can be determined by comparing the two ends of the stroke —the deeper, sharper end is the finish of the stroke. The end of the gouge stroke is away from the worker, that of the knife stroke toward him (fig. 14b,c).

Style, together with quality of line, often conveys an immediate impression of incising technique. Boldness and simplicity of style, the prominence of short, straight, or slightly curved strokes, a certain limitation of line direction combined with angularity and asymmetry of trough of the line may leave one certain that the design was executed by a different type of tool than that ordinarily used. Yet to prove that either a gouge or a knife was employed demands detailed observation and sometimes experimentation to test means of producing certain effects. Invariably the question arises, Are such inquiries justified—are we not falling prey to the fascination of minutiae? There is no simple answer. Sometimes technique is significant and sometimes it is not. It depends on its standardization and distinctiveness and on how firmly it was established. Various tools may have been used indifferently or certain ones chosen in order to produce particular effects, and the resulting style may have been accepted and perpetuated. Even the use of more than one tool—a point for intricate lines, a gouge or knife to accent or emphasize certain lines, for example—may characterize a style of incising. More than one tool was employed, in some instances at least, for the type of decorative technique called plano-relief, in which the background of design is cut away, leaving the design in the plane of the original surface. In certain types, the figures were outlined with a point and the background was cut away with a knife or a narrow chisel-like tool. As long as a technique is standardized, whether it be simple or involved, it may afford useful data because it offers a fruitful means of comparing types. For example, if one type appears to be an imitation of another, one must inquire the nature of the similarity. Is it a case of imitation of certain effects with a distinct native technique or was a new technique learned along with the adoption of new stylistic elements? When techniques are analyzed and compared, the discussion of the relationships of pottery types can be more explicit and convincing.

This review should serve to emphasize the student's obligation to state the basis of his identification of incising technique. Proof is often lacking because of the nature of the evidence, and rarely will study of a small collection or a few vessels be conclusive; whereas the accumulated observations of a number of workers will at least build up strong circumstantial evidence. If in publication deductions are stripped bare of the observations on which they rest, we are robbed of this cumulative data.

Painting techniques. Methods of applying color for the decoration of a vessel surface can be defined in terms of order of painting and firing, manner of utilizing color of the vessel in design, and details of application. With respect to sequence and heating, there are three basic techniques of application: before firing, after firing with no further heating, and after firing with secondary heating. These methods are adapted to different types of paint; thus, the best-known examples of unfired paint are minerals that change color on firing (such as cinnabar, malachite, and limonite). Consequently, recognition of technique is reduced to identification of pigment (see p. 389).

The basis of identifying certain paints as postfiring with secondary heating is the fact that these paints, which are in the form of carbon, can be burned out on reheating at temperatures below the range of most pottery firing. Such paints were originally an organic substance, most likely a plant extract, applied after firing because clays with low base exchange capacity do not prevent oxidation in firing. The secondary heating would have been just sufficient to char and convert them to carbon. The identification of this technique is therefore a matter of determining the oxidation temperature of a carbon paint. The standard ceramic practice of painting before firing is either recognized by firing changes in the paint, such as the sintering of an iron oxide (see p. 174), or inferred by eliminating the other, more specialized procedures. The condition of certain paints may not indicate whether or not they have been fired. Ferric oxide, for example, may not undergo change and, when fired, lacks bond no less than when unfired, whereas a red ferruginous clay is bonded by the clay which requires firing for hardening.

The basic technique of painting designs by applying pigment with a brush presents no problems of identification. If one considers details of brushwork, however, various observations can be made. One can appreciate the questions that arise in interpretation when he considers the factors that affect line quality: viscosity of paint, grain size of pigment if it is insoluble, type of brush, method of handling the brush, and the potter's skill. The length of a stroke is affected by the spreading quality of the paint and the capacity of the brush. Degree of uniformity in width of stroke and thickness of the paint throughout the length of the line are also affected by spreading quality of paint. The effects of paint composition on line quality are reviewed under "Paints and Glazes" (p. 170), and this discussion will be limited to evidences of the way in which the brush was used.

A pigment that is thin or has poor covering power often reveals individual brush strokes and overlapping of lines, from which certain characteristics of painting can be recognized. Brushwork, although seemingly a detail, may be marked by peculiarities that distinguish a style of painting (fig. 16). An example familiar to the Southwestern archaeologist is the extension of brush strokes beyond the point of juncture of separate strokes, which is a distinguishing mark of Kana-a Black-on-white. Other peculiarities of line give hints as to manner of using the brush: number of strokes that compose a broad line; sharpness of angles at points marking change in line direction, which indicate whether the brush was lifted to make a series of separate, short strokes or used without lifting in one free, unbroken stroke; presence or absence of guide lines and net structures used as boundaries in painting solids; and variation in line width with change in direction of continuous strokes, a style that follows from the use of the side of the brush and maintenance of a constant position of brush with relation to surface.

When two or more pigments are used, the question of order of application arises. Of particular interest is the sequence of painting outlined figures filled with a contrasting pigment. The preliminary drafting of outlines to be filled constitutes a different approach to design from that in which bold masses are blocked in first and afterwards outlined to point them up. Psychological factors may be involved; in one case, the tendency is to emphasize correctness of outline; in the other, interest is centered on the balance and relation of masses. Even such a detail as the care exercised to confine a color within outlines—interest in working accurately to the boundary or the indifference that allows daubing beyond it—may indicate not alone the psychological traits of the individual painter but also the standards of a stylistic tradition.

In the study of brushwork, sporadic characteristics attributable to individual differences should be segregated from the constant features that reflect established techniques. This can be done only by studying the variable and persistent features

FIG. 16—BRUSH TECHNIQUE
Methods of painting a broad line. a: Single stroke of a broad brush. *b:* Two overlapping strokes of a narrow brush. *c:* A band outlined and filled. **Differences in sharpness of lines painted with.** *d:* Separate strokes for each direction. *e:* A single stroke without lifting the brush when turning an angle. **Use of guide lines.** A wavy line painted—*f:* without a guide line; *g:* with a guide line (Kana-a Black-on-white ware). The guide line can be recognized by the fact that it cuts across the troughs of the waves. **Use of preliminary lines or net constructions as guides for repeat elements.** *h:* A running line (zigzag). *i:* Section of net (crossed zigzags). (Bands from Samarran-style pottery from Matarrah.) **Effect on line width of changing direction of lines without changing position of brush.** *j:* Painted with a single stroke, dragging across the bristles to the right, pulling downward with the bristles, dragging across to the left (copied from Vinaceous Tawny ware, Benque Viejo, British Honduras). *k:* Painted for contrast with *j,* with a stroke for each direction, all made by pulling the brush in line with the bristles. **Extension of stroke beyond junction of lines.** *l:* Kana-a Black-on-white.

FIG. 16

in collections of sufficient size to show frequency of occurrence reliably. Consequently, the importance of examining large samples cannot be overemphasized.

When color of the vessel surface is incorporated as an integral or primary part of design, a specialized painting technique may be employed. This subject can be approached through the concept of positive and negative styles, terms here used with reference to the effect of ratio of dark and light in painting and not to method of applying paint. If there is a predominance of darker values, or if normal value relations are reversed and parts that are ordinarily light are dark and vice versa, the design is considered negative. The effect is most clearly brought out when figure and background are plainly differentiated. The background is darker than figure in a negative pattern. This relation of values can be produced by: (1) painting the background around the figures, which retain the light slip or body color of the vessel; (2) painting the figure with a temporary protective material, applying an allover coat or wash of darker color, and subsequently removing the protective material to expose the figures in the surface color of the vessel, a technique hereafter referred to as resist painting; (3) painting light figures on a darker slip or surface. It is important to know the diagnostics of these techniques because one of them, resist painting, is specialized and has an interesting distribution in the New World (see Curry, 1950, for listing of occurrences). This technique is sometimes referred to as negative painting, but the term is ambiguous and terminology will be simplified if we recognize that we have two distinct things, a class of design distinguished by the reversal of ordinary relations of dark and light, and a technique of decoration which involves the use of a temporary protective coat and permits the application of color as a wash.

The use of a light paint on a darker ground is an easily recognized, minor technique that can be dismissed with a few words. The paint is always a suspension, usually a whitish or light-yellow clay, and therefore has body and can generally be identified by its relief. If it is thin and its relief is not clear, careful scraping will reveal the color of the background paint beneath it.

It is more difficult to distinguish resist from background painting because on both, the untreated vessel surface constitutes the light part of the design and the same kind of pigment can be used for background color in both. The distinction is in method of application, not in paint composition. Attention has been called to similarity of design style and paint color of resist decoration as it is known from different areas—South America, Mesoamerica, and the eastern United States (Willey and Phillips, 1944). It does not follow, however, that these characteristics afford sound basis for identification. In considering style, it is important to remember that resist technique affords the easiest and quickest way of producing certain negative patterns. If an area is to be filled with dots or circles, for instance, it is much simpler to paint the dots with a brush than it is to paint the background around them. There would be no reason for using resist technique unless it had an advantage of this kind, although when it was once developed, its use may have been extended to other patterns for which it offered no advantage. It is possible that general similarities in design are explained, in part at least, by such practical considerations. This factor cannot be weighed, however, until there is a thorough, systematic comparison of styles in the various areas.

Students familiar with resist-paint decoration identify confidently most specimens, although a sample often includes some doubtful sherds. Color of the background is often mentioned as a criterion of identification. Although line quality can afford proof of resist painting, there is nothing in the nature of the paint itself, which is carbon, that defines technique. It so happens that this colorant appears to have been used consistently for the background of resist-painted design, and that the ware is often associated with types decorated in mineral pigment from which it is quite distinct in appearance. But if these resist-decorated sherds occurred with types having design painted in organic black, composition of the background color of resist would cease to have diagnostic value. With respect to style and quality of line, the characteristics that are difficult to define but are intuitively felt undoubtedly rest on the fact that the light figures offer greater economy of effort in painting; the pattern is such that the figures could be most easily produced by confining brushwork to the light parts. This observation affords at best only circumstantial evidence. There are, however, certain characteristics of lines and pattern that prove that the light parts were painted with resist material (fig. 17). These diagnostics do not occur on all sherds, but it is none the less important to seek and record them.

The color of the body or slip, which generally constitutes the pattern of resist-decorated pottery, is variable, but the applied coat is either black or gray, often a pale gray. Sherds from the Maya area (Copan, Honduras; Quirigua, Chipoc, and Nebaj, Guatemala), Teotihuacan, Mexico, and Angel Mound, Indiana, which I have examined, all have a gray or black coat that oxidizes readily at relatively low temperatures (500°–600°C). This temperature range is, I believe, lower than that within which the vessels were fired, a relation indicating a postfiring technique. There is little doubt that the color is due to carbon black, but it could have been produced in various ways: by applying some organic substance such as a plant extract after firing and reheating the vessel just enough to char the paint; by rubbing some form of carbon such as soot onto the surface, as is done in present-day decoration of gourds in Guatemala (McBryde, 1943); or by smudging the vessel. In each case the deposit of carbon would be readily oxidized. The manner in which it was produced has more than passing interest because of possible derivation from the technique of textile dying known as batik. A wax is usually employed in batik to prevent parts of the textile from absorbing dye, and wax would afford a satisfactory protective material in pottery decoration also. Its use in the decoration of gourds strengthens the probability of its ceramic use. Willey has suggested in conversation that the use of an organic extract for the gray may have been influenced by or derived from the practice of textile dying. It is noteworthy that the black pottery paints of those parts of the Maya area where resist technique occurs are mineral (iron-manganese ore), and therefore the choice of colorant for resist decoration was not influenced by ceramic technique. If the black were obtained by smudging, it would, of course, be impossible to use wax or any material that would melt, and archaeologists who have favored this theory have suggested that clay was the resist material. This hypothesis offers no parallels to batik technique other than the fact of protecting parts of the design while a wash is applied.

The method of producing the background color of resist decoration is not easily explained by direct analysis, but there are observations that have a bearing on it, particularly the appearance of the edge of the line and uniformity of color. In the specimens that I have examined there is great variability in appearance of the edge of the gray areas. On some specimens it is sharp and has the same intensity as the main body of color; on others it has an indistinct, cloudy, or blurred appearance. This haziness sometimes suggests diffusion of a liquid paint in the clay beyond the line of application. It is known from the study of fired organic paint that this effect occurs more frequently on certain clays than on others; consequently, it does not occur on all specimens. The only explanation of a blurred-

FIG. 17—DIAGNOSTICS OF RESIST TECHNIQUE

White represents the parts painted with resist material in all except *b* and *d*. Patterns were copied in white paint on black paper to obtain the quality of brushwork. *b* and *d* painted in black to illustrate contrast in character of outline when the background is painted. *a,c,g,h* copied from illustrations of sherds from Angel Mound, Indiana; others copied from sherds: *e*, Copan, Honduras, *f*, Teotihuacan, Mexico, *i*, Nebaj, Guatemala. *Shape of ends of background spaces formed when parallel lines join a transverse line*. *a:* Note square, sharp ends of background spaces. *b:* Painted in black with square-tipped brush to reproduce the quality of background spaces of *a* as nearly as possible. Note difference in sharpness of corners. *Alignment of the ends of series of parallel lines*. *a:* Ends of background spaces (black) are cut off evenly by the transverse line. *b:* When these background lines are painted, there is no guide and their evenness depends on the skill and care of the painter. Their alignment is rarely as true as that of background cut by a painted transverse. *Form of ticks made with a round-tipped brush*. *c:* Lines and ticks painted in white. *d:* Background painted with a round-tipped brush for comparison with *c*. It would be excessively difficult to duplicate the effect by painting the background. *Joining of elements when the medium overflows the intended area of application*. *e:* Dots in a panel have flowed together. This error would not happen were the background painted. *Blob left at the beginning of a stroke by a full brush: f. Extension of end of brush stroke beyond the outline: g. Orderliness and pattern of brush strokes*. *h:* In the band at the lower left, the black spaces lack regularity of form and position, but downward-curving crisscrossed lines can be traced in the white. *Simplicity of draftsmanship*. *i:* The white figures are made with four broad, short strokes. To outline them and paint the background would require delicate work with a very fine brush.

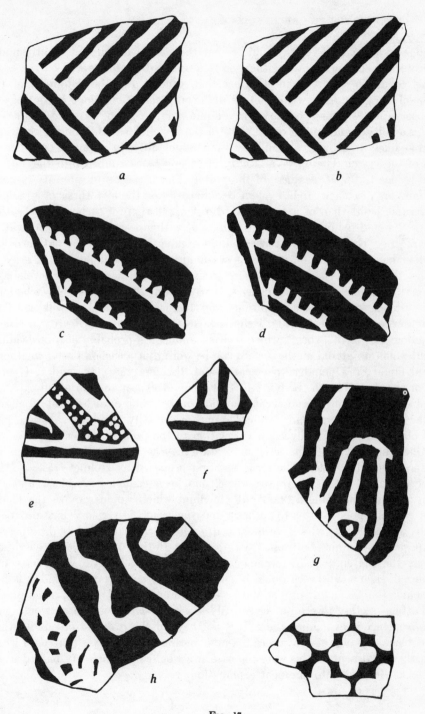

FIG. 17

line edge on a smudged vessel would be that the carbon penetrated slightly under the protective coat, which was either too thin or failed to adhere well on the edge. Such a condition would be local rather than general and the definition of the outline of the gray areas would not be uniform, a condition which is contrary to my observation. With respect to color, a liquid paint might be streaked or uneven, and this quality would appear on all parts of the vessel. A smudge, on the contrary, would be likely to show local uniformity but might differ in intensity on different parts of the vessel. The only variability of carbon black rubbed into the surface would be due to the carelessness of the potter. The variation in intensity of color from faint gray to black can be explained more easily on the hypothesis of a carbonized organic paint than of a smudge or direct application of carbon. Overheating the vessel would oxidize a charred paint, and, with uncertain control of heat, a range of grays comparable to those of fired organic paint would be obtained. On the other hand, it would be a very poor smudge that would produce a gray as faint as that which characterizes many resist-decorated specimens. In this connection it may be well to emphasize that carbon is a very stable substance under ordinary atmospheric conditions and temperatures, and it will not fade through exposure or weathering. References to the color as faded are, therefore, misleading. The term "worn," which is often applied, is probably also misleading. A paint which stands out on the surface can be worn, but a carbon black, whether a charred liquid or a smudge, penetrates and discolors the clay, and it is only worn or abraded when the body itself is. We cannot expect to gain a full explanation of technique from the observations that can be made on a handful of sherds, but the gleanings from many examples may eventually yield the answer, provided observations are analyzed with relation to the problem of technique.

One other fact regarding resist decoration may be significant. The decoration was once called lost color. The term was first proposed by Holmes (1888, p. 113) on the assumption that the entire vessel had been coated with black and the design produced by using a "take-out" medium which would remove the black. There is no support for this hypothesis, but the term "lost color" has also been used by archaeologists who have described a substance that faded or disappeared on exposure to the air (Lothrop, 1936, pp. 9, 13; Butler, 1951). This observation suggests the presence of an organic substance such as a dye which was not carbonized; such a substance would be subject to solution and decay, and it is not improbable that remnants of it would be oxidized on exposure to the atmosphere.

Potters' methods were not necessarily so simple and uniform as would suit our convenience in explaining them. It is not beyond the realm of possibility that carbon black was obtained by more than one means and that dyes were used without further treatment. If this were the case, we would be completely baffled if we tried to fit them all into one neat explanation.

Usulutan ware, which occurs principally in the pre-Classic horizon of the Maya area, illustrates a negative style obtained by a variant technique. The characteristics of this decoration will serve as an example of the questions raised by an obscure technique and ways in which hypotheses may be tested. This decoration has characteristics that could be explained by resist painting, but it differs from the black-wash class just described in color and style of decoration. (The term "wash" seems less ambiguous than "paint" because the application was probably an allover coat.) The design is distinguished by the prominence of straight or wavy parallel lines in sets, executed with a multiple-pointed applicator. Lines and other elements of design are in the white or cream color of the body or slip; the background is light red or orange. The lack of constancy of slip is explained by the fact that the ware is made from different body clays, some of which have a light color comparable to that of the slip. Identification of the technique of this decoration as resist painting has been questioned because sherds with comparable colors have, in place of pattern, irregularly disposed splotches and cloudy areas that were not painted.

Before we consider the ways in which these effects might have been obtained, peculiarities of the red background color should be noted. The colors are those of ferruginous paints, but the relief characteristic of such paints, which are suspensions, is generally lacking. The exceptional sherds that show relief of the red color may represent imitations of the standard technique by potters who did not fully understand it or lacked the requisite materials. The red of typical specimens also has a luster comparable to that of the elements of design that are in the original clay surface. Such luster and lack of relief are characteristics of paints applied as solutions, but the iron oxide paint or materials from which iron oxide might be obtained are insoluble and hence are applied as suspensions and have relief. The properties of Usulutan red might be obtained by using a thin coat and polishing it, but if this ware is decorated by resist painting, the resist material would interfere with polishing. Another possible explanation is that a wash of an alkaline substance was used instead of an iron-bearing material. The red color would then be caused by the reaction of alkali with the clay, liberating iron oxide, which would be oxidized in firing (see p. 385). We have an example of this effect in Pueblo pottery, where the source of the alkali is an organic paint and the red color was developed by accidental oxidation. Examples of this reaction are uncommon, not only because the ware was normally unoxidized, but also because only certain clays liberate iron upon the application of alkali. This occurrence suggests an explanation of Usulutan red. Like Pueblo ware, it may have been painted with a plant extract that contained sufficient alkali to react with the clay. Its color shows that it was fully oxidized in firing, and the clay, which is an exceptionally fine cream or light buff, may well have had the requisite composition. It is tempting to toy with this hypothesis that an organic paint was applied on such a clay, since the probability that the paint of black-wash pottery was a plant extract suggests how the effect of alkali on certain clays when oxidized might have been noted and utilized to obtain color combinations such as those of Usulutan, but the props are easily knocked from this theory. Aside from the fact that the black wash was unfired, Usulutan antedates the black-wash resist style in Mesoamerica. Before spinning such theories, we should obtain more direct evidence of the nature of the red. This is an instance where chemical analysis would afford a definitive answer. If the red is caused by iron oxide released from the clay, then a quantitative determination should show identical percentage of iron in the red and light material. If, on the other hand, the red has a higher percentage of iron, a pigment must have been added.

To return to the question of the light part of the pattern, resist painting would explain satisfactorily the method of obtaining the negative effect of Usulutan ware. Painting a pattern with temporary protective material places no restriction on composition of background wash or on the sequence of painting and firing. The resist material has served its purpose as soon as the background color is applied, and the time of its application is determined by whether or not the background coat will withstand firing. Shook and Kidder (1953, p. 100) call attention to peculiarities of the light part of Usulutan patterns which pose questions regarding technique, and they "have wondered if the light lines might not have been drawn with a liquid, presumably an acid, that altered the color of the slip." The peculiarities include weakness of line contrast within some areas, spreading of lines, apparent marks of running and smearing, and cloudy areas. The latter sometimes occur on vessels which lack pattern but have the characteristic colors and vessel shape of Usulutan. The suggestion of chemical action on the slip recalls Holmes' "lost color" theory (1888, p. 113). It might seem to be given some point by the fact that leaching effects are sometimes observed on sherds buried under tropical conditions. Light, wavy markings on red-slipped ware suggest contact with rootlets and subsequent solution of ferric oxide brought about by action of organic acids. It does not follow from this effect, however, that potters could have used a leaching process because soil acid would have acted over a long period, whereas the potter depends on immediate or short-period results, and it is questionable what acids for quick leaching were available to the potter. Strong mineral acids applied cold to the surface of Usulutan sherds do not affect the color. Shook and Kidder (1953) refer to my suggestion that etching effects might be observed if acid had been used. The term "etching" is misleading because an acid would not attack the clay substance appreciably; what I had in mind was the destruction of luster if the surface were rendered porous by the removal of iron oxide. After seeing examples of "rootlet"-marked sherds some years ago, I dismissed the suggestion because leached and unleached areas are indistinguishable in luster. Resist painting offers a more tenable explanation of Usulutan decoration than leaching or bleaching as its mechanics are well established and have been used to obtain Usulutan-like effects, whereas we do not know of an effective manner of bleaching the red slip. Running, spreading, and smearing could occur with either medium. Cloudy Usulutan has not yet been studied. Firing-clouds that extend over both line and ground show that decoration was applied before firing.

As an example of different color combinations in resist paint, polychromes from Piedras Negras, described and illustrated by Butler (1935), and Chipoc types, illustrated by Smith (1953), might be cited. Paint composition of these has not been reported.

Resist painting, one of the most specialized methods of color decoration, has been reviewed in detail to illustrate the observations that have a bearing on technique. Microscopic examination may in some instances play a more prominent role, as for example in determining order of application of coats and methods of outlining figures in stucco decoration (see Kidder and Shepard, 1944). In general, hypotheses regarding technique will suggest specific observations by which they can be tested, and experiments designed to reproduce effects often serve as further tests.

FIRING

The final stage of pottery making is the crucial one; it tests the soundness of the potter's work, it determines the serviceability of the ware, and it affects its attractiveness. The Americanist deals principally with wares fired without a kiln. Although this technique is relatively crude and simple, it admits of variation in provisions for firing (a pit, a grate above ground), in type and amount of fuel, length and rate of heating, and length of the stage in which draft and temperature necessary for oxidation are maintained. Furthermore, prehistoric pottery shows a wide range in the properties affected by firing temperature and atmosphere. It is important, therefore, to know how much can be learned about firing methods from these properties.

Wares differ greatly in such properties as hardness, strength, color, and porosity. The question is, Can firing methods be judged reliably from these properties? Expressions such as "overfired," "underfired," "fired in reducing atmosphere," or "fired in oxidizing atmosphere" are not uncommon in pottery description, but the last two are interpretations, not simple descriptions, and it is well to consider their reliability.

Judgment of effects of firing and inferences regarding firing methods. It is important to distinguish at the outset expressions regarding firing that refer only to the appearance or properties of pottery from those that postulate a condition of firing. In other words, we should not confuse description of the effects of firing on pottery with deductions regarding firing method. For example, it is one thing to say a vessel was overfired and quite another to say it was fired at a high temperature. Defects such as bloating or deformation will indicate overfiring, but the temperature at which different clays mature varies over a wide range; therefore, overfiring does not necessarily indicate that an exceptionally high temperature was attained but simply that the temperature was too high for that particular clay. Likewise, to say that a piece of pottery was not oxidized is quite different from saying that it was fired in reducing atmosphere. We can easily determine whether or not the pottery was oxidized, but to prove that it was fired in reducing atmosphere is quite another matter because clays differ in their requirements for oxidation; some are nearly oxidized in the raw state, others may contain a large amount of carbonaceous matter and other impurities requiring long oxidation. Also, length of firing and temperature, as well as atmosphere, affect the degree of oxidation.

Paradoxical as it may seem on first thought, we can decide *how well* a vessel was fired much more easily than we can learn *how* it was fired. The reason is that the properties of pottery show directly the effectiveness of firing but not the method of firing because the same firing conditions will produce different results with different clays. A temperature that will render one clay dense and hard will leave another open and porous, and a firing atmosphere that will bring out a strong clear color in one clay will leave another gray.

It is important to know how well a vessel is fired and to judge whether or not potters were turning out a good product. It is even more important to know how effectively potters were working within the limitations imposed on them by the materials they had, to judge the stage of technical advancement they had reached. For example, we can learn if pottery is soft by merely scratching it. But the question is, Does this property indicate that it was poorly fired or is it soft because it is made from a refractory clay that would not become hard within the potter's temperature range? We can determine empirically by firing experiments whether or not the pottery could have been fired harder or to a clearer color within the temperature range which we know to be attainable in simple, open firing. Such tests offer a means of evaluating the pottery and the potter's methods. The importance of such evaluations should not be underestimated even though the tests give no absolute data on firing temperature and atmosphere. The technical standards of a people and the effect of technical excellence on the demand for a ware, as indicated by the extent of its trade, are matters of direct interest in relation to the economics of pottery making.

To emphasize the significance of such inquiries is not to disregard the value of information regarding the actual conditions of firing. However difficult to secure, data regarding firing method are important in any study of the development, persistence, and spread of techniques. But these introductory remarks should give a hint of the difficulties and uncertainties involved in ascertaining firing method from the properties of pottery. The difficulty rests in the fact that the properties of pottery are affected by a number of independent variables which can be summed up as the physical and chemical properties of the clay, and the temperature, length, and atmosphere of firing.

The nature of combustion.   In order to appreciate the difficulties involved in judging how pottery was fired, it will be well to review briefly the conditions that affect clay in firing. First, we may consider the basic facts with regard to combustion. It is hardly necessary to point out that fuels differ greatly in physical and chemical characteristics. Although we can disregard gaseous and liquid fuels and concentrate on solid fuels, we still have to recognize that there are marked differences among them. The various kinds of wood burn very differently, as anyone who has watched a campfire well knows. Some woods have a quick, hot flame, others burn slowly; some give off black smoke and have a sooty flame, others burn with little smoke and have a clean flame. The intensity and persistence of the flame varies, depending on the volume and nature of the gases formed; and the color of the flame is affected by incandescent, colloidal carbon and by the salts that are volatilized from the ash. Then there is the difference in density of the charcoal formed from different woods, and even the amount and texture of the ash affects the way charcoal burns. Some ashes are loose and light enough to fall or be carried off, leaving the charcoal exposed to the air; others cling, forming an insulating coat that reduces the rate of combustion.

Differences in the way fuels burn suggest their complexity. The compounds in coal, for example, are known to number in the hundreds. From the standpoint of combustion, however, all the complex fuels can be considered mixtures of three elementary fuels: gaseous hydrocarbons, solid carbon, and a mixture of carbon monoxide and hydrogen. When wood burns, for example, volatile products are first driven off and decomposed to the gaseous elementary fuels, leaving behind solid carbon, the charcoal. It should be understood that the hydrocarbons include gases having a considerable range of chemical compositions and properties. Also, as I have just indicated, charcoals and other forms of solid carbon vary in their physical properties, yet the members of each class of elementary fuel have common characteristics.

Combustion is in all cases a process of oxidation, and when it is complete, the end products are carbon dioxide and water. The intermediate products and the way they are formed differ for each class of fuel and also for the members of each class, depending on temperature, the relative amount of oxygen in the atmosphere, surface of the fuel exposed, and the presence or absence of catalysts. For example hot charcoal unites with oxygen from air passing over it to form carbon dioxide, carbon monoxide, and an intermediate physicochemical complex that breaks down into these two oxides. At low temperatures carbon monoxide may be the principal product of combustion. At high temperatures carbon dioxide will be formed, but it may be reduced wholly or in part to carbon monoxide, depending on the relative amounts of carbon and oxygen and on the time of contact between carbon dioxide and carbon. As another example, the hydrocarbons burned with sufficient oxygen have a smokeless flame and pass in rapid succession through several intermediate products to formaldehyde, which in turn breaks down into hydrogen and carbon monoxide, or water and either carbon monoxide or carbon dioxide, depending on the amount of oxygen present. Under other conditions the hydrocarbons, particularly the higher ones, break down into carbon and hydrogen, and the carbon appears as smoke and soot. This process of decomposition is known as cracking. Temperature influences the way in which the hydrocarbons decompose. Both forms of decomposition can take place simultaneously, but conditions usually favor one over the other.

This brief review will suggest the complexity of the reactions occurring in combustion and the various factors that affect the composition of the intermediate products. The reader who is interested in pursuing the subject further is referred to Haslam and Russell (1926).

The atmosphere in direct firing.   This simple description of combustion will suggest how variable the gases that surround pottery during firing may be. We speak of firing atmosphere as being oxidizing or reducing. When there is a good draft affording an excess of oxygen over that required to burn the fuel, the atmosphere will be oxidizing, which means that, given the requisite temperature range, carbonaceous matter in the paste or soot on the vessel surface will burn out; then after removal of carbon, which has a stronger affinity for oxygen than does iron, the iron oxides will be brought to their highest state of oxidation. If, on the other hand, there is insufficient oxygen for complete combustion of the fuel, and reducing gases (carbon monoxide, hydrogen, hydrocarbons) that rob other substances of oxygen are present, carbonaceous matter in the paste will remain unburned; and at certain temperatures, iron oxides will be reduced to a lower state and their color effect will be gray instead of red. Not infrequently when there is insufficient draft, the fuel will give off smoke containing colloidal carbon, which will cause sooting or smudging of the pottery. The reactions in either an oxidizing or a reducing atmosphere will be more or less intense, depending on the composition of the gases, the relative volume of the active gases, the temperature, and the period of reaction. When firing atmosphere is fully controlled, it can also be made neutral, neither yielding nor taking oxygen. In open firing there is always a mixture of gases; only by rare chance and then momentarily would the reducing gases formed in the burning of the fuel be fully oxidized, leaving no excess oxygen in the process. Nevertheless, there may be conditions in which there is little exchange of oxygen between the atmosphere and the constituents of the pottery because there is only a slight excess of oxygen and neutral conditions are approached or temperatures are too low for oxidation to occur.

In open firing, the atmosphere will be continually changing during different stages of combustion and with shifting draft and air currents. When wood first starts to burn, the volatile constituents are driven off and reducing gases will be present; with poor draft and overfueling, they will be excessive, but the temperature range will generally be low and the gases may have little effect. When the wood is burned to charcoal, the fire will be smokeless, and with sufficient temperature and draft, the atmosphere will be oxidized. Unevenness in color of pottery reflects the fluctuations in firing atmosphere that occur as air currents shift, gases mingle and swirl about the vessels, and flames play upon them.

A suggestion of the variable percentage of oxygen and reducing gases which are present when there is partial control of draft is given in Table 10. Samples for these gas analyses were taken from experimental firings in a jug-shaped pit, the form and dimensions for which were based on pits found in Pueblo ruins. Although the prehistoric pits were probably not used to fire pottery, a pit allows more control of atmosphere than is possible with open firing and hence is convenient for experimental purposes. The fuel for these firings was juniper wood, and the fire was kindled on the floor of the pit at one side of a flue. Both oxygen and reducing gases are present in the samples analyzed, but the difference in their ratio during different stages of firing is considerable, and they show that the atmosphere may be strongly reducing when fresh fuel is added and nearly neutral or oxidizing when the fuel has burned to charcoal.

Interpretations of evidences of firing atmosphere. The color of pottery usually indicates in a general way whether or not it is oxidized. The effects of firing atmosphere on color were first brought to the attention of Southwestern archaeologists by H. S. Colton (1939) in a paper that has had considerable influence on pottery classification and general theories of cultural relationships in the Pueblo area. Colton described the effects of refiring sherds and advanced the hypothesis that clear colors—yellows, buffs, reds—indicate that pottery was fired in oxidizing atmosphere; grays, that it was fired in a reducing atmosphere. I have previously mentioned the difference between the statements that pottery is not oxidized and that it was fired in a reducing atmosphere. The state of the paste with respect to oxygen is easily established by refiring a fragment in air. The temperature should be high enough to burn out carbon and to bring iron oxide to the ferric state but should not be appreciably higher than that at which we believe the pottery was fired. The range of 700°–750°C is satisfactory except for the very

TABLE 10—ANALYSES OF GAS SAMPLES TAKEN FROM EXPERIMENTAL FIRINGS

NUMBER OF SAMPLE	FIRING METHOD	STAGE WHEN SAMPLED	TEMP. °C	DRAFT	PERCENTAGE OF GASES DETERMINED				
					CO_2	O_2	CO	H_2	HYDRO-CARBONS
1	Pit kiln	Early, black smoke	630–790	Moderate; direct	17.0	1.3	3.5	0.4	..
2	Updraft kiln	Early, black smoke	600	Moderate, direct	11	8.4	2.4	..	2.4
3	Pit kiln	Early, black smoke	800	Strong, direct	19.4	0.4	10.0	1.0	0.4
4	Updraft kiln	Early, no smoke	565	Moderate	5.7	11.5	..	3.2	0.9
5	Pit kiln	Near temp. peak	950–870	Moderate	6.6	7.2	0.3	5.0	..
6	Pit kiln	Near temp. peak	810–830	Moderate	19.3	0.6	1.7	..	..
7	Pit kiln	Near temp. peak	745–740	Flue 2/3 closed	18.9	0.5	2.4	0.8	..
8	Pit kiln	Past temp. peak	620–600	Flue luted	16.6	1.6	3.8	..	..
9	Pit kiln	Past temp. peak	610–560	Flue luted	16.4	2.6	6.8	4.0	..
10	Pit kiln	Past temp. peak	540–512	Flue luted	14.3	0.8	2.2	1.7	0.3

low-fired wares. If the pottery contains carbon or carbonaceous material, it will usually become lighter and clearer with five minutes' heating within this range, but half an hour or longer may be required to oxidize it fully. The length of firing for this test cannot be fixed because the requirements of each paste for oxidation must be established individually. A chip from a sherd can be fired five minutes, drawn and cooled to compare its color with that of the original, and, if necessary, reheated successively until there is no further change. The test is best performed in an electric resistance furnace with a thermoelectric pyrometer for heat control. This simple thermal test is satisfactory for the majority of low-fired wares. It may be necessary to oxidize at higher temperatures for well-fired wares. If there has been vitrification, the test is not applicable because the constituents of the clay are protected from contact with oxygen.

If there is no change in color of the paste on refiring in air, it was originally fully oxidized. What does this fact show with respect to firing atmosphere? The final effect of firing was oxidizing, but we know from the nature of combustion that in a direct firing the atmosphere is not oxidizing in the early stages of firing when a large volume of volatile matter is released from the fuel. It is the end result of firing that we observe. Whether the oxidation period was long or short, and whether the atmosphere during this period was weakly, moderately, or strongly oxidizing can be determined only if we have some of the original clay and test its requirements for full oxidation. The expression "fired in oxidizing atmosphere" when used to describe pottery that has a clear color suggests a firing atmosphere that is uniform throughout firing, one that is fully defined with respect to intensity or length of oxidation. These are false implications. The vessel which has a clear-colored, fully oxidized paste may differ from an unoxidized gray one only in length of firing or the stage of firing at which it was drawn.

If pottery is gray, there are several possible explanations of its color: it may have been made from a highly carbonaceous clay that was not oxidized in firing, it may have been smudged, or it may actually have been reduced. In the first case there is an insufficient supply of oxygen; in the second, carbon is deposited; in the third, oxygen is taken from constituents of the clay. These distinct reactions may or may not take place simultaneously. Reducing gases and fine carbon are frequently present at the same time so that both reduction and sooting take place; on the other hand, there may be sooting without reducing or vice versa or lack of oxidation without either sooting or reduction. How can the effects of these different conditions be distinguished? Intentionally smudged pottery is usually black. If slightly or imperfectly smudged, it may be gray, and often it will be mottled or uneven in color, but unevenness does not always show in sherds. Moreover, clays do not absorb carbon equally. Texture and porosity have a marked effect on absorption; some clays become gray under conditions that turn others black. Therefore, a more reliable criterion than depth of gray is needed to distinguish the sooted or smudged vessel from one made of a highly carbonaceous clay that has not been oxidized, or, in other words, to distinguish carbon that was originally present in the clay from that which was deposited in firing. Ease of oxidation affords some clues. The rate at which carbonaceous matter in the clay can be oxidized is highly variable and depends on its state and the texture of the clay. Nevertheless, that which is in the clay is held more strongly than the light, loose carbon that is deposited in the pores when smoke penetrates the ware. A short firing at 500°C may be sufficient to clear a vessel that has been smudged. In some instances a sherd will fire to a lighter gray at this temperature but will require a higher temperature for complete oxidation. It is probable that the oxidation that takes place at the low temperature is that of the carbon deposited in firing, and if two stages of oxidation are demonstrated, the probability is increased.

A carbonaceous clay that has not been oxidized and a clay in which iron oxide has been reduced will both be gray. How can the two be distinguished; that is, how can we prove that reduction has actually taken place in firing? When a clear color is brought out by refiring pottery, we do not prove that it was reduced in firing but only that it was not oxidized. In discussing the black ware of Egypt, Lucas (1948, p. 430) makes the statement that "early ancient black pottery was fired in a primitive manner in an open fire with an atmosphere that cannot have been a reducing one." He defines a reducing atmosphere as "being not merely the absence of the usual complement of oxygen, or even the momentary presence of small proportions of reducing gases, but the presence of a considerable propor- tion of such gases operating over a somewhat lengthy period of time." It is im- portant to recognize the distinction between the absence of a strongly oxidizing atmosphere and the presence of a reducing atmosphere. Do we have any proof that reduction took place in primitive, direct firing?

The gray and black-on-white wares of the Pueblo area are generally described as being "fired in reducing atmosphere," but it should be clear from this dis- cussion that their colors alone do not prove that reduction has taken place. They may have been made from a carbonaceous clay that was not oxidized. The fact that many sherds have black cores and white outer zones shows that there has been partial oxidation—enough to burn out some of the carbonaceous matter but not enough to bring the clay to a state of complete oxidation in which it is generally buff-colored, as is shown by refiring samples in air. Although the effects on a carbonaceous clay of an atmosphere that is reducing and one that is nearly neutral cannot be distinguished by inspection, there is clear evidence in the properties of the black iron oxide paint that at least some Pueblo black-on-white ware was subject to reducing conditions (see p. 175). Another ware that shows the effects of reduction in firing is Plumbate. In this instance the properties of the slip are significant. Soft, underfired slips are red or orange, whereas hard, vitrified ones are gray. The paste is carbonaceous, but there is no evidence that the slip clay is; and the gray colors have been duplicated by refiring red sherds in an atmosphere of carbon monoxide. Reduction of ferric to ferrous oxide, which is a violent flux, is believed to explain the vitrification of the slip.

These two instances of reduction are special cases. Ordinarily color of paste alone does not constitute proof that reducing conditions prevailed. Lucas (1948, p. 430), in attempting to refute the theory that Egyptian black ware was reduced, used a simple test to demonstrate the presence of carbon. A finely powdered sample of the sherd is mixed with lead chromate and heated. When the gas that is evolved is passed into lime water, the presence of carbon dioxide derived from carbon in the paste is indicated by a milky precipitate. But even though carbon occurs and is the chief colorant, the lower oxide of iron may also be present and contribute to the gray color. The magnetic oxide could have occurred in the raw clay or have been formed by the reduction of ferric oxide during firing. Since, in the majority of cases, it is difficult to prove that firing atmosphere was reducing, it is advisable to describe gray ware as unoxidized rather than as fired in reducing atmosphere.

We have considered the significance of clear colors and grays. There is an intermediate range of colors of low chroma—browns, tans, and drabs. These are generally red- or buff-firing clays that are incompletely oxidized. Any carbonaceous matter that may have been present has been burned out, but the iron oxide is not fully oxidized. Occasionally, however, comparable colors are found among fully oxidized clays. Pastes in this color range should be refired before their state of oxidation is judged.

White clays that are free from iron oxide are the same color whether fired in oxidizing or reducing atmosphere, provided there is no deposition of carbon. Pure white clays are not common, however, and many clays which are whitish when reduced change to a warm cream or light buff when fully oxidized. Whitish pastes should therefore be refired to determine their state.

This discussion of evidences of firing atmosphere has been with reference to studies in which only pottery is available. More specific deductions regarding firing atmosphere can be drawn when the raw clay from which the pottery was made is also available because its requirements for oxidation can then be determined. The instances when we can prove that we have the very clay that was used for a prehistoric pottery type are rare (see p. 155 ff.). The general characteristics of the clays of a region may be significant, however. In the San Juan drainage, for example, carbonaceous clays are abundant and widely distributed in Cretaceous formations. In the study of La Plata pottery a series of clays from different parts of the La Plata drainage was tested and their firing properties compared with those of the pottery of the region. The clays are preponderantly buff-firing, and refiring sherds brings out a comparable range of colors; also the black cores of the sherds indicate that the clays were originally carbonaceous (Morris, 1939, p. 251). These types belong to the class of ware that has been contrasted with the brown wares of the Mogollon area to the south. When we compare the pottery of the two areas, it is important to remember that the clays are basically different and reflect differences in the ceramic resources of the two regions. The southern pastes are darker gray when reduced than the northern ones; therefore, they offered less incentive to check oxidation or to reduce in firing. The contrast in the pastes of the two areas illustrates the importance of understanding the firing properties of clays before concluding that color differences in pottery types are due primarily to differences in method of firing.

Estimations of firing temperature. We have considered how the great variability of clays in their requirement for oxidation complicates judgment of firing atmosphere. Likewise the wide differences in the maturing point of clays render unreliable judgments of firing temperature based on direct observation of firing properties. The hardness, the density, the ring of pottery may indicate that it was well fired, but they do not show how high it was fired. One clay may be matured or vitrified at a temperature which leaves another soft enough to be scratched with a fingernail. In consequence of this circumstance it is possible to compare pottery types with respect to quality by direct observation, but their relative firing temperature cannot be determined without knowledge of their firing behavior. Estimates of firing temperature therefore require laboratory tests. There are three general classes of data that may be used: changes in optical properties of the clay, thermal changes in mineral inclusions, and changes in the physical properties of the body. These data set a limit to the temperature range within which a type was fired, but they do not enable one to determine the exact firing temperature.

Optical properties of the clay can be used only for relatively low-fired wares. If the clay minerals have not lost their crystalline structure, the temperature at which it is destroyed can be determined, and an upper limit is thus placed on the original firing temperature. Length of heating, as well as temperature, affects decomposition. In testing pastes, a rapid rate of heat increase and a slow rate can be employed to establish a range for the upper limit. It is a reasonably safe inference, however, that the rate of direct firing was rapid.

Examples of thermal changes in minerals have been discussed under nonplastic inclusion (p. 30 ff.). These thermal changes may suggest the possibility of establishing what might be called a mineral thermometer. Undoubtedly with further work on thermal properties of minerals, more points can be fixed on the scale, but in most cases these thermal changes, like those in clay minerals, will set limits or indicate possible ranges but will not mark exact temperatures. Another obvious limitation of the mineral thermometer is the fact that the diagnostic minerals are not always present. The thermal effect which is of greatest interest to archaeologists, since it can be observed with a hand lens, is the decomposition of calcite. It is important that the conditions and meaning of this change be understood (see p. 30).

Since the physical properties of pottery undergo progressive change with rise in temperature, these properties would seem to offer a means of estimating temperature that would always be applicable. Matson (in Griffin, 1951) has emphasized the usefulness of color changes in this connection. He has also used other physical properties, particularly shrinkage (in Greenman, 1937). These thermal effects appear to offer simple, straightforward, and universally applicable means of judging firing temperature, but there are sources of error that limit their usefulness and reliability. Two factors should be considered when estimating firing temperature from change in paste color: original state of oxidation of the paste and rate of color change on heating. Gray or black ware may be oxidized at or below its original firing temperature or a temperature higher than that of the original may be required. White-firing clays undergo no color change on firing. Consequently, all white, gray, and black pottery is unsuitable for judgment of firing temperature by color change on refiring. Caution should also be exercised in drawing deductions from clays in the brown and tan range because these may be incompletely oxidized. The second factor that limits the usefulness of color is the fact that when oxidation is complete at a low temperature there may be no further perceptible change for several hundred degrees. The darkening of the buffs, reds, and browns on refiring is due largely to reactions of iron oxide that occur when the paste begins to sinter; therefore, low-fusing clays will afford the possibility of making closer estimates than will refractory clays. Matson (in Griffin, 1951, pp. 107–08) has described the sequence of colors for an iron-bearing, calcareous clay which passes from red through buff to olive. This is a type of clay which is exceptional for its range of firing colors.

There are sources of error in the interpretation of thermal changes in other physical properties also. Porosity affords a clear illustration. In general, it increases during the dehydration and oxidation periods and decreases as the ware matures. The increase during oxidation is due largely to the burning out of carbonaceous matter, which is, of course, affected by time and atmosphere as well as temperature. If pottery is not fully oxidized, it will undergo an increase in porosity on refiring but this does not show that the original firing temperature had been exceeded. The carbonaceous matter might actually be burned out at a lower temperature than the original if the atmosphere originally was not oxidizing.

Firing shrinkage accompanies decrease in porosity and becomes most pronounced as a ware matures and commences to vitrify. In certain stages of firing, however, expansion rather than contraction may occur. It may be caused, in some cases, by volume change in minerals when they pass an inversion point. Quartz is the only common material having a low temperature of inversion that may occur in considerable volume in pottery, but its effect on the expansion of pottery has not been fully investigated.

The sources of error in estimating firing temperature from changes in physical properties must be understood in order to avoid hasty and ill-considered deductions. They should not discourage the student, but rather stimulate him to seek as many lines of evidence as possible.

VESSEL SHAPE

The study of vessel shape can be approached from the standpoint of function, aesthetics, or taxonomy. Function has the appeal of human interest; the purposes of vessels tell something of the activities and customs of the people who used them. Who would not find it more interesting to sort sherds into such groups as cook pots, water jugs, food bowls, paint jars, and incense burners than to classify them as hemispheres, cylinders, simple-silhouette and composite-silhouette vessels? But the relationship between use and shape is rarely unique. The same shape may have a variety of uses, and conversely the same purpose may be served by many forms. Furthermore, we do not know all the uses prehistoric peoples had for pottery and we are often at a loss even to guess the purpose of particular forms. Consequently, function is not a satisfactory criterion for general classification. I would emphasize, however, that it does not follow from this condition that the study of function is unfruitful or unimportant. There are various indirect means of learning how some vessels were used, as, for example, by the conditions under which they are found, by their contents, and from scenes of murals and codices that show vessels in use. Ethnological studies may also be valuable in indicating the relation of shape to function. In order to judge the range of variation and the constant features in vessels used for particular purposes, ethnological data should be extensive because specialization will vary from culture to culture. Linton (1944), in a study of cook pots, has given a striking illustration of the broad implication of differences in form within a functional class. Vessel function is something to test the archaeologist's alertness to indirect evidence and his resourcefulness in checking and interpreting it.

The aesthetic aspects of vessel contour and proportion have received little attention in the archaeological field. We can best consider the scattered studies that have been published after reviewing the broader aspects of vessel shape.

In the American field, concentration on the establishment of chronological frames of reference has been reflected in the study of vessel form. Emphasis has been placed on the description and naming of shapes with the object of using them as criteria for the identification of periods of occupation. There is, of course, a direct relation between the development of a style and the range and detail of its features. The more varied and specialized shape becomes, the more useful it is to the taxonomist. Consequently, in those regions where shape styles are well developed, vessel form takes a prominent place in ceramic classification. In the Mesoamerican field, for example, specific shapes have been used extensively and most successfully as an aid in chronological ordering and in equating cultural horizons. As a result of this circumstance, efforts to systematize classification and standardize nomenclature have been directed largely toward the establishment of a common terminology for specific shapes and for vessel parts; also, the importance of recording proportions for descriptive purposes is well recognized, as is shown by the customary reporting of height/breadth ratios. The broader shape categories, which should serve a complementary purpose in facilitating comparative studies, have received less attention. Thus far, interest in broad classes has centered largely around definition of common shape names—such as jar, bowl, dish, and plate—in terms of contour and proportion. It is hardly an exaggeration to say that this nomenclature has been built up by concentration on a set of words rather than by systematic study of the characteristics of vessel shape. This approach is not adequate for comparative studies, since distinctive shapes alone do not afford sufficiently inclusive basis for tracing the history of style or comparing the influence of one style on another. In proposing a different system of classification, I do not minimize the usefulness of such words as bowl and jar; indeed, our shape vocabulary would be seriously impoverished without them. But the advisability, even the practicability, of establishing strict limits for words which have long been used loosely may be questioned.

Data on shapes of various horizons and regions have accumulated to the point where an efficient filing system for illustrations is required. The need for an inclusive method of classification is thus doubly urgent. The system I shall outline was developed while working on a code for a punched card file, which has served to test its practicability.

SHAPE ANALYSIS AND CLASSIFICATION

A general scheme of classification should be drawn up in terms of the basic characteristics of form as such. Functional references are too uncertain to be included in such a scheme, and finish, which has sometimes been introduced in shape classification, is irrelevant. The obvious approach is a geometric one. We are concerned primarily with vessel proportion and contour. Proportions are easily calculated and expressed as ratios. Contour is more difficult to describe, but there are two obvious approaches: analysis of the general characteristics of contour, and comparison of specific shapes with geometric figures.

A basic concept of the analysis of vessel contour, introduced by Birkhoff (1933), is useful in drawing vessel form as well as in classification and description. Birkhoff considered the points of the vessel contour on which the eye rests (fig. 18).

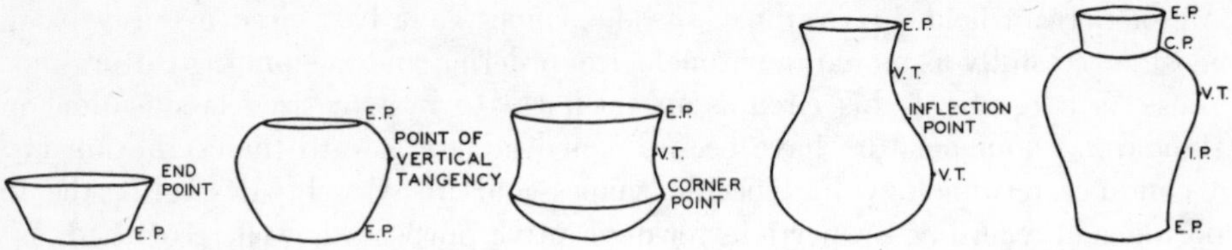

FIG. 18—THE CHARACTERISTIC POINTS OF A VESSEL PROFILE

These "characteristic points," as he called them, are of four types: (1) end points of the curve at base and lip, (2) points where the tangent is vertical, as, for example, points of maximum diameter on a spheroidal form and of minimum diameter on a hyperbolic form, (3) points of inflection where the curvature changes from concave to convex or vice versa, (4) corner points where the direction of the tangent changes abruptly (there is a sharp change in contour).

Fig. 19—
THE LOCATION
OF AN
INFLECTION
POINT

Although Birkhoff's terminology is new, the characteristic points of a contour are generally recognized, with the exception of the inflection point. It is important to understand how to locate this point because its position is definitive and it marks a fixed division of the vessel. One can test its position by moving a straight edge as tangent along the contour of the vessel profile. As the line follows a convex section it rotates in one direction. When it reaches the inflection point and commences to follow a concave section, its direction of rotation is reversed (fig. 19). The stronger the curvature, the more easily the position of the inflection point is recognized by eye, but no matter how slight the curve, a change in its direction can always be demonstrated by this simple, mechanical test. An example will illustrate the usefulness of the inflection point. If a jar has a smooth curve instead of an angle between neck and body, the point at which the neck rises is unmarked and consequently judgments of the height of the neck will differ; but the vessel will have an inflection point which establishes an unequivocal division and affords a means of calculating relative proportions.

The fundamental importance of these points is reflected in the fact that vessel dimensions are calculated from them. Thus, diameters at orifice, at the equator of a spheroidal body, and at a body-neck angle are measurement at end points, points of vertical tangency, and corner points, respectively. The characteristic points differentiate contour types and degrees of complexity of contour, and each of the points establishes a basic shape class (fig. 20).

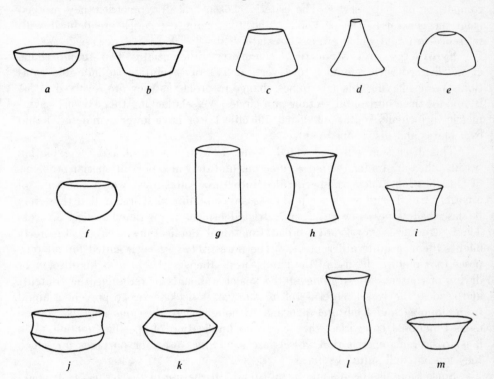

FIG. 20—SHAPE CLASSES DEFINED BY CHARACTERISTIC POINTS

a-e: Vessels having end points only. The sides extend continuously inward or outward without reaching a point of vertical tangency. Unrestricted forms (*a,b*) are common; restricted forms (*c-e*), rare.

f-i: Vessels having a point of vertical tangency. The point approaches a medial position in common restricted forms (*f*) and the hyperboloid (*h*). The cylinder is a special form with an infinite number of points of vertical tangency. The flaring-sided vessel with the start of its wall vertical has a point of vertical tangency coinciding with the end point at the base (*i*). In the hemisphere, a point of vertical tangency coincides with the upper end point.

j-k: Vessels having a corner point. These are characterized by an angle in the contour and include both restricted and unrestricted forms.

l-m: Vessels having an inflection point. These have recurved sides. When a point of vertical tangency is introduced below the inflection point, the form is more complex (*l*).

With this general concept of contour for reference, I will outline a broad classification based on symmetry, structure, contour type, geometric shape, and proportion, taken in that order. In any system of classification, the criteria chosen and their relative order are determined by convenience, the object of the study, and the relations or properties that are deemed significant. The purpose of the present classification is to establish a general method for the systematic comparison of shape styles. The criteria chosen are all geometric, they proceed from the general to the particular, and the major categories are defined with reference to limits which are easily established.

Symmetry and structure. Symmetry differentiates two major shape classes defined with reference to a vertical axis of revolution (infinite-fold rotation). Vessels having this axis do not change in profile as they are revolved about it, and all their horizontal sections are circles. Vessels lacking this axis are asymmetric (principally imitations of natural objects) or have lower symmetry, as do oval plates and disc-shaped canteens.

This discussion will be devoted to vessels with a vertical axis of revolution because they are by far the more numerous and they also present special problems of classification. They can be divided into three categories, which for want of a better term, I shall call structural classes. For preliminary designation they may be described as vessels with: 1. unrestricted orifice, 2. restricted orifice, 3. neck. These structural classes have broad functional implications; that is, the form adapts them to quite different uses. The unrestricted vessel is suited for all purposes that require the use of the hands inside the vessel and also for display or drying of contents. Restriction of the vessel wall aids in retaining the contents and renders the vessel more useful for storage. A neck serves to prevent a liquid from slopping and facilitates pouring. Although these divisions may be spoken of as functional categories, they carry no implication of specific function. Also it is to be remembered that vessels are sometimes used for purposes for which they are not well suited by form.

Since there has been some inconsistency in the use of the terms "restricted" and "unrestricted," and sometimes a neck is not easily delimited, I shall draw on geometric concepts to define the structural classes more precisely and shall qualify the terms and introduce new ones when necessary. The restricted orifice is generally defined as having a diameter less than the maximum vessel diameter; the unrestricted, as having the maximum vessel diameter. Some writers have used the two terms to refer to different degrees of constriction, a usage probably adopted for convenience in the study of a group of vessels lacking open forms. It is not recommended because it disregards the simple, logical, easily identified limit in the series; that is, the point at which the vessel walls are vertical. Spreading to vertical walls mark the unrestricted vessel; converging walls, the

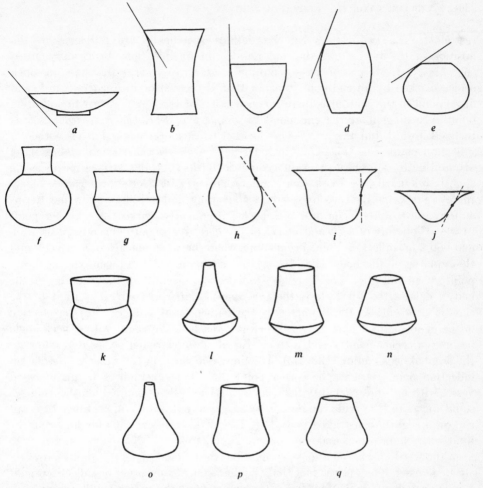

FIG. 21—THREE STRUCTURAL CLASSES

a-e: Distinction between the unrestricted vessel (*a-c*) and the simple restricted vessel (*d,e*). A vertical tangent (*c*) marks the limit of the unrestricted form.

f-j: Distinction between dependent and independent composite and inflected vessels. As long as a corner point lies above the major point, the vessel has an independent, restricted form (*f*). When the two points coincide, the shape becomes unrestricted, composite (*g*), or dependent restricted, according to the slope of the upper section. The vessel with an inflection point above a major point is also an independent restricted vessel (*h*). When the tangent at the inflection point becomes vertical or is inclined outward, the form is unrestricted (*i,j*).

k-q: The distinction between a necked vessel and an independent restricted vessel. Exceptions to the general correspondence of these two classes result from the fact that the first is defined by proportions, the second, by characteristics of contour. As the corner point on the general form is moved outward, the neck becomes wider and wider until it ceases to have the proportions associated with a neck (*k*). Independent restricted vessels therefore constitute a more inclusive class than necked vessels, but there are rare composite shapes with slender upper sections which suggest a neck although the form is dependent rather than independent (*l*). The shape is directly related to familiar dependent, composite forms (*m,n*). Inflected vessels corresponding in proportion to (*l-n*) are all independent because the inflection point lies above the major point (*o-q*).

restricted. The two classes can be defined specifically by reference to the position of the tangent at the end point, rim modifications being disregarded (fig. 21a-e). In terms of basic contour, the *unrestricted vessel* has an open orifice marked by an end-point tangent that is vertical or inclined outward, and at no point in the contour is there a constriction marked by a corner or inflection point. The tangent at the end point of *simple* and *dependent restricted vessels* is inclined inward, but the profile also lacks a constriction marked by a corner or inflection point. The third class includes most neck vessels. I might define it by attempting to describe a neck in geometric terms, but this strikes me as being slightly unethical. It is like taking common property for a private purpose. I shall therefore describe the class by reference to contour and introduce a few new terms as they are required. The base of a neck is frequently marked by a corner point (angle at juncture of neck and body) or, if there is a smooth curve between neck and body, an inflection point occurs somewhere between constriction of neck and the equator of the body (fig. 21f, h). This characteristic of contour, a corner point or an inflection point above a *major point* (point at the equator of the body), defines the third class, the *independent restricted vessel*. The limit of the class is clear cut. As the diameter at the corner point is increased, the position of the major point is approached. When it is reached, the vessel with a neck angle becomes a corner-point vessel with restricted or unrestricted orifice depending on the original neck contour (fig. 21g). The limit is defined in the same way when an inflection point replaces the corner point and the transition is to an inflected vessel with an unrestricted orifice (fig. 21i, j). This definition avoids the troublesome question, How wide can a neck become before it has the appearance of a tall rim on a slightly constricted body (fig. 21k-q)? The answer calls for an arbitrary limit where impressions and concepts are bound to vary. Moreover, it is better to keep the word "neck" as a loose term. The word "independent," applied to a restricted vessel, refers to the fact that the diameter at the corner or inflection point is independent of, or distinct from, the diameter at the major point. In contrast, there is coincidence of these points on the restricted-orifice vessel having a corner point, and it is therefore referred to as a dependent form. In place of the three approximate designations—1. unrestricted orifice, 2. restricted orifice, 3. neck— we therefore have: 1. unrestricted vessels, 2. simple and dependent restricted vessels, 3. independent, restricted vessels. These concepts are easily applied since they are defined in terms of simple geometric limits.

Contour and specific shape. The three structural classes are each subdivided by contour type, which is defined by reference to characteristic points as: simple, composite, inflected, and complex. This classification is illustrated with vessels taken from various cultures and periods of the Old and New World, in order to indicate its inclusiveness (fig. 22). Exotic shapes and some that are

UNRESTRICTED VESSELS

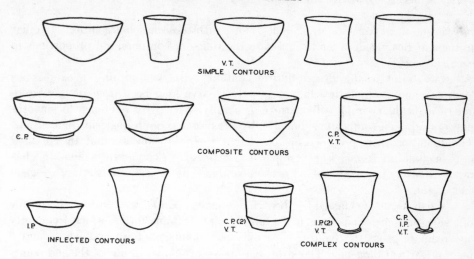

SIMPLE CONTOURS

COMPOSITE CONTOURS

INFLECTED CONTOURS

COMPLEX CONTOURS

SIMPLE AND DEPENDENT RESTRICTED VESSELS

SIMPLE CONTOURS

COMPOSITE CONTOURS

INFLECTED CONTOURS

COMPLEX CONTOURS

INDEPENDENT RESTRICTED VESSELS

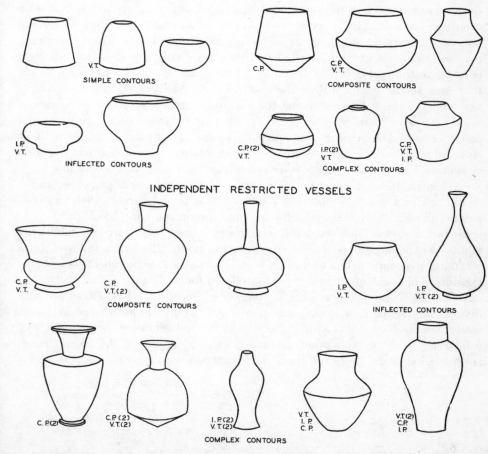

COMPOSITE CONTOURS

INFLECTED CONTOURS

COMPLEX CONTOURS

Fig. 22—A GENERAL SYSTEM OF SHAPE CLASSIFICATION

rare or absent in America are included along with those which are entirely familiar to the Americanist in order to illustrate the range of contours and proportions in each class.

Two terms in this description of contour types will recall the expressions "simple" and "composite silhouette," which have long been used in the Meso-american field. A simple silhouette is generally defined by reference to smooth-ness of outline; a composite silhouette, by the presence of an angle in the contour. The definitions here proposed are consistent with this concept, but they extend it to include all forms. For example, the expression "composite silhouette" has rarely, if ever, been applied to necked vessels, but its extension is both logical and useful.

When forms are classed by their characteristic points, we consider the profile of a side, noting the positions and type of points. Simple forms, which frequently approximate geometric figures, have only end points, or both end points and a point of vertical tangency. The latter may be coincident with one of the end points or separate (see simple forms under unrestricted and restricted vessels, fig. 22). Composite forms have a corner point, an angle in the contour which marks the juncture of two parts of the vessel, each of which is often comparable to a section of a geometric form. The composite contour may or may not have points of vertical tangency, but inflection points are absent. Inflected vessels have convex and con-cave sections joined by a smooth curve; they are characterized by an inflection point. Like composite vessels, they may or may not have vertical tangents, but they lack corner points. Either the composite or the inflected vessel may have two points of vertical tangency and the maximum number of points on vessels of these classes is therefore five. Vessels with two or more corner or inflection points or with both corner and inflection points are classed as complex. This class includes many variations of common forms resulting from a change in direction of curvature or abrupt changes in radius of curvature and direction of line.

This classification and count of points applies to the vessel proper, exclusive of rim modifications or supports, a limitation that is necessary to maintain con-sistent classification. Pedestal supports and prominent rim modifications do constitute a part of the vessel contour, however, and they introduce additional points. All points are counted in the description of the character and com-plexity of the contour, but to include points at rims and pedestals in basic shape classification would result in grouping unrelated forms.

The four contour types—simple, composite, inflected, and complex—are sub-divided on the basis of shape and proportion. Many simple shapes are most easily described by reference to geometric forms, and geometric reference is well established in shape description, as for example in the use of the terms "hemi-sphere," "cylinder," and "spheroid." But potters were not constrained by mathematical specifications. Furthermore the very plasticity of clay tempted them to vary shape and to originate new forms. It is not uncommon for a potter to start a vessel by laying rings one above another over a basal disc to form a cylinder and then by using a tool of proper curvature to press out and stretch the sides until the cylinder is transformed into a spheroid. A little experimenting with clay is sufficient to convince anyone of the ease with which one shape can be derived from any other. The potter's complete freedom in forming and modifying shapes raises the question whether or not geometric terms are generally applicable to hand-modeled pottery. In other words, is there a great range of nongeometric shapes with only a few shapes that approximate mathematically defined forms or is there a tendency for vessel forms to cluster around geometric shapes as norms? Aside from the problem of classification, this question is interesting in itself. It indicates the desirability of making extensive comparative studies of shape before adopting a nomenclature. The question of conformity to geometric norms will have to be answered independently for the pottery style of every culture.

In an extensive review of Mesoamerican pottery it was found that the majority of shapes can most easily be described by reference to geometric forms but there is no reason to expect them to be mathematically perfect. There are other styles in which geometric reference is not adequate. Meyer (1945, p. 304), in a diagram of what he calls "the most fundamental forms of vessels and their names," includes with defined geometric shapes such as the sphere, ellipsoid, cylinder, cone, and hyperboloid, other forms either natural or functional that are not mathematically defined, as pear-shaped, bell-shaped, egg-shaped, drop-shaped, plate-shaped, dish-shaped, and bag-shaped. Meyer's outline of forms applies especially to classical and Old World pottery.

The geometric approach is simple and convenient whenever it is applicable. A system found satisfactory for the American field will serve for illustration. In this system there are three solids—sphere, ellipsoid, and ovaloid—and three surfaces (forms with open ends and undefined limits)—cylinder, cone, and hyperboloid —that serve for reference (figs. 23, 24, column a). All of these forms are mathematically defined except the ovaloid (egg-shape). The ellipsoid can be used with the long axis horizontal or vertical; the ovaloid, in upright or inverted position. I would emphasize that vessel shapes approximate these forms or are most easily defined by reference to them; the terms do not imply identity.

Simple shapes with restricted orifices are formed by cutting the solids above their equators; corresponding unrestricted shapes terminate at or below the equators of the solids (fig. 23, columns b and c). The derivations are clearer in the restricted shapes, and the difficulty of recognizing the form of unrestricted vessels increases as they become shallower; in particular, sections of ovaloids lose their distinctiveness when they are cut below their points of maximum

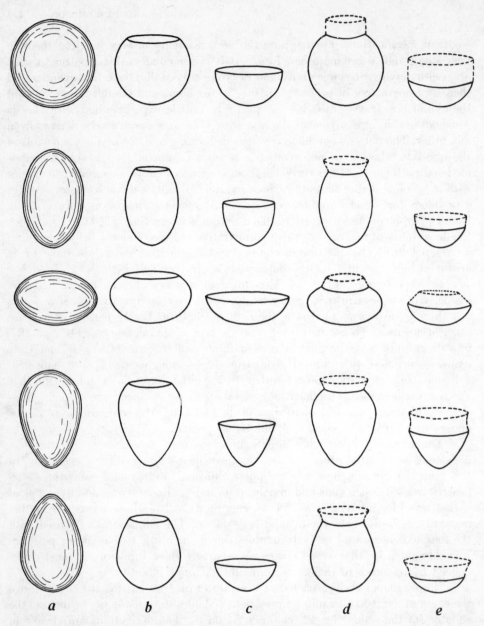

FIG. 23—GEOMETRIC SOLIDS AS REFERENCE NORMS FOR VESSEL DESCRIPTION: SPHERE, ELLIPSOID, AND OVALOID
Simple restricted and unrestricted forms (columns *b* and *c*). Sections of these solids combined with sections of other solids or of surfaces (dashed outlines) form independent and dependent composite vessels (columns *d* and *e*).

diameter (fig. 23, column *c*). Vessels with simple convex contours that do not conform closely to mathematical solids are best designated as sections of spheroids.

The hemisphere is the ideal form of many bowls. With various modifications it tends to approach other simple shapes. If curvature is decreased at the base and increased near the rim, it resembles a section of an ellipsoid with long axis horizontal; when these changes are reversed, it assumes the contour of the same form in vertical position. Although some vessels are comparable to a section of an ellipsoid, simple convex shapes are generally between it and the hemisphere or

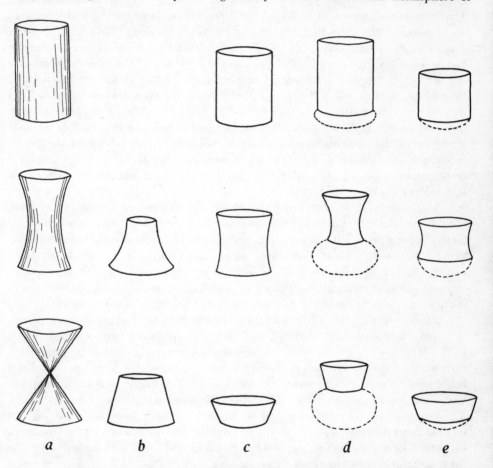

a   *b*   *c*   *d*   *e*

FIG. 24—GEOMETRIC SURFACES AS REFERENCE NORMS FOR VESSEL FORMS: CYLINDER, HYPERBOLOID, AND CONE

The cylinder marks the limit of unrestricted forms. Either restricted or unrestricted forms can be obtained from the hyperboloid and cone, depending on the part of the form used (columns *b* and *c*). Combined with sections of solids (dashed outlines), these surfaces form independent or dependent composite vessels (columns *d* and *e*).

sections of it. The ellipsoid in vertical position is unstable, and its section in horizontal position is shallow. The depth/breadth ratio of the hemisphere cannot exceed .5, but greater relative depth is obtained by extending the sides as a straight wall resulting in a nongeometric shape. The depth/breadth ratio of the hemi-ellipsoid with major axis vertical also exceeds .5.

Of the shapes that are comparable to geometric surfaces, the cylinder is always necessarily an unrestricted form, whereas the hyperboloid and cone can be used for either class, depending upon where the surface is cut (fig. 24, columns *b*, *c*). The unrestricted sections are much more common than the restricted, which have an acute angle at the base that makes them difficult to clean. This form also has smaller capacity than convex forms of equal over-all dimensions. The cylinder can be converted by imperceptible degrees into the hyperboloid, and the two forms are not always distinguished in current nomenclature in the Mesoamerican field. A hyperboloid is often referred to as a cylinder because a type defined by specialized supports and decorative style varies in shape from cylindrical to hyperbolic. The fact that in this style an ambiguous or borderline form—a hyperboloid without strong curvature—is common does not mean that the distinction between the hyper-boloid and the cylinder is unimportant. There are other styles in which one form or the other is closely adhered to; unless the two are recognized, the degree of standardization may be ignored.

Many complex vessels are composed of parts which are derived from these same basic forms. Probably the most familiar example is a jar with spherical body and cylindrical neck, but there are innumerable combinations among both restricted and unrestricted forms of dependent vessels and among independent restricted vessels (figs. 23, 24, columns *d*, *e*). All such vessels are described with reference to the sections of the geometric figures of which they are composed. This group includes the vessels classed in current usage as complex-silhouette vessels.

Proportion.   Over-all proportion has sometimes been given a more promi-nent place in shape classification than it has in the system here outlined. Thus, in the Mesoamerican field, limits of basic forms have been defined by proportion rather than contour. The order in which these two aspects of form are considered is not solely a matter of personal judgment of relative importance or of compara-tive homogeneity of the classes established. Convenience is also a consideration. The contour type can be identified by inspection, the proportion must be cal-culated from measurement. In so far as contour and proportion are related, the difference between the two approaches is minimized, and with either order the same specific classes are obtained in the end.

Irrespective of the place of proportion in a system of nomenclature or taxonomy, its importance as a feature of shape should not be minimized, nor its relation to contour and function disregarded. It will be worthwhile first to con-sider the relation of proportion to stability.

The limiting factors in the proportion of a vessel are its functional requirements. It is natural to think of the necessity for stability as setting a definite limit on relative height; the taller a vessel, the more easily it tips. But the stability limit is not constant because some vessels were handled more than others. One cannot afford to have in daily use jugs and bowls that are easily upset. A vessel made for decorative or ritual purposes is subject to fewer hazards, and a certain extravagance may therefore be expressed in its proportions. Then again, some vessels are held in stands or suspended, and these may be unstable in form.

The stability of a vessel is determined by its shape, the distribution of its weight, and the breadth of its base. Obviously the taller the vessel, the larger its upper portion, and the narrower its base, the less stable it is. Degree of stability has a direct relation to the position of the center of gravity, which is easily determined empirically. When a body is suspended from a point, the center of gravity lies on a vertical line which passes through the point of suspension. If the

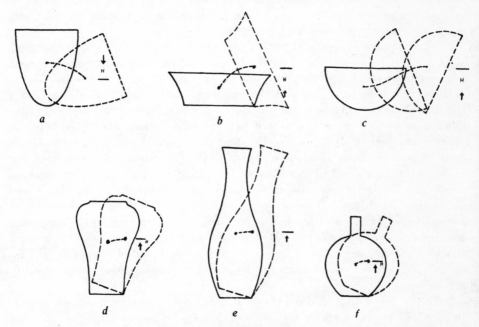

FIG. 25—VESSEL STABILITY

Center of gravity marked by a point; course traced by this point when the vessel is tipped indicated by a dashed line; position of the vessel when it is in unstable equilibrium, dashed outline. The vessel is in stable equilibrium when the center of gravity must be raised to tip it (*b*), unstable when tipping lowers it (*a*). The hemisphere rolls on its side instead of rotating on a point (*c*). Different forms compared with respect to the distance through which the center of gravity must be lifted to bring the vessel to a position of unstable equilibrium (*d-f*).

body is suspended successively from two different points, an intersection of verticals is obtained that marks the center of gravity. A body is in stable equilibrium if its center of gravity is raised when it is tipped, unstable if the center of gravity is lowered (fig. 25a,b). The lower the center of gravity, the more stable the vessel. The toy figure that bobs up when it is pushed over is weighted to make its center of gravity lowest when it is upright. Dr. Kenneth M. Chapman has called my attention to the fact that certain forms of Chihuahua polychrome vessels have the same peculiarity. Provided the walls are uniform in thickness, the height through which the center of gravity must be lifted to bring it outside a point of support gives one indication of the relative stability of vessels (fig. 25).

There are a few basic relations between shape and proportion. The vessel height/orifice diameter ratio of .5 is set by the hemisphere and of 1.0 by the sphere. Although a complete sphere does not occur as a vessel shape, the neck height of a spheroidal jar often compensates for the section of the sphere removed in forming the throat. Consequently, many low-necked jars approximate 1.0 in over-all proportion. In certain styles this proportion is maintained by combining a low body with a tall neck and vice versa.

The proportion range of structural and contour classes varies somewhat from style to style. To suggest the kinds of relationships that may be found, the over-all proportions of vessels that are illustrated in eight reports on Mexican and Mayan pottery have been estimated and the frequency distribution plotted graphically (fig. 26). One can easily recognize the forms in which stability requirements have affected proportion. Function, as well as geometric relations, limits the depth of unrestricted vessels. It is noteworthy that flaring-sided and composite vessels have lower norms than the sections of a spheroid. The only unrestricted form that is characteristically tall in this class is the cylinder, which places no limit on proportion. The height/breadth ratio in the upper range of the cylinder is well above that which generally characterizes a utility vessel. The simple restricted forms show distinct variations in contour with change in proportion, suggesting considerations of stability. Low shoulders are most frequent on tall vessels; high shoulders, on low ones. The difference in proportion range of composite and inflected independent vessels appears to reflect function rather than stability requirements.

In the description of vessel shape, it is customary to report over-all proportion (height/orifice diameter for unrestricted vessels, height/maximum diameter for restricted dependent and independent vessels). How much farther the analysis of proportion should be carried obviously depends on complexity of contour, size and range of the sample, and purpose of the analysis. Over-all dimensions fully describe the proportion of only a few special shapes; the more complex the contour becomes, the greater the inadequacy of this basic ratio alone. The characteristic points mark the position of horizontal and vertical dimensions of the vessel that are significant. A height/orifice diameter ratio takes dimensions at an upper end-point, but there are only two common shapes in this class which, when mathe-

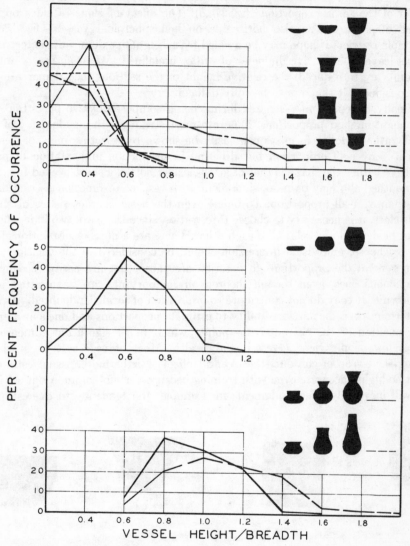

FIG. 26—THE RELATION OF CONTOUR AND PROPORTION:
VESSEL SHAPES FROM MESOAMERICA

Key illustrates averages (not norms) and extremes in over-all proportions and variations in contours at extremes.

matically true, are fully described by it, the cylinder and the hemisphere. This proportion alone does not describe the section of a cone because the cone introduces a second end-point diameter, and if either orifice or base is chosen for the calculation of an over-all proportion, the form does not appear commensurate with a cylinder of the same proportion (fig. 27a,b). The effect of slope of sides on impression of proportion is also noticeable on hemispheroidal vessels (fig. 27c,d). The simple restricted shape may be defined by a height/maximum diameter ratio, but this leaves the relative diameter of orifice undefined. When corner or inflection points are introduced, the relative height of the sections they demarcate has to be considered if shape is to be fully defined.

Finally, independent restricted forms, being composed of two parts that are independent in their proportions, illustrate most strikingly the inadequacy of the over-all ratio to define form, as can easily be shown by selecting pairs of vessels identical in over-all proportion but differing in proportion and relation of parts (fig. 28). Whether the shape is that of a tall-necked bottle, a short-necked jug, or a wide-mouthed olla may be more significant with respect to function as well as to shape than over-all proportion. To define even the basic characteristics of shape for this class, it is necessary to choose three ratios, since there are two independent parts to be defined and related to each other. There are a number of relations from which to choose, and visual impression should be considered in the decision.

In general the proportions to describe are those that are easily recognized. Inconspicuous ones, even though theoretically important, can be omitted once it is shown that they do not contribute to impression of form. Undoubtedly, training determines in some measure ability to estimate proportions and one's awareness of the position of the characteristic points which mark significant dimensions. Perhaps few people view a vessel analytically. Most of us see it as a whole, noticing the sweep of contour, the over-all effect. Furthermore, visual estimates cannot be highly accurate even with training because certain common optical illusions will inevitably affect judgment; for example, the tendency to overestimate

FIG. 27—THE EFFECT OF CONTOUR ON JUDGMENT OF PROPORTIONS
Proportions should be judged before reading this caption. Over-all proportions: a and b both 1, c and d both .66.

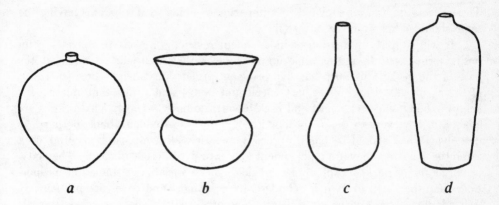

a   *b*   *c*   *d*

Fig. 28—INADEQUACY OF OVER-ALL PROPORTION TO DEFINE INDEPENDENT COMPOSITE VESSELS
Forms taken from Chinese procelain. *a,b:* Extremes in neck size and throat width. *c,d:* Extremes in neck height.

vertical distances in comparison with horizontal, and the effect on judgment of converging or diverging lines, an example of which is seen in flaring-sided vessels (fig. 27).

Contour may also influence judgment by suggestion. This effect is well illustrated in the impression of relative shoulder height on bodies of spheres and ovaloids. (The term "shoulder" is here applied to the point of maximum diameter—point of vertical tangency—of a restricted form; the area above this equator, which some writers call the shoulder, is referred to as the "upper body.") If the body is spherical, the base unmodified, and the throat (base of neck) one-quarter the diameter of the shoulder, the ratio of shoulder height to body height is .51; in other words, the shoulder is raised very slightly when the neck is narrow. But when the throat is nine-tenths the width of the body, the ratio is .69; as the throat approaches more nearly the diameter of the body, the shoulder rises rapidly. The shoulder height of a spheroidal body is therefore quite variable, depending on the relative width of the throat and flattening of base. But surprisingly, this variation is not conspicuous. We perceive the form rather than the relative position of the shoulder, and the form suggests a medial shoulder height. Generally, vessels which appear to have a high shoulder are inverted ovaloids with distinctly stronger curvature of upper than of lower body. And when the base is lowered by flattening, which brings the shoulder nearer the mid-point, the ovaloid still appears to be high-shouldered. The shape of the erect ovaloid has an opposite effect. It gives the impression of a low shoulder regardless of modifications of the ratio of heights made by slicing off an upper section. Again, this is because of our concept of the form.

These effects are best appreciated by comparing ovaloids with spheroids having the same shoulder height/body ratios (fig. 29).

It will simplify discussion of independent restricted vessels to consider composite forms first, taking as an example a jar with a well-marked angle at the base of the neck. This form has five principal proportions: height/breadth ratios of the entire vessel and of its part (neck and body) and ratios that relate neck height to body or vessel height and neck breadth to body breadth. Three ratios are adequate, however, to define proportions uniquely, provided shape of parts is described. They should be based on easily measured dimensions. Body and neck catch the eye since they are independent and entirely different in shape. The body, usually a major part of a spheroid or ovaloid, is less variable in shape and proportions than the neck, for which cylinders, hyperboloids, and cones are particularly well adapted. These forms are difficult to compare with respect to proportion. If the diameter is measured at either orifice or throat, flaring and tapering necks of identical proportion will be quite different in appearance because judgment is influenced by convergence or divergence of the walls (fig. 30, a-c). It might

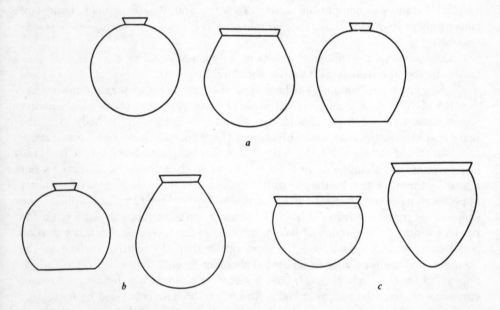

FIG. 29—THE EFFECT OF CONTOUR ON IMPRESSION OF SHOULDER HEIGHT
The ratio of shoulder height to body height. a: Body forms left to right: sphere, upright ovaloid, inverted ovaloid. Relative shoulder height all .45. b: Body forms: sphere with section removed to form flat base, ovaloid. Relative shoulder height, both .54. c: Body forms: sphere with section removed to form wide throat, inverted ovaloid. Relative shoulder height, both .75.

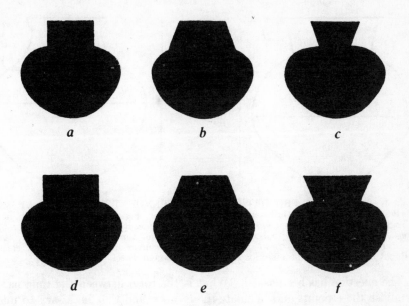

FIG. 30—EFFECT OF CONTOUR ON JUDGMENT OF NECK PROPORTIONS
a-c: Height/orifice diameter constant (.55). *d-e:* Height/average neck diameter constant (.47).

seem that a truer basis of comparison would be obtained if an average diameter is calculated, but this is time-consuming and does not completely compensate for differences in contour. The importance of a proportion depends partly on its variability, and unfortunate necks are more variable than bodies. As an indication of the range, a series of cylindrical necks on Mesoamerican vessels was analyzed. A lower limit of .2 was arbitrarily set to distinguish neck and rim. The height diameter ratio of the majority of necks is between .3 and .7. There are not many above 1.0, but the ratio runs as high as 1.6.

The troublesome calculation of a neck proportion can be avoided by establishing the relation of neck to body with two ratios: height neck/height body, diameter of throat diameter of body. For the third ratio, either body or vessel proportion can be used (fig. 31).

The inflected independent vessel is comparable to the composite one, with the inflection point taking the place of the corner point at the base of the neck of the composite form, and the same relations hold for both. It is hardly necessary to discuss complex vessels because the principles that have been outlined apply equally to them; that is, characteristic points demarcate their significant parts, and choice of ratio will depend on visual impression. It is especially important with this group to distinguish primary and secondary points.

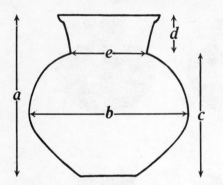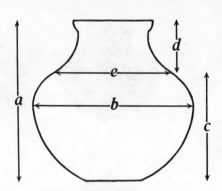

FIG. 31—DEFINITIVE PROPORTIONS OF INDEPENDENT RESTRICTED VESSELS
Proportions of composite and inflected vessels and of their parts: Height to breadth of vessel,
a/b; height to breadth of body, c/b; height of neck to breadth of throat, d/e. Alternate proportions: Ratio of neck height to body height, d/c; ratio of throat diameter to body diameter,
e/b. Either set will define the form. The same five measurements are required for each. Note
that throat is measured at the inflection point on an inflected vessel.

The question has been asked, "What is the ratio between the time necessary
to establish these points and calculate these ratios and that necessary to make an
outline drawing of a pot?" Actually, the characteristic points are an aid in making
the outline drawing, as I shall show (p. 253 ff.). The principal justification of the
ratios, however, is that they serve a different purpose from the outline drawing,
which shows the appearance of only a single vessel. (I am excluding the diagrams of
average and extreme forms in a series because these have to be based on calculation
of proportions.) The calculation of proportions is necessary in order to summarize
adequately the characteristics of a group of vessels and show the degree of their
variability. The drawing of individual specimens cannot serve this purpose even
when the group is small enough to allow illustration of all forms because one cannot
summarize from visual impression alone the characteristics that serve as a basis
for systematic comparison.

The number of proportions or indices reported will depend on the purpose of
shape analysis. If the object is merely to distinguish low, medium, and tall vessels,
the over-all index is all that is needed; but if a systematic comparative study of
contours and proportions is to be made, more precise definition is required, and
the indices that have been discussed will spare many needless words of description
and will give impetus to stylistic study by rendering data in the standardized form
necessary for satisfactory comparison.

On reading a first draft of this chapter on form, Dr. A. V. Kidder made two
observations which he labeled "irrelevant":

"It seems to me that, in general, undecorated wares are more pleasingly
shaped than those that bear ornament, particularly appliqué."

"As cultures advance (whatever that means), doesn't shop practise, mass production, increase, bringing a wider divergence than existed, when potting was a routine housewife's task, between utility and fine wares, the former becoming more highly standardized and less meticulously finished, the latter, more varied and more carefully made? This seems to have happened in post-Classic Mexico."

Impressions of this kind gained from an extensive study of form seem to me distinctly relevant for they illustrate the kind of generalizations that can be tested and developed by the type of shape analysis I have outlined.

Elaborations of rim.   Rim is here defined as the margin of the vessel orifice. When the wall is carried to the lip without break in smoothness of contour or change in thickness, the limit of rim is indefinite and its height, indeterminate. This is the "direct rim." Only when the margin is elaborated in some way, as by thickening or a sharp change in wall direction or both, is the rim set off as a distinct part of the vessel.

Probably no other feature or aspect of vessel shape has received the attention that has been given to rim. This emphasis is explained in part at least by the prominent place of sherds in archaeological ceramic studies. It is not uncommon for the rims from a stratigraphic test to be saved for detailed analysis while body sherds are discarded with only a count. Rim sherds are considered especially important because they usually reveal more about vessel shape than body sherds and when elaborated they become diagnostics of style. For shape analysis, the arc of the rim affords means of calculating orifice diameter, unless the arc at the lip is very short. The slope of the upper part of the vessel can also be judged, and unrestricted and restricted orifices distinguished, provided the rim is properly oriented—held with the plane of the lip horizontal (see p. 252).

The value of rim sherds in classification stems from the fact that the vessel edge can be shaped, reinforced, and elaborated in many ways, taking on a variety of forms. The classic example of a stylistic sequence established primarily by rim analysis is Kidder's study of Pecos Glaze-paint ware (Kidder and Shepard, 1936). Kidder found that the rims of these types, which have a time span of nearly four centuries, underwent consistent and distinct modifications, and hence they serve to establish the relative chronological position of sherds collected in surface survey. Kidder's work at Pecos stands as one of the earliest examples of the use of stratigraphic method in the Southwest, and the nature of his data made possible a systematic analysis of rim shape. His results gave great stimulus to the study of rim forms and were no doubt responsible in large measure for the detail with which rims are often described and illustrated.

The more or less logical evolution of rim elaboration which was found at Pecos and which characterizes the Glaze-paint types of the upper Rio Grande valley does not seem to occur frequently, but even in the absence of a sequence, rim forms may be a useful diagnostic of type. This fact needs no emphasis; rather, attention should be directed to means of reconstructing shape more fully by including other classes of sherds in shape analysis. For example, diameter at base, equator, and spring of neck, as well as at orifice, can be calculated from sherds. Correct orientation is essential; that is, the arc at the given point must be in a horizontal plane. These sherds then show a part of the silhouette as effectively as does a rim fragment.

Variations in shape of rim profile are almost numberless. Certain well-marked forms have been named, but our concept of this feature can be organized better by considering the variables than by reviewing terminology. There are just two basic variables: direction in relation to contour of the vessel side, and thickness. The rim may be direct, that is, follow the general outline of the vessel side, or it may deviate more or less abruptly from it, either by a curve or an angle, and the direction of deviation may be inward or outward, up, horizontal, or down. Thickening may take many forms and there are at least seven secondary variables (fig. 32).

Not all rim forms are of equal significance. Many were functional or decorative, and accepted style would seem to have dictated shape as long as the modification was on a visible surface. But concealed thickening on the interior of a restricted-orifice vessel results merely from the chance redistribution of excess clay when the rim is shaped. Another sweep of the potter's fingers might have produced a different shape. The custom of illustrating rim in profile gives point to this caution. This type of illustration is practicable because the archaeologist deals

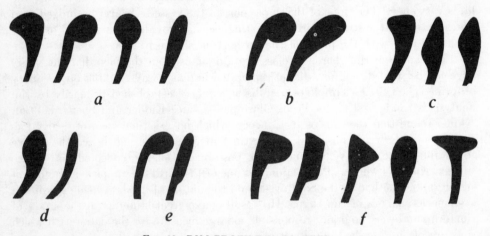

FIG. 32—RIM PROFILE VARIABLES
a: Position of thickening with relation to vessel wall: interior, exterior, interior and exterior, indeterminate. *b:* Junction of thickened part with wall: abrupt, gradual. *c:* Point of greatest thickness: at lip, low, medial. *d:* Ratio of rim thickness to wall thickness. *e:* Relative length of thickened part. *f:* Shape of thickened part.

largely with sherds. The profile permits a simpler and more exact representation than is possible from a perspective view, but it is well to remember that the maker and user of the vessel may never have noticed the characteristics of the profile.

The rim may be a means of strengthening the orifice, of modifying form for functional purposes—pouring, lifting, and retaining liquids—or of affording a decorative effect. It is in some instances an elaboration comparable to a flange or molding, and not infrequently a flat, everted rim bears some simple grooved or painted decoration. The rim is, therefore, an element of function and style that cannot be omitted from the over-all picture. The question is, Does the profile enable us to visualize surface appearance, and do we picture it with facility? Since the profile shows both interior and exterior outline at once and also gradual thickening that is not perceived in the perspective view, it will give the impression of greater diversity of form than is obtained by surface view; a rim appears to have more individuality in profile. On the other hand, grooves are more noticeable on the surface than in scaled profile. A groove that decorates a lip or marks the edge of a thickening may hardly be perceptible in profile. Often, however, the groove is exaggerated in depth for emphasis in the profile drawing. Simple rims are not difficult to visualize in perspective from profile, whereas aberrant forms often are and may even leave one questioning the reliability of the drawing. Illustrations that show profiles side by side with shaded perspective drawings take care of the problem of style visualization satisfactorily.

The profile drawing not only gives a more clear-cut picture of the rim than does the perspective view, but it also shows variations in form that may not be appreciated from an exterior view. It is well to consider extent of visibility in the surface view because variations in the form of the concealed part will be fortuitous unless they were functional. This caution applies, especially to the underside of a flaring or everted rim and to the inner side of the rim on restricted orifices. A well-stylized rim may be a very useful diagnostic in classification, but a minor variation may be a minutia which is meaningless in the study of style.

Reference to rim variables is useful for description but it does not differentiate techniques of shaping rim. Even though form and technique cannot always be correlated, when a technique can be identified it affords a significant basis for the establishment of types. The only distinctive feature of the direct rim is the lip, which will vary in shape depending on the manner of finishing the edge. When the lip is finished by hand, the position of the thumb and fingers will determine whether it is rounded, tapered, or squarish. A lip trimmed with a straight-edged tool will have a flat surface, either horizontal or oblique. The form of the lip is a minor variation, and some pottery types lack well-defined lip contour. The flat lip is specialized and therefore more distinctive than the rounded.

The principal question of technique is whether the rim was formed by manipulating the edge of the wall and redistributing clay or by adding coils. Wide-everted and flared rims may have been built out, whereas short ones could easily be formed by turning the edge of the vessel wall. Also a moderate increase in thickness may be obtained by scraping the sides to bring excess clay to the margin or by leaving the final coil unflattened or by adding coils to the edge. When a thickened rim tapers smoothly into the wall, it is impossible to determine technique of thickening. Abrupt thickening indicates addition of coils or fillets. If welding is imperfect, the number of coils can be determined from a fractured section. These details of technique are not observed frequently enough to afford a basis for classification, but all evidence of this kind is worthy of recording.

AESTHETIC ASPECTS OF FORM AND METHODS OF COMPARING FORM STYLES

The aesthetics of vessel form is a subject the archaeologist may well approach with misgivings. Aside from the fact that there are no generally recognized standards for judging the aesthetic qualities of shape, the suitability of much prewheel pottery for such a study may be questioned. There is little doubt that most vessels served a useful purpose and that shape was adapted to and limited by function. Aesthetic considerations would enter in different degrees in the making of a cook pot and a ritual vessel, and we may never know when people started making pottery primarily for its decorative value. In consequence of these circumstances, one cannot expect to reach sound conclusions by gross comparisons of vessel shapes in different cultures or periods because one may not be comparing aesthetic preferences as expressed in line and proportion but merely the response to different needs for containers.

The requirements of stability, as well as of function, have a limiting effect on form. On first thought, stability might seem to be an influence that could be ignored because it is a common factor, but this is not the case; as we have seen, a high degree of stability is more important for some kinds of vessels than for others, and stability requirements can be disregarded when a stand or rest is used. Also with regard to function there is a further condition: there are critics who will insist that beauty is found in perfect adaptation of shape to purpose; the adaptation has an intrinsic worth. With all these complications it is no wonder that most of us have shied from pronouncing aesthetic judgments.

When the qualities of vessel form are discussed, evaluations are usually expressed in terms of personal response. The reader may sympathize with the enjoyment expressed, envy it, or dismiss it as self-induced hypnotism. Whatever the reaction, as long as individual appraisals differ widely, personal evaluations do not offer a basis for broad analytical comparisons.

In only a few instances, mainly in the study of highly developed, sophisticated styles, have evaluations been based on specific criteria. An example is Hambidge's study of classic Greek vases (1920). Hambidge worked on the theory that the Greeks, in designing, used certain mathematical proportions, mainly ratios derived from irrational numbers, for which special aesthetic appeal and particularly a dynamic quality are postulated. The parts of a vase silhouette are analyzed and compared to determine what pattern of rectangles will enclose them. We need not consider what the probabilities are that the Greeks used the constructions suggested or the extent to which these particular proportions contribute to the pleasing qualities of Greek shapes. The theory cannot be tested or applied in aboriginal American ceramics because there is not a remote possibility that Indian potters were aware of these proportions. Hambidge's study is mentioned only because he used specific criteria.

Of more direct interest is the study which Birkhoff made of Chinese vase forms (1933, pp. 67–86). He based his analysis on the position of the four types of characteristic points, drawing a network of verticals and horizontals through these points and calculating proportions. He believed that ratios of 1:1 and 2:1 could be appreciated. Such ratios between verticals or horizontals or between verticals and horizontals of the network he considered "elements of order" contributing to the aesthetic value of the form. He also considered certain relations of tangents: perpendicularity and parallelism in directions other than the vertical; vertical characteristic tangents at end, corner, or inflection points; and characteristic tangents or normals that pass through an adjacent *center of a vase* ("a point of the axis of symmetry lying on a horizontal line of the characteristic network of maximum or minimum breadth").

These criteria illustrate the relationships that may be recognized by a mathematician. It is doubtful that they are ordinarily recognized or estimated. It seems improbable, for example, that horizontal and vertical dimensions can be accurately compared by eye because of the well-known optical illusion which exaggerates vertical distances. Also it is questionable if the position and relation of all tangent lines can be visualized clearly enough to judge perpendicularity or parallelism. But Birkhoff himself probably would not have claimed that all these comparisons could be made visually. In fact, he questioned how recognition of them affects aesthetic judgment and expressed the opinion that the effect is slightly adverse because "in all fields of art it is the intuitively felt relationships that are most enjoyed" (1933, p. 86). The aesthetician and the psychologist should be best prepared to determine if these relations impart qualities of contour and proportion that are intuitively enjoyed. Birkhoff was not fully satisfied with this method of aesthetic measure because he recognized three categories of aesthetic factors: regularity of outline, utilitarian and conventional requirements, and definite geometric relationships between dimensions. The first factor, though formal, is difficult to define exactly; the second is connotative and beyond precise analysis; and the third is the only one of which his theory takes precise account.

Despite the fact that conditions affecting vessel shape are discouragingly involved and that the methods of analysis which have been applied are not adequate, one cannot dismiss the subject easily. To thumb through illustrations of vessels of various times and places—Chinese, Classic Greek, Middle Eastern, American Indian—is to feel the fascination of line and proportion, and even though one is aware that his responses are influenced by the aesthetic tradition of his time and by his training, he feels that there are qualities of shape that have strong appeal and have been appreciated by people of different cultures. Nevertheless, it seems to me that the archaeologist's task is to attempt to understand the qualities of form rather than to pass judgment on them. The comparative study of form is within his field.

Comparisons of form styles of different periods or regions are more often directed to specific similarities or differences in a few outstanding forms than to the characteristics of styles as a whole. Incomplete comparisons may be misleading, for similarities do not necessarily indicate direct derivation or extensive influence of one style on another. There are many possible explanations of similarity in form from different pottery-making centers, for example: imitation of a particular shape or of a special feature, such as a pedestal or handle, that appears on one form while others are unmodified, introduction of a cult requiring distinct shapes that are adopted without affecting the main ceramic output; parallel, independent development in response to widespread change in custom, as in culinary practices following the introduction of a new agricultural product; opening of trade resulting in mutual stimulation as well as imitation of the forms that are exchanged; and extension of political domination involving control of craft forms. Whatever the causes of similarity, they are best understood when the style is analyzed as a whole.

Birkhoff's method of defining contour offers a broad, objective means of making comparisons. Characteristic points mark the boundaries of principal vessel parts and lay off dimensions from which proportions are calculated. These are the points where direction of wall changes. The quality of contour—its smoothness and gentleness of curvature or its sharpness and decisiveness of line—is determined by the kinds of points it has and their positions. Birkhoff (1933, p. 73) also mentions a means of estimating degree of curvature. For every point on a curve of variable curvature there is a circle that most closely fits. The curvature of this *tangent circle* can be defined by the reciprocal of its radius, which also serves as a measure of the curvature at the given point on the profile curve. The basic geometric forms employed may also offer a useful basis for generalization and comparison. The number of characteristic points in the various shapes is one measure of the complexity of a style. Others are elaborations (supports, rims, etc.) and functional additions (handles, spouts, and covers), both of which can be considered in relation to contour.

In order to deal with comparable form classes when describing characteristics of contour and proportion, it is desirable to identify functional groups as far as possible. Criteria for establishing functional categories of prehistoric pottery are meager. Probably finish has been most widely used. It is customary to recognize two classes of pottery: one variously called utility, culinary, coarse, or unslipped ware; the other, finely finished, decorated, or service ware. The specific features by which they are distinguished are not constant. In addition to refinement of finish (polishing and/or slipping) and presence of decoration, thickness of wall, texture of paste, and quality of workmanship may all afford some basis for judgment. Despite variability of criteria, the distinction between the two classes is usually clear-cut; they meet different requirements and therefore do not intergrade. The utility vessel is usually unslipped and unpolished. If the paste is coarse, the surface is likely to be hand-smoothed without scraping. Fine ware may be slipped or unslipped, but if unslipped it is generally well polished.

The two classes are convenient for preliminary sorting, but they are extremely broad and not strictly functional. In some cultures, the rougher wares will include ritual vessels along with common household utensils. For example, many Mexican and Mayan incense burners are comparable to ordinary cook pots in paste texture and surface finish. Therefore, these major groups defined by finish should be further subdivided with reference to all available direct or indirect evidence of function. It is within these relatively uniform classes that detailed comparisons can be made.

To summarize, characteristics of form that have a bearing on aesthetic quality include proportioning, relation of parts, handling of curvature, and complexity of contour (number and type of characteristic points). The degree of conformity to certain proportions may reflect the extent to which certain canons of form style were defined and accepted within a culture. Detailed studies would be made not for the purpose of passing aesthetic judgment but to understand a style, and to obtain well-defined means of comparing styles.

METHODS OF ILLUSTRATING FORM

For purposes of illustration, there is probably no substitute for a good photograph. It gives a normal view and shows at once shape, decoration, and workmanship. By any other means of representation some of these qualities, especially workmanship, are lost, and even the relation of design to form is omitted when the two are illustrated separately. This is not to minimize the advantages of other methods of illustration and of concentrating attention on particular aspects.

There are a few simple facts to consider in rendering shape photographically. To avoid distorting contour and relative proportions, the level of the lens should be at approximately the mid-point of the vessel. Other views may be desirable to show decoration or special features, but this is the standard view to illustrate form. If a vessel has tripod supports, it is important to show the degree of inclination of the foot and its spread in relation to the diameter of the vessel. The stability which the tripod affords can be judged only when the vessel is in the position that brings one foot in profile. This view of the support is very likely to give the vessel an unbalanced, awkward appearance and is sometimes avoided for this reason, but in so doing essential data are sacrificed.

The lighting of a photograph should be as natural as possible. Difficulty arises, however, when the source of light is above the equator or point of maximum diameter since the part below is thrown in shadow. Often the simplest solution is to invert the vessel, but photographs obtained in this way are rarely satisfactory even though taken at the level of the vessel's mid-point because the lighting is unnatural. Shadow can be cut much more satisfactorily by setting the vessel upright on a ground glass that is lighted from below.

When shape is illustrated by a drawing, a sectional profile is frequently used. This convention may follow from the extensive illustration of rim profiles. Theoretically this type of illustration serves two purposes: it illustrates the shape in outline and it shows variations in thickness of the wall resulting from method of construction. Representation of wall thickness, however, is largely a convention, since there is generally no record of calipering. Obviously measurement of thickness at rim gives no basis for drawing the profile of the entire vessel; in a hand-modeled vessel, wall thickness will vary with the form and its method of construction. When the wall is pressed out to increase curvature, it will be stretched and made thinner. At angles, such as base-side and neck-body junctures, there is generally thickening of the wall. These details of construction are interesting, but a complete record for every specimen is hardly justified. The representation of the wall section therefore serves no purpose; furthermore it distracts the eye and interferes with judgment of proportions. In fact, the question may be raised if the silhouette is not more satisfactory than outline for the representation of basic shape, despite the extreme contrast of black and white.

For rim illustration, the advantages of the profile are obvious. There are, however, two precautions that must be observed. First, the sherd must be accurately oriented—that is, placed in the position it would occupy if the vessel were set level—otherwise contour and depth will be misjudged. It is customary to sight along the edge of the rim to bring the arc into horizontal position. Orientation is facilitated by holding a transparent plate against the rim because the plane of the plate is more easily judged than the level of the rim. Also extent of contact, which shows evenness of rim, can be seen at a glance. A plate of plastic can be used as the guide, and if it is inscribed with a series of arcs of graded curvature, it will also serve to estimate rim diameter. When a rim profile is being drawn, it is convenient to have a box with a glass end, against which the rim can be placed squarely. A little sand in the box will hold the sherd in position.

It is an unfortunate circumstance that there is no way of knowing whether or not illustrated rims were accurately oriented, but large series of variable shapes illustrated with uniform orientation raise doubt. A horizontal line at the lip indicates that the archaeologist was at least aware of the importance of orientation, but it may distract the eye and mar the effect of profile, and it can become a mere convention that is no guarantee of accuracy. Obviously there are rims that cannot be accurately oriented, because of either shortness of the arc or irregularity of the line of the lip or both. Such sherds should not be illustrated, at least not without indicating that orientation is indeterminate.

The second cause of inaccuracy in rim recording is irregularity of break. Only when the break extends vertically from the lip and when it cuts squarely through the wall can the profile be reliably recorded. If the break is slanting or irregular, it will distort the curvature of the profile; if it is oblique through the wall, it will increase the apparent thickness. Sherds fracture differently, depending on texture, homogeneity, and density of the paste, and direction of breaking force. Consequently a natural break will not always meet the requirements for profile drawing. Ideally the section should be cut, but a saw is seldom available. In case a break is unsuitable for drawing, a more reliable profile can be obtained by sighting along the outline of the properly oriented sherd than by using an irregular break, but outline drawing has the disadvantage that measurement of wall thickness must be taken to draw the inner side. Also with certain forms, as strongly recurved rims, the entire exterior may not be visible.

Although the artist's eye, a ruler, and calipers are usually relied on for drawing the vessel profile, various special mechanical devices have also been used. Probably the best known is the pantograph proposed by March (1934, p. 45). This traces the vessel outline but has the disadvantage of bulk and weight if one is working on museum collections.

The fundamental relation of characteristic points of vessel contour suggests a relatively simple method of drawing the profile. The co-ordinates of the characteristic points can be located, and the connecting lines then drawn in by eye. The co-ordinates of intermediate points can be taken if necessary; that is, if the vessel is large and the contour between characteristic points is not smooth. I have tested this method by placing tracing paper over a full-sized drawing of a vessel, marking the points and tangents at the points, then asking a person who had not seen the original to complete the outline. The result was checked by again placing the tracing paper over the original. The closeness of the outline was surprising.

A simple device for measuring the co-ordinates of points of the contour was tested in the study of Plumbate ware. A base in which a meter scale has been set is provided with an upright scale and a second upright carrying a sliding horizontal scale that passes directly in front of the vertical scale (fig. 33). The vessel is set against the upright, which is taken as the zero abscissa. The base is, of course, the zero ordinate. The abscissa for the end point at the base, which is on the zero ordinate, is read from the scale at the base, and the ordinate for the point of maximum diameter, which is on the zero abscissa, is read directly from the vertical scale. The end of the movable horizontal scale is then brought to the other characteristic points, and the co-ordinates of these points are read from the

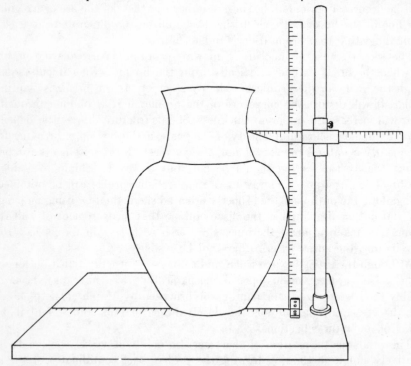

FIG. 33—A DEVICE FOR DRAWING VESSEL PROFILES
The base of the vertical tangent at the point of maximum diameter marks the origin for plotting. Co-ordinates of the other characteristic points are read from the upright and horizontal scales. The scale on the base assists in reading diameters of shoulder and base. The upright can be removed for convenience in transportation.

horizontal and vertical scales at their intersection. If instead of recording the numerical values of these points one plots directly on co-ordinate paper, time is saved, and, since the curve can be completed at once, any error in reading is immediately checked. In plotting, the abscissa is read from right to left. If one person takes readings and a second person plots, profiles can be drawn very swiftly.

This gives the contour of one side of a vessel. If forms were perfectly symmetrical, it would be sufficient to read the abscissa of the base at its far side from the scale on which it rests and to duplicate the curve from this point. In the study of Plumbate ware, forms were idealized by mirroring one contour on the plane passing through the mid-point of the maximum diameter. All major diameters—base, shoulder, and orifice—were measured directly. If the profile of both sides is desired, the maximum diameter is read. If this is not at an end point, it can be obtained accurately by placing a scale across the orifice and sighting to bring the two scales in line with the point being read. This diameter establishes an abscissa zero on the opposite side. The points are marked on the base of the vessel, where it rests on the scale, and the vessel is turned to bring the opposite side in contact with the vertical upright; a second set of points is read, these being plotted with reference to the second zero abscissa and to its right instead of its left.

The uprights of the frame used for vessel measurement are made detachable from the base to facilitate transportation. In the study of Plumbate ware this method proved practicable, and through its use attention was drawn to characteristics that might otherwise have escaped notice. For example, I found that the central axis of jars is frequently inclined to the vertical; that is, the planes of the throat, shoulder, and orifice are parallel but the plane of the base is inclined to them. This peculiar form of asymmetry would result from removing the vessel from a support while it was moist enough to yield and setting it down firmly on a flat surface without exercising care to keep it level (Shepard, 1948, p. 14). Recording the position of characteristic points facilitates study of profile, and this method of drawing automatically gives all measurements needed for calculation of proportions.

DESIGN

The archaeologist well knows how much decoration adds to the value of a sherd when it is used as a means of classification and correlation. Beyond this is the importance of pottery design in the study of the development of decorative art. The record is rich and varied because pottery offers two distinct media, the plastic and the graphic. In both of these the potter had considerable latitude and freedom of expression. Ceramic art affords insights of the life and psychology of a people by its qualities as well as by its subject matter. The tastes and concerns of both the simple craftsman and the artist have found expression in pottery decoration. There are common articles of daily use—food bowls, water jugs, and cook pots—on the one hand, and on the other, ritual vessels required for solemn ceremonies and vessels made as offerings to important personages during life and upon death. Pottery decoration shows the trials of the beginner, the work of the expert, the efforts of the copyist, and the expression of the creator. It is for us to try to recognize each for what it is and to free ourselves of narrow habits of evaluation in order to read the record.

Description and analysis of decorative style are related and dependent phases of study because we seek to understand the basic qualities of a style, and these are not shown by superficial appearance alone. Recording design and analyzing it, however, are distinct tasks. One involves only the use of adequate means of reproduction, the other requires an understanding of the qualities of artistic expression and leads to interpretation. The problems of recording are the mechanical ones of illustration. If the archaeologist wishes to leave design study to the student of art, he is free to do so, but recording is a responsibility that cannot be slighted.

THE RECORD OF DESIGN

There is little need to argue that, in so far as practicable, the record of decoration should be graphic rather than verbal. Decorative design is a form of expression, and verbal description is a translation in which too much meaning and quality are lost. These remarks apply to the description of individual examples for which it may be said that graphic representation is primary, verbal comment secondary. When large numbers of designs are reported on, it becomes necessary to summarize characteristics; to point out their range of variation; to distinguish typical, distinctive, exceptional, and aberrant features; and to consider relationships and their significance. Discussion is then essential and illustration often must be limited to a portion of the series.

The record of decorative design should have the accuracy and detail necessary to serve those who wish to make an independent analysis of style or a thorough comparison of one style with another. This is essential because we are only beginning to formulate methods of analysis and criteria of classification. The sensitive emotional responses and perceptions of the artist and the habits of systematic and logical dissection and persistent questioning of the analyst should each have a role in the development of this field.

For purposes of illustration, both photographs and drawings have their peculiar advantages and disadvantages. Although photogravure or halftone reproduction of the photograph is more expensive than a linecut of an ink drawing, the cost of the draftsman's time should be counted against the drawing. Weighing against the accuracy, detail, and speed of the photographic method are distinct disadvantages: (1) the view is limited; one photograph cannot show the entire decoration of many common vessel shapes; (2) the photograph gives a more or less distorted or foreshortened view, depending on the curvature of the field and on the type of lens used; (3) the photograph shows stains and abrasions and is useless when wear has left the design indistinct.

The drawing is free of these limitations, but there are disadvantages peculiar to this method of illustration. Basic is the mechanical or geometric problem of maintaining correct spatial relations when design from the surface of a three-dimensional, curved vessel is transferred to paper. One has only to visualize a hemispherical bowl with its sides slit and laid flat like the peel of half an orange to appreciate the problem. The adjustment that must be made and its effect depend partly on the characteristics of the decoration. If the motifs are naturalistic, their size and proportion are fixed, and increase in background areas may not be conspicuous. Geometric design, on the other hand, often has more intimate spatial relations; that is, both painted and unpainted areas may form integral parts of the design. The true balance of dark and light and even the proportions and contours of forms are lost in this case if the figures are copied exactly, leaving unpainted areas to take up the extra space. The importance of making correct adjustment for this class of design cannot be overemphasized.

The camera automatically makes the adjustment necessary to maintain spatial relations but in the process throws in foreshortening. The effect of foreshortening was greatly reduced in the photographic method devised by Wesley Bradfield for illustrating Mimbres bowl designs. He constructed a special box using a wide-angle lens and enlarging paper instead of film. The large size of the paper negative enabled him to bring the lens close to the bowl and also afforded the opportunity to supply by projection of lines the missing parts of incomplete or worn specimens. The process can be used for photographic reproduction or reduced to black and white for linecut, and it undoubtedly offers the best solution of this general problem. The superior rendering of design can be seen in the illustrations of *Cameron Creek Village* (Bradfield, 1929). That the process has not generally been adopted is doubtless due to the fact that it requires special photographic equipment and has been described only briefly (Bradfield, 1925). When design is drawn freehand the copyist's sense of the balance of black and white, his trained appreciation of spatial relations, is perhaps the best guide to correct rendering, but to make a reliable reproduction from a strongly curved surface requires exceptional judgment.

Another inadequacy of drawings is in the rendering of quality of technique. Drawing is independent of this disadvantage only when diagrammatic or formalized illustration serves to bring out certain features of design. The difficulty of illustrating technique is increased when it is necessary to use a medium different from the original, as in a pen-and-ink drawing of an incised design. A comparable medium and technique should be used whenever feasible. The quality of a painted design can be maintained better when copied with a brush rather than a pen.

Another factor that complicates faithful rendering is the difference in effect of design on an irregular, curved surface and on a plane, even one. The illustrator discovers to his surprise that a meticulous reproduction of the irregularities and imperfections of a design gives an impression of greater crudity than the original possessed, since on the vessel there is some compensation for irregularity of line in the unevenness of surface.

The representation of polychrome design in black and white reproduction, that is, the differentiation of color and relative values, is a problem that has been satisfactorily solved by Kidder. It was once customary to use various symbols, such as hachure, crosshatching, stippling, etc., to indicate different colors. This method involved a tedious drafting job to produce a linecut that was confusing in its effect because the symbols conflicted with the pattern and taxed the reader to recall the meanings and visualize the effect, and often failed to carry the impression of relative values of different colors. Kidder found that a photogravure reproduction of a water-color painting shows the distinction in value of different colors (see illustrations in Smith and Kidder, 1943). If the vessel is well preserved, a photograph of the original is adequate and superior for illustration of draftsmanship and technique. It is necessary to resort to the water-color painting only when the surface is worn, colors are faded, or the design cannot be reproduced photographically without distortion.

Another special problem is that of rendering incised designs to give the effect of pattern and value. This type of decoration is basically a monochrome technique in which differences in relief throw a shadow in the line of the design. To render the incised lines full width in solid black gives a false impression of the balance of ground and pattern, whereas an outline of the edges of the trough is often confusing. If, however, the design is drawn with wax pencil on textured paper such as coquille,the correct relation of ground and figure can be illustrated and the process requires hardly more time than ink drawing.

The various considerations that I have reviewed suggest the special purposes of both photography and drawing. The drawing can be used to present the results of analysis and generalizations regarding the features of styles. At best it can be made a satisfactory means of illustrating individual specimens, and whenever design is faint or incomplete, it offers the only recourse for effective illustration. But some photographs should be included in the record to illustrate such features as quality of linework, spatial relations, and the effect of surface texture, features that are shown only with difficulty or not at all by a drawing.

Beyond the selection of appropriate methods of illustration are possibilities of relating photography and hand rendering in the actual process of analysis and illustration. An outstanding example is Dr. Hugo G. Rodeck's use of positive transparencies to obtain accurate drawings of the life forms from Mimbres pottery. Rodeck projects the positive image under a table and reflects it upward with a mirror placed at an angle of 45° to a glass set in the table top. The image is then copied on vellum tracing paper. Any desired enlargement can be obtained, and focusing is facilitated by placing the projector on a track which is pushed back and forth from the position of the copyist. Devices such as this greatly increase accuracy and at the same time reduce cost of illustration.

DESIGN ANALYSIS

The attempt to classify pottery decoration teaches one the difficulty of drawing sharp lines between the naturalistic, the conventional, and the geometric or between the symbolic and the abstract or purely decorative. By naturalistic we understand the representation of an object as it appears in nature, but such representations are far from photographic; they are rather abbreviated renderings, the form of which is conditioned by the skill of the artist and by the style and conventionalities with which he is familiar. For example, the representation of a human figure may be unnatural in posture or proportion in consequence of the artist's disregard of perspective or the figure may be distorted to fit a field. There will be simplifications; and straight line may be substituted for curved line, or features and ornaments may be conventionalized as symbols of particular beings. At what point does the design become conventional; how many modifications and what particular ones distinguish the conventional?

The distinction between the symbolic and abstract or decorative is no less difficult to draw, though it offers a different problem. By following a series of conventionalizations in the representation of a symbolic object, it is sometimes possible to recognize meaning in a geometric figure, but when the record of the history of a design is lacking, there is no proof of its significance. Consequently, one can rarely feel confident in classifying the design of a prehistoric people as simply abstract or decorative. We can only insist that the meaning of design should be sought whenever possible.

The problem of classification can be simplified by distinguishing the connotative and the formal aspects of design and by recognizing that they can be studied independently. By connotative I refer not only to what is represented, but also to its meaning in the culture—not alone the identification of a serpent, for example, but also an understanding of what the serpent signified or symbolized to the people who represented it. By formal aspect I refer to those qualities that define style. To separate the connotative and formal factors is not to deny the existence of relationships between them but rather to recognize the needs for different methods of study.

It follows from the nature of the connotative aspects that fixed rules of guidance for their study cannot be outlined. The subject matter is rich and varied, and the purposes of decoration are diverse. A design may represent an object of deep significance—a rain or fertility symbol; it may portray an important being—a cultural hero or a god; it may commemorate an event, describe the activities of a people, or tell a story. The design may bear a direct relation to the use of the vessel, or it may have a magical significance; it may be used because of its associations, because of interest in the subject or appreciation of its decorative value. There is a reciprocal relation between interpretation of design and knowledge of its cultural matrix; the better the culture is understood, the easier and more certain the explanation of the decoration, which in turn contributes to knowledge of the culture.

The formal aspects of design include its adaptation to vessel shape, composition or structure, use of elements and motifs, and such characteristics as symmetry, relation of figure and ground, and balance of dark and light. These are factors that determine to a considerable extent the quality of design, and fortunately they can be described, in part at least, from inspection alone. Moreover, it is possible in many cases to arrive at a common basis of judgment of them, which is extremely important if we are to understand and use the results of one another's analyses.

The different media of decoration present different problems of style analysis. Plastic decoration runs the gamut from simple surface texturing through simple and complex incised and plano-relief design, which is in effect graphic, to modeling in the round, which often finds its richest expression in the representation of human and animal forms. Painting likewise varies from simple to complex in both geometric and realistic styles. I shall not attempt to consider the formal factors that can be studied in all these classes of design but shall confine my discussion mainly to one class—graphic geometric—with the purpose of suggesting some of the possibilities that can be explored and the extent to which it may be possible to reach common agreement. Geometric design was chosen partly because we have greater wealth of illustration of it than of most of the other classes. Various approaches have been made in this field and progress has been sound, but there are still important aspects of design that we do not know how to describe precisely and perhaps qualities of which we are only half aware. One can discuss problems of analysis and make suggestions, but to lay down a full and final procedure is out of the question.

Field of decoration. The potter's first step in decorating a vessel is to choose the area that will receive the ornamentation. There are a few simple, obvious considerations that usually, though not invariably, influence the choice. One is that of visibility from a normal viewing position. There are seeming exceptions, some of which can be explained. The design on the underside of a Greek kantharos may not be visible as it sits on a museum shelf, but it would show to advantage when the cup is raised to the lips. Again, a Pueblo prayer-meal bowl may be painted over the entire exterior, including the base on which it rests, but it was a sacred object, not decorated simply for the pleasure of its owner.

Ordinarily, realistic figures are not painted across an area of strong curvature or across an angle in the profile where they cannot be seen from one position without distortion. In addition, these surfaces may be more difficult to paint. Certain surfaces, such as the nearly flat floor of a plate and the side of a cylinder which is straight in the vertical direction and has uniform curvature in a horizontal direction, are especially well suited to figure painting. This circumstance undoubtedly explains why these forms were so frequently chosen for this style of decoration. But there are exceptional instances in which surfaces with a sharp change in contour are chosen, an example being the red- and black-figured Greek amphora with the field of decoration extending across a strongly curved or angled shoulder.

Angles in a vessel contour form natural limits for areas of decoration, and the field is often framed more formally than when the contour is smooth. The Greek amphora affords a good example of this relation since it occurs in two contours. The vessels are similar in proportion and shape, but one has an angle at the base of the neck, the other a smooth curve and an inflection point. Both are decorated with figures in approximately the same position on the upper body, but on the corner-point vessel the field is generally bordered by a geometric band at the base of the neck, which is treated as a separate field in geometric style, whereas the inflected vessel often has a figure without bordering band and the neck is left undecorated (fig. 34). Flat, everted rims on bowls suggest a bordering band by their form. The basal flange of classic Maya polychrome has the same effect. The flange did not originate in painted ware, but was developed and extensively used in it, forming a prominent frame at the lower margin of a band. This relation suggests the extent to which a vessel shape may affect the plan of decoration and the possibility of reciprocal relation.

Although the vessel form influences the position of design in ways such as I have suggested, it also leaves the potter considerable freedom of choice in the position and extent of the area to be decorated, in the proportion of dark and light, and the relation of plain and patterned surface. These factors have a marked effect on style. The potter's latitude in space treatment can be illustrated by the decoration of bowl interiors of Pueblo pottery (fig. 35).

FIG. 34—THE EFFECT OF VESSEL SHAPE ON THE BOUNDARIES OF THE FIELD
OF DESIGN
Two forms of the Greek amphora illustrate how an angle in a contour delimits a field and influences formality of framing.

Some of the questions to consider in describing the relation of decoration to shape will serve as a summary.

Relation of position of design to visibility:
Can the entire design or a complete unit of it be seen from a single viewing position?
Are areas not normally in view decorated?
Relation of contour to field:
Is the field limited by sharp changes in contour, as by an angle between body and neck?
Are areas of slight curvature chosen in preference to those of strong curvature?
Are secondary elements such as rims, moldings, or flanges given special attention, or do they serve as formal borders?
The vessel as a field for design:
Does the vessel surface serve as a ground for design or is the design merely an embellishment of the vessel?
Is there a relationship between formality of design and the part of the area decorated?

Are different classes of design associated, a different part of the vessel being used for each, as naturalistic on jar body, geometric on the neck?

FIG. 35—EXAMPLES OF SPACE TREATMENT OF A BOWL INTERIOR
a: Some basic structural subdivisions of the field. *b-d:* The symmetry of the field: *b*, radial; *c*, rotational; *d*, unsymmetric eccentric. *e-g:* Use of dark and light: *e*, light value predominates and has the effect of background; *f*, dark and light play similar roles; *g*, dark and light form complementary patterns.

Composition and structure. It is logical to commence the study of design with an analysis of the manner in which it was planned, that is, to identify the original outlines and the major divisions of the field. Various well-defined plans or methods of space breaking will be discovered in this way; and often they will furnish a key in the search for derivations and developmental stages in the history of style. Also, relationships between construction and such features as symmetry and balance of dark and light will become evident. To follow through the potter's steps in composing and elaborating the decoration of a vessel, to ascertain in what order the lines were drawn, gives one a feeling for design which can never be gained by fitting it into a ready-made scheme of classification.

In many designs the decorator's procedure in outlining and treating space is simple. It may involve only the repetition of a motif, the elaboration of a line, or the panelling of a band and the subdivision of its rectangles. In such cases methods of construction are obvious at a glance. When design is complex and particularly when secondary lines are given more weight or prominence than the primary structural ones, it becomes necessary to study in detail the characteristics of lines and the relationship of parts.

The most direct indications of method of composition are to be found in the relation of painted lines, particularly in continuity of line and overlap of brush strokes, features that show up more plainly with some pigments than others.

FIG. 36—ANALYSIS OF THE BASIC STRUCTURE OF DESIGN: ILLUSTRATIONS FROM CLASSIC MIMBRES BLACK-ON-WHITE

Paneling. a-d: Basic division of the band laid off with four bars, *b.* A common method of band subdivision is here rendered inconspicuous by using unlike pairs of bars and joining adjacent ones by secondary Z-like space dividers, *c,* thus incorporating the paneling bars into the design. The subdivisions of the panels are outlined and the spaces broken by simple geometric figures, *d.* This is a relatively simple composition, and analysis of structure is largely a matter of separating by inspection primary and secondary space dividers. *General alignment of elements suggesting three possible schemes of space divisions. e-j:* Paneling, *f.* This layout can be dismissed because the lines are not continuous from frame to frame. Three long sweeping curves that outline overlapping lunar segments, *g.* The smoothness of one of these curves suggests this layout, but a distinct jog in the line on the right and lack of smoothness at several other points casts doubt on this explanation of basic structure. Independent elements drawn from inner and outer framing lines, *h.* This use of marginal dividers is clearly indicated in other Mimbres compositions. Framing these marginal elements is consistent with Mimbres technique, *i.* The remaining spaces are subdivided by simple geometric figures, *j.* A feature that might throw this analysis into question is the smoothness with which the lines of the X's continue the curve of the lines that frame the inner sides of the pendent rectangles suggesting the basic strokes indicated in *g.* The character of this line holds the key to the method of composition. Inspection of the vessel (the present analysis is based on illustration) should show whether or not these lines are continuous. *Design built up from a central zone. k-o:* There are no lines running from inner to outer framer. Elements erected on the framers may be marginal dividers (cf. *h*) or final fillers of a design that was started in the central zone of the band. The smoothness and trueness of the central arcs suggest that diamonds were first drawn in opposite sides of the band, *l,* and connected by arcs, *m.* On each arc stepped figures and triangles are erected in rotational balance, *n.* From this point the completion of the design is a matter of outlining these central figures and breaking spaces.

Overlapping affords incontrovertible evidence of the order in which lines were drawn. Abutment of lines offers a sound clue also. If a set of lines ends against another line, the single line is primary. When parts are completely independent, indirect evidence must be sought. Some clues that have been found useful are illustrated in figure 36. Any line that runs through from edge to edge, subdividing the

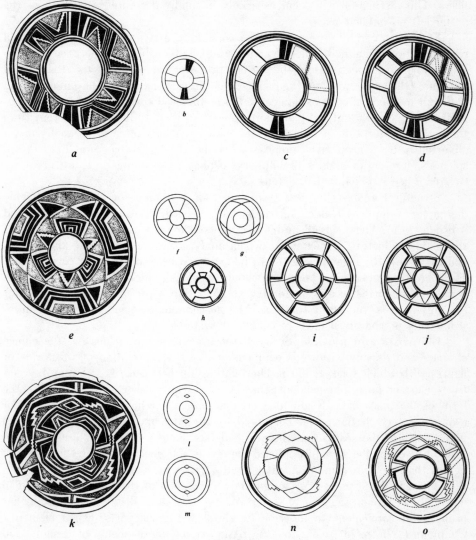

Fig. 36

field, is a possible structural line drawn in laying out the field. The parts of the design drawn first are usually familiar elements or regular figures, and are generally evenly spaced and more symmetric than figures that were drawn later as space fillers, since the latter are adapted to areas that bear the accumulated inaccuracies of freehand composition. Odd-shaped elements are likely to be background fillers. This distinction will occur especially in solidly decorated styles where the potter left no unfilled spaces.

Even with careful study it may be possible to arrive only at a hypothetical reconstruction of method of design composition. It then becomes necessary to distinguish between construction (the potter's procedure in executing the design) and structure (the apparent plan, the main spatial divisions, and the relation of parts). Different methods of composition can often be followed to produce the same composition (fig. 36e-h), and the plan as it appears to us may be quite different from the potter's conception of it because secondary elements may intentionally or inadvertently have been given emphasis, leaving the basic structural lines inconspicuous, just as an artist's preliminary strokes in outlining a figure are later covered when it is painted in detail.

Structural analysis has been employed in a number of studies of Pueblo design, for example by Kidder (in Kidder and Shepard, 1936), Chapman (1936), and Amsden (1936). These classifications were devised for the description of particular styles. They illustrate the extent to which analysis can be systematic and logical, and they show the ingenuity that can be exercised in reconstructing composition. These are the respects in which they should serve as guides and standards. There is no general inclusive system for the classification of design structure, and for the present it is important that there be direct and independent analysis unrestricted by preconceived ideas of particular systems.

Elements and motifs. Study of the basic structure of design—the choice of space and its subdivision—is complemented by a description of the forms or figures with which space is filled. The relationship between the two may be relatively close or fairly independent; that is, the layout restricts or determines the form of the parts of a design to a greater or less extent. There are styles, for example, in which the potter composed by dividing and subdividing space and filling parts of the scaffolding thus formed (see Kidder in Kidder and Shepard, 1936). But often the structure is used merely as a frame for a figure or group of figures that are drawn independently of it.

The significant parts of a design and the method of their analysis depend in no small measure on the type of design. When the style is strictly geometric, it has been found convenient to describe its simplest regular parts, called elements. Chapman (1936, p. 18) refers to "the basic, irreducible elements of design" and illustrates their identification in his study of Santo Domingo Pueblo pottery.

Simple designs are often composed of arrangements of one or more elements. In more complex design the conspicuous or seemingly significant parts are groups of elements. Bunzel (1929) pointed out that the Zuni potter in painting design does not think of elements as we break them down but rather of motifs. Examples drawn for her by a potter were intricate figures. They may or may not have symbolic significance or be named, but they are the units with which the potter composes. In using them she apparently thinks no more of the individual elements of which they are made up than we think of the letters in using a word.

In the analysis of prehistoric pottery it is not always possible to recognize the potter's motifs, but the repetition of arrangements of elements on the same vessel and their appearance on other vessels will at least be significant. Because of its greater complexity, the motif is necessarily more varied and distinctive than the element. The same simple geometric figures appear again and again in various styles. Their usefulness in analysis depends on the complexity of the style. The simpler the style, the greater the probability that the element is the basic decorative unit, and the more significant it will be. The more complex the design, the greater the probability that the units of composition are combinations of elements. The concept of the element has been especially helpful in the study of sherds because a small part of design shows in the fragment when motifs and structures do not. The sherd at best, however, gives a sketchy and incomplete record of design and it would be unfortunate if dependence on sherds should dictate methods of analysis.

In order to simplify and standardize description a nomenclature of elements and motifs has been widely adopted by Southwestern archaeologists (Douglas and Raynolds, 1941). Brainerd's adoption of the terms "line enrichments" and "fillers" (Beals, Brainerd, and Smith, 1945) suggests the advantage of classifying elements according to their function in design. This is a possibility that calls for further exploration.

Structure and motifs constitute in a sense the morphology of design. They reveal in many cases the artist's procedure and illuminate the relationship of design styles. There are also qualities or properties of design. Artists use such terms as rhythm, balance, unity, harmony, but these qualities are not easily defined. The trained artist can evaluate a composition with respect to them, but he cannot measure them, nor are judgments always consistent. We need methods of analysis and description that are free of variable individual aesthetic taste. Our aim is to recognize qualities that can be consistently described regardless of personal preference. The review which follows covers some aspects which have been extensively tested and others in which the approach is experimental.

Symmetry. Probably there is no other quality of design that lends itself as readily to precise definition as symmetry. In fact, the possibilities of regular spatial arrangement have been worked out mathematically by students of atomic structure who, as a pastime, have applied the principles they use in the study of complex three-dimensional space to band and allover patterns (Buerger and Lukesh, 1937). I will review the subject briefly since I have considered it at length elsewhere (Shepard, 1948a).

The symmetry of single elements or motifs is familiar. There are only three classes—bilateral, rotational, and radial—and we see innumerable illustrations of them in geometric figures and the forms of nature. Examples of bilateral symmetry are found in an isosceles triangle, a pansy, and a human figure; of rotational symmetry, in a parallelogram, a triskelion, and a swastika (nature eschews this class of symmetry); of radial symmetry, in a square, a daisy, and a starfish. The characteristic which they possess in common is that a fundamental part is repeated regularly about an axis. Each class is defined by the motion employed in repetition. In the bilateral figure it is mirroring; in the rotational, it is rotation about a point with an even number of repetitions within a revolution. The radial figure combines both reflection and rotation. All that is required for symmetry classification is identification of the fundamental part and of the motion by which it is repeated. The fundamental part may be an unsymmetric area or part of an area or a segment of a line, but it is always the unique part of the pattern from which the entire composition can be generated by regular repetition of a motion.

Elements and motifs are symmetric with respect to a single axis (a line), or a point, or intersecting axes, and are referred to as finite designs. If a series of axes is taken to repeat the figure again and again along a straight line, a band pattern is produced. It may appear as a regular serial repetition of symmetric elements or motifs, but examination shows that the same motion that produced the individual figure also projects it from one point to the next. There are axes between the figures as well as within them. The necessity of extending the pattern in a straight line limits the number of times a motion is repeated about an axis. Rotation is limited to twofold because this is the only degree that will extend the fundamental part in a straight line. Higher-fold rotation is meaningless with respect to band symmetry, but translation is added to reflection and rotation, and the various combinations of motions result in seven different types of regular band patterns, each defined by its characteristic motion or motions (fig. 37). Examples of these are common in geometric design and are easily recognized when one looks for the essential motion of repetition. Probably the best way to learn them is to experiment, choosing a few simple asymmetric elements and designing bands in each of the seven classes.

Regular band patterns are important because they are so frequently used in pottery decoration, and one should be thoroughly familiar with them. They do not exhaust the possibilities of symmetric arrangement, however. We can go further and repeat the fundamental part in two directions to form a surface or allover pattern. Again new combinations of motions are possible and the total number of regular allover pattern types is seventeen. These have been well illustrated by

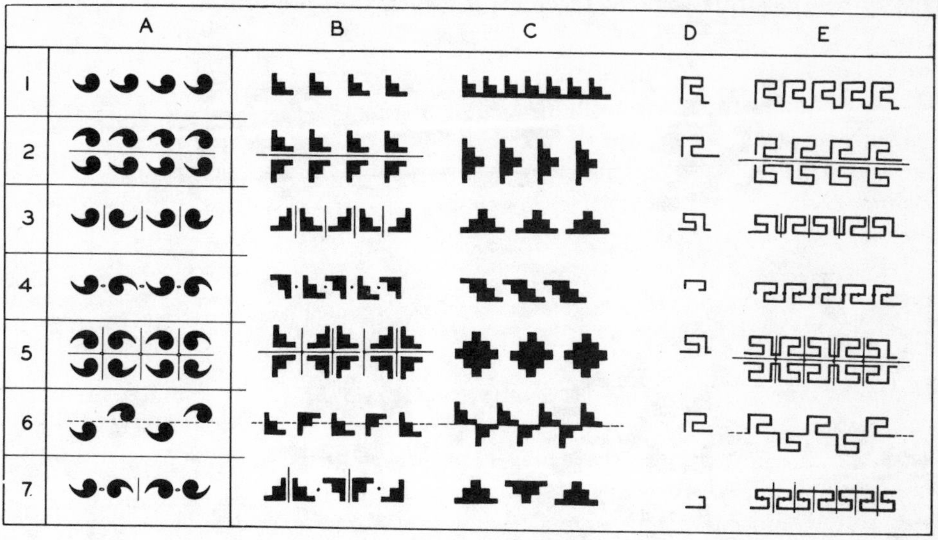

	A	B	C	D	E
1					
2					
3					
4					
5					
6					
7					

FIG. 37—THE SEVEN CLASSES OF REGULAR BAND PATTERNS

These classes are defined by the motion employed in repeating the fundamental part of the design. *Column A.* A diagrammatic illustration. The comma represents the fundamental part. The motions are indicated as follows: solid line—axis of reflection; dotted line—axis of slide reflection; small ellipse—axis of bifold rotation. The characteristic motions of the classes are as follows: (1) Translation. The fundamental part is moved without change in orientation. (2) Longitudinal or horizontal reflection. This class involves translation as well as reflection. (3) Transverse or vertical reflection. Repeated reflection alone produces the band. (4) Bifold rotation. The fundamental part is swung around the axis through an angle of 180°. By repeating this motion at regular intervals, the pattern is extended in a straight line. (5) Longitudinal and transverse reflections combined. This has the effect of a series of radial figures. (6) Slide reflection or screw motion. Patterns of this class should be viewed vertically to appreciate their symmetry. They are composed of alternating left and right images. (7) Alternate rotation and transverse reflection. The latter motion may be most noticeable, but the quality of design is influenced by rotation which has the effect of inverting alternate figures. *Columns B and C.* The seven classes are illustrated with a simple step figure as the fundamental part. The position of the axes with relation to the figure (whether they impinge on the fundamental part or are spaced) does not affect the symmetry, but it alters the form of the figure that would be identified as the element or unit of design. In B, axes (indicated by lines and dots) are separated from the fundamental part. In C, some axes impinge forming solid figures, others are spaced. Note that in Class 6, the axis runs through the figures in Column B and impinges in Column C. Had it been spaced, it would have spread the elements vertically, forming a wider band. The seven classes can be employed for continuous-line design, no less than for block design. A series of comparable patterns is shown in Column E produced from the fundamental parts shown in Column D. Note that these parts do not always correspond to the unit that would be selected as the element of the design. The tendency in viewing these bands is to see a series of simple repeats and to neglect the characteristic or intrinsic motion.

In classifying the symmetry of a pattern, it is necessary first to identify the unique or fundamental part, which is always unsymmetric and from which the entire design can be generated by employing the characteristic motion that defines the symmetry of the class.

several authors (Birkhoff, 1933; Buerger and Lukesh, 1937). Allover patterns are much less frequent on pottery than bands, but they do occur and are even cut to the area of a band in some instances. A few examples taken mainly from Pueblo pottery will illustrate some of the ways in which they are formed (fig. 38).

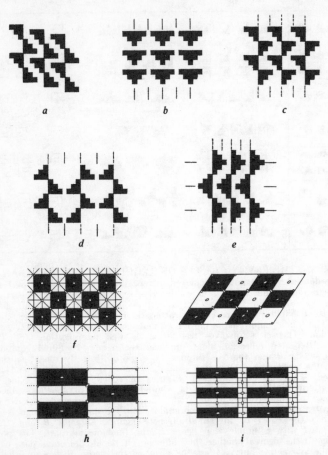

FIG. 38—EXAMPLES OF THE REGULAR ALLOVER OR TWO-DIMENSIONAL DESIGN
Symbols for axes the same as in fig. 31. In allover design, two-, three-, four-, and sixfold rotation can be employed, and reflection and slide reflection axes can be used in various ways. The patterns are constructed on nets of which there are five that are consistent with repeat operations (the parallelogram, rectangle, diamond, equilateral triangle or hexagon, and square). Three of the five patterns here developed from a step figure occur in Pueblo pottery. (a,d,e; cf. Brew, 1946, figs. 59c, 60a, 60d respectively. The symmetry of fig. 60a is imperfect. Instead of alternate reflection and slide reflection axes, it has only a central axis of reflection, combined with slide reflection axes.) It is noteworthy that the class represented by a, which employs only bifold rotation, is most common in Pueblo allover design. In this class, the spatial relations are such that a meander can be laid off in the ground. When reflection or slide reflection is used this characteristic is lacking. Aside from design covering a surface, sections of two-dimensional design are sometimes used as bands. Four simple examples from Mesa Verde Black-on-white design are illustrated (f-i).

The classes of symmetric pattern that have been defined for the three spatial categories of design can be proved to be inclusive. Every symmetric design belongs to one of them, and each is precisely defined by the motion or motions of the fundamental part. The fact that the system is inclusive and that types are discontinuous and unequivocal makes symmetrical design a paradise for the classifier. But we can be reasonably certain that the potter did not think of design in terms of the motions of a fundamental part. This being the case, we may well ask what significance symmetry classification has in the study of design. Is it merely an artificial system that we impose, or is it something that man is aware of in his environment and copies intuitively as he uses natural forms as models, or does it follow from the structure of design itself and from regular arrangement?

The suspicion of artificiality can be dismissed at once because nature affords a wealth of prototypes for symmetric figures and patterns. The form of higher animals, of most leaves, and of some flowers is bilateral. Many lower animals and many flowers have radial symmetry. A stem with opposite leaves can be viewed as a band formed by longitudinal reflection. A stem with alternate leaves and a line of footprints have slide reflection. The innumerable examples of symmetry in our environment may foster the liking for regularity and order because symmetric arrangement seems to be ubiquitous in decorative design. Furthermore symmetry often follows from the structure of design, and it may even result from the manner in which a vessel is held and turned as it is painted. The designer, whether sophisticated or not, considers manner of repetition when composing and introduces variety by changing the orientation of a figure, by swinging it around, or by inverting it, even though he does not define these operations in mathematical terms. The extent to which consciousness of order in nature influences arrangement and the part which experimentation with form and repetition has played in the development of symmetric design is a question not easily answered, but there can be little doubt that both are in some measure responsible for the prevalence of symmetric figures and patterns.

Intuitive feeling for symmetry, that is for the motion implicit in repetition, is perhaps nowhere better illustrated than in rotational band patterns. Twofold rotation extends the pattern and keeps it in a straight line by turning it 180° with each repetition, whereas a threefold rotational figure can be used in a band only by translating it; when a fourfold figure is used, half its motion is lost (fig. 39). If band patterns were composed as simple, serial repeats of elements or motifs without feeling for their implicit motion, one multiple might be used as often as another. Actually, however, twofold rotation is very characteristic of band patterns, and higher-fold figures are comparatively rare.

The importance of symmetry in design analysis is indicated, not alone by its prevalence, but also by the difference in decorative styles that suggest variable preference for certain classes of symmetry. Even when examples of all classes can be found within styles, relative frequencies often differ enough to set the styles apart. Brainerd (1942) was the first to point out that there is a very high proportion of

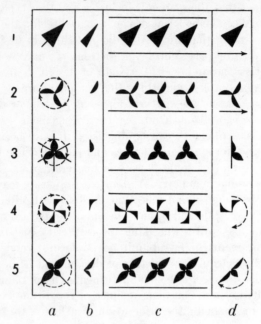

FIG. 39—THE SYMMETRY OF MOTIFS AND BANDS COMPARED

a: The motions of a single motif. b: The fundamental part of the motif. c: A regular band formed by the repetition of the motif. The symmetry of the band differs from that of the motif because certain of the motions that can be employed for single figures will not form a band. The fundamental part of the band (d) therefore differs from that of the motif. Note that in a band, oblique bilateral figures (1) and threefold rotational figures (2) can only be translated; threefold radial figures (3) are reduced to transverse or longitudinal reflection if they are symmetrically placed (one axis vertical or horizontal) or to translation if their position is unsymmetric (all axes oblique); fourfold rotational figures (4) and oblique biaxial radial figures (5) are reduced to bifold rotation.

bifold rotation in Pueblo design, whereas in certain Mexican and Mayan styles slide reflection is prominent. The question is, Do these differences reflect preferences for the suggested motions and rhythms or is symmetry a by-product of structure? One can demonstrate for himself that symmetry is independent of the form of the element by choosing as a fundamental part any element and constructing with it designs in all the symmetric classes, but some patterns will, of course, be more familiar or seem more satisfying than others. More convincing is the fact that the same element is used in different symmetries in different styles. Among the Pueblos, for example, the scroll is almost invariably used in bifold rotation arrangement. On the other hand, in Mesoamerican styles the scroll is often used in slide reflection. Not infrequently it springs from a wavy line like tendrils on a vine. In a study of Plumbate style, I found this type of arrangement persisting even after the design element had been so modified that it was subordinated to a nearly symmetric secondary element (Shepard, 1948a, p. 68). This suggests that the feeling for arrangement may be stronger or more persistent than interest in a figure.

The relation of symmetry to structure can easily be demonstrated with band designs which for convenience can be divided into three classes (fig. 40): (1) Arrangements of elements or motifs without base lines or preliminary subdivisions of the area of the band. The fundamental portions of the design may be attached to or framed by straight lines. (2) Designs developed on base lines which are symmetric. The band is framed or unframed. (3) A structural plan involving subdivision of a strip laid off by framing lines. In the first instance, the artist starts with elements or motifs, and there is no structural plan which restricts symmetry. One may say

FIG. 40—TYPES OF BAND CONSTRUCTION

a: The band is composed of separate, independent motifs. *b:* The band is developed on a continuous line. *c:* A framed band is subdivided or laid off by structural lines. Examples drawn from Santo Domingo design.

that here the symmetry of the band constitutes its structure, and it may be a conscious concern of the potter, particularly when employing the less common arrangements of slide reflection or alternate reflection and rotation. If the design is developed either on a base line or in the subdivisions of a strip, the structure itself will belong to one of the seven classes of symmetric band patterns and will thus restrict, but not absolutely determine, the symmetry of the finished band. The relation in the case of a subdivided band is shown in figure 41 with examples of structures employing four symmetry classes. Horizontal-transverse reflection, represented by vertical paneling, is by far the most common. This structure places no restriction on the symmetry of the band because the panel embodies the motions employed in all the other classes of symmetry. In all instances, the extent to which symmetry is modified by structure depends upon the number of motions included

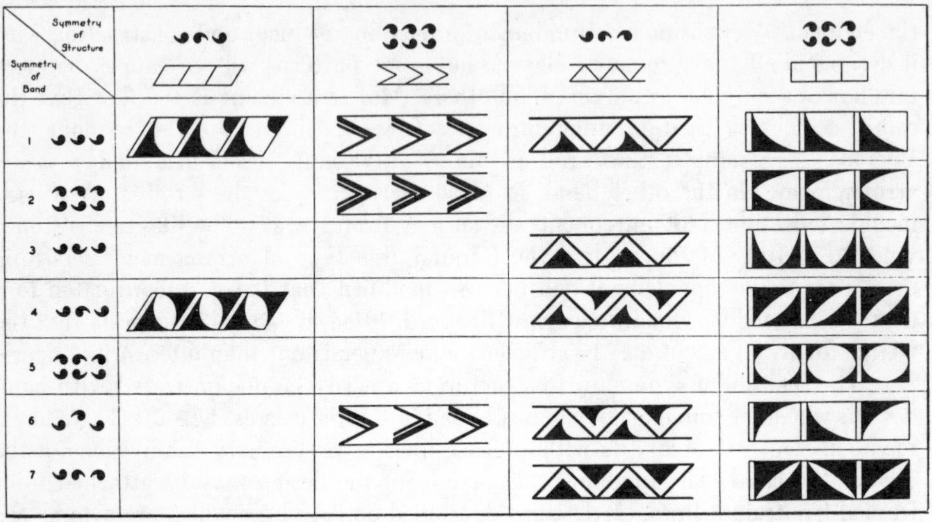

FIG. 41—EFFECT OF BAND STRUCTURE ON THE SYMMETRY OF THE PATTERN
A symmetric pattern can be developed with each of the motions implicit in the structure, and other motions cannot be employed. If the structure has only one motion in addition to translation, only two pattern types can be developed (first column, translation and bifold rotation). When all motions are included in the symmetry of the structure, the band can be developed in any of the seven pattern classes (last column, transverse-longitudinal reflection includes all the motions that can be employed for band patterns).

in the structure. If there is just one motion in addition to translation, as in transverse reflection (Class 3), or bifold rotation (Class 4), there are just two possibilities for the final band; that is, the design can be developed in the symmetry of its structure or this can be reduced to simple translation.

The same principles hold for design developed on a base line. Probably the most frequent of such lines are zigzags and wavy lines which have reflection and rotation (Class 7). Also frequent is the crossed zigzag which has transverse and longitudinal reflection (Class 5) that places no limit on symmetry of development. It is clear from these examples that there are relations between structure and symmetry, and still the designer usually has considerable freedom in choice of symmetry within the common band structures. It is important to consider the relationship in order to determine the extent to which symmetry was prescribed and also whether or not the highest symmetry which the structure afforded was used. Before concluding that a high frequency of occurrence of a given class of symmetry reflects a preference for it, we should ascertain whether or not this type of symmetry is dependent on a standard structure or appears with distinct structures. The relations between symmetry and structure are reciprocal. Description of a composition is incomplete without a record of the manner of arrangement of the fundamental part of the design, and symmetry affords the most satisfactory means of defining the arrangement of design composed without preliminary layout. Symmetry may therefore be considered an essential aspect of construction.

Elsewhere (Shepard, 1948a) I have considered empirically in some detail the problems of symmetry analysis. Many of the points mentioned here are illustrated more fully there. Only a little experience is required to learn to distinguish the three spatial categories of design. The criteria are the motions of the arrangement itself, not the form of the field nor the extent of the surface covered. A finite design can cover the entire surface of a bowl, for example, and a regular allover design can be restricted to a small circle in the center, or cut to a strip that forms a band. A series of transverse bands covering a surface becomes a regular allover design when the figures in contiguous bands bear an orderly relation to each other. In all cases it is the motion of the design which determines its symmetry, just as the internal structure of a substance, not its outward form, determines whether or not it is crystalline.

The classification of design that is perfectly symmetric is simple and straightforward, but symmetry is rendered imperfect in a number of ways resulting in design which is distinct from that which is basically unsymmetric. Deviations cannot be ignored; moreover, the manner in which design is rendered unsymmetric often throws light on the history of a style. It will suffice here to mention briefly some of the principal ways in which symmetry is degraded.

Lack of skill in drawing or laying out the space for design is a common cause of secondary asymmetry which as a rule is easily recognized. Irregularity and uncertainty of line marks the work of the beginner or the poor painter. A common cause of irregularity is the crowding or stretching of a unit of design to fit an unequal space at the close of a band. Occasionally, drafting is so careless that one cannot be certain whether the intent was to draw a symmetric pattern or not. This is particularly true when simple elements are used in composition since there is then little structure by which to judge the plan.

Free rendering and indifference to exact repetition is very likely to result in variation in position or form of a detail in basically symmetric designs. Quality of line and regularity of spacing usually enable one to distinguish between free composition such as this and crude drawing. Secondary modifications of a symmetric structure often suggest that the potter was more interested in qualities of design other than perfect symmetry. A clear-cut example is to be found in the solid filling of one half of a bifold rotational design and the hatching of the other half, a device not uncommon in Classic Mimbres Black-on-white design. The rotational effect is much less clear because of the change in value, but the potters were more interested in an equal balance of solid and hachure than in symmetry. In other cases the elaboration of a design is not in conformity with the basic symmetry. In this instance the potter had a familiar stock of devices for elaboration and evidently used them without awareness or concern for their effect on symmetry. The details that destroy the symmetry of a design may also be introduced with conscious intent as when they form part of a symbol.

There are also purely mechanical factors that limit choice of symmetry and these were sometimes disregarded by the potter; for example, either a sector or a segment of a bowl interior is a bilateral field and is not suitable for rotational figures, but potters accustomed to rotation sometimes forced it into such a field. Adaptations of this kind are frequently found in wide bands of Classic Mimbres Black-on-white design.

These various features that influence the symmetry of design require thorough analysis and considered interpretation. A simple tabulation of symmetry classes will seldom be adequate because the record should show: (1) the frequency with which symmetry is affected by careless or free draftsmanship, minor elaborations, introduction of dark and light in the balance parts of a design, and distortions resulting from adaptations of design to unsuitable field shapes; (2) whether symmetry is normal and simple or complex, as when elements of different symmetry are combined, units of a band are altered, finite symmetry is reduced by linear repetition, regular band design is converted to finite by closing a wide band, or regular allover design is reduced to a band; (3) the relation of symmetry to field shape, structure, and dominant elements.

The value of symmetry in design analysis rests on a number of facts. It lends itself to precise definition and is independent of connotative factors; these conditions afford a basis for common agreement in classification. It bears a relation to design structure and, being an essential aspect of arrangement, often affords a concise means of describing it. It is not directly determined by method of composition but has an important effect on the quality of design, especially on its dynamic or static effect. Finally it has wide application, and the differences that styles show with respect to it suggest that it reflects psychological factors. To one unfamiliar with it, a verbal description may make it appear difficult and confusing, but only a little experimentation with design is necessary to correct this impression.

Motion and rhythm.   The terms "static" and "dynamic" are often used in art criticism, but the characteristics that impart a feeling of rest or motion are difficult to define precisely—or at least it is difficult to weigh the relative effect of the various factors. Aside from connotative factors, characteristics that are recognized as imparting a sense of motion are oblique line direction, figures that appear to be in unstable equilibrium or unbalanced, and continuity of line. In addition, there is symmetry which plays a primary role because motion is implicit in the repetition of the fundamental part of the symmetric pattern. This fact has not been fully appreciated owing largely to failure to recognize the significance of rotational arrangement. The effect of symmetry is shown most clearly by the contrast between bilateral and rotational patterns (fig. 42). Vertical reflection produces

FIG. 42—MIRROR AND ROTATIONAL SYMMETRY CONTRASTED WITH RESPECT TO DYNAMIC QUALITY

The effect of the motions implicit in these two classes of symmetry illustrated by pairs of designs copied or adapted from pottery. *a,b:* Early Pueblo (Alkali Ridge, Utah). The rotational design (*b*) changed from curvilinear to rectilinear to make it more nearly comparable to the bilateral design (*a*). The effect of swirl is more pronounced when the base lines are curvilinear, as in the original. *c:* Figures from a Symmaran bowl interior rearranged in mirror symmetry. *d:* The original rotational arrangement of the figures used in *c*. In this instance, the portrayal of a running animal emphasizes the dynamic effect. *e,f:* Scroll designs from Coclé, Panama. The contrast is less pronounced in these designs because the scroll is in itself dynamic. Furthermore, the bifold rotational arrangement does not have as strong torque as the three- or fourfold rotation arrangements illustrated in *b* and *d* respectively. In a band, the bifold rotational design carries through in a wavelike motion, whereas the bilateral design forms a series of units in static balance.

perfectly balanced parts that seem to be braced back to back, giving the impression of support and stability; in other words, a static effect. A rotational figure or pattern, on the other hand, seems to have torque; one visualizes it swinging about its axis or flowing forward in a wavelike motion, hence its dynamic quality is pronounced. Do these impressions indicate that symmetry affords a simple means of judging the dynamic quality of design? Obviously not, for some rotational designs are more dynamic than others, and unsymmetric design can also be dynamic. We must therefore consider the effects of such factors as direction and continuity of line and balance. Patterns in which all factors except one are held constant, in so far as possible, serve for comparison. In continuous-line design, for example, different symmetries can be introduced while maintaining uniformity of line direction (fig. 43). The difficulty of maintaining constancy of all but one variable brings out certain inseparable relations. For example, oblique lines in bilateral design must be equal in both directions, whereas in rotational pattern they are unequal, giving dominance to one direction (fig. 43, A3 and B3).

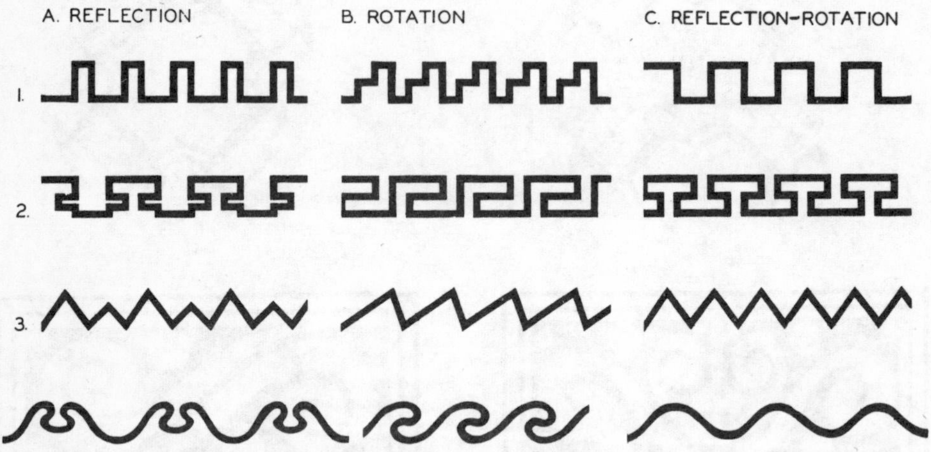

FIG. 43—CONTINUOUS-LINE PATTERNS COMPARED WITH RESPECT TO DYNAMIC QUALITY

In the rectilinear patterns the same line direction has been maintained in each series with emphasis on the vertical in (1), the horizontal in (2), and the oblique in (3). There is an unavoidable difference in complexity, or number of changes in line direction per unit, but the inequalities are counterbalanced in the different series. A transverse axis of reflection gives complete balance of the right and left halves of a line segment; one direction cannot be favored over the other (Column A). The opposite relation holds for bifold rotational design, one direction must be more strongly emphasized than the other (Column B). This difference is inherent in the symmetry. The reflection-rotation patterns have balance of line direction, but they also have an axis of bifold rotation which carries the bilateral unit into itself when it is swung half-way around (Column C). Even though the bilateral effect catches the eye first in these patterns, they have a dynamic quality lacking in the simple reflection patterns.

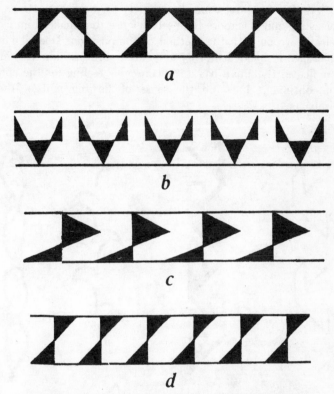

FIG. 44—THE EFFECT OF MECHANICAL BALANCE
     ON THE DYNAMIC QUALITY OF DESIGN
These patterns have been composed with the same elements
of design and the oblique is emphasized in all of them.
They differ in symmetry and mechanical balance. *a:* Bilateral figure in stable equilibrium. *b:* Bilateral figure in
unstable equilibrium. *c:* Unbalanced, unsymmetric figure.
d: Bifold rotational figure with mechanical torque. From
a mechanical viewpoint the stable bilateral is more static
than the unstable, and in so far as lack of balance creates
a dynamic effect, the asymmetric figure which is strongly
off balance is more dynamic than the unstable bilateral which
can be tipped either way. The rotational figure introduces
the effect of torque. Instead of falling, the figure swings about
its axis or swings into the position of the next figure.

An interesting fact that is brought out by these experiments with continuous-
line design is the familiarity and wide distribution of those having bifold rotation
or rotation-reflection. The Wall of Troy, the simple meander, the T-line, oblique
and regular zigzags, and wavy lines are ubiquitous in design, whereas comparable
line patterns in bilateral symmetry are very rare. If, after searching far for examples,

one falls back on his own invention, he is likely to produce patterns that are distinctly displeasing, and it is more than self-defense that makes him feel that something is basically wrong with the method of composition. Does it not seem likely that the difference in incidence of dynamic and static symmetries in continuous-line design indicates that man has an unconscious feeling for the consistency and harmony of continuous line and the sense of flowing motion that rotational symmetry imparts?

FIG. 45—THE DYNAMIC QUALITY OF SLIDE REFLECTION
Dynamic quality is strongest when line direction is upward and thus consistent with the motion of the symmetry. When transverse lines are emphasized (lower left), the effect is ambiguous.

The concept of balance in design is, in part at least, a mechanical one. Consciously or unconsciously, we view a figure as though it were an object sitting upright. Balance, in this sense, is not independent of symmetry (fig. 44). The structure of the bilateral figure gives it static balance, when its axis is vertical. Other positions in which it is unstable are rare because the distinct quality of its symmetry is lost. In contrast, the rotational figure in an unbalanced position appears to have torque. Each figure or unit of design in a rotational pattern seems to swing into the next, whereas unbalanced bilateral or asymmetric figures in comparable patterns appear to be falling.

We have contrasted the effects of rotational and bilateral symmetry on dynamic quality. It may be well to review briefly the effects of combinations of motions in other regular band patterns. In two (fig. 37, nos. 5, 7), both reflection and bifold rotation are used. In one instance, they are combined to produce a radial unit; in the other they are used alternately. In both arrangements the dynamic quality of the pattern is less pronounced than that of the simple rotational pattern, but they do not have the static effect of simple bilateral design. When reflection is introduced on the longitudinal or horizontal axis of the band (fig. 37, no. 2), balance and stability are no longer inherent in the symmetry (unless the band runs vertically). Instead, these arrangements often seem to emphasize direction by pointing along the horizontal. If they appear more satisfactory when they point to the right rather than the left, it is perhaps a reflection of our reading habit.

Slide reflection (fig. 37, no. 6) is unique in its quality. Since it is composed of alternate left and right images, it should be viewed in vertical rather than horizontal position to appreciate its quality (fig. 45). It then has the effect of forward or upward progression, and the concept of empathy is applicable because in walking we move with alternate right and left steps. Probably the comparative rarity of this symmetry is due to the fact that bands are generally used in horizontal position and this symmetry then loses much of its effectiveness.

We have not exhausted the factors that impart the feeling of motion in design. A composition that is unsymmetric may be definitely dynamic (fig. 46). An eccentric balance that is sometimes referred to as occult and a flow or cursiveness of line contribute to the impression. There are also connotative factors, even in geometric design. The suggestion of something that has swift motion such as lightning or waves, will be dynamic. On the other hand, there are features that slow the motion of dynamic design, as elaborations that distract attention from the dominant direction, or vertical bars or panels that interrupt the continuity of pattern.

It should be clear from this discussion that many factors influence the sense of motion in design. We cannot weigh each and set it down in a neat, inclusive scheme such as we have for symmetry, but since symmetry is fundamental in rhythm and motion, it affords a standard base from which to proceed in analysis.

Spatial relations. If it were possible to recognize categories of design defined with respect to spatial relations that are independent of both structure and elements or motifs, we would have another broad basis for analysis and comparison. This discussion is in the nature of an exploratory excursion into the subject. The concept of figure and background affords an entering wedge. The aspects of perception involved in the distinction between figure and ground have been investigated by Gestalt psychologists (see Koffka, 1935), who have experimented with the features that cause an observer to direct his attention to certain parts of a design and to regard the remainder of the space as background.

Many factors influence perception of figure, including meaning, form, ori-

FIG. 46—DYNAMIC QUALITY OF FLOWING LINE AND ECCENTRIC
BALANCE
From a Celtic mirror.

entation, value, position, elaboration, and size. Not the least of these is meaning. We can differentiate representations of natural objects, symbols, and abstract figures, but there will not be complete agreement regarding these classes because knowledge of symbolism is not shared equally by everyone, and our understanding of it is continually growing. There may even be doubt of the representation of the natural object when the style is simple and sketchy, but these doubtful cases are exceptional. As long as meaning is attached to part of a design, whether it be imagined or is recognition of the depiction of a natural object or symbol, that part is always seen as figure. It is in geometric and abstract design that the problem of figure-ground relation arises, and we can therefore confine our illustrations to this class.

There are three ways of perceiving the spatial relations of geometric design: (1) The same parts of the design are always perceived as figure. (2) Different parts of the design are perceived as figure at different times depending on the viewer's attention, association, preparation, or interest. (3) No distinction between figure and ground is perceived; all spaces are integral parts of the pattern. These impressions do not afford a satisfactory basis for design analysis because of individual differences in perception. This difficulty also holds for the classification I have proposed elsewhere (1948a, pp. 261–63). Some people are more likely than others to attach meaning to ambiguous forms; furthermore the various factors that influence perception—especially form, value, and position—may be conflicting in their effect and observers will weigh them differently. We must have a common basis for analysis, and the question is whether the various factors that influence perception afford a satisfactory means of distinguishing spatial categories. I shall review these factors without attempting to follow the psychologist closely in either terminology or illustration. Ideally, illustration should be drawn from patterns differing only in the factor under consideration, but this is not always possible as the variables are not all independent. The class of allover design in which the entire area is divided into identical figures or spaces (patterns developed on a net) enables one to hold shape constant while examining the effect of value or orientation. This is a specialized class of design but it occurs in many styles of ornamentation (fig. 47a-f). Bands can be divided into identical areas also, either by lines running from border to border or by a longitudinal line such as a zigzag or meander (fig. 47g-l).

It is important to recognize that knowledge of technique of decoration plays a role in perception. It is natural to think of the applied line or area as constituting the meaningful part of the design. We are more accustomed to positive than to negative design and generally assume that the potter intended the modified part of the surface to stand out; consequently, it appears to stand out as the significant part. If we know that black represents paint in an illustration, we are predisposed to see it as the figure or pattern; whereas a person who does not have this association may see figure-ground relations reversed. Since perception is influenced by suggestion, it would be advisable for the reader to look at figures 48–53 and form his own judgments before reading text and captions.

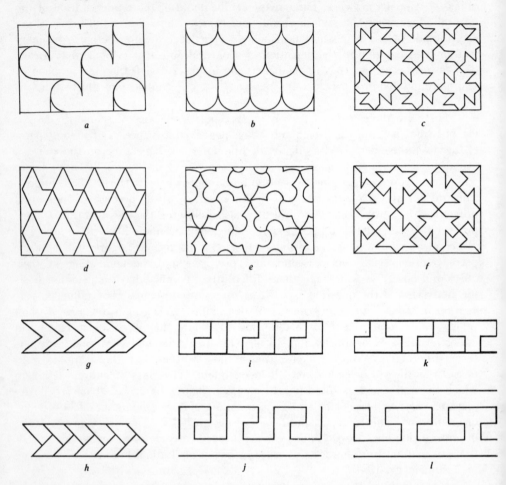

FIG. 47—NET PATTERNS

Allover patterns composed of areas identical in shape. *a-c:* Orientation identical. *d-f:* Orientation varied. Motions: *a,* translation; *b,* reflection and slide reflection alternating; *c,* fourfold rotation; *d,* slide reflection; *e,* threefold rotation, reflection and slide reflection; *f,* bifold rotation and reflection. Band patterns composed of areas of identical shape. *g-i,k:* Areas formed by transverse lines. *j,l:* Areas formed by longitudinal lines. *g:* Areas identical in orientation. *h-l:* Areas differ in orientation. Motions: *g,* longitudinal reflection; *h,* slide reflection; *i,j,* bifold rotation; *k,l,* rotation-reflection.

Value is a factor which influences perception of figure and ground, but its effect is variable. This is best shown in a net pattern of areas identical in orientation as well as in shape. A black-and-white checkerboard may be viewed as a mosaic in which black and white are complementary and equally prominent (figure and background are not differentiated) or as black squares against a white ground or vice versa. One value does not necessarily or invariably predominate over the other and we cannot assume uniformity of perception. On the other hand, value influences perception directly when it is used to relate areas or emphasize familiar arrangements (fig. 48a). It can also determine whether lines or areas are perceived in a pattern (fig. 48b).

a

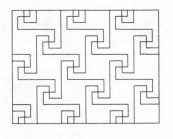

b

FIG. 48—FIGURE-GROUND PERCEPTION: THE EFFECT OF VALUE
a: Different figures and arrangements brought out in a pattern of overlapping circles by the use of contrasting values. Contrast assists in the organization of elements. *b:* Line design converted to areal design by value contrast (ceiling decoration, Thebes).

Spatial relations are fundamental in figure-ground perception. We conceive of the background as lying behind the figure and therefore surrounding it more or less completely. The effect of enclosure can be recognized in many geometric patterns from pottery decoration (fig. 49). A particularly interesting example is that of the stylized scroll so characteristic of the pottery of Coclé, Panama (fig. 42e, f). Scrolls are painted in such a way as to leave unpainted scrolls. The effect of enclosure is emphasized by the extension of the outer sides of the painted scrolls to frame the space. Here spatial configuration is very likely to outweigh the effect of value and knowledge of technique.

The Coclé scrolls suggest that space configuration may be a dominant factor in determining figure-ground perception. This is probably true in classes of design in which there is complete enclosure of one area or group of areas by another. Obviously there are many types of design for which this generalization cannot hold. In patterns constructed on a net, for example, the articulation of spaces is such that there is a reciprocal relation of parts. Each area may be said to be enclosed by several others and in turn contributes in like manner to their outline. In less regular patterns there are many complex designs composed of areas in two or more values that are not differentiated by enclosure (fig. 49g). Complex areal configurations such as these obviously do not afford means of differentiating figure and background.

Psychologists have studied the effect of orientation on perception, testing the tendency to favor the vertical and the horizontal over the oblique with a circle divided into eight sectors (fig. 50a). The effect of orientation can also be demonstrated by net patterns (fig. 50b, c). When a figure is oriented on the vertical it is often in its most familiar position and also the position that suggests balance and maximum stability (fig. 50d, e). The effect of stability influences judgment when there is a choice between two vertical positions. This effect is enhanced, of course, when the figures suggest a natural form (fig. 50f, g).

Symmetry influences figure-ground perception because regularity and repetition aid in organization of images. This factor cannot affect simple, symmetric band patterns in which all spaces are symmetric, but it may be a determining

---

FIG. 49—FIGURE-GROUND PERCEPTION: THE EFFECT OF ENCLOSURE
a: Diamonds against a background. b, c: Background reduced to spaces that form opposed isosceles triangles. The diamonds may still tend to dominate as figures in both positive and negative treatments because they are enclosed by the marginal triangles. d: Enclosure affecting both diamonds and opposed triangles. e: Effect of enclosure in Santo Domingo band design. Coves in opposed corners of a panel are a common motif (see Chapman, 1936, pl. 26). Here they carry as background by enclosing the central space. f: Modification of e to show effect of enclosing the cove elaboration. g: Complex Santo Domingo band with parts of both values enclosed, producing an anomalous effect.

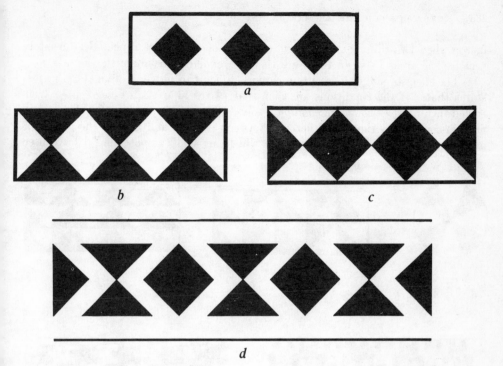

a

b

c

d

e

f

g

FIG. 49

factor when two different symmetric elements or motifs are repeated alternately because the areas between them are thereby rendered unsymmetric (fig. 51).

The effect of size on perception is more difficult to judge. Koffka (1935, p. 191) states that, "If the conditions are such that two field parts are segregated from each other and *double representation ensues*, then *ceteris paribus*, the figure will arise in such a way that the difference between its area and that of the ground is a maximum, or still simpler: the figure will be as small as possible." I have used

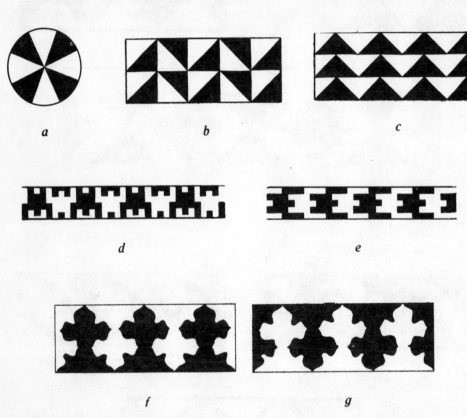

FIG. 50—FIGURE-GROUND PERCEPTION: THE EFFECT OF ORIENTATION
a: A comparison of the relative prominence of vertical and horizontal directions and the oblique. Does the black of the white cross stand out? *b,c:* Identical triangles, both patterns symmetric (*b,* horizontal slide reflection; *c,* vertical reflection). If *b* suggests a mosaic and *c* rows of black triangles, perception is influenced by differences in orientation and stability. *d,e:* Geometric patterns composed for experiment. The suggestion of Atlantean figures is fortuitous. Compare the vertical and horizontal arrangements with respect to figure-ground effect. *f,g:* If the first pattern appears positive and the second appears negative, the effect can be attributed to the suggestion of stability (14th century Moorish silk).

a   *b*

FIG. 51—FIGURE-GROUND PERCEPTION: THE EFFECT OF SYMMETRY
Band patterns composed for illustration. *a:* Vertical reflection, a variation on the standard pattern used by psychologists. *b:* Bifold rotation. The alternation of figures having different motions would also form irregular intervening spaces.

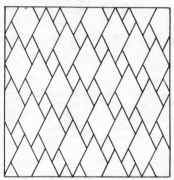

a

b

FIG. 52—FIGURE-GROUND PERCEPTION: EFFECT OF RELATIVE SIZE
a: Allover pattern composed for illustration. This represents an attempt to main-tain constancy of all factors except relative size, but contiguity of the large diamonds introduces another difference. The relative prominence of the two diamonds can be further tested by introducing a dark value, first in one size and then in the other. If the same size stands out in both instances, the in-fluence of size on individual perception has been demonstrated. *b:* A band composed for illustration. Figures have close similarity but not identity of form. Black, taken as the dominant value, was introduced in the large areas in op-position to the effect of smaller size.

an allover pattern to test the effect of size and have found no uniformity of judg-ment regarding it (fig. 52a). Absolute, as well as relative, size should be con-sidered because it undoubtedly plays a role in perception when an area becomes too large to see without eye movement.

Elaboration of any part of a field attracts attention and may favor it as figure. This result seems obvious, particularly when the embellishment suggests natural or meaningful forms (fig. 53a, b, c, d). When the ornamentation is purely geometric, however, the effect may be ambiguous because elaboration can be perceived in relation to different parts of a field. Consequently it does not always afford a reliable means of distinguishing figure from background. If a symmetric decorative detail is confined to the boundary between areas, as in serration, it is related equally to both. If elaboration takes the form of elements extending from one area into another or of small detached and enclosed elements, it can be perceived as an extension or distribution of areas having the same value or it can have the effect of openwork in the area that encloses it (fig. 53e, f). In instances of this kind, elaboration does not identify the figure; instead it is the figure that organizes the elaboration. In addition to the factors that we have reviewed, general organization of the field, the relative unity of parts of the same value, will play an important role in perception.

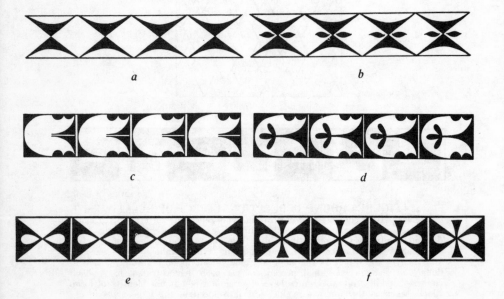

FIG. 53—FIGURE-GROUND PERCEPTION: EFFECT OF ELABORATION
Pairs of bands from Santo Domingo pottery illustrating the effect of introducing an elaboration. The negative diamonds in a tend to appear as background when a black leaflike element is added, b. In c a central white area is enclosed and can be perceived as figure. In d it is replaced as a center of interest by the black element. e: A variant of the diamond-and-triangle pattern in which the teardrops can be perceived as eyelets or appendages. f: The addition of an elaboration that tends to center attention on the black.

This discussion of factors affecting figure-ground perception will indicate the complexity of the subject and the impracticability of relying on individual impression for classification. These factors can be partially analyzed, at least, but since they are numerous and often subtle in their effect, it would be premature to suggest their use in classification. This does not mean that the subject is unimportant. The pronounced influence which the relation between line and mass and the characteristic configuration of spaces have on style is generally recognized.

The fundamental nature of figure-ground articulations is indicated by their relation to structure and symmetry. As a suggestion of correlations, a few distinctive categories of composition may be mentioned: (1) Separate elements or motifs are drawn within a field. Such design will generally be unambiguous. There will be complete enclosure, and the effect will be of figures lying against a background. The same relation holds if the field is painted in such a way that separate, enclosed areas are left unpainted; the only difference being that the pattern is negative rather than positive. (2) The field is subdivided geometrically or laid off in a regular net, and certain parts are chosen for filling or elaboration. If the spaces laid off serve only to frame a field, as in the simple paneled band, the effect may not be fundamentally different from that of the first class. When the lines serve as scaffolding for design, they restrict its structure and symmetry. This method of composition often produces ambiguous designs and designs that appear as mosaics of contiguous figures because all areas of the field are integral parts of it. (3) The space around basic elements or motifs is subdivided and elaborated until the entire field is filled. This type of composition is common in Classic Mimbres black-on-white ware (fig. 36). Complete filling of the field may give the design built up by accretion a superficial resemblance to that developed on a net, but the difference is fundamental. The use of a net is a mechanical method of construction resulting in repetition, whereas the unguided blocking in of space is a free method that allows scope for variation and originality. In consequence of this freedom, the effect on figure-ground perception is not easily predicted. The relative weight and value of different parts may emphasize figure, or values and forms may be balanced in such a way that the design as a whole appears as an intricately meshed unit.

These categories of composition represent distinct approaches to the problem of decorating a field. To draw independent motifs is quite different from laying off a framework and tinkering with it to obtain interesting effects. Despite the difference, which seems basically psychological, these classes of composition are not always sharply differentiated, and more than one method may be employed for the same design. The analysis of composition then becomes a challenge. In any case, the characteristic spatial relations of a style can best be understood when they are studied in relation to method of composition.

The use of value. The effect of value in pottery design depends first on the contrast between paint and vessel surface. It is most pronounced when white ware is painted in black and least noticeable in polychromes employing paints and slips that are close in value. It is hardly likely that potters using slips and paints having strong contrast were unaware of the effect of value. Certain Pueblo potters, for instance, have expressed the opinion that too much black is not good —"it makes the pot look dirty."

Everyone would probably agree that value can be an important aspect of design; but without a satisfactory means of analysis, we cannot describe the characteristic way in which it was used in different styles. We speak of positive and negative patterns and of ones in which dark or light predominate, but such broad expressions are hardly adequate for detailed comparisons. It may clarify the problem of analysis to consider the observations that can be made with respect to a very simple design.

In a black and white checkerboard the two values are approximately equal in area, are uniformly distributed, are used in spaces of identical shape, and convert a network of lines into a pattern of masses.

We have mentioned first the actual ratio of areas in the two values. This is an obvious method of description which is very simple for a design constructed on a net, but tedious for elaborate design. Parenthetically, it may be well to point out that the black and white squares of a checkerboard are not exactly equal in area because the width of the line in which the net is laid off is added to the area of the black. Often the difference is not noticeable, but if the squares are small and the line wide, the difference should be taken into account; consequently, the judgment of percentage of dark and light even in these patterns is not simple after all. There are various ways in which the ratio of value can be compared in more complex design. In composition of masses or areas, one can trace the design on cardboard or tin foil, cut out each part, and weigh accurately all pieces of each value. A method comparable to this was used at one time by petrographers in comparing the areas of different constituents of thin sections. Another possibility is to spin the copy of the design rapidly enough to fuse the areas and match the value obtained—the average of the dark and lights—against a standard. This would be the more satisfactory method because it is applicable to line as well as to mass. A difficulty with these methods is that of maintaining the true value relations when copying design from a curved surface. This problem has been mentioned in the discussion of the design record (p. 257). It does not enter if the surface is straight in one direction, but does require careful attention if there is marked curvature in two directions.

These methods of estimation are tedious and would not be applied extensively.

With a judicious selection of design, however, they furnish a quantitative basis of comparison.

A mechanical estimation of the percentage of dark and light taken alone is obviously inadequate for description. Two black and white patterns that give the same gray when fused may produce entirely different impressions of value because of differences in disposition of value in the field. Distribution and position are both factors to consider. The effect of value differs depending on whether it is massed or scattered and, if massed, on whether it occupies the center or the margins of the field. A massing of value might show when the design is fused as zones of different grays; and this is the nearest approach to a quantitative statement of distribution of value that occurs to me, although experimental work might well suggest others. This use of fusion raises the point of the shape of the field in any test of this kind. A circular field of design offers no problem; but if the field is any other shape, a circular section must be cut from it in such a way as to represent correctly the ratio of values.

A fundamental question regarding value is whether the figure or the background is darker—the relation of value to configuration; in other words, whether the design is positive or negative. This brings us back to the problem of identification of figure, and it also raises the question of the definition of positive and negative design. If the design is unambiguous, there is no question of its classification with relation to value. A light background produces positive pattern because this is the normal relation in painted design. Painting the background or at least applying a darker color to it, as in resist technique, reverses normal value relations and gives negative design. But supposing we are unable to decide which part of the pattern is figure and which is background, how can we judge whether the design is positive or negative? We probably could agree that patterns constructed on a net in which values are identical in form and approximately balanced are neither positive nor negative. It might be argued that for other classes of ambiguous design, dominance of the darker value or the enclosure of lighter by the darker value marks a negative pattern. For the present, however, it would seem advisable to limit the terms "positive" and "negative" to unambiguous patterns. When there is uncertainty, values can be compared with respect to such factors as form, enclosure, orientation, regularity and simplicity of the areas they occupy.

If this discussion of value does not go beyond a suggestion of the difficulties that must be met, it should not be construed as indicating that analysis of this aspect of design is impracticable, but rather as reflecting our inexperience with it. Once systematic comparative and experimental studies are made, new possibilities will occur to us.

Fig. 54

ANALYSIS OF A GEOMETRIC STYLE ILLUSTRATED

An example of the analysis of a familiar style of geometric design will serve to summarize and perhaps clarify some of the points raised in this discussion. I have chosen Mesa Verde Black-on-white because it is well known, and a large collection of vessels has been fully illustrated (Morris, 1939). Morris' systematic classification of the band patterns has facilitated the analysis. This outline makes no pretense to completeness. It only records the characteristics and some of the relative frequencies of features that can be observed in these illustrations. A few vessels are illustrated here to suggest quality of line and relation of dark and light (fig. 54).

Principal surfaces decorated and limits of the field (fig. 55). The field of decoration, including framing bands, usually extends to the rim of bowls and mugs. The upper body constitutes the zones of decoration of jars. Necks are plain or banded. Decoration extends from the base of the neck approximately to the equator of the vessel or to the level of the handles which may be slightly below.

Differences in these forms with respect to contour and area of visibility from a normal viewing position have not had a pronounced effect on the layout. Thus, essentially the same band decoration is often found on mugs, of which only sections can be viewed from one point, and on bowl interiors which are completely visible. The curvature of the bowl necessitated contraction of the lower half of a band, but adjustments were made without giving the impression of crowding. The limitation of view of the band on a mug does not give the impression of incompleteness partly because the units of design are small and the repeat pattern is usually clear.

Jar designs appear to have been planned with the vessel viewed from the top. A square rather than a circle sometimes limits the field at the base of the neck, and a curious feature of some of these plans is the lack of orientation of the square with relation to the handles. When encircling bands are used, they differ from the bands of smaller vessels in size and boldness of elements, but the area is treated as a single zone and not broken into multiple bands such as occur on approximately a third of the mugs. Independent figures or motifs which would constitute a complete decoration for the side of a jar or mug are absent, except for minor secondary decorations on bowls.

FIELDS OF DESIGN

FIG. 55

Structure of the field (fig. 56).   The field plan of nearly two-thirds of the bowls is an encircling band on the interior side wall. Other structures cover the entire interior. Fourfold division is slightly more common than bifold. An unsymmetric treatment is standardized and less frequent. Mugs are always banded; ladles are treated like small bowls. Jars are too few to justify generalization.

Bands.   The study of bands is based on 189 examples illustrated by Morris. Two-thirds have seven or more repetitions of the unit of design. The minimum number is four. Four to six repeats may have the appearance of single motifs but the effect is often destroyed by inequality in length of one unit, suggesting that the potter drew units in sequence without first laying off space. No correlation between band width and number of repeats was noted.

Subdivision of the band into compartments is infrequent, but geometric areas are often suggested by repeat units that fill the band space (*d*). Triangular, rectangular, and diamond areas are most common. Striping, with or without secondary elaboration (*a*), net patterns—including "fence rails," diamonds, and parallelograms (*b*), and running bands (*c*) are next in order of frequency (10–15 per cent). Less numerous are unit-width strips of nets, defined by structure but probably composed with reference to marginal elements (*e*). Vertical paneling is rare and generally associated with crude workmanship. Some transverse lines that are integral parts of motifs may have been drawn first (*f*). Figures surrounded by open space are as rare as paneling. Band subdivision by lines having slide reflection is rare but distinctive (*g*).

Fourfold fields.   Quadrate (*h*) and offset quadrate (*i*) division is most frequent. The same methods of subdivision are used in both (*l*), the many-cycled volute being typical. A modification of *h* (*h'*, bifold), emphasizing rotation, is rare. Conversion of *i* to the elementary lines of a swastika-like motif (*j*) with elaborated terminals (*m*) gives rise to a minor group of complex and varied designs. Morris (1939, p. 240) calls attention to comparable motifs on jars, the central square outlining the throat, the arms interlocked on the sides. Crossed bars (*k*) are rare and the designs simple. Some fourfold fields (*h* and *i*) are reduced to bifold symmetry by different elaborations of alternate sections; in consequence, bifold designs preponderate over fourfold.

Bifold fields.   Two classes are represented—a bisected field (*n*), the halves generally filled with heavy-line volutes, and bold scroll motifs in hachure (*o-q*). An S is the simpler of the rotational arrangements (*o, p*). The complexity of the motif in which scrolls are joined at right angles (*p*) suggests that the central black bar ending in scrolls was drawn first. Side arms rising from it interlock with the hachured scrolls on either side, but here one is willing to leave order of construction to the potter. In the radial arrangement the hachured motif is central and may have been drawn first (*q*).

Unsymmetric fields.   These are rare, being represented by spirals, solid or solid-and-hachure balanced, that fill the field (*r*).

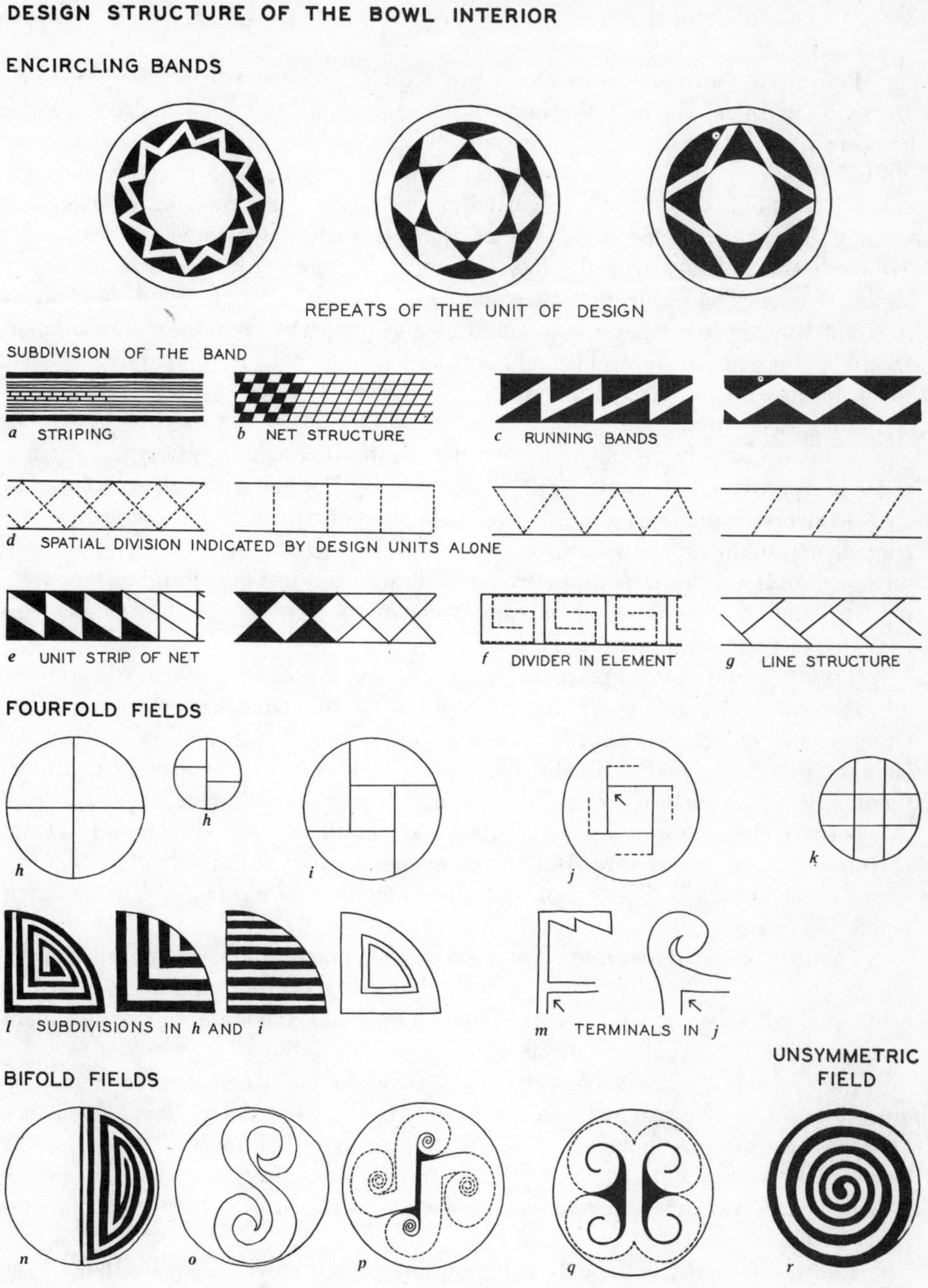

DESIGN STRUCTURE OF THE BOWL INTERIOR

ENCIRCLING BANDS

REPEATS OF THE UNIT OF DESIGN

SUBDIVISION OF THE BAND

a   STRIPING   *b*   NET STRUCTURE   *c*   RUNNING BANDS

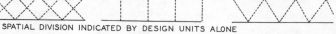

d   SPATIAL DIVISION INDICATED BY DESIGN UNITS ALONE

e   UNIT STRIP OF NET   *f*   DIVIDER IN ELEMENT   *g*   LINE STRUCTURE

FOURFOLD FIELDS

h   *h*

i

j

k

l   SUBDIVISIONS IN *h* AND *i*   *m*   TERMINALS IN *j*

BIFOLD FIELDS

UNSYMMETRIC FIELD

n   *o*   *p*   *q*   *r*

Fig. 56

Principal elements and their position in repeat units (fig. 57). Triangles occur in nearly half the bands. They are generally solid and set on the banding lines; often they are the only element. When directly opposed, they outline parallelograms or diamonds (*A*-1, *C*-1), thus creating a negative pattern. When alternated, they form a negative zigzag (*A*-2, *C*-2). Paneling is suggested when either basal angles or apexes of right triangles are connected (*A*-3, -4). Although the isosceles triangle does not occur in these arrangements, it has a higher frequency of occurrence than the right triangle. Careless painting changes the right triangle to a scalene, but well-drawn examples of the form are uncommon except as the base of keys. The common key arrangement is comparable to that which forms a zigzag (*D*-2), but joining of opposed keys often breaks continuity of the negative line.

Volutes—usually rectangular, less frequently triangular, rarely rhombic—occur in approximately 25 per cent of the bands. Double rectangular volutes in open sequence or interlocked are typical (*G*-3, -4). The form which carries out the triangle-and-diamond space arrangement (*G*-1) is uncommon. The rarity of true meanders in the series is noteworthy and follows from use of S-form volutes resting on banding lines (*G*-3, -4). Triangular volutes are comparable to isosceles triangles in their arrangements (*F*-1, -2).

Triangles and volutes occur in 70 per cent of the bands. Standardization of arrangement and consistent marginal position of the triangles are noteworthy. Other elements are of minor occurrence. The stepped figure is essentially an elaborated right triangle (*B*) and follows through comparable arrangements although the zigzag pattern is rare. The diamond, a common negative element, is rare as a positive element. Squares, rectangles, and parallelograms occur mainly in net patterns and are here distinguished from elements painted individually. A curvilinear scroll is rare in bands but not uncommon in other fields. Circles occur mainly as space breakers.

Elaborations of design. *Space breakers.* These emphasize parallelism of line in large areas. Subdivision of a field that departs from the original outline is exceptional. In small solid elements, the space breaker is an eyelet independent of the outline but symmetrically placed.

Elaborations of lines and borders. Single and double ticked lines are common, dotted lines rare. Negative effects are formed by opposed ticked lines. Brickwork lines are conspicuous in bands, outlines, and as parts of motifs. When hastily painted, they become parallel ticked lines and the transition sometimes occurs on a single line. Serrate lines are uncommon. Ticking is the principal marginal elaboration of solid elements.

Fillers. Hachure is the only common filler. Its line width equals that of the outline and its direction varies with the form of the area. It parallels a side of small triangles, is oblique in horizontal bands, vertical in oblique bars, and symmetric with respect to elements and large fields. Cross hachure and stippling are very rare.

PRINCIPAL ELEMENTS AND ARRANGEMENTS

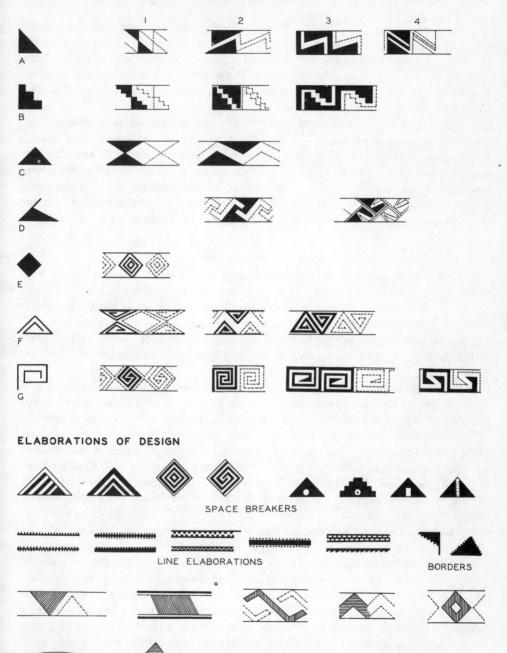

ELABORATIONS OF DESIGN

SPACE BREAKERS

LINE ELABORATIONS

BORDERS

FILLERS

FIG. 57

Line and area (fig. 58*a-h*). Prominence of line and linear elements and rarity of large areas with complex outline appear to be general characteristics of the style. The potter's interest in line is further attested to by its elaboration (ticking, etc.) and by the use of multiple outlines. A rough measure of the relative prominence of line or linear elements and area in bands can be obtained by distinguishing patterns composed of linear elements alone, area alone, and a combination of the two. Since both black and white are integral parts of design, it is necessary to consider what form the unpainted, as well as the painted, part takes. Banding, hachuring, and other fillers are counted as area: minor elaborations are disregarded. In the following tabulation, L equals line, A equals area, the first letter stands for black, the second for white, italics for illustrations. Four of the nine possible combinations (L-A, L-LA, A-LA, LA-A) are represented by from one to three examples, which are considered aberrant and omitted from this tabulation.

Combinations:	L-L	A-L	A-A	LA-L	LA-LA
No. of occurrences:	23(*a*)	34(*c*)	41(*b*)	57(*d*)	11(*e*)

It is noteworthy that the unpainted part of the pattern is reduced to line in all except two groups, one of which (A-A) includes net designs formed by filling spaces in a scaffolding of lines. The distribution is clearer when black and white are broken down separately percentagewise: black occurs as line in 14 per cent of the bands, as area in 46 per cent, and as line and area in 39 per cent; white occurs as line in 69 per cent of the bands, as area in 25 per cent, and as line and area in 7 per cent.

Line is no less prominent in full fields than in bands. The simple volute that reduces ground to linear proportions is prominent in fourfold and bifold fields (fig. 56*l*, *n*). The use of striping and hachuring as the sole decoration of quadrants of fourfold fields is also noteworthy (*f*). Bold hachure motifs are often linear in their proportions and either serve as outlines (*g*) or are themselves emphasized by single or multiple outlines (fig. 59*j*). The figures impinge on the banding line, and background area is crowded into small marginal spaces. Still another illustration of the linear tendency of the style is the use of patterned stripes in allover design (*h*).

Dark and light (fig. 58*i-u*). The relative proportion of painted and unpainted area can be judged from geometric relations, but value contrasts are very much lower on the vessel than in the reproduction because of the grayness of the pottery paint (see fig. 54). Dark and light are approximately equal in net patterns in which lines were painted with a narrow brush (*i*, *k*), but, through carelessness or intent, the paint was often allowed to overlap the outline; the pattern then becomes definitely negative (*q*). Volutes constitute a second major motif group in which values are often balanced (*l*, *m*), though variation in width of line may give one value or the other dominance. In view of the frequency with which unpainted surface is reduced to line (*n-p*), it is not surprising to find that bands in which black dominates are most numerous. Estimated from geometric relations, the proportion is 61 per cent. Dominance of white in bands is exceptional (*r*).

Hachure and other fillers having the effect of a third value, gray, occur in a fourth of the bands. The simplest are hachured bands. Bands in which hachure is combined with white alone (*s*) or with black line and white areas are uncommon. Generally, white is reduced to line, and hachure and black dominate as balanced figures or areas (*t*). Usually when areas in the two values are opposed and fill the field, black is lightened by eyelets or by striping. In full-field patterns, hachure often appears in the dominant motif (*g;* fig. 59*j*); less frequently it is used in large enclosing areas (*u*).

LINE AND AREA

DARK AND LIGHT

FIG. 58

Spatial relations (fig. 59*a-k*). Net patterns and negative effects both tend to produce design in which either black or white can be perceived as figure. Bands of this class are prominent, whereas those in which only black appears as figure are exceptions. But trial sorts by different people have demonstrated the impracticability of basing classification on figure-ground perception. The potter's approach is taken as an alternative. To the potter commencing to paint, the white slip of the vessel is ground. Once having laid off a field, how did she use the ground? Three methods of composition can be distinguished: (1) Ground was used as area *within* which to paint figures; it completely surrounds figures and is less simple in form and less organized (*a, b*)—a rare class. (2) The area was laid off by simple, regular lines, and alternate spaces were filled, leaving ground in geometric areas comparable or identical to the black (*c, d*). These represent a fourth of the sample and are principally net patterns. The less familiar patterns illustrated were not constructed on a net although both could be. The geometrically minded will see in *d* a strip of an allover hexagonal net, but it was constructed on a horizontal line crossed by a zigzag. (3) By fitting painted areas (black and/or hachure) and filling space, ground was reduced to line or to a linear element (*e-h*). Subgroups (equally well represented in the sample) are illustrated: *e*, the fitting of marginal areas creates a negative continuous-line pattern, zigzags being typical; *f*, fitting and connecting marginal areas create negative, segmented line; *g*, involution and interlocking of linear elements create balancing line elements in white; *h*, fitting of marginal and central areas reduces white ground to an outline. This use of white is well illustrated in full-field scroll patterns, in which white emphasizes the motif (*j*). Classes 2 and 3 include the majority of bands. It is exceptional for white to play a more complex role as in *i* where it appears as a zigzag, a net element and ground of a dotted field, and this follows from unusual space breaking in a structurally typical continuous-line pattern. Designs in which fillers are used in all spaces to create the effect of textured or gray areas, thus eliminating white as a value with distinct spatial relations, constitute a distinct but minor group (*k*).

Symmetry and dynamic quality (fig. 59*l-n*). All seven classes of band patterns are represented in the sample but there is strong preponderance of rotational symmetry (58 per cent in a sample of 142; the second highest class is rotation-reflection—17 per cent; Classes 4, 5 and 7, all employing rotational motion, constitute 82 per cent of the sample [Shepard, 1948a, pp. 242–51]). With this summary, we may inquire if the style has pronounced dynamic quality, basing the answer on the relation of symmetry to other factors that contribute to this effect. Line direction and continuity are easily defined. Oblique line (dynamic) appears principally in triangle patterns and many of these also introduce continuity of line (dynamic), but the isosceles triangle and the regular zigzag (reflection-rotation) are favored over the more dynamic right triangle and oblique zigzag (bifold rotation). Volutes, which are the principal element in bifold rotation patterns, employ vertical and horizontal line more frequently than oblique, and the meanders which represent the characteristic resultant line pattern are extremely rare. Another quality that tends to carry the eye from one unit to the next may be called repeat emphasis. When the unit either lacks distinctiveness or holds the eye by its elaboration, this quality is weak. Many-cycled volutes illustrate lack of distinctiveness of motif and, in bifold fields particularly, they tend to carry as linear fillers.

Designs from three fourfold structures will illustrate these various effects: *l* has weak repeat emphasis but the curve of the structural lines and the direction of the acute angles of the volutes contribute to the effect of rotation; *m* has marked differentiation of field sections but repetition is interrupted by alternation of motifs; *n* has a central motif with strong repeat emphasis, but the dynamic effect of the design as a whole is subdued by the radial symmetry of the margin.

SPATIAL RELATIONS

SYMMETRY AND DYNAMIC QUALITY

Fig. 59

Dynamic effect cannot be defined as simply as some of the factors that contribute to it, but it is clear that the effect of rotational symmetry was not extensively or consistently emphasized in this style.

* * * * *

This analysis was undertaken for the purpose of testing the extent to which the qualities of geometric design can be described in nonsubjective terms. The style itself has dictated the direction analysis has taken, and although the attempt to define qualities may seem to have broken down to a description of the mechanics of composition, they are not irrelevant to style. Had the style been different, analysis would undoubtedly have taken a different turn. One cannot assume that a procedure that has proved useful in one case will have general applicability. Common principles should guide analysis, but I cannot overemphasize the fact that one should never allow himself to become caught in the machinery of analysis.

A study such as this can be made only from a sizable collection of entire or restorable vessels. Obviously it would be impossible to use sherds alone. Moreover, this survey includes features that have not been considered in the study of "style" when the object has been to assign sherds to a type. In the accepted procedure for typing sherds, attention is centered on features that will aid in differentiation. The range of these features is strictly limited by what can be recognized in the fragment of design which the sherd shows; hence the prominence of "elements" of design in this method of study.

The fact that this experimental outline departs from the method which has been accepted generally in the Southwest does not imply that it has no contribution to make to pottery classification. Fragments of design which are obscure or meaningless when viewed alone can be recognized or read into the design as a whole when it is known, and thus the study of vessels can extend considerably the usefulness of sherds. But this is not the primary purpose of the broader study of style, which collections of whole vessels permit.

It is the history of design—the waxing and waning of traits, indications of origination, examples of outright borrowing, the reflections that design gives of the interactions between peoples—that deserves more attention. Certain of the features of Mesa Verde style that have been pointed out may be peculiar to it. Others are common Pueblo traits but may be more or less well represented in Mesa Verde than elsewhere. To distinguish the common and distinctive features would require the same kind of analyses of other Pueblo styles, but it would be a step in the direction of a systematic study of design history.

The words "design analysis" recall to my mind an exhibit I saw some years ago at a well-known art institute. A class in art analysis had chosen famous paintings and illustrated diagrammatically such elements as value, color, form, and line. One diagram in particular seemed to express the spirit of the work. It outlined the principal areas in a portrait and was labeled "the amoeboid spaces." The title was perfectly descriptive, but unfortunately there was no explanation of the significance of amoeboid spaces in a portrait.

The analytical approach holds certain promises and, with them, serious warnings. Analysis promises the opportunity to penetrate beyond the superficial to the fundamental, to recognize aspects that would not otherwise be appreciated, to examine the interrelationship and mutual effects of the parts; and perhaps the most important, analysis promises sound ground for common understanding and agreement. Despite all this, analysis can be directed to the inconsequential aspects of a subject and to aspects that are irrelevant to our interest; so it can lead to sterile effort if its results are not critically evaluated.

In the study of pottery decoration, we have no direct way of knowing what the design meant to the potters—whether it was symbolic or purely decorative, whether it represented something of great significance to them or was merely a traditional form of ornamentation. But these are things we would like to know, and for which we should always seek and can often find indirect evidence. In analyzing the style of decorative art, in seeking clues to what it reveals of a people's psychology, we should not forget that we are dealing with a mode of expression.

IV. Problems of Pottery Classification

USES AND LIMITATIONS OF THE TYPE CONCEPT

IT IS probably safe to say that the archaeologist's chief concern with pottery at the present time centers about the problems of classification. Classification is the chore that confronts him at the end of every field season, and, laborious though this is, the remarkable effectiveness with which pottery has been used to establish relative chronologies makes it incumbent upon him to follow established and tested procedures. The importance of summarizing and generalizing ceramic data was recognized when the worth of the potsherd for relative dating became apparent and description of individual specimens no longer served the requirements of reporting. Now, after some years of trial and debate, archaeologists have arrived at a considerable degree of standardization in taxonomic procedure. Nevertheless, the theory of classification and the accepted taxonomic unit, the pottery type, are currently being critically and extensively re-examined, which is a healthy and promising sign. It is not my intention to review in detail the various positions that have been taken, but rather to look at the problem of classification from the standpoint of a technologist, considering what aid knowledge of material and technique may offer and also speculating on the possible ramifications of taxonomy when its purposes are extended.

It is well to recall at the start that the task of sherd classification, like the schoolboy's mathematics, affords valuable training and discipline. In handling sherds by the thousands and sorting out groups distinguished by common features, the archaeologist becomes familiar with the range of variation in diagnostic features; he notices that some properties vary simultaneously, others independently, that some have a wide range of variations, others a narrow one, that some are relatively stable, others change abruptly. Even though he does not attempt to analyze and explain these observations, they give him a realization of the possible diversity in appearance of pottery made by the same basic methods, and they alert him to the risk of mistaking superficial resemblances for the marks of identical technique or composition.

Two main steps are involved in sherd classification. The first is the recognition of features that establish a hypothetical relationship for a group of sherds. This is not a simple thing to do when vessels are reduced to fragments and one must deal with small pieces of different parts of differently shaped vessels and tantalizing fragments of design, and when surface features show not only the variations resulting from individual differences in craftsmanship and accidents of production, but also the effects of usage and of weathering. After the selection of groups distinguished by common characteristics that presumably reflect basic rather than chance distinctions, the second step is to create a unified picture for each group by determining the norms in variable features and by collecting and interpreting the fragments of shape and design.

Archaeologists had the benefit of this kind of experience for some time before the pottery type was formally defined and rules for naming it agreed upon. The early definitions of the type were general in that they specified uniformity in certain features but left judgment of what is meant by it to the classifier. They were also theoretical in so far as definitions and standards were drawn up without full regard for the practicability of their application. For example, uniformity of paste was usually prescribed, regardless of the fact that it is often impossible to identify temper with the unaided eye when texture is medium or fine; also unity of decorative style was usually included, although it is not easily proved from sherds alone. In so far as theoretical standards were at variance with experience, they were only a façade for the actual business of classification; nevertheless these early efforts to formalize classification served to introduce a common system of nomenclature and some standardization of description.

The early attempts to systematize ceramic classification, which, especially in the Southwest, were accompanied by prodigious activity on the part of taxonomically inclined archaeologists, drew sharp and often well-founded criticism because of the disproportionate time and effort devoted to pottery, the extremes to which splitting was carried, and the tendency to turn to the biological sciences for guidance in concepts of classification. These general objections gave way in time to a more philosophical approach to the problems of classification and to a critical examination of the causes and effects of the artificiality of the pottery type.

Since the pottery type is a generalization from many fragments and since there may be no individual example including all of its features, it is not infrequently referred to as an abstraction. Also the pottery type is artificial in so far as it is selected to serve as a means of outlining relative chronologies, a purpose that has no relation to the conditions of production or original functions of pottery. Any feature that changes in time, irrespective of its possible meaning or lack of meaning to the makers and users of pottery, is accepted as a criterion of classification. This approach to the problem of classification plus reliance on sherds, which can give only an incomplete and fragmentary record, results in acceptance of arbitrary limits between types. Limits seem necessarily arbitrary because experience in sorting sherds has created the impression that ceramic change is a very gradual process. A type defined from sherds in one stratigraphic level will differ slightly from the norm of similar sherds in higher and lower levels, and if such a series is traced far enough, the deviation becomes sufficiently great to justify the definition of another type. The point at which the limit between the two is drawn rests with the taxonomist's judgment because of the gradualness of transition. It follows that the definition of the type depends on the point in time chosen for sampling. A comparable relation holds with respect to areal variation. Therefore, even though the type is considered a node in a ceramic tradition, the limits of its variability in either time or space may be said to be defined more or less artificially.

Although this aspect of pottery classification has been effectively set forth by a number of writers (Phillips, Ford, and Griffin, 1951; Rouse, 1939; Krieger, 1944; Brew, 1946; Ford, 1954; Steward, 1954), not all archaeologists are agreed that the type is primarily a creation of the taxonomist. The belief persists that it is in some measure a cultural entity. In so far as aspects of technique and stylistic tradition are used as criteria, the type has some basis in reality, irrespective of the classifier's perceptions, and some archaeologists have gone so far as to consider that the type is "discovered." Even though this concept is diametrically opposed to that of the type as a fabrication of the archaeologist, both are extreme positions.

It is interesting to note that archaeologists are probably in closer agreement regarding acceptable procedures for classifying sherds and naming and describing types than with regard to the meaning of the type, and in consequence the same types are used by different students for distinct purposes and with different ideas of what they actually represent. It is tempting in this connection to draw attention to the contrast in biologic taxonomy. Sears (1950, p. 51; quoted by permission of Charles Scribner's Sons), in discussing the effects of the theory of evolution, writes: "The naturalists of the 18th and early 19th centuries had vastly improved the techniques for classifying plants and animals. But until the doctrine of evolution emerged as more than a shadowy guess, the basic theory and purpose of their efforts were almost as primitive as the motives of the tribal medicine man collecting herbs. It is enough for him to tell the kinds apart and have names for them." The theory that all organisms are related by common descent challenged the taxonomist to discover the degree of relationship between them and to express it in classification. It was thus a keen stimulus to research and a unifying force. Contrast this situation with that in archaeology, where the pottery type is referred to as ". . . a named abstraction, representing a combination of selected characters, susceptible of recognition from sherds alone." Stated even more specifically, "An artificial, albeit useful, creation of the classifier, the pottery type has at this state of being little, if any, correspondent cultural 'reality,' present or past" (Phillips, Ford, and Griffin, 1951, p. 66). To be sure, there are some theoretic concepts underlying the present definition of the type, but they appear to be more nearly rationalizations than independently tested hypotheses that afford a unifying principle. Perhaps the nearest approach to a hypothetical meaning of the type that would have supplied a guiding principle is implicit in the definitions common in the thirties that specified uniformity of material, technique and style, thus assuming that the type represents pottery made by people using the same materials and methods, influenced by the same stylistic tradition, and employing pottery for the same purposes.

The fact that such a unit of classification is not at present recognized may be taken as evidence of the impracticability of establishing it with the methods now being used and the approach and point of view which is now prevalent. Such a type, which might be called a cultural type, would have distinct advantages, even for the student setting up a chronological frame of reference, for although he concentrates on those features that mark a difference in time, all such criteria are related in some way to pottery composition, technique, or style, or to a combination of them. The taxonomist is dealing with cultural features whether he recognizes them as such or not, and lack of recognition of this circumstance is at the root of much of the difficulty that leads to the definition of pottery types that are primarily the product of the particular sample the archaeologist is handling and his individual impressions and judgment.

Actually, many pottery types are not strictly morphological, historical-index types (i.e., defined only by outward appearance and with specific reference to those features that have value for marking the passage of time). Temper has been accepted as a primary criterion of classification in the Southeastern taxonomic system; organic and iron oxide paints, marks of paddle-and-anvil technique, and color as affected by firing conditions are important criteria in the Southwest. These are technical and cultural features, and the type is moving toward a cultural entity in so far as such criteria have been introduced. But this approach has not been followed as consistently, as critically, and as fully as it might be. Despite the fact that much has been written on the subject of the artificiality of the pottery type, the underlying cause of artificiality, the habit of viewing pottery as a physical object abstracted from the essentials of its composition and the method of its manufacture, in other words, the persistent tendency to ignore the role of the potter, has not received the criticism it deserves. It is indeed strange that pottery should be studied without considering its relations to the people who made it. There is, of course, more than one explanation of this apparent blind spot. Composition and marks of technique have not been used extensively as criteria, partly because of inherent difficulties of analysis and identification. The lag cannot be attributed to any disinclination on the part of archaeologists to introduce such features when they once are familiar with the complex factors involved and can recognize them with confidence, nor can irrelevance of these features to the problems of classification be claimed.

There are three distinct obstacles to the use of technological features as classificational criteria: (1) identification of materials often requires laboratory facilities; (2) evidences of some important techniques are difficult to recognize or, in some cases, they actually leave no identifiable mark in the finished vessel; (3) physical properties are often influenced by both composition and technique and hence their interpretation may be uncertain. The difficulties are formidable and the extent to which they can be met should be accurately gauged to avoid waste of time with impracticable procedures or, at worst, self-deception. The possibilities of identifying materials and techniques have been covered in some detail in the section on pottery analysis, in which limitations and unexplored methods and criteria have been pointed out. Especially pertinent is the fact that laboratory analysis often directs attention to properties that afford means of identification by inspection, properties whose significance might otherwise be ignored or misinterpreted. The pigments of Pueblo Black-on-white ware are an example (see p. 385 ff.), and there are many comparable instances in temper identification. In the case of techniques, both greater familiarity with the methods of living potters and experiments planned to test the effects of various processes will multiply the number of criteria that can be used. The difficulties of interpreting physical properties must be met by more thorough understanding of the nature of ceramic materials and of the effects on them of firing. Identification of technical features and judgment of the causes of properties are not necessarily laborious or time-consuming tasks. The need is for understanding of basic principles rather than for rules of procedure. For example, one might enumerate and contrast the characteristics by which organic paint can be distinguished from black iron-oxide paint, but if the student understands the properties of solutions and suspensions in relation to pottery paint, he has the key and need not clutter his mind with particulars that can be derived by simple deduction. Furthermore, with adequate background and experience, recognition of many features may become a matter of second nature no less than are the sortings which the archaeologist is accustomed to make.

The study of technological features offers at least three distinct advantages in pottery classification: (1) it directs attention to the human factor by making one think in terms of what the potter did and thus aids in the definition of a taxonomic unit in terms of cultural factors; (2) it enables the student to distinguish chance or accidental variations from significant ones resulting from change in material or technique, thus lessening dependence on random criteria chosen because of conspicuousness and ease of recognition or from conventional practice; (3) it offers simple criteria for delimiting types. Since this is one of the principal difficulties in classification, it may be well to illustrate the possibilities.

Before considering the limits suggested by technological analysis, as compared with those generally employed by the taxonomist, let us examine the causes of artificiality of limits. One type appears to be transformed into another by gradual modification, irrespective of whether the type is defined by superficial appearance or by technical and stylistic features. This circumstance suggests that the cause lies in the nature of the material rather than in the way it is handled by the taxonomist. Apparent continuous change is explained theoretically by the slow rate of improvement in the early stages of culture, a rate which is conditioned by meagerness of the stock of fundamental knowledge and by discouragement of individual initiative through weight of tradition. No less important is the fact that abrupt change in one feature is often rendered inconspicuous by the prominence of features that are stable and therefore exhibit only the variations that result from lack of standardization and individual differences in skill. This is only part of the picture, however. When one considers ceramic change in terms of materials and processes, he is reminded of many examples of qualitative and discontinuous quantitative changes that mark limits recognized by the taxonomist but not arbitrarily set by him, as are those in a series that show continuous quantitative differences.

Tempering material affords a simple and familiar example of qualitative change. One class of tempering material does not grade into another. There is a clear and complete break between such materials as sand, sherd, shell, and rock, and if two or more of them are mixed by the potter, the practice does not constitute intergradation but rather marks a change in custom. Again, if there is a discontinuous range in texture within one class of material (e.g., fine and coarse sand with medium sand unrepresented), a natural division is present. If, on the other hand, there is a continuous textural gradation within a single kind of tempering material, temper is not a satisfactory criterion of classification because any division will be arbitrary. In choosing tempering material as an example of the three kinds of change, I do not mean to imply that temper necessarily has chronological or cultural significance, although it may have either one or both. It will mark geographic source if it is peculiar to one region and absent from surrounding territory, and it will reflect custom if potters chose it in preference to another material equally accessible and suitable. Not infrequently, however, a particular temper was used too long to have value as a marker of periods or developmental stages; nevertheless in simple, plain ware it may be the outstanding feature that changes in time. Furthermore, a change in temper may or may not be coincident with a change in style: a region in which a uniform style is established may include districts with distinct natural resources that will be reflected in pottery material, or different styles may develop within an area having the same geological formations and similar resources.

Before this illustration of technological limits is carried further, it may be well to point out parenthetically that ever present possibilities such as these, which must be constantly tested, raise classification above the dead level of a task that can be guided by simple rules of thumb; it becomes a spur to curiosity, a challenge to resourcefulness, and a means of holding our sights to the human element in the problem.

Clays, no less than classes of tempering material, differ both qualitatively and quantitatively, but, as we have seen, the fineness of their texture, their impurities, and the fact that their property ranges overlap make them more difficult to use in classification. Among physical properties, color is a conspicuous and familiar example of overlapping ranges. Close color resemblance of pastes or slips may be merely fortuitous in consequence of the wide range developed by most clays when subjected to varying firing conditions. Two late pottery types from the Hopi country in the Pueblo area illustrate the kind of questions that such variations pose. Sherds can be selected to show an almost continuous blending of color from Jeddito Black-on-orange to the following type, Jeddito Black-on-yellow. What does this color range mean? That a series of clays was used, each differing slightly from the previous, or that there was a gradual change in firing technique? Thermal tests have disproved both of these possibilities, since they have shown that one type is made from a red-firing clay, the other from a buff-firing one. The fact that some sherds of each fall between the norms of the two raises the questions if they both fire to similar colors under certain conditions or if a clay having intermediate properties was occasionally used. Appropriate observations and tests can supply the answers. One of the most serious criticisms of the claim that classificatory division is necessarily arbitrary is that it destroys the initiative for such questioning and analysis.

Throughout the list of pottery materials and techniques, one finds examples of qualitative and continuous and discontinuous quantitative variation or change. The major classes of pigments, for example, are qualitatively different but within a class composed of two or more essential substances in a natural mixture, such as an iron-manganese ore, there may be found a continuous quantitative variation; nevertheless, the ore from any one source is usually limited in composition range.

The techniques of building and shaping may be said to vary qualitatively. Coiling does not develop by imperceptible steps from modeling, for instance. On the other hand, the same pottery may employ both techniques, even for the different parts of the same vessel. Although this will complicate classification, it is an example of versatility, not of gradual change in technique. A parallel case is found in the paddle-and-anvil and the scraping methods of shaping the vessel and thinning its walls. Methods of surface finishing, such as wiping, scraping, polishing, and slipping, may all be difficult to identify under certain circumstances not because one leads step by step to another but rather because we may be uncertain of the distinguishing marks. A surface may be abraded, a slip may be masked by deposition of carbon, the luster that marks the polished surface may have been destroyed by firing shrinkage, or the polishing tool may have been applied so sketchily that the term "polished" seems unmerited. Although distinctions may be blurred by these incidental features, actually each technique involves the employment of different classes of tools and different manipulations to produce certain mechanical effects that mark the technique more or less clearly.

Firing methods raise entirely different questions and are more difficult to use as criteria of classification. In the first place, firing produces chemical changes in pottery material that affect its physical properties. These physical properties not only show wide ranges of continuous variation but are also influenced by original composition of the clay as well as by firing temperature and atmosphere. Consequently, the latter cannot be deduced simply and directly from a study of physical properties. This point has been covered in the sections on physical properties and firing methods. A specific example will show how it may be handled in classification. The slip color of Plumbate runs a wide color gamut in both the oxidation and reduction ranges, some surfaces can be scratched with a copper coin, others are not marred by quartz, some are dull and matte or badly weathered, whereas others have a fine vitreous luster. How can properties with such a range be used as criteria for classification? Should the pottery be classed as a single type or broken down into subtypes? If it is a type, should it be classed as reduced or oxidized? Analysis has given us hindsight which tends to blur the memory of how confusing these questions were, and we do not know how many of the soft, reddish sherds were handled without a suspicion of their relation to the hard, gray, vitreous ones. Analysis showed that the chemical composition of the slip clay was unusual, and observations of the relation of color to hardness, together with thermal tests, indicated that the distinctive properties resulting from vitrification were developed by reduction. Plumbate was recognized as a valuable historical-index type before it was analyzed. The results of analysis may be said to have established it as a technological type, and when it is viewed as a sampling of potters' trials with a special method of firing that brought out distinctive qualities of an unusual clay, the range in its properties no longer presents a meaningless continuum but instead records technological history. Granted that this record does not interest the archaeologist using Plumbate sherds as an "index fossil," it nevertheless makes the type a more effective tool for his purpose since it gives significance to a striking variability of properties which, when unexplained, are a source of uncertainty and error. Plumbate is a favorable example because of its distinctive materials and specialized techniques. In general, it may be said that as potters' methods are developed, the qualities of pottery become correspondingly distinctive, and the taxonomist's task is in turn facilitated. It would be unfortunate if our ideas of the possibilities of analysis, classification, and interpretation were dominated by familiarity with the simplest stage of ceramic development with which we deal.

The fact that certain changes in material and technique mark what may be called natural limits does not mean that they will necessarily afford useful criteria in classification. They are not always conspicuous; furthermore, a succession of minor changes may leave the choice of a dividing line difficult. In other words, a limit based on qualitative or discontinuous quantitative variation is not an artificial break, but given many such changes, the choice made from among them may be arbitrary. On the other hand, when several such changes occur simultaneously, the break is not only clearer but is also likely to be significant in terms of ceramic history.

The technological approach has been stressed in this discussion because it offers unexploited possibilities and because, in the majority of cases, evidence of technique does not suffer from fragmentation of pottery as does that of shape and design. This emphasis carries no implication of relative importance of technique and style as reflections of culture or as means of classification. Both are fundamental and neither can substitute for the other. A basic distinction that should be borne in mind, however, is that choice of material is limited by natural resources, and the properties of material have an effect on technique, whereas shape and decorative style are free of these restrictions. This point is mentioned because technical features are sometimes misinterpreted as unconditioned cultural expressions.

The relative usefulness of style and technique in classification has sometimes been compared on the basis of postulated difference in their rates of change. There is some theoretic ground for the idea that style changes more rapidly than technique. When the best clays, tempers, and pigments that a locality offers have been discovered, there is no incentive to try others. Practicability is a primary governing factor in technique, and the number of choices that potters have is often limited. Style, being free of these restrictions, may be less stable. Despite this circumstance, particular examples can be mentioned in refutation no less than in confirmation, of this idea of relative rates of change. Furthermore, the systematic analysis and comparison necessary to support broad generalization has not yet been made. Regardless of the outcome of such comparisons, both aspects of pottery have definite progressive steps which are useful in classification as well as significant in ceramic history.

This inquiry into the nature of ceramic change might logically be carried through shape and decoration, by reviewing such features as proportion, contour, functional features, and elaborations of vessel form, and field, structure, elements, organization, and symmetry of design, but we would be dealing in part with interrelated qualities some of which have not yet been specifically defined. In this respect, style is more difficult to analyze than technical features that can be treated in terms of distinct materials and successive steps in a process. A detailed review is not needed, however, to recall that some stylistic traits, no less than technical ones, vary qualitatively. Symmetry of design affords a clear-cut example.

At the present time the taxonomist's major problem regarding style is not differentiation but the more elementary one of obtaining adequate samples. One of the most serious criticisms that can be made of the pottery type is that it is generally defined principally, if not entirely, from sherds, which means that physical properties, many of which are of secondary importance, are given more prominence than features of style. It may seem unfair and unrealistic to criticize a procedure which is dictated in some measure by circumstance, but there is risk that we may forget that opportunities for studying style are not as limited as they once were. In the course of years of excavations, many collections of vessels have been made that offer untapped sources for stylistic study. In most cases the specimens in such collections can be correlated with types defined from sherds. As I have argued elsewhere, such studies and correlations would illumine the fragments of decoration and shape that sherds preserve, just as the mental image of a picture puzzle often enables one to visualize where the individual piece fits.

The limitation of ceramic study imposed by the type concept as at present employed is serious because of the tendency to allow this one unit of classification to dominate analysis. We think and talk largely in terms of types; moreover, we treat the named type, once it is published, as though it were as well established as a biological species. This attitude may be an insidious holdover from the time when biological models were accepted for pottery classification. In any event, I would emphasize that the condition of the average pottery sample and particularly the incompleteness of stylistic data make of the pottery type a tentative, hypothetical class to be re-examined, corrected, and amplified from time to time as evidence accumulates; a class that may be split or combined with another, redefined, or discarded. It is a category in the process of formulation instead of a fixed standard of reference.

The objection may be raised that acceptance of the type as tentative would leave us at loose ends or throw us into confusion. But there is no alternative except self-deception; as long as evidence is incomplete, definitions must be correspondingly so. As for the confusion that would result from recognizing that we do not possess a neat and final system of classification, that is our situation, and there will be very much less confusion if we admit it and proceed accordingly. When this fact is ignored, confusion is increased by reporting new material solely by reference to published types, many of which are incompletely defined. The familiar practice often means loss of data on areal or chronological variation and on style. Furthermore, it substitutes a process of matching for the independent analysis by which the validity of the type must be established.

Generalizations regarding pottery types named to date call for qualification because equal reliability and significance have not been insured by rules of nomenclature and standard forms of description. Type samples on which descriptions have been based have differed greatly in size and representation of areal and temporal variation. In addition the classes of pottery that have been given type status do not all have the degree of technical specialization or the stylistic elaboration that permits easy differentiation and interpretation. Finally, the different concepts of the type which archaeologists have held and the diversity of their aims have also contributed to lack of uniformity. Consequently, although some types are represented by collections that have accumulated over the years and have been studied independently by different workers, other types await the amplification and critical review necessary to establish them reliably.

This brings us back to the question of the actual meaning of the type and the purposes it can serve in archaeological research. If it is considered as only a sorting group selected for the convenience of the student attempting to define a chronological sequence, no cultural significance is claimed for it. This is a cautious definition; it makes no claims that might be refuted. But the purposes that types have served indicate that they are more than meaningless divisions. Cross dating and identification of intrusives rest on the long-accepted belief that pottery from different localities can be distinguished. Studies of trade in pottery, of the spread of styles and techniques, and of the influence of one style or tradition on another are made by using the pottery type. One measure of its cultural significance is its usefulness for these purposes. The problem of recognizing classes of pottery which represent the products of people using similar materials and technique and following, within a given period, the same stylistic canons is more challenging than the chore of separating sherds by appearance for the sole purpose of chronological ordering. Nothing is lost in seeking to discover classes that have cultural significance, for they can be useful in chronological ordering, no less than the artificial type. But it is essential to recognize them as approximations and to test them repeatedly in the light of new evidence.

The pottery type, whatever its defects and potentialities may be, does not serve adequately all lines of ceramic investigation. A series of types takes one through ceramic history by jumps instead of by steps, and it is the periods of transition that are skipped because they are often short compared with periods of stability in ceramic practice, and hence the sherds that represent transitions are not only relatively few in number but also difficult to classify; they suggest aberrant specimens or extremes in the variation range of the type defined with respect to peak development. By habitually thinking in terms of norms, we forget the possible meaning and importance of divergent specimens. Typological classification is at best a clumsy means of studying periods during which new techniques were introduced and style was in flux; the chances are that causes of change and the course of development will be blurred or obscured by the typology. The need is to analyze in detail the particular features that underwent change, considering the nature of change—how the persistent features compare with the new, if new materials and methods were adopted simultaneously, if technical development was accompanied by stylistic change, what steps were passed through before an innovation became established, and if new features can be attributed to imitation of intrusive pottery, to adaptation of foreign techniques or styles, or to native invention.

Specific features offer effective means of studying the history of both style and technique because they direct attention to significant characteristics by which the course of development can be followed in greater detail and more sensitively than is possible when reliance is placed on a class defined from generalization of many features.

In the last analysis, specific features are the criteria on which the type or any other classificatory unit is based. In mentioning their place in ceramic interpretation, I would also stress the importance of understanding the factors that condition them. This approach insures that they will be chosen not at random but systematically, and not for mere conspicuousness but for pertinence. In view of the importance of distinguishing between environmental and cultural factors and of differentiating persistent modifications from normal fluctuations, it may be worthwhile to list controlling factors: (1) Natural resources—clay deposits, materials suitable for temper and pigments, and fuel. The extent to which this is a limiting factor—that is, the range of choices which the environment offers—will vary from locality to locality. The choice of material will affect principally the physical properties although it may have other influences also, as when a strong plastic clay permits the production of a thin-walled ware or when a variety of pigments stimulates experimentation with polychrome effects. (2) Properties of ceramic materials. This factor will also affect primarily the physical properties, but the variety of physical and chemical changes that clay undergoes on firing allows wide variation in pottery made from the same clay. (3) Common knowledge of the potter's craft, established techniques, practical requirements for pottery, and accepted standards of the community to which the potter belongs. These will determine in large measure the selection of material, the general methods of production, the quality of workmanship, and the range in vessel shape and decoration. (4) The individual potter's capacity, experience, skill, taste, independence, and originality. This is a cause of secondary fluctuations in workmanship—in vessel symmetry, fineness of surface finish, certainty of line in decoration, and uniformity of firing. It is also a possible source of innovation in choice of materials, method of production, and concepts of form or of ornamentation. (5) Accidents of production. These will cause sporadic variations, mainly in physical properties. The effect may be recognizable as accidental or it may be so unlike that of the normal product that the relationship will not be apparent. (6) The direct or indirect influence of foreign techniques and styles. These may bring about a great variety of permanent changes, and their adoption may be accompanied by more or less experimentation and by various modifications.

In summary it may be said that stabilizing factors are both environmental (natural resources setting limits on quality of clay and range of pigments, etc.) and cultural (the techniques, standards of workmanship, and stylistic traditions accepted by the community). The causes of persistent change or development may be traced to the individual (discovery of new materials or methods and creation of new elements of style) or to foreign contact, which likewise can influence both style and method of manufacture. Causes of minor variations and meaningless fluctuations are individual (accidents of production, variations in skill affecting physical properties and workmanship, and innovations that are not accepted by the group)

This outline may suggest one answer to the ever-troublesome question of how fine a distinction should be recognized in defining the pottery type. We are concerned primarily with cultural factors; a criterion must, therefore, be consistent in occurrence. If it is sporadic or if we can show by technical analysis that it represents an accident of production, it is not a valid criterion.

Although chief reliance in classification is placed on the pottery type, other categories and concepts have also been introduced, some of them broad, others related to specific aims, some derived from the type, others independent of it. Ware, one of the older and more familiar group terms, is often loosely employed. It has been variously defined as: (1) A broad class based on some prominent feature such as color, decorative technique, or function (e.g., red, incised, culinary ware). This usage, which carries no implication of common location, age, cultural relation or similarity of features other than that named, is consistent with that of commercial ceramics as illustrated in the terms "earthenware," "glazed ware," and "hollow ware." (2) A synonym for type. There is a factor other than that of carelessness behind this usage. In some cases it has expressed distrust of hasty and premature naming of pottery types. A broad class designation was temporarily employed pending more precise definition. The critical evaluation of the type that has been made in recent years should help correct this situation. (3) "A group of more or less similar pottery types," "a group of types which consistently show the same methods of manufacture" (Colton, 1953, p. 50). Ware characters listed include firing atmosphere, method of construction, kinds of temper, surface treatment, and paint constituents. (4) A ceramic group in which all attributes of paste and surface finish remain constant (Guthe in March, 1934, p. 6; cf. Cole and Deuel, 1937, p. 290). The last two definitions reflect the background of the archaeologists who proposed them. In the Southwest, large classes of pottery distinguished by degree of oxidation or by type of paint are familiar, and also expressions such as black-on-white and corrugated ware have been used for many years. Colton considers this usage consistent with his definition although the early workers were not thinking in terms of types, neither had they identified paint or paste composition. In fact, the inclusion of the latter criterion would seem to be dictated by desire for consistency more than by practicability because often the temper of Pueblo pottery cannot be identified without microscopic aid. On the other hand, paste classes are readily recognized in the Eastern United States because their texture is coarse, a fact which explains the definition of ware in this area. These two definitions are consistent in so far as they group types having in common certain conspicuous features of manufacture. They suggest an archaeological equivalent of the modern ceramist usage of the term. The confusion that would result from insistence on narrow restriction of the features that define the class should be clear. The implications of the class will depend on the technique of manufacture by which it is defined. If it is basic and widely distributed (e.g., smudging) or influenced by natural resources (e.g., volcanic ash temper), it will not have the implications of derivation or connection that a highly specialized technique does (e.g., resist decoration). The fact that an adjective naming the diagnostic feature is employed with the word ware should help prevent misunderstanding of the significance of the class. It should be clear that difficulties will arise if particular features or sets of features are singled out as invariable criteria or if certain implications are assumed *a priori*. Although ware is always a broader class than type, it does not by definition represent a uniform level of generalization, as long as the diagnostic techniques differ in distribution and degree of specialization and either one or more may be designated (e.g., untempered ware, Fine Orange ware).

The concept of a pottery style is an example of a class which summarizes likenesses and differences of a special aspect of pottery. In the study of artistic development or relationships, this class is more satisfactory than the pottery type, which, being defined with reference to all conspicuous distinguishing features, introduces irrelevant criteria and may subdivide the style unnecessarily. Moreover, in order to trace the interactions of technical methods and aesthetic standards in ceramic history, each must be analyzed independently; we cannot recognize their interplay if we are bound by classes defined with respect to both. Although the term "style" is employed freely in the discussion of pottery, and we would be hampered without it, its connotations have received relatively little attention. Often a particular assemblage of concrete features is designated by it rather than qualities common to those features. A style of form usually means a group of associated shapes rather than the qualities of contour and proportion that they possess in common. Likewise a design style is frequently defined in terms of component elements and motifs. The criteria and methods of stylistic description have received surprisingly little attention in comparison with the thought and discussion that have been given to the pottery type, but to the extent that shape and design analysis have suffered from our dependence on sherds, identification and interpretation of style have necessarily lagged correspondingly. This situation is not altogether deplorable; it is wise to pursue stylistic classification cautiously and tentatively until the foundations of analysis are well established.

The technological counterpart of a style, a cluster of associated or of interdependent techniques, has not to my knowledge been introduced in ceramic analysis although particular features of manufacture have played a role in interpretation in so far as a number of archaeologists have indicated the significance of their distribution. This situation has no relation to the possible usefulness of a technological unit of classification; the lack of such a category can be attributed to the comparative recency of technological analysis, the difficulties of field identification, and the trend of ceramic research. The significance of what might be called a technological tradition is something to be tested in future studies.

A number of ceramic categories used in sherd analysis have been described and illustrated by Colton (1953). Some of these have been more widely used than others. The "series," a sequence of pottery types that are known to follow one another in time, is a familiar class. This and the "ceramic group," comprising contemporaneous pottery types occurring in sites of short occupation within a limited area, are employed in relative dating and are defined from association and stratigraphic data. The "index ware," on the other hand, is an interpretative class, being defined as a ware including more or less similar types used for cooking and storage "which are peculiar to a certain prehistoric tribe" (Colton, 1953, p. 67). Here we are on controversial ground. The assumption that the sharing of basic techniques of manufacture indicates the kind of relationship implied by the term "tribe" may well be questioned. Aside from this objection, the definition of this class raises the problem of distinguishing evidences of basic techniques of manufacture from effects of environmental restrictions of ceramic resources, particularly when techniques are judged from physical properties. This problem calls for more study than it has yet received. Colton's definition of the "analogous pottery type"—contemporaneous types having the same style of design but belonging to different wares—suggests a stylistic category cutting across type, but he introduces an ethnic connotation in this term, also.

Two concepts, the horizon style and the pottery tradition (Willey, 1945), developed by archaeologists working in the Peruvian field are important because they have stimulated interest in cultural and functional interpretations of style. The horizon style is a broad concept based on evidence of all techniques that reflect widely expressed artistic influences. As long as pottery constitutes only one of its components, this hypothetical class serves to relate ceramic art with the art of other cultural manifestations—weaving, stone carving, architecture, etc. —which is a strong point in favor of the concept. The validity of a horizon style defined solely by general resemblances might be challenged in view of the present status of stylistic studies, but in the Peruvian field evidence is strengthened by introducing an independent factor—the relative position of the style in a sequence compared from region to region. Willey (1948) has presented a functional interpretation of the concept. The pottery tradition is defined with reference to long-time historical relationships. In contrast to the horizon style which expresses only coeval spatial relations, the pottery tradition summarizes temporal relations, refers specifically to pottery, and is not limited to style. According to Willey (1945, p. 53), "A pottery tradition comprises a line or a number of lines, of pottery development through time within the confines of a certain technique or decorative constant." The technical or decorative constants supply the guide to derivation giving assurance that the variables observed have the direct relation necessary to constitute a significant development. The first attempts to recognize pottery traditions may result in rather vague and simple reconstructions, but all such efforts perform a valuable service in pointing up the need for more meaningful pottery analysis and description.

It is apparent that the American archaeologist has introduced enough concepts in ceramic classification to serve many purposes. In general, the prerequisites of a workable classification are adequate sampling together with a method of analysis which springs from clear understanding of ceramic principles and is formulated with direct regard to the purposes of the study undertaken. The fixed hierarchy of criteria that have sometimes been proposed to simplify and standardize classification has no place in this approach. If our purpose is to recognize the unique and meaningful qualities of a culture's ceramic products, the classes we seek have no such limitations. Many different criteria and many combinations of them may be significant, depending on their implications in a given case and the constancy of their occurrence. In a sense, we have been too objective in our attitude toward pottery; we have treated it as a simple physical thing and, as I have said before, we have well nigh forgotten the role of the potter. Even though we are interested in pottery primarily as one of the expressions of culture, we should be more conscious of the human factor than we generally are, and we will be reminded of it continually as long as we question the meaning of ceramic properties, seek to understand techniques, and study style in its entirety.

USES OF PUNCHED CARDS IN POTTERY STUDY

Files of illustrations have become essential for systematic study of pottery styles. The time has passed when a student, after thumbing through a few reports, could speculate on distributions and correlations with confidence that he had reviewed all available data. The difficulty now is that once a file has adequate coverage, it becomes self-defeating if it is handled with an ordinary indexing system because all such systems are based on a single classification, whereas pottery illustrations must be sorted in many ways—by provenience, horizon, type, shape, decoration, technique, and associations, to name only major headings. With a single indexing system, card-by-card sorts must be made for classifications other than that used in filing, or cross files must be maintained. Hand sorting is far too time-consuming, and cross files mean expensive duplication. For example, if a file is indexed by provenience, occurrence by region and site is made the key and determines how the file can be used. This permanent arrangement serves the student when he wants to know what was found at a given place or if some particular trait or type is represented there; that is practically all it does. It is not even efficient for the study of geographic distribution of traits because this requires first a systematic search for given traits, which means card-by-card sorting with a file that is not indexed for this purpose. The dilemma is fully resolved by punched cards which, with a well-planned code, enable one to sort quickly and simply for a large number of items or to rearrange the file according to any one of a number of systems of classification. Another distinct advantage of punched cards is that the labor of refiling cards is eliminated. There is no need to store cards in any particular order because the next time they may be used for a different purpose.

Two systems of punched cards are widely used, machine-sorted and hand-sorted. This discussion will be limited to hand-sorted cards because their relatively low cost makes them available to every student and their flexibility adapts them to a wide variety of purposes in the analysis of archaeological material. These cards, which come in a variety of sizes, in standard form or specially printed, are provided with holes around the margins. When the meaning assigned to a hole is recorded by a given card, the hole is clipped through to the edge, forming a notch. The cards are sorted with a skewer-like tool or tumbler from which the punched cards drop. For details regarding the mechanics of sorting and general principles of coding, the reader is referred to Casey and Perry (1951). As the holes are only on the margins, the greater part of the card is available for recording observations, descriptions, references, etc., and for attaching illustrations.

The simplest form of coding, termed "direct coding," assigns a meaning to each hole. The cards on which this meaning is coded (punched) drop out from the pile with a single pass of the tumbler. If this method alone is used, only as many meanings can be coded as there are holes. The capacity of the card is greatly expanded by "numerical coding" for which holes are used in combination. With the most commonly used numerical code, which has a "field" of four holes numbered respectively 7, 4, 2, 1, combined punching (adding numbers) permits coding any number from zero (no punch) to 14 (all holes punched). Very large numbers can be coded by using a series of such fields, one each for units, tens, hundreds, etc. As an illustration of this system, consider the coding of pottery types. By taking eight holes for direct coding, one can code only the same number of types. With an extensive file covering a large area and a long time-span, there may not be enough holes for all types (e.g., a 5-by-8-inch card has 100 single-row holes). In contrast, by coding numerically and using four holes for units and four for tens, 149 types will be coded with eight holes, and 1499 with 12 holes. Another possibility is to use one field for ware and a second for the types within each ware. This allows a possible 196 types from eight holes if there are 14 types within each ware. The limitation of numerical coding is that only one number in any one field can be coded on any one card; that is, data must be mutually exclusive to be coded in this way. By judicious combination of direct and numerical coding and by assignment of major divisions to one field and subdivisions to another, an extensive code can be drawn up. This is where there arises the temptation to devise a code so involved that the sorting advantage of the punched-card system is lost. When one studies how to get as much as possible on the card, one begins to crowd in items that are unimportant. It is essential therefore first to review the uses of the file and to analyze thoroughly the data to be coded.

From among the purposes for which vessel illustrations are consulted, I will consider the following in relation to the problem of coding: (1) Identification. This will include: (a) Comparison of vessels of unrecognized type or style with well-established types or styles possessing the same features. The file would be sorted for the outstanding features of the unknown to make systematic comparisons. Sorting might also be made by a guessed type for verification. (b) Ascertaining of the stylistic context of various individual features or parts of features exhibited by sherds. For example, one might want to know the shape or shapes on which a distinctive rim or support occurs within a given pottery type, the effigy of which a certain appliquéd or incised ornament is an insigne or the designs in which a particular motif occurs. For such purposes the file would be sorted by a great variety of stylistic features. (2) Determination of geographic and chronologic distributions. This would not be an end in itself, but might be used—in the case of geographic distribution—to determine the extent of trade in pottery from a given center, to study the spread of a stylistic influence, and to search for the pottery components of a horizon style. Chronological distribution would be examined to recognize index types, to study the genesis and development of styles, to search for pottery traditions. In any case, the sorting would be not by period or location but by diagnostic features. (3) Correlation. This will include chronological correlation established by means of index types and correlations of stylistic features to study the sources and relationships of well-established styles, the former requiring sorting by types, the latter by features of style. (4) Summarization of: (a) Stylistic features of a type from all reported examples, (b) Geographic and temporal variations of a type or style, (c) Stylistic characteristics of a period or region. Sorting would be by type; type, style, and specific features; and period and region, respectively. The data required for these various purposes can be obtained in part from written description, as for example the record of distributions; however, illustration serves all these purposes far more effectively than the written word. The most carefully phrased description of a design motif cannot create the image that a simple drawing gives from a glance; and even when we feel sufficiently familiar with features to name them, there is still the element of uncertainty because of differences in usage and frequent looseness of terminology. The advantages of a file of illustrations are therefore obvious.

To summarize the coding problem, the enumerated purposes of a file require sorts by: (1) pottery type, (2) vessel shape, (3) particular features of vessel shape, (4) design style, (5) elements, motifs, and qualities of design, (6) decorative technique, (7) geographic location, and (8) chronological period. This list suggests the number of cross files that would be required to handle the material with an ordinary indexing system. It is also noteworthy that for the purposes mentioned, sorts by stylistic features would be needed most often and that these cannot be adequately handled with a single-index filing system because we have to deal with two different expressions of style—in shape and in decoration—and a great many independent features within each. In coding for a punched-card system, each classification should be considered as a distinct problem; in every case the student has to analyze and classify his data, bearing in mind its relation to his objectives. By way of illustration, I will mention a few considerations regarding the various classifications listed.

Pottery types, being mutually exclusive, can be coded numerically. It is necessary only to estimate the number that the file will probably contain in order to reserve sufficient space for them. It is important to avoid hasty or premature type assignments, for they will cause confusion and error. This warning points up another advantage of the punched-card system: with multiple indexing a card can be entered as soon as it is classified with respect to any one index and its classification and punching can be completed at any subsequent time, whereas in a file with a single index, a card cannot be entered until it is fully classified. In a file of vessel illustrations, features of shape and decoration can always be coded by inspection, and provenience would normally be given, whereas pottery type or stylistic type may be uncertain and chronologic position undetermined. But the use of an incompletely coded card in sorting for specific stylistic features often aids in its type classification. To return to the file, it is generally desirable to code for some broad category in addition to type, as for example, ware or such classes as plain, unslipped, unpolished; plain, polished, unslipped and slipped; unslipped with plastic decoration; painted, unslipped and slipped. These groups can be expanded if desired by introducing color designations, but it is important to keep the classes mutually exclusive in order to code numerically. If these groups are broad and fundamental, they will serve as a preliminary sort for type, thus multiplying the number of types that can be included and giving them a useful organization. When there are no more than seven classes, three holes (4, 2, 1) are sufficient, or for three classes, two holes. An additional class (0, no punch) can always be obtained if all specimens can be classified. One should bear in mind, however, that small fields greatly reduce the number of sorts per hole (two two-hole fields give six sorts as compared with 14 sorts for one four-hole field). Nevertheless one often has to deal with small classes; purpose of classification and requirements of the material, not the maximum number of sorts that can be obtained, are the primary considerations.

The coding of vessel shape requires considerable study. It deals with one of the principal categories of information an illustrated file affords and must cover contours and proportions that vary continuously over a wide range; in addition it must include many special features, both functional and ornamental. A simple alternative is to code numerically for particular standardized and well-recognized shapes, allowing space for the list to grow. This might be sufficient for certain limited purposes, as in the use of chronological indices, but it would be far too incomplete for systematic study of shape style. It would also soon become unwieldy as it would be unorganized. To suggest one way of solving the problem, I will outline a code based on the method of shape classification previously discussed (pp. 225–48). This requires seven groups of holes as follows:

A. Structural class (see p. 228). Numerical, 2 holes, 4 sorts.
B. Major subdivision of the above classes by vessel proportion, contour, or symmetry depending on the structural class. 1 hole, 2 sorts.
C. Basic vessel shape. Numerical, 3 holes, 8 sorts.
D. Rim or neck form. Numerical, 4 holes, 15 sorts.
E. Supports. Numerical, 4 holes, 14 sorts (note that 0 cannot be used to designate a type of support because vessels without supports will be unpunched).
F. Handles and lugs. Numerical, 3 holes, 7 sorts (0, no handles).
G. Special features. Direct, 3 holes: spouts, covers, flanges (these are not mutually exclusive).

These 20 holes take up one side of a 5 3/8-by-8-inch card (the extra 3/8 inch, equivalent to two holes, is gained by the elimination of tabbed dividers). If all features coded occurred in all possible combinations, there would be a total of 345,600 classes, many times more than one would care to handle in a single series, whereas classification yields simple, quickly learned groups and affords the important advantage of permitting direct or short numerical sorts for various special features, which permits independent tracing of their distinction and study of their correlation with basic shape.

A partial expansion of the above outline will indicate the possibilities of the general system and also serve to bring out certain points to consider in coding. The expansion will differ depending on the area covered by the file. For detailed, localized study, major culture areas would call for different subdivisions, depending on the extent of development and elaboration, the preponderant forms, and the significance of form with respect to areal distribution and chronological stylistic variation. The example given was developed in the study of a series of Mesoamerican vessel shapes. The expansion of the first two fields is basic and broadly applicable:

A. Structural class
  With an axis of revolution
    0. Unrestricted vessels.
      B. 0. Low to medium, .5 and under; 1. Tall (ht/br. > .5).
    1. Simple and dependent restricted vessels.
      B. 0. Low to medium, .85 and under; 1. Tall (ht/br. > .85).
    2. Independent, restricted vessels.
      B. 0. Corner-point vessels; 1. inflection-point vessels.
  Without an axis of revolution
    3. All forms.
      B. 0. Effigies; 1. Geometric forms.

The order in which classes are coded may be determined by logical relations which aid in remembering the code or by efficiency in punching and sorting. If the latter consideration is paramount, zero will be used for the most numerous class, thus obviating the need of punching. For the same reason the smallest will be coded as 3 as it requires two punches. In the above example, the order is one of increasing complexity, which by coincidence meets requirements of efficiency in punching.

In the C field, specific contours are coded by reference to geometric norms and characteristic points of the contour, reserving one sort for extremes in proportion. Depending on shape style, various subdivisions might be made in this field or an extra hole added from one of the feature sorts—rims or supports. For the Mesoamerican series the assignments for the first two classes were as follows:

A. 0. Unrestricted vessels
  B. 0 and 1
    C. 0. Sections of spheroid
       1. Cylinder or symmetric hyperboloid
       2. Upper nape of cone
       3. Upper section of hyperboloid
       4. Corner-point forms with convex base and flaring sides
       5. Other corner-point and complex forms
       6. Inflected forms
       7. Extremes in proportion
          (B-0 ht./br. < .2; B-1 ht./br. > 1)

A. 1. Simple and restricted dependent vessels
  B. 0 and 1
    C. 0. Spheroids, medium proportion
       1. Spheroid, extreme in proportion
          (B-0 ht./br. < .5; B-1 ht./br. > 1)
       2. Ovaloid
       3. Inverted ovaloid
       4. Lower nape of cone, other forms without corner or inflection points
       5. Corner-point forms
       6. Inflected forms
       7. Complex forms

Both these groups are divided by the B sort into low-to-medium and tall vessels. Except for extreme proportions (sort C-7), this sort is optional because the same shape classification is maintained for the entire range. Aside from its simplicity, this coding is advantageous for the study of shapes having average proportions near the middle of the range, but independent coding would give a more uniform distribution because contour does vary with proportion.

The third structural class, independent restricted vessels, is more complex in contour and less variable in proportion than the first two; consequently, the B field is used to separate two major contour types, the C field to classify body forms, and the D field for "necks" instead of rims. Since these codes follow the geometric principles outlined in the discussion of form classification and since details of coding will vary from area to area, there is no need to outline the expansion.

The fourth structural class, vessels lacking an axis of revolution, is generally small compared with the others but includes a much wider range of shapes. The B field makes a primary separation of representational from geometric shapes. For the former, subject is coded in the C field and for the latter, vessel symmetry. As this is a shape classification, the effigy vessels include only those that lack a vertical axis of revolution; that is, basic shape is modified by representation of the natural object. The subject classification is introduced in the C field only because it determines form. All effigies having a vertical axis of revolution are classified with their respective geometric vessel forms. The general classification of effigies is coded under decorative style and a sort of this field brings together the various types of effigies from all shape classes.

Fields D-G, coded for special features, are self-explanatory. The number of holes assigned to each, as well as their coding, will vary with the degree and direction of shape elaboration in a given area. In the study of Mesoamerican vessel forms, the coding of rim form was guided by the variable outlined in figure 32. Coding of special features has several advantages; in particular it permits direct and detailed sorting in the study of their distribution and their correlation with basic vessel shape. This is important because they are often useful diagnostics of an index style or type. This coding also facilitates rapid sorting for special shape types; basal-flange bowls, for example, would be located most quickly by sorting flanged vessels first, and the same advantage would hold for all vessels having distinctive secondary features. It is impracticable to attempt to obtain complete sorts for every possible vessel shape because of the complexity of form. It is far better to combine several rare and related features and to hand sort a few cards than to adopt a code so involved that it becomes unmanageable. For this reason, specific features are extremely useful for fine sorting; at the same time the relative frequency of any one should be considered in deciding whether or not to code it separately.

This code for vessel shape is only analytical. It does not give any hypothetical groups by shape style. Various associations of shape are obtained, however, by the coding of other data. A sort for pottery type will bring out the full range of shapes in a general ceramic class, and geographic and chronological sorts will be used in the study of spatial and temporal distributions or relations of vessel shape.

Pottery decoration presents an even more difficult coding problem than shape, or rather it presents many such problems, but generally they will not all arise in any one area. The student of Southwestern pottery, for example, deals primarily with painted, geometric design. In Mesoamerican, both decorative technique and style of decoration cover a much wider range. When this situation arises, stylistic analysis can be made a subsort under major decorative techniques; e.g., painting, modeling, incising, etc. There is then the question of differentiating such classes as representational or naturalistic, symbolic, and abstract design. The difficulty is that criteria of these classes have not been fully defined. Broad classes, such as these, are generalizations that should be developed from systematic analysis and not allowed to predetermine its directions and limits. Of course, striking likenesses and differences will suggest stylistic groups before thorough or complete analysis is made, but these classes will rarely be defined with the exactness and certainty that is necessary for coding. Premature coding of style would defeat one valuable purpose of a punched-card file; that is, by facilitating analysis it should contribute to a more satisfactory definition of stylistic classes. It is entirely feasible to code for particular features and qualities of design as primary sorts rather than as subsorts of a hypothetical, general class. For example, one might code fields numerically for such data as: line (rectilinear, curvilinear, and mixtilinear); use of line and mass (discrete strokes, continuous line, mass alone, independent line and mass, and outlined mass); patterns of repetition; life forms; features; postures of figures; insignia; and costume etc. Various kinds of conventionalization could then be separated without recourse to a class with ill-defined limits. This method of approaching design coding forfeits the advantage of the extra fields obtained when subclasses are introduced, and when the file includes both geometric and distinctly naturalistic design, much detail is lost if a uniform code is used because some characteristics will not be shared and others will be developed differently. One of the difficulties of preliminary classification arises when highly conventionalized forms occur. One way of meeting it is to consider the occurrence of certain formal elements of design (e.g., geometric structure, patterns of repetition, symmetry, etc.) as diagnostic of a conventional-geometric class. In the subsort of this class, space would then allow for design meanings—life form, symbols, etc.

A general consideration in the coding of design features is whether or not they are mutually exclusive and can be coded numerically. Some, such as design structure and symmetry, are very easily coded in this way, whereas others, such as elements and motifs, have to be coded directly, and judgment must be exercised in coding them. The number of elements is so large that they can easily take up more space than their significance justifies. It would not be necessary to point out that it is wasteful of space to code simple, ubiquitous elements, were it not for the emphasis given them by our dependence on sherds.

The subject of design coding is left with these brief suggestions because we are not yet fully prepared to outline procedures for design analysis. Various styles will suggest special requirements, and solution of problems will be facilitated if the file does not include too many styles and decorative techniques. The use of a punched-card file should accelerate progress in this field because it makes possible ready comparison of the large number of design features that must be covered in any extensive, systematic study and for which the single index system is entirely inadequate.

Method of coding geographic location will depend partly on the extent of the area covered, but it is generally advantageous to code subarea or region and then site. Regions can be defined in physiographic or cultural terms; modern political divisions, although more definitely defined than either of these, are irrelevant and would not ordinarily be considered. Physiographic boundaries are more easily established than cultural ones and, in so far as cultural relations are influenced by physiography, they will afford significant groupings in addition to a convenient preliminary sort. If it is desirable to sort by cultural area and if boundaries have not been established, nuclear sites can be punched and those that are uncertain left unpunched until their position is established. This will affect the coding of site as will be explained in a moment.

The question of entering cards that are incompletely classified and punched has to be considered in relation to the purpose of the file. If a reference file of fully documented material is desired, such cards will not be included, whereas a file to be used as an analytical tool can include incompletely coded cards provided they record significant stylistic data. It is important, however, to avoid adding cards having relatively little information because they increase the labor of sorting.

Site presents no problem of classification except the choice between numerical and alphabetic coding. With numerical coding, sites are numbered serially as they are entered in the file, and an alphabetic list with code numbers is kept. The mechanics of alphabetic coding and sorting are similar to those of numerical. The letters a to m are coded as the first 13 numbers of a four-hole field, the second half of the alphabet is coded in the same field using a fifth hole which is punched when the letter falls between n and z. Any letter can be sorted out by needling first the n-z hole and then the four holes of the field, or the entire file can be arranged in alphabetic order with nine needlings. This is done by first separating the two halves of the alphabet with the *n-z* punch. The *a-m* pack (on the needle) is then sorted in order 1, 2, 4, 7, and after each sort the dropped cards are placed at the back of the stack and sorted with the rest of the pack. This will place the first 13 letters of the alphabet in order; the process is repeated for the *n-z* stack. Except for omission of the *n-z* punch, numerically coded cards are arranged in the same way; that is, by needling the four holes in turn they fall into numerical order from 0 to 14. Parenthetically, I might call attention to a distinct advantage of numerical coding for arranging a file according to a system of classification. The 15 divisions which are obtained by needling the four holes of a numerical field would require 15 needlings if coding were direct. Although numerical ordering has no meaning for sites numbered serially as entered, alphabetical ordering is useful when cards from several sites are to be drawn from the file because the same number of holes are needled in ordering the entire file and sorting for a single item, although more cards are handled in the former process. In general, therefore, when more than one item is desired from a numerical field coded in logical sequence, it is quicker to arrange the file than to sort for individual items.

Numerical and alphabetic coding each have advantages and limitations for coding sites. Numerical coding yields complete separation of site cards with no extras; however, the code must first be consulted for site number, and it is also necessary when adopting the code to estimate in advance the number of sites that will be included in order to reserve sufficient space for growth of the file. Alphabetic coding does not give a single site sort but drops all sites with the same initial letter or first two letters if first and second letter are coded. If site is coded as a subsort under region, the number of sites covered by a numerical code will be multiplied by a factor determined by the number of regions, in the case of uniform distribution. This can be done only if all cards are coded for region when entered in the file. The alphabetic site code, however, can be used either as a primary or secondary sort, and it will, therefore, allow introduction of sites unclassified with respect to cultural area.

Theoretically, coding for chronological classification offers no difficulty because periods, being mutually exclusive, can be coded numerically. The chronological position of much important material is uncertain, however, and systems of relative chronology are subject to modification. Coding a card on insufficient evidence can only lead to difficulties. It is often advisable, therefore, to allow space for chronological classification but to delay coding until temporal relations are well established.

The importance of giving more attention to entire vessels in the study of style suggested the example chosen for this discussion. The reader will think of many other applications. The system is especially useful for bibliographic files because of the possibilities of coding subject matter.

This review will have suggested some of the pitfalls of coding. The punched-card system is a simple mechanical means of sorting cards that can be coded in a variety of ways for any purpose one chooses. At best, it can be a tremendous time-saver, thus enabling us to do things we otherwise could not afford to do. But the mechanical system itself does not ensure this advantage. Its effectiveness is dependent on clear definition of purpose, sound analysis of material, and a well-planned code.

THE PLACE OF STATISTICAL METHODS IN POTTERY ANALYSIS

Statistical methods may be said to play a double role in archaeological ceramic analysis. In the guise of simple, familiar calculations they are accepted by everyone as part of the established routine, but when they appear as new and complicated formulations they are likely to arouse suspicion and controversy. This reaction is understandable, but not altogether reasonable or fortunate. Archaeologists who have used statistical methods have warned that they "can answer a problem objectively only in terms of the data submitted" and that their "only connection with reality is by way of the systematics from which the manipulated symbols are taken" (Brainerd in Griffin, 1951, p. 117). This being the case, the familiar, simple procedure is subject to error no less than the new and difficult one. It may be argued that the errors are more easily detected in one than in the other. Actually, the "obvious" often throws us off guard. For evidence that we can be deceived, we have only to recall how often percentage frequencies of occurrence are reported from samples too small to yield reliable results. Yet, it is a very simple matter to determine the effect of size of sample and size of proportion on the reliability of this universally used measure. Curves have been published from which probable error or standard error is read directly (see Brainerd in Beals, Brainerd, and Smith, 1945, p. 166; Shepard, 1942, p. 237). The archaeologist should familiarize himself with this type of curve and make its use habitual. But the question of reliability goes back of this to methods of analysis. No mathematical formulation can rectify faulty analysis or confusion of cultural, individual, and environmental factors.

The fact that I have been principally concerned with technological ceramic research and have not specialized in the highly technical field of statistical analysis explains why I leave the subject with a few references. This treatment carries no implications of value judgment but merely reflects a disinclination to discuss methods to which I cannot bring direct experience.

It is noteworthy that archaeologists who have introduced mathematical for-mulations have generally worked with the assistance of or in collaboration with trained statisticians; in other words, they have not simply substituted figures in borrowed formulas. Robinson (1951) and Brainerd (1951) proposed a method for chronological ordering which they tested on undocumented collections. Their method has since been further tested empirically in the analysis of California collections (Belous, 1953). The proposal made by Spaulding (1953) for a statistical method of defining artifact types precipitated considerable controversy, partly perhaps because the concept of the artifact type is itself a controversial subject. Brainerd (in Griffin, 1951) has presented a suggestive review of the uses and limita-tions of mathematical formulations in archaeology. Additional references will be found in the bibliographies of these articles. All of these efforts are encouraging because they indicate a readiness on the part of archaeologists to seek out new technical methods which will give more sensitive measures and more reliable bases for common judgment than inspectional methods alone can ever be expected to afford.

V. The Interpretation of Ceramic Data

W HEN THE ceramic specialist attempts to evaluate the place of ceramics in archaeology, he may well be suspect of having prepared a defense or simply of arguing for the importance of his work. Protests to the contrary are useless; it is for the reader to judge if the specialist has viewed his subject in perspective, recognizing the limitations of his approach, accepting valid criticisms of his methods, and examining carefully the general assumptions on which his deductions are based.

Perhaps the most frequent criticism is that the archaeologist has become preoccupied with pottery to the neglect of other classes of evidence. A moderate statement is that of Clark (1952, p. 205): "The significance of pottery for the understanding of prehistoric society can easily be overrated, though the variety in which it can be fashioned and its great durability, when compared with many other categories of material equipment, makes it peculiarly suitable for classification. It must always be remembered that pottery was only one of many substances used to make containers and that even when it had come into use it was not everywhere the most important of these."

It is possible that the stage of ceramic development with which a critic is most familiar bears some relation to the severity with which he judges the fault of overemphasis. The more advanced ceramics are—the better potters understand how to select clays, the wider the range of their pigments, the greater their control of firing, the more varied their adaptations of shape to use, and the more refined and elaborate their decorative style—the more a vessel has to tell about its makers. This is only part of the story, however. If cultural development is consistent, advancement in other aspects of culture will be commensurate with that in pottery, and a constant relation will be maintained; hence the original criticism will still hold. On the contrary, if within the handicraft stage of industry pottery has greater potentiality for elaboration and refinement or if it develops more rapidly than other crafts, relative values will not remain constant. When greater stress is placed on one aspect of culture than on others, it may mean that that aspect gives richer returns. It is also true, however, that in the pursuit of a discipline, students are subject to mutual stimulation and emulation that at times give the guiding techniques and aims the appearance of fad.

There is no need to weigh probabilities. The neglect of pertinent and fruitful categories of archaeological data cannot be justified by any amount of rationalization. To acknowledge this fact is not to depreciate the value of ceramics. There is nothing mutually exclusive in the study of the various aspects of a culture, and one of our basic problems is to understand their interrelations as fully as possible. This observation suggests that in a review of the present aims of ceramic analysis it is pertinent to inquire if ceramic data are being adequately integrated with data from other sources or if their collection is in danger of becoming an end in itself. Ceramic studies have not escaped the accusation that taxonomy and the publication of so-called objective data are sometimes made ends in themselves. Criticism of failure to interpret the results of a method does not necessarily discredit the method itself. I have elsewhere argued that it would be unfortunate to lose sight of the importance of common standards and precise techniques through entirely justifiable rejection of meaningless display.

The purposes of ceramic analysis are diverse, but certain basic assumptions carry through a number of them. Taxonomic systems depend on the concept that a people's standards and traditions have a sufficiently strong influence to maintain a certain degree of uniformity and thus produce recognizable styles. If changes in technique and style are gradual and consistent, they will reflect the passage of time and a relative ceramic sequence can be defined. As a corollary it is sometimes assumed that the rate of change is greater in style than in technique, although this idea has not been tested by extensive comparisons based on precise criteria. A further assumption is sometimes made that in the absence of stratigraphy, morphological or typological features will reflect the direction of history, but the pitfalls of this premise are now generally recognized. Continuity of style is often interpreted as one evidence of continuity of population, and sudden change in style as indicative of shift in population. Typological similarities are analyzed in terms of the relationship of cultures and their influence on one another. When intrusive pottery can be identified, it is used to establish the contemporaneity of occupations and to trace trade relations.

Some of these assumptions have been challenged more often than others. Perhaps it is the reliability of identification of intrusives that has been questioned most frequently within recent years and since this has direct bearing on several distinct phases of ceramic interpretation, it may be well to examine the grounds for identification before proceeding to the specific uses of ceramic data. The other generalizations can best be examined in relation to particular objectives.

THE IDENTIFICATION OF INTRUSIVE POTTERY

Neither the archaeological importance of intrusives nor the reliability of many identifications will be questioned, yet the possibilities of identification in general have been questioned more frequently since the introduction of technological methods of analysis. When laboratory methods added the evidence of composition and technique to that obtained from style and general appearance, they not only reduced uncertainty; they also labeled as probably intrusive, pottery that had hitherto been accepted as indigenous. It is understandable that archaeologists should view this development with caution. The evidence is circumstantial and generally derived from procedures that are not shared by the field man. But more is involved than unfamiliarity. Technologists themselves have from time to time voiced warnings. It is extremely important therefore that the nature of the evidence and its limitations be clearly understood.

Let us first consider the archaeologist's identification by direct inspection. There are two possibilities: recognition of a well-defined style or type of known source, and tentative classification of unfamiliar sherds as intrusive because of their rarity and distinctness from the principal types of a site. In the absence of knowledge of distribution, rare or unique sherds can be listed only as unknowns or possible intrusives. Judgments are usually based on surface features which are recognized without technical aid. In the identification of an unknown by its resemblance to a familiar pottery type of foreign origin, the chances of error are greatest when the type is unspecialized and when reliance is placed on only one or two criteria. Clever imitations may also be mistaken for intrusives. It is difficult to estimate how serious these sources of error are because these identifications are not as a rule checked by independent means. In the case of an intrusive of unknown source, the basis of judgment is not likeness to something foreign but rather difference from that which is assumed to be indigenous because of its abundance. The fact of rarity in itself throws into question the local origin of a type, but other causes of scarcity should always be weighed. There are: (1) examples of individual inventiveness and originality—the unusual experiment with new materials or new ideas in form or decoration that did not gain acceptance; (2) accidents of production, especially from rare, high temperatures, which may alter the appearance of a pottery type beyond recognition; (3) the scarcity of essential materials, such as pigments or slip, which limit the volume of production; (4) the production of a ware for special purposes for which quantity is not demanded, as for ritual use or mortuary furniture for the ruling hierarchy; (5) a period of first appearance or of imminent disappearance of a type. In the last case, error of identification can be checked when the sequence of types and styles of an area is established.

Technological identification of intrusives rests on recognition of foreign materials or techniques rather than on style or general appearance, a fact that indicates the importance of using these two lines of approach as a check upon each other. A conspicuous advantage of the technological approach is that it adds a factor, the source of raw materials, that is independent of style of supposed local and intrusive pottery; yet this is the line of reasoning that is frequently challenged. Two criticisms are made: first, local resources cannot be investigated thoroughly enough to rule out the occurrence of any given raw material, and, second, even though the raw materials do not occur locally, they, rather than the pottery, may have been imported. The difficulties of proving the origin of materials are sometimes so considerable that it is impracticable to pursue this line of evidence alone. We cannot hope to know the resources of a site or a region with the thoroughness of natives who spent their lives there. Yet geological maps and some knowledge of the principles of occurrence and association of rocks and ore bodies are no small compensation. Moreover, sole reliance is never placed on probable natural occurrences of materials. It is the distribution of pottery with the material in question taken in relation to known sources that is generally considered, and strong circumstantial evidence can be built up in this way.

The question of importation of the raw material presents a different problem. Here we can argue regarding probabilities, remembering always that we may overlook some condition or reason that seemed important to the native potter. The likelihood of importation is greatest in the case of materials used to finish or decorate the vessel, especially pigments and slip clays that are prized for their color. Materials used in large quantities are less likely to be transported long distances, unless local sources are entirely lacking. Clays are widely distributed; only infrequently would it be necessary for potters to go far for body clay. Although clays differ greatly in their properties and although it is conceivable that either high standards or tradition would lead potters to import clay long distances, such instances in historic times are the exception rather than the rule. Temper, of all ceramic materials, is the least exacting in its requirements; consequently, nonplastic materials are the least likely to be obtained in trade or from a great distance. This circumstance coupled with the great variety of substances that are suitable and the ease with which they can be identified, gives tempering material exceptional values as a means of spotting the possible intrusive. But potters were not always guided by consideration of efficiency of production. In the absence of scientific theory, tradition and habit held control, and it may well be argued that people who had migrated might still follow the practices of their ancestors. If this were the case, it would be the entire output of pottery, rather than a small amount, which would contain foreign temper, unless we assume that there were only a few exceptionally conservative potters among many. This may suggest a tangle of qualifying circumstances. Actually, however, these are mainly the consequence of following one line of evidence exclusively. Correlation of stylistic and technical data will often clarify sources before one is pushed to this extreme.

One of the difficulties of weighing the sources of error in the identification of intrusives is that these errors are usually discussed in general terms. References are made to itinerant potters or an isolated example of the importation of ceramic materials is cited, but there is no attempt to determine frequency or weigh the importance of such factors. The impression is thus created that identification is necessarily uncertain and unreliable. It may clarify this question to set down the various possibilities. In addition to pottery and raw materials, traditions of technique and style may be brought into one pottery-making center from another, and each has a number of components; thus materials include body clay, tempering material, slip clay, and pigments; and there are techniques of selecting and preparing materials, of vessel forming, finishing, decorating, and firing, and style in shape and design. An entire group of ceramic practices may be borrowed or certain ones may be selected and combined with local elements. New techniques and styles may be introduced by foreign settlers or natives may imitate a foreign style.

Many of these possibilities (Table 11) are familiar to ceramic students because they are known among present-day prewheel potters. Potters marry into other pottery-making villages and either continue to follow their native traditions or adopt those of the potters among whom they settle. Materials are traded or exchanged and used in various ways.

None of these possibilities can be ruled out completely, but some are much more likely to occur than others. It is noteworthy that among all the possibilities listed, there are only two under which locally made and intrusive pottery are indistinguishable; first, when immigrant potters continue to obtain all of their materials from their native pottery-making center and likewise continue to follow their native technique and styles in all particulars, and second, when local potters obtain foreign material and copy perfectly foreign techniques and styles. There is also the opposite case in which the immigrant potters succeed in following local tradition in all its particulars and their product is then indistinguishable from that of native potters. Under all other circumstances there are, theoretically at least, clues for the identification of foreign, imitative, and heterogeneous types. This is a matter to which we will return.

The first question is, How serious are the failures to distinguish intrusive from indigenous types? This depends on the kind of interpretations that are made as well as on the relative number of specimens involved. If deductions regarding the contemporaneity of, or contact between, two pottery-making centers are drawn, the validity of conclusions will be the same whether the pottery is intrusive

TABLE 11—THE POSSIBILITIES OF ERROR IN THE IDENTIFICATION OF INTRUSIVE POTTERY

Foreign Element	Materials	Technique and Style	Differentiation Means
A. Materials obtained from another pottery-making center	I. Used alone	a. In local tradition	Distinguished by technique and style
		b. Imitation of foreign tradition	Identification depends on imperfection of imitation
		c. Mixed techniques and/or styles	Identified by local elements of technique and/or style
	II. Used in combination with local materials	All of above possibilities	Identified by local materials, supported by elements of local technique and style in *a* and *c*
B. Foreign potters working in the local center	I. Importing their native materials	a. In their native tradition	Indistinguishable from an intrusive from their native center
		b. Technique and style modified by local tradition	Identified by local elements of technique and style
		c. Local tradition adopted	
	II. Using some native and some local material	Any of above possibilities	Identified by local materials, further confirmed by elements of local technique or style in *b* and *c*
	III. Using only local materials	a. In their native tradition	Identified by material
		b. Native tradition modified by local tradition	Identified by material, further confirmed by local elements of technique and style
		c. In local tradition	Indistinguishable from local types
C. Foreign style adopted by local potters	I. Importing foreign material		Duplication of A I b
	II. Combining local and foreign materials		Duplication of A II b
	III. Using only local materials		Identified by materials

or was made by immigrant potters following their native tradition or by local potters imitating the foreign style. Contemporaneity and contact are essential in all cases. If, however, we are concerned with a question of economics—the volume of trade in pottery—then locally made pottery in a foreign style will be a source of error. Speculation alone is of little avail because whatever the probabilities, there can be no universal rule. It does not follow, however, that the question of source is unanswerable. The general ceramic picture may afford clues. For example, if the foreign type is of excellent quality and is followed in later levels by a poor imitation made from local materials, the original, local imitation is ruled out, and the decision rests between trade pottery and immigrant potters following their native practices to the letter. In some sites which have been studied the very number and diversity of foreign types would cast serious doubt on the hypothesis that they were made by immigrant potters, for such an explanation would demand an extremely conglomerate population. Again, distribution and frequency of occurrence of the types have a bearing on the probabilities. Wide distribution and decrease in frequency of occurrence with distance from the center of highest concentration is a common phenomenon. To explain pottery showing such distribution as the work of immigrant potters requires that we assume the existence of a large number of transient potters with absolutely fixed ceramic traditions. If potters migrated any distance they might reasonably be expected to try out the materials of their adopted home, and absence of expressions of the foreign style in local materials would argue against the hypothesis of immigrant potters. When these various possibilities are considered in relation to specific cases, the indications are often more convincing than reasoning on the basis of generalities. These remarks are intended simply to indicate some of the lines of evidence that may be followed.

These generalizations apply to the few cases where there could be identity of the intrusive vessel and the one made locally in the same tradition. Table 11 suggests that in all other cases there is mixed tradition which offers means of distinguishing the locally made vessel from the import, whatever the combination of its elements. The question is, How practicable is such identification and what are the chances of error? The identification of features of technique and style, in so far as they can be judged by direct inspection, does not involve a great deal of time or labor. This advantage may be somewhat offset by the fact that these features are often so imperfectly or incompletely preserved in the sherd that their recognition is difficult. The basic materials, on the other hand, are just as indestructible as the sherd itself, but their identification usually demands the use of laboratory equipment and may be slow and costly or rapid and simple, depending on the nature of the materials and the techniques employed. The discussion of analytical techniques and of methods of identifying materials (pp. 138–81) should afford a basis for evaluation.

We have considered the suspected intrusive that can be compared with a well-defined foreign type. Sherds that are recognized as different or strange but cannot be compared with any type known at the time are often more numerous. They may be either of an unknown foreign type or at least influenced by such a type, or accidents or experiments in local practice. Field examination may leave one at a loss to decide whether the differences are significant and indicative of origin or merely accidental variations. Microscopic examination, however, often shows that strange-looking sherds contain materials different from those in pottery typical of the site and, at best, material that, judged by general geological knowledge of the region, are unlikely to have been derived from local sources. Such sherds can be labeled only possible or probable intrusives until such time as comparative material becomes available, but as soon as they are recognized in more than one site they can be used for cross-dating, provided they are sufficiently distinctive to admit of positive identification. On the whole, technological analysis is likely to turn up a greater number of these suspected intrusives than is stylistic study simply because technical evidence suffers less than stylistic when the vessel is reduced to potsherds. The limitations of the technical approach are most apparent when the same geological formation occurs over large areas and ceramic resources are similar. It is disappointing when a source of suspected intrusives cannot be postulated, but this is inevitable in the first stages of investigation in any little-known area, and it will suggest the advantages of determining by survey methods the distribution of basic techniques and materials.

By way of summary I would point out that Table 11 should serve to emphasize two principles: first, the importance in any investigation of the source of pottery of searching out and evaluating distinct lines of evidence and particularly of correlating the evidence obtained from the study of materials, techniques, and style; and second, the value of studying features in terms of processes. These principles should be borne in mind in reviewing the various uses of ceramic data.

THE USE OF POTTERY FOR RELATIVE DATING

The archaeologist must devote a great deal of time to whatever evidence he can gather of the relative age of his finds because a chronological frame of reference is essential to give archaeology historical perspective. In the absence of recorded dates or material that will yield absolute dates, he turns to the study of changes in the form of artifacts for the record they bear of the passage of time. In view of the fact that potsherds occur in great abundance and exhibit many variables, it is not surprising that they should afford a primary means for setting up a relative chronology. At present this is probably the dominant object of ceramic studies in American archaeology.

Among the various ways in which pottery is used for relative dating, we might distinguish the definition of a chronological sequence for a site or region and the establishment of contemporaneity of occupations. The latter is by far the simpler and more direct procedure of the two, but it gains significance from the former.

A CHRONOLOGICAL SEQUENCE

Methods for intensive study of pottery with the object of defining a time sequence have undergone considerable refinement and elaboration in recent years. Data are drawn from collections made during excavation of stratified deposits and in surface reconnaissance. One class of material usually supplements and extends the other. The order of the levels that are cut through in excavation shows the direction of time, and it is desirable to choose sites with long occupations in order to include as many steps of cultural development as possible. When sole dependence is placed on surface collections, relative age must be inferred indirectly, and the task of correlation is simplified when there is a series of sites of short occupation having just enough time overlap to relate them. The sherds collected are studied in order to chart the passage of time from the order of appearance, peak of popularity, and disappearance of pottery types, styles, or traits.

The principles and generalizations on which such studies are based have been outlined and discussed by Ford in several publications (1951; Ford and Willey, 1949; Phillips, Ford, and Griffin, 1951). They include assumptions regarding the populations of a region, the nature of ceramic or cultural change, and the manner in which the pottery type can be used as a measure of change. Generalizations regarding the distribution of populations and cultures are suggested by the special conditions presented in the particular region under investigation. For example, it may be assumed that the composition of a population was stable with respect to a general area within which there was frequent shifting of individual village sites, or that at any one time there was cultural uniformity within a given, restricted region. Such postulates are accepted as working hypotheses until they are disproved.

Of broad application are the assumptions regarding the pottery type and the nature of ceramic change. Cultural change is conceived as occurring gradually and continuously, and the pottery type is considered a means of recognizing this change. The artificiality of much pottery classification and frequent reference to the pottery type as an abstraction follow from the assumption that pottery as a phase of culture represents a continuous stream of development and that changes in style and technique occur so gradually that the potters themselves were not aware that they were taking place. It follows that the selection of particular segments of this stream as time markers is an arbitrary process. One set of limits is as valid as another, provided each of them demarcates segments that serve the purpose equally well. As Ford and Willey have stated (1949, p. 40), "As a type is primarily a space-time measuring tool, its validity depends solely on how well it serves for its end purpose." The artificiality of the system will be accepted as long as it gives results, and the question to be considered is not the usefulness of such methods, since that has been demonstrated, but rather if they can be made more effective. Basic assumptions should be examined from time to time to ascertain whether the reliability or efficiency of the system is reduced by erroneous inferences or limited by failure to use pertinent data.

In the section on taxonomy I have touched on the problems of classification, arguing that some ceramic features exhibit continuous variation, others discontinuous variation, and that the degree of artificiality of a system depends partly on whether a point of discontinuity is taken as a boundary or a break is made in a continuous series. Ordinarily the approach in taxonomy is empirical and any readily recognizable feature that changes with the passage of time is accepted as a suitable criterion. The pottery type is defined by a number of criteria, some of which vary continuously while others change discontinuously. Doubtless the fact that the type is based on an assemblage of traits which do not change simultaneously influences the impression of continuity of variation.

This observation raises the question whether the apparent continuity of change is conditioned by method of classification or rests on a quality inherent in the early stages of ceramic development; at least, we might ask to what degree each factor is operative. The same principles do not necessarily apply to the history of technique, shape, and design, and the question therefore breaks down into three parts. In considering the technical aspect, two quite different factors should be clearly distinguished: quality of craftsmanship and manner of utilizing materials. These two factors cannot be equated. Potters' skills, or perhaps it would be better to say standards of workmanship, fluctuate; they are spurred, sustained, or allowed to decline with the changing interests and values of the society. The acquisition of skill is a process of learning which is going on among individuals continuously, and the level of excellence we attempt to evaluate is the average that is struck between beginners and the experienced, between the inept and the expert, but perhaps the range of variation is not as great as might be expected. The beginner's pots, when too crude, may not have been fired; the individual who was too clumsy would not follow the craft. The standards that are accepted for a craft tend to set limits on the acquisition of skill, and there are limits inherent in the nature of the techniques—a vessel wall can be just so thin before it is impractical; evenness and symmetry are properties having states of perfection; with a given method of polishing, a clay will acquire a certain degree of luster, no more; and so on. Even though perfection may not be attained, the individual potter with reasonable aptitude needs only application to approach it. Manipulative skill, therefore, does not seem to be a force that guarantees continuous, consistent progress.

Intelligent use of material is quite a different thing. It rests on the understanding gained by cumulative experience and advances by unpredictable discoveries; the potter's readiness to note and use the unexpected is important for progress. This may consist in finding a new material—a better clay or pigment —or in hitting on a more effective technique—an easier way to polish, a method of obtaining higher temperature or better control of firing atmosphere. If the cause of a new effect accidentally obtained is unknown, there will be a period of trial and error experiment before it can be reproduced at will. The acceptance of a new practice may be immediate or hesitant and slow, but the time required for either control or introduction is likely to be short compared with that during which it is practiced in standardized form. This is fundamentally the way ceramics advances technically in its early stages. The innovations may be trivial or fundamental, they may occur frequently or only at long intervals. Shifting interests and needs and the force of mutual stimulation have their effect but do not guarantee continuity or uniformity in rate of progress; they may operate sporadically.

If the technical quality of pottery can be said to advance through the potter's acumen in learning from the fortunate accident, the history of vessel shape would seem to be controlled in part by a people's need for containers for particular purposes. The appearance of basically new shapes must reflect, in part, at least new ways of doing things—the adoption of a new method of food preparation, or a different ritual practice. The potter's interest and pleasure in form may also enter, but are likely to be reflected in such features as subtlety of contour and secondary modifications such as rim form rather than in size, basic shape, and proportion. Do these forces result in continual change so gradual that potters are unaware of them? Would any one suggest that potters learned to make comales by deriving the shape through imperceptible modifications of a food bowl?

If vessel shape is conditioned by considerations of utility and pleasure in form, pottery decoration may be said to be influenced by beliefs and by concepts of the ornamental and perhaps through play of fancy. Beliefs may dictate subject matter—the choice of symbols, the gods that are represented, or perhaps such general rules as avoidance of natural forms and restriction to the geometric. Style is a complex and subtle thing, and one hesitates to speculate on the causes of changes in decoration in view of our limited data on the history of design styles. Nevertheless, I would argue that it is not a foregone conclusion that change is gradual; in fact the nature of elements of style casts doubt on the idea of gradual transitions. Could rotational symmetry be derived by gradual modification of bilateral, or a band design originate from a quartered field?

This general line of reasoning might be pressed one step further by following the course of ceramic history in an area for which there is absolute dating. It would be interesting to do this systematically and thoroughly for the Southwest. A few suggestions may serve to indicate the possibilities. The history of basic techniques can be followed most easily; it appears to be marked by early development of techniques which were comparatively stable for a long period. A contrasting slip and polishing appear early in the south, while black iron oxide and organic paints were discovered in the first ceramic period in the north and have continued in use to the present time. The technique of reducing or preventing oxidation in firing likewise dates from the beginning of the craft in the north and was followed so consistently for hundreds of years that changes in firing method are not apparent from the general appearance of the black-on-white pottery. The production of black ware by smudging also came in early and persisted locally. With respect to materials, there are pronounced areal differences in composition, conditioned in part by natural resources, whereas successive changes over a period are less noticeable. Against this background, however, some innovations in technique stand out. Conspicuous among these is the shift from black-on-white to red and buff wares in central Arizona in the 14th century. This change, which has been attributed to the introduction of coal to replace wood, could have taken place with half a dozen trial firings with the new fuel. The rate of change may not have been affected as much by the time required to learn the technique as by the readiness of potters to accept it. Another innovation is marked by the discovery that lead ore will make a vitreous paint. In this instance, the conditions for producing a special effect which must first have been obtained accidentally are complex; it was essential to have a pigment with sufficient flux and also firing temperature high enough to cause fusion. After the first accidental discovery was made, trial and error experimentation was necessary before these two factors would be recognized and a reliable technique established. Sporadic appearance of vitreous paint on a matte-paint type that antedates the first well-standardized glaze-paint type of the Rio Puerco of the West gives evidence of repeated accidental production preceding the discovery of a reliable method. The course of development of the technique in the Rio Grande Valley was somewhat different because Rio Grande people had obtained the Western glaze-paint pottery in trade and were therefore familiar with the idea and possibly had learned something about technique. Consequently their principal problem was the discovery of local sources of material. The important point in this illustration is that in neither case did change take place by small increments. Potters either made an accidental discovery or strove for an effect, and as long as they were successful, adoption was rapid.

We need not follow the argument through pottery shape and decoration. It is sufficiently clear that the concept of change which has arisen from practical experience in sorting and classifying sherds is not in agreement with what may reasonably be expected on theoretical grounds and from general knowledge of the nature of ceramic processes. Man is the recipient of sudden insights and fortunate accidents which sometimes change his ways of doing things or his habits of thinking; taken in sum, these experiences affect the course of his progress. If this is true, why does it appear that ceramic development is a continuous stream moving imperceptibly but certainly? There are doubtless a number of different reasons. In the early stages of ceramic history, the effects of discoveries are often difficult to recognize since they are of a simple order. The problem of interpreting ceramic change is rendered more difficult by the fact that different things have superficial resemblances and things that are essentially identical are so variable that they may be easily mistaken as different. Our habit of thinking abstractly about pottery instead of seeing it in terms of processes adds to these difficulties. Finally, the fragmentary state of the sherd record blurs telling parts of the picture and blots out others. The test of methods of using pottery for relative dating is in experience. Minor errors of interpretation may escape notice but there is little ground for doubting that the main outlines are correct. This can be true even though some assumptions regarding the mode of culture change are open to criticism.

The advantage in the use of the pottery type for such studies lies in the fact that it is defined with reference to a great many criteria. Local differences in ceramic resources and minor fluctuations in technique and standards, as well as the definite improvements necessary to progress, cause variations in these characteristics. The type offers a great many more steps in a scale than would the group of traits by which it is defined considered separately, because of the many possibilities of combination. The value of the type is established, but method of classification is still subject to refinement, and consideration of causes of traits should increase precision and serve as an independent check.

One of the bothersome details of sorting types is the tendency to let boundaries shift. The fact that a workable scheme is based on the treatment of classes of pottery as abstractions without close analysis of the significance of variables in terms of the processes and cultural forces acting on them would seem to exaggerate the difficulty unnecessarily. The analysis of evidence of processes is not offered with the thought that it would necessarily supply a simple key. Traits are not always easily analyzed nor their causes self-evident, and the properties that vary discontinuously are not always the most conspicuous or the most significant. Nevertheless, this approach offers sufficient promise to merit trial with various kinds of collections.

Aside from the question of underlying theory, statistical considerations, especially of sample size and conditions that affect normal frequency of occurrence, are primary concerns of archaeologists using pottery to establish a relative chronology. The soundness of conclusions is dependent on them no less than on the significance of the traits chosen for classification.

THE ESTABLISHMENT OF CONTEMPORANEITY

The use of intrusive pottery to prove that sites were occupied simultaneously is both a simple and a familiar process. Obviously it is requisite that the pottery types selected for the purpose have a short time span. The value of a ceramic "index fossil" increases with range of distribution. In the discussion of the identification of intrusive ware, I have called attention to the fact that inferences regarding relative time are the same regardless of mode of distribution. Certainty of identification is another question, but it is noteworthy that a type which enjoyed wide distribution did so by merit of distinctive features; this very fact gives assurance that it will be more readily identifiable than the average type. The possibilities of erroneous identification are not to be discounted, however, and every feasible means should be used to check suspected intrusives. Another cause of error may be the preservation of many generations of the rare intrusive vessel as an heirloom. Although there is a record of the preservation of glaze-paint vessels in a Rio Grande pueblo for some 250 years, such occurrences are not likely to be frequent; moreover, it may be possible to check the contemporaneity of a type with its deposit when a number of intrusive types occur.

An entirely different approach to the problem of establishing contemporaneity is that based on general similarity of certain traits in pottery of different regions, a similarity that is construed as indicating spread of styles or techniques from a common source. Regional modifications may occur but do not obscure the fundamental traits. The principles involved in such relative dating have not as yet been fully defined, and to a large extent conclusions are based on individual judgment, but the fact that students reach the same conclusions independently establishes confidence in the method.

As a means of establishing contemporaneity, pottery has advantages over other kinds of artifacts because of the variety of its features and the richness of its development. A critique of this method of relative dating might commence with an analysis of pottery traits made with respect to their significance; in other words, what kind of similarities can be fortuitous and what kind are least likely to occur independently? A basic distinction may be made between traits that are conditioned mainly by properties of raw material and those that follow primarily from technique. An example will suffice to illustrate the point. Color is probably the principal physical property that has been used extensively in comparative studies, yet it is conditioned primarily by the composition of the raw clay, and natural resources determine the kinds of clay from which the potter could select. It seems a truism to point out that color may have no temporal or cultural significance since clays that fire to identical colors occur in areas having no connection, and the same types of clay were used over long periods of time. Nevertheless, the very prominence of color tempts us to give it more weight than the facts of occurrence justify. When we come to the combinations of color in a polychrome ware, the element of selection plays a far more prominent role, and similarities in color combination have proportionately more weight.

A second general distinction to be made is that between general techniques or general effects obtained by a number of related techniques and specialized techniques or effects obtained in one particular way. The former, of which polishing and smudging are examples, are widely distributed geographically and temporally. The latter, of which reduced iron oxide paint and resist decoration are representative, are restricted in occurrence. Obviously, the more specialized a technique, the more weight it carries in comparative studies. A comparable distinction might be made between simple, widely distributed stylistic traits and the more elaborate and restricted ones.

We have considered the relative significance of various ceramic traits, but usually pottery types rather than individual features are compared. Since the pottery type is defined with reference to an associated group of traits, it generally affords more specific evidence of contacts than individual features. Still, there are marked differences in the specialization or development represented by pottery types, and resemblances between simple types are less reliable indicators of a connection than are those between evolved types; in other words, the significance of similarities between types must also be weighed. This circumstance brings us back to the individual features by which the type is defined and therefore emphasizes the importance of considering their significance and weighing them accordingly. It seems to me that this relationship enables one to appreciate more fully the value of understanding ceramic principles and practices.

POTTERY AS A CLUE TO THE INTERACTIONS AMONG PEOPLES AND CULTURES

Since pottery is traded and man is imitative, it should be possible to recognize the influence of ceramic traditions on one another. We have to take care that we do not say, by a slip of the tongue, the influence of cultures on one another. Perhaps that would be a reflection of wishful thinking. Even while we admit the foolishness of allowing pottery to loom too large in our concept of culture, the use of pottery to establish relative chronologies—the setting up of "ceramic periods"

—tends to establish in our minds a close association that sometimes verges on substitution. Anyone without this background might well ask why special significance should be attached to a change in the shape of a cook pot rim or the application of slip on a food bowl. Such refinements may not even have had direct connection with a people's food habits, to say nothing of their political and social conditions or their religious beliefs.

It is not surprising that one of the most direct challenges to some of our common assumptions regarding the value of pottery in the study of culture history comes from a review of pottery made during periods of major political upheaval and social adjustment. Tschopik (1950), in a study of the Aymara of Peru, sought evidence of the influence of Inca dominance and of the Spanish conquest. He drew on historic records and on traditions of the immediate pre-Spanish period for the outline of political events and then compared pottery of these periods with pre-Incaic pottery, carrying the comparison through to present-day ceramic practice. He concluded that Inca and native Cuchito ceramic styles remained distinct and standardized during the time of Inca dominance, roughly a century; that Aymara pottery from the refuse of the colonial period could not be assigned to either Incaic or colonial periods with certainty, except for association with sherds of Spanish wine and olive jars, glaze ware, and tile; and finally that present-day Aymara pottery preserves ancient techniques and forms. Although he does not claim that no changes took place, he considers persistence more striking than change and writes (p. 217): "This observation seems of particular significance since it is a well-known archaeological platitude that pottery—the plastic art *par excellence*—is so sensitive to modification from generation to generation that it acts almost like a cultural barometer in reflecting change. Yet the Aymara ceramic tradition has been conspicuously insensitive and resistant to change throughout 500 years of drastic acculturation."

This is a sobering report for the archaeologist who has looked on pottery as a primary means of studying the contacts between peoples. In view of its importance, it is unfortunate that data on the traits showing continuity and the nature of the changes that did occur are not fully recorded. But the fact that Tschopik's comparisons are not detailed or specific does not lessen our responsibility for re-examining common assumptions regarding the value of pottery for the study of cultural relations.

To assume that man has necessarily taken full advantage of the freedom of expression that clay affords would indeed be naïve. The fact that clay allows him to give rein to his originality may have influenced the shape of vessels less than traditional patterns and customs that called for certain kinds of containers. But, if it is naïve to assume that the potter's art necessarily mirrors political or social conditions, it would also be hasty to accept the conservatism of the Aymara as universal or to generalize from one instance. Too many variables are involved in the relation of conqueror and conquered and in the effect of contact and conquest on arts and crafts to allow simple generalizations. Conquest followed by benign rule may stimulate people through the introduction of new techniques and styles, but an oppressive rule may cause a decline in the finer expressions of ceramics; again, conquest may leave the ceramic tradition untouched. The fact that a people comes under the domination of foreigners does not necessarily give cause for change in the shape of the cook pot, although the introduction of new food habits could, and conquerors can demand tribute in native wares or specify that pottery like their own be produced; or the religious rituals they impose may or may not require new kinds of ceremonial vessels. The results of conquest necessarily depend on the extent to which the ways of life of the two peoples differ—their relative advancement—on the reasons for conquest, the kind of administration the conquerors establish, and on the attitude of the conquered—their interest in and evaluation of the new things brought in by the conquerors. In view of these factors, it is not surprising that conquest may, under certain circumstances, have little effect on the ceramic output of a people. To return to the Aymara example, it is noteworthy that contact with the Inca and the Spanish is shown by intrusive pottery in the refuse heaps; moreover, the persistence of native ceramic tradition is in itself an illuminating commentary on the effects of conquest on crafts and customs of the common people, something that tradition and the historic record often slight.

It would be desirable to have a great many more studies employing the classes of data that Tschopik used, and it would be especially advantageous if studies could proceed from historically documented periods backward into the times for which we have only the sketchy and often cryptic records held by material remains. But more often than not the archaeologist steps directly into some prehistoric time. and when his material represents an extended period of occupation, he is likely to be confronted with striking changes in ceramic styles and techniques. This familiar situation is the opposite of that described by Tschopik, and the archaeologist must be prepared to interpret it. He cannot assume *a priori* that ceramic development is self-contained; consequently he must be prepared to recognize effects of foreign influence. Although the interactions of ceramic traditions may be a humble phase of cultural interplay, they are still part of the picture. Moreover, they are not likely to take place without concomitant effects in other aspects of culture, and since the ceramic evidences of contact often catch attention, they can serve to alert the student to other signs of foreign influence.

Study of the interactions of ceramic traditions is not only a much more complicated matter than establishing contemporaneity of sites by intrusive pottery, it is correspondingly more stimulating. Perhaps we have been too easily satisfied at times with broad generalizations regarding cultural relations and influences. When these concepts are invoked on the bare ground of superficial similarities or a few specific resemblances among artifacts, the words "influence" and "relationship" begin to lose their meaning. The question is, How can similarities be analyzed and interpreted? We are not now concerned with identity, which means exchange, but with those resemblances that may reflect something that was done in response to a foreign stimulus. It might be helpful to distinguish attempts to copy a foreign pottery type from adaptations of elements of the foreign ceramic tradition; also the effects of local resources and customs on the borrowed elements should be studied. When the nature of the borrowing is thus defined, its effects through a period of time can be followed with more certainty.

Pottery offers a rich field for comparative studies because of the variety of styles, techniques, and material it presents. The first question is, How can change that results from native origination be distinguished from that due to foreign influence? Obviously, knowledge of the ceramic tradition in those regions that are possible sources of influence should be familiar to the analyst. Rarely is knowledge sufficiently complete to cover all material, and therefore native innovations can rarely be postulated with the same confidence as response to foreign influence when its source can be demonstrated. Intrusive pottery can serve as a guide to possible sources of influence. The student then starts with some kind of similarity to a known foreign type or element of the foreign tradition. Assuming this advantage, one can consider the possible variability of the copy and how adaptations or modifications of a foreign element can be recognized. The distinction that is made here is essentially that between reproducing an object and borrowing an idea. The copy may be more or less true, depending on similarities of local and foreign materials and the extent to which new techniques are understood and mastered. Vessel shape and pattern of decoration are free from the restrictions that composition of material places on such features as color of body, slip and paint, quality of surface finish, thinness of vessel wall, etc. The copy must therefore be marked by close similarity in both shape and design, but may only roughly approximate physical properties. Materials will differentiate the copy from the import, and deviations in technique may reflect the firmness with which certain practices are established. The adapted element is more difficult to recognize because it may be modified and, in any event, is associated with local elements which tend to disguise it. The borrowed idea may relate to function, style, or technique. For example, a religious symbol introduced with a cult may be executed in native materials and with native techniques that are quite distinct from the original; a new vessel shape may be accepted along with a different method of food preparation without modifying customary methods of finishing and firing, regardless of their departure from those of the original; a new technique such as slipping, polishing, or the use of superior temper can be introduced without accompanying stylistic change. In mentioning these simple, hypothetical cases, I do not mean to imply that single features will necessarily be neatly lifted out of context and incorporated into local practice. It is fortunate that elements are not likely to be adopted singly because the greater their number, the more certain the evidence of their source.

Some such questions as I have suggested should be asked in order to define more precisely the nature of the relationships among pottery traditions. It may never be possible to know the political relations of the peoples whose pottery we analyze, but the effects of contacts on craft history offer a rich and ramified field for investigation, and, most important, the craft is not something set apart from other activities of the people; hence the possibilities of recognizing interconnections will always be a challenge.

THE POTTER'S CRAFT AS AN ASPECT OF ECONOMICS

General considerations suggest that pottery would not be traded extensively among people with a simple system of transport. It is fragile and bulky, it is not a necessity, and it is not likely to be as highly prized as stones or metals that serve for ornaments. It might be a thing of wonder to people who had never seen it before, but among people who had learned the craft, there would not seem to be sufficient demand to establish trade. Yet conditions among present-day pottery-making people belie seemingly reasonable deductions. If one wanders about a Rio Grande Valley pueblo on a warm, summer evening, glancing furtively in the open doorways as he passes, he may be surprised by the number of vessels from other pueblos which he sees. More telling are ethnological records of relations among pottery-making people of Mexico and Guatemala. In many instances the potters of a village are truly professionals, giving most of their time to the craft and depending on it for a living. In some cases, more pottery is produced for trade than for home use. In talking with these potters, one is reminded of their concern for the cost of materials and what they will earn for their time. They do not lavish time on elaborating wares that will not bring a good price because of their technical inferiority. Often pottery is distributed by professional traders, and the price for which it is sold depends partly on the distance it has to be carried. It can be taken just so far before it comes in competition with pottery from nearer villages.

This is a far call from the primitive craft stage in which each family makes all its own utensils. It cannot be argued that contact with an industrial society is responsible for the place of pottery in the economics of Guatemalan villages, for the craft has deteriorated in quality, and demand has decreased as pottery has come in competition with cheap articles of commerce. Moreover, there are indications enough of extensive trade in prehistoric times with types such as Thin Orange, Fine Orange, and Plumbate spread from the valley of Mexico in the north to Guatemala and even beyond in the south, distributions best explained by the hypothesis of trade.

Although intrusive pottery has been a valuable means of correlating occupations in different parts of Mesoamerica, the economic relations which it suggests have received relatively little attention. It may well be said that at present our picture of trade relations in the area is sketchy. Probably intrusives and suspected intrusives have been reported for every major excavation, but the territory covered by many of the pottery types that have been recognized among traded wares has not been plotted, nor have estimates of the volume of trade been made.

There are, of course, many questions that the archaeological record cannot answer completely or perhaps at all, but until questions are asked, resources for answering them are unprobed. A review and analysis such as Clark (1952) has given for prehistoric Europe suggests the challenging possibilities. The very connections and causes that Clark has reconstructed or suggested highlight the importance of studying economic relations as a whole rather than subtracting pottery and concentrating on it alone. One will then consider the relation of exchange in pottery to exchange in other goods—the extent, for example, to which need for one commodity developed demand for another or conditioned the direction of trade in it.

The argument that there may be extensive trade in pottery even though, on general grounds, it does not seem to be well suited for transport should not be mistaken for a conclusion regarding the relative importance of pottery as a commodity of exchange. I have mentioned it by way of emphasizing neglected possibilities. We are well aware of the fact that pottery was not necessarily an important trade commodity. Roys' account of trade in his *Indian Background of Colonial Yucatan* (1943) is a reminder, for pottery is not included among the articles he discusses. Anyone dealing with archaeological materials realizes that the near-indestructibility of potsherds gives a false impression of the importance of ceramics in the over-all picture of crafts and commerce. This circumstance makes it imperative to give due allowance for possible perishables such as foodstuffs, textiles, wooden objects, and feathers, and also to give the most careful attention to the less distinctive imperishables. Kidder's notes on the artifacts of Uaxactun (1947) are a reminder of the data that stone artifacts may afford.

Pottery may be taken as the springboard for a study of economic relations if one remembers its limitations. To plot the distribution of well-established intrusives for an area wherein there is considerable diversity of style and technique is a natural first step. There are then a number of questions relating specifically to pottery that would follow.

By what means was pottery distributed? Did potters themselves carry it, did buyers journey to pottery-making centers for it, or were there middlemen? Historical accounts and tradition refer to a merchant class in Mesoamerica, but such records do not prove that all pottery was distributed in this way nor do they prove that a merchant class existed when ceramic exchange began or that the two sprang up simultaneously. The archaeological record does not give promise of throwing light on such a question, although one may speculate on the possible relations between a merchant class and volume of trade, and may seek evidence of differences in volume of trade in different periods.

What types of pottery were traded most frequently and most extensively? Were certain functional categories favored? Was elaborately decorated ware most popular and to what extent was plain utility pottery exchanged? Are there indications of preference for wares of superior technical quality? These are questions with which the archaeologist feels more at home.

The functional approach has general interest, but its possibilities are limited by sketchy knowledge of function of various forms. In so far as function can be inferred with reasonable confidence, this lead should be followed. The comparison of different ceramic categories may seem to be asking the obvious, but it would be a grave mistake to assume that only the most showy or the best-finished wares were traded. There is, in fact, reason to give more attention to the simple, utility wares. The lack of distinctiveness of this class of pottery leads to neglect of evidence and an incomplete picture. This fact can be appreciated by the technologist because every now and then unique paste composition shows that some plain, inconspicuous sherd of utility ware came from a distant source.

It is clear, even from the present state of knowledge, that in Mesoamerica the most elaborate and showy wares are not always the most widely distributed. There may be more than one explanation of this situation. Aside from the question of function—the possibility that vessels made for ritual purposes would not be traded—there are practical considerations. Some of the most elaborate polychromes are technically inferior. The paint and slip are soft and the paste is friable. Not only would they break easily in transport but their surfaces would easily be marred, and abrasion would destroy their value.

The comparison of pottery types with respect to technical quality is direct and the results are conclusive. It is noteworthy that the three types that are probably most widely distributed in Mesoamerica, Thin Orange from the Classic period, Fine Orange and Plumbate from the post-Classic, are technically outstanding although they do not compare with many of the polychromes in elaborateness of decoration. The distinctiveness of the paste composition of Thin Orange and Plumbate and their technical homogeneity leave no ground for doubt that each originated in a single center. The extent of territory over which they are distributed and the numbers in which they are found suggest that they were produced in larger quantities for trade than for home use. Were it not for the effigies of Thin Orange, a monochrome type, its style might not attract attention. It is well finished and either plain or slightly decorated with simple incising and punctation. One may find simplicity of form and decoration pleasing, but not all Mesoamerican people were puritanical in their tastes, as is shown by the ornateness of many types. The most striking characteristic of Thin Orange is its strength and extreme thinness of vessel wall. Fine Orange is distinguished technically by a very dense, fine-textured, hard paste. It attained high craftsmanship but nevertheless is simple in style compared with many of the polychromes. Plumbate with its semivitreous glaze, its interesting color range, occasional iridescence, and extreme hardness is beyond question the most outstanding technically, not only of the three but of all Mesoamerican wares. Apparently it was also the most extensively traded. The wide distribution of these three types points to the possibility of a general preference for pottery that is technically superior. This question of valuation can be followed easily in the study and comparison of types known to have been traded with those which are restricted in distribution. Trade is inevitably influenced by conditions such as the relations between peoples, sources of conflict, and complementary crafts or resources, which are independent of the demand for quality in pottery. If, despite these factors, trade pottery shows a consistently high technical standard, it would seem indicative of conscious selection on the basis of serviceability.

The relative popularity of different kinds of pottery will reflect general standards and valuations. There may be also regional differences in standards and preferences, and it is of interest to know if people who were making pottery for trade met special demands. If this question seems to suggest a degree of economic advancement we are not accustomed to associate with prewheel potters, it may be well to recall Clark's discussion of the trade with Arctic hunters carried on by Swedish boat-axe people who controlled the source of flint in Scania. Clark (1952, p. 252) comments: "It is understandable that the southerners should have sought to obtain what they wanted of the Arctic hunter-fishers by developing a line of trade already established in the north, and it is most interesting to observe that nine-tenths of the flint celts are gouges resembling the stone ones which form an integral element in the circumpolar cultural zone. Evidently the boat-axe people found it easier to create a market in flint artifacts by reproducing forms already familiar to the natives of the northern territories. Indeed, there is little doubt that the flint gouge was manufactured originally for the Arctic market and was taken into use in southern Sweden, Denmark and contiguous areas as a result of acculturation—a reminder that cultural borrowing no more flows in one direction than does trade itself."

When a well-defined pottery type is widely and extensively distributed, it may be possible to obtain large enough collections from different regions for systematic comparison. Samples adequate for statistical study are necessary to demonstrate either presence or absence and significant differences in proportions. When such differences are found, they may reflect either selection from the range of forms, finishes and decorative elaborations normally produced in a pottery-making center, or actual response of potters to trade demands through modification of technique or style. The style of a type as it is known in its center of production can be compared with that of the same type where it occurs as an intrusive, and the latter can be compared in turn with native types. Differences in the first instance and similarities in the second would afford grounds for postulating that demand had affected production. Within the Mesoamerican field, Plumbate has seemed to offer the best opportunity for following this question. From the standpoint of distribution and size of collections, it is exceptional, but lack of knowledge of its center of production has been a disadvantage. The review that has been made was limited to the type alone, which was an unnecessary restriction (Shepard, 1948, pp. 113–14). Of the several differences in distribution that were noted, the comparatively high proportion of effigies of Mexican gods in the Valley of Mexico seemed most significant. Since Plumbate potters are believed to have been Pipil people of Mexican origin, these effigies may have held an integral place among the various vessels they normally made. It is not surprising that people who worshipped the gods represented should obtain the effigies in greater number than the peoples of Guatemala and Salvador who had a different pantheon. In this case, consequently, the distribution suggests selective trade but does not afford basis for postulating that trade modified the style of the pottery.

Another question to consider is the relation of natural resources to the growth of pottery centers. Did communities or regions where pottery was made not only for home use but also for trade have access to superior clay or rare decorative media or was it the potters' skill, the excellence of their decoration that made their ware popular beyond the limits of their own village? There is no reason to expect an either/or answer. A high quality clay can arouse a potter to greater effort, and new experiments and special skills will not find full expression in poor materials. The people who made Thin Orange pottery had developed exceptional skill, but they could not have made such delicate, fragile ware without clay having exceptional workability and dry strength. Plumbate slip clay has unusual properties but it was through special firing that its qualities were brought out. It does not follow, however, that the question of the relations between natural and human resources is pointless. A constant balance does not necessarily result from a direct relation such as this. Valuable resources may be neglected on the one hand; on the other, potters may be stimulated by needs and desires that are independent of the color and workability of their clay or the quality of their pigments. Consequently, each set of conditions calls for independent analysis and for survey of local resources along with the analysis of pottery.

These various questions may suggest studies of pottery that is readily recognized as foreign to the local ceramic tradition—pottery that generally occurs in minor proportions and presumably was not essential to the domestic economy but merely supplemented the local output. Such pottery can be identified in the field by simple inspection because it is conspicuously different from the common types.

No less pertinent to the subject of the economics of the potter's craft is the question of specialization and exchange within a region where pottery appears to be stylistically uniform. Such uniformity is generally considered indicative of the sharing of technical and stylistic standards by a group of pottery-making communities. But ethnographic records remind us that a comparable distribution of pottery types may be brought about by various trade relations: one village may supply all the pottery for the settlements of a region; a number of villages may produce distinctive pottery in consequence of special resources and unique local tradition, and general distribution and intermingling may be brought about by exchange; the production of certain essential forms may be general and a few villages may specialize in more elaborate types made for trade.

How can similarity arising from a common tradition and actual identity resulting from a single source of supply be differentiated? Paste composition holds the most promising key whenever there are different geologic formations and ceramic resources within the region under consideration. The answers are not simple or self-evident, however, for the question always arises whether pottery or raw material was brought into a village. As I have suggested in another connection, requirements and availability of the material have a bearing on the question. Minerals that are rare and treasured will be sought at a distance if necessary; those for which substitutes are abundant are less likely to be, and when the material belongs to a class of which the varieties could be recognized by a petrographer but not by the potter—sands from different drainages, for example—the chances that the potter will go beyond the nearest source of supply are very slight indeed. Consequently, detailed analyses are often required. The strength of the circumstantial evidence that can be obtained will also depend in part on the number of villages making pottery. When centers in different parts of an area are each making special types of pottery that are intermingled by trade to give the appearance of homogeneity, evidence is found in contrast of local materials from different localities and decreasing frequencies of occurrence with distance from point of origin. Although distance from source of supply would affect the quantity of raw materials transported no less than that of pottery, it is the nature of materials as well as the number of them derived from the same source that is important. Generalizations such as these are not as convincing as, and often less suggestive than, examples. An illustration of local specialization and extensive trade, which will serve to indicate the importance of geologic diversity and reinforcement of one line of evidence by another, is afforded by the glaze-paint area of the Upper Rio Grande Valley (Shepard, 1942).

These suggestions and comments on the economics of pottery are offered, not without realization of the difficulties involved in the identification of intrusive pottery. This is a first consideration. Were it impossible or impractical to identify intrusives, the questions that might be raised would be subjects for speculation, not points that could be tested by observation and correlation of data. Prediction regarding the practicability of identifying trade pottery is likely to be unconvincing. It is only through studies in which there is thorough sampling and systematic analysis that the reliability and value of such investigations can be weighed.

CONTRIBUTIONS OF POTTERY TO THE STUDY OF CULTURE HISTORY

POTTERY AS SOURCE MATERIAL FOR THE STUDY OF DECORATIVE ART

The archaeologist generally deals with design as a criterion for the classification of pottery types. He uses it along with various physical properties to establish time markers and is therefore concerned with the typical. He learns to make the most of potsherds, recognizing telltale design elements and key fragments of structure. This is a far call from the approach of the art historian, who looks upon ceramic decoration as one phase of the aesthetic expression of a people and studies it in relation to others. To him, that which is rare has a significance, no less than the typical, for it may represent the work of the original artist unconsciously establishing the canons of a future style. Since the art historian is concerned with subtleties of style and the complete artistic expression, his study demands entire vessels. Sherds are of secondary importance, their value depending largely on how clearly their place in the whole can be visualized. At its best, pottery affords a rich field for the art historian and his researches in turn form an important chapter in cultural history.

It may be well to recall the range of artistic expression which pottery affords. Its purposes, together with its technique and form, are diverse. At one extreme are simple embellishments that have no relation to a vessel's function. Gouged fillets or incised zigzags relieve the plainness of a cook pot, but the stew is just as savory without them. At the other extreme are elaborately painted and modeled ritual vessels. Modeling can transform the vessel into the image of a god, and the presence of the proper symbols may be essential to the efficacy of the ceremony. Ceramic art is then religious art.

Paralleling the diversity of purpose of pottery decoration are differences in proficiency and specialization of the decorator. As long as pottery making is a household craft, its decoration is popular art; it represents prevalent standards and average tastes and it includes the expression of the beginner and the inept along with that of the capable and experienced. When specialization occurs and household industries become trades, decoration is in the hands of a few proficient craftsmen who, bringing their full time and energy to their work, may develop a skill akin to that of the artist. They work largely within the tradition of their culture and are influenced by popular demands, but their specialization also gives them responsibility for the standards of their trade and may thus partially free them from the grip of tradition and give them some incentive to originate. Still another possibility is the appearance of specialists in decoration. An artist, rather than the potter, paints the vessel. One is reminded of the famous San Ildefonso potters, Julian and Maria Martinez. From the archaeological field there is the example of Maya stucco-painted pottery with figure painting in a style comparable to that of mural and codex painting (Kidder, Jennings, and Shook, 1946, p. 218 ff.). Although these suggestions are in part speculative, there is no question of the differences in the decorator's status, which means that pottery affords a wide sampling of aesthetic expression. One of the first problems that arises in the study of style is to learn, if possible, whether one is dealing with folk or professional art.

The diverse purposes of ceramic decoration and the differences in experience and position of the decorator are matched by the choice of decorative techniques which pottery affords. Probably no other industry affords the opportunity for exercise of a comparable range of techniques. Weaving limits decoration to a two-dimensional field and imposes mechanical limitations on the forms of design. Picking out a design stitch by stitch is quite a different thing from painting or carving it freely and swiftly in response to impulse and mental image. Wood, soft stone, and bone can be carved or engraved; but they are harder than clay, they cannot be molded or modeled, and some of them do not hold color well. Metal likewise presents obvious restrictions. Clay, on the contrary, lends itself equally well to plastic and to graphic art.

Still another advantage of pottery lies in its abundant occurrence and frequent replacement, which means that the history of a style can be followed in detail. Studies of early art often reflect a predisposition to inquire into the beginnings of things. There are many theories of the origin of art—original, brilliant, and stimulating, but speculative and inconclusive because direct evidence is lacking. This fascination with origins sometimes distracts our interest from more fruitful fields. It is a temptation to argue that the student of early art should curb his ambition somewhat and give relatively more attention to the course of development and the influencing factors during periods for which there is ample evidence. The specialist who brings experience and sensitiveness to this field and who studies pottery decoration in relation to other forms of art makes a contribution to archaeology and cultural history as well as to his own field, for he has an unusual opportunity to study the causes of change and to follow the influences of foreign contact.

CERAMIC DEVELOPMENT AS A PHASE OF TECHNOLOGICAL HISTORY

When artifacts are analyzed in order to evaluate man's technological advancement, it is usual to consider their function—as far as it can be ascertained or inferred—their form and variety, and the quality of their workmanship. Less direct, but no less pertinent, is the extent to which they reflect the craftsman's understanding of the peculiar properties of the substances with which he works. This approach is especially important in the field of ceramics because the potter modified clay in so many ways and actually changed it to a different kind of material in firing. Consequently, pottery gives evidence of the intelligence with which man has used materials, and of his understanding of their potentialities. This is a neglected field of research, partly because of its technical nature and partly because the establishment of relative chronologies has been a consuming task in recent years. Nevertheless, archaeologists have occasionally ventured to make estimates of technological development on the basis of various properties or on apparent degree of specialization.

Perhaps the most common basis for judging stage of ceramic advancement is the refinement and elaboration of pottery. A series of wares such as unslipped plain, slipped monochrome, and painted polychrome may mark sequent stages in a ceramic history. Such a scheme of classification has the advantages of simplicity and ease of recognition of criteria, but it does not constitute a technological approach; the monochrome pottery, for example, may be more sound than the polychrome.

Pottery-making methods offer a more direct means of technological evaluation. Hand-modeling, casting, and throwing on a wheel or open firing and use of a kiln represent major steps in progress. These changes, however, mark only the main outline of ceramic history, and one might work in a large field, such as American Indian ceramics, and yet be confined to one or two stages. For finer divisions we turn to the various specific properties.

Certain basic technical qualities are common to all classes of pottery. These include strength, hardness or resistance to abrasion, porosity and permeability, degree of freedom from defects, and uniformity of color. There are also properties that can be judged in relation to the adaptation of a vessel to its function: one might cite as examples low thermal expansion for a cook pot, permeability for a vessel intended to keep water cool, low porosity for a vessel used for storage of liquids. Finally there are properties that determine the success of special effects, such as fit of slip, permanence of paint, and completeness of vitrification of glaze.

The definition of properties such as those enumerated constitutes an evaluation of technical quality. There is a fundamental difference between describing the technical properties of pottery and defining a stage of technological development. Evaluation of technical quality is a comparatively simple matter of defining end results without regard to the means by which they were attained. The specimens hold a tangible record that is easily read if reliable methods of analysis and measurement are chosen. This is merely a selective kind of description. On the other hand, judgment of technological progress is approached from the viewpoint of the potentialities of materials and the purposes and requirements of the artifacts made from them. It is necessary to consider the potter's resources, the properties of raw materials, and the techniques that were employed. This is not merely a matter of identifying methods, but of understanding their effect on the quality of the product.

Comparison of the technical quality of pottery of different periods or places is a comparatively straightforward procedure, but the establishment of the superiority of one ceramic complex over another does not necessarily prove that there was also superior knowledge and technical skill, or actual ceramic advancement. Clays differ so greatly that they may be responsible for considerable differences in quality for which the potter deserves no credit.

One of the first questions the ceramist asks is, To what extent were the properties of pottery affected by the quality of available ceramic materials? Only when this relation is defined can we judge how intelligently and skillfully the potter worked within the limitations imposed by natural resources. To take a few examples, when pottery is exceptionally strong or resistant to abrasion, is the fact to be attributed primarily to the fusion point of the clay or to firing methods? When vessel walls are unusually thin, were plasticity and dry strength of the clay conditioning factors or should the credit go principally to the potter's skill? To ask these questions is not to imply that properties of pottery can be attributed solely to either quality of clay or expertness of the potter; neither can be entirely independent of the other. But no matter how direct the relation may be, the effects of one must not be mistaken for those of the other.

In view of this problem, a thorough study of technical development requires that the ceramic resources of a pottery-making center be studied and the properties of available clays and pigments tested. If an archaeological program includes technological pottery analyses, the ceramist should plan for such a survey, and, in any event, the excavator should always be alert for samples of ceramic materials that may be found in excavation.

The potter's methods do not all have equal significance for an evaluation of technical advancement; for example, different methods of building a vessel may cause less variation in its properties than methods of firing. A fundamental question, therefore, is whether or not pottery was fired well enough to mature the clay, thus obtaining low porosity, high strength, and uniformity of oxidation or reduction. Provided a sherd has not been leached by the action of soil waters, refiring will show the potentialities of the paste within the potter's temperature range. A temperature of 950°C, for example, might be taken as a standard. Measurement of changes in physical properties on refiring affords means of judging the effectiveness of original firing. It is important to remember, however, that strength, hardness, and low porosity were not always sought. In a ritual vessel, for example, they may have been sacrificed for high luster or bright colors. It is therefore desirable to consider properties in relation to function. In this connection, it is well to recall that technical properties affect both usefulness —durability, adaptation to function—and attractiveness, that in fact the same property may contribute to both. The smooth surface is not only more pleasing to the hand and eye than the rough one, it is also easier to keep clean. The skill exercised to obtain symmetry of form simultaneously contributes to thinness and uniformity of vessel walls. There is no need to draw a line between utility and aesthetic quality, however, if the point of approach is the intelligence with which materials are used and processes employed to gain particular effects.

The fact that this type of investigation is intensive and specialized points to the importance of studying it in the general context of the material aspects of culture and placing this in turn in the culture as a whole, as far as it can be reconstructed. Different crafts and the knowledge and skills on which they depend do not necessarily develop at a uniform rate, since the needs and interests from which they spring do not follow a simple course. Moreover, natural resources may favor one craft more than another, just as the stimulating effects of cultural contacts do not act equally on all of them. Consequently, in judging the stage of a people's technological advancement, it is imperative to balance ceramic data with that of other industries. This insistence is motivated by more than the desire to avoid distortion, because the activities of a people are not unrelated nor without their effect on one another. The artifacts that are left us present the challenge to find evidences of these interrelations.

* * * * *

Some of the lines of investigation here proposed are untried. We have been occupied with the task of ordering objects in time and space, arrangements which are essential to an adequate understanding of origins and relations. Although pottery has served as a handmaiden in this task, it is also an integral part of the cultural content. Ceramic technology should serve to reveal some of its facets in this context and to bring it into focus with the concerns of man.

In the long course of his history, man has been learning to understand his physical environment and to make himself at home in the world. At first he learned by shaping and altering for his use and convenience the materials nature offered. Thus the simple tools and utensils that he left not only tell a story of technological progress, but also hold the imprint of early steps toward the sciences. It can hardly be said that we are pushing evidence too far if we look at pottery in this light, for the archaeologist is forced by his dependence upon material remains and the consequent meagerness of his data to probe carefully and fully and to bring all his gleanings together in order to discern their meaning. Thus the various special interests which pottery arouses contribute to a common endeavor.

Ceramic Terms Referring to Materials, Properties, and Techniques

NOMENCLATURE is a subject that has been taken with relish, scorn, facetiousness, indifference, and seriousness, according to individual temperament. One man is impatient with what appears to be quibbling, another dislikes compromise and resents arbitrariness, still another becomes earnestly concerned with the benefits of common usage and eager to help tidy the household.

Whatever a person's attitude may be, the need for an occasional, critical review of terminology will be brought home to him when he considers the various ways in which the technical terms that aid—and encumber—our discipline have worked themselves into our vocabulary. There is coinage by individuals having a happy faculty for that art, borrowing from other sciences forced by the exigencies of the moment, and studied or groping selection. If a word expresses a fertile idea or sharpens perception, its place is assured; but then again there are words that seem to have wormed their way into our vocabulary simply because they have been drummed into our ears. Sometimes there is just a suspicion that we enjoy an easy way of impressing the layman or that we are willing to accept a veil for our ignorance. After all, we do have to talk occasionally about things that we do not understand, and an impressive word is a simple face-saving device. We are scarcely aware how these processes of incorporating terms into usage go on, but, sooner or later, some conscientious individual calls for systematization. Then the difficulty of the task that is presented depends, in no small measure, on whether or not our terminology has grown like Topsy or submitted to the discipline of guiding principles.

These remarks are not made in a spirit of cynicism or scorn. There is a genuine and legitimate satisfaction in the use of precise and well-established terms. Beyond that, we bear an obligation in our choice and employment of technical terms because words are the tools by which ideas are assembled and the direct means of communicating them. It is with this thought that I would like to consider a few principles that might guide efforts to improve terminology.

Discussion of terminology brings out the attachments and repulsions most of us have for particular words. Odd, chance associations tend to build up an emotional attitude of which we are comfortably unaware until it is disclosed by our disagreement with another person. Besides being a source of difficulty in conferences on terminology, individual attitudes toward words block the general acceptance of any system of terminology which a group of experts adopts. One way to break this block is to give more thought to clarification of concepts, understanding of the processes designated, and testing the theories and assumptions implied. This, it seems to me, is a basic principle. Consider how easily two people can fall into debate over the choice of a word for a given technique, when a correct understanding of the nature of the technique would leave no ground for argument. This circumstance is a reminder that contributions to terminology come indirectly through discovery no less than through formal discussion and action. Fresh insights are likely to come unannounced, in the flash of a moment. We cannot decide that we will sit down in conference at 10:30 Wednesday morning and have new ideas. Consequently, the results of conferences on terminology are more likely to be critical than creative. Formal discussion may be an effective means of pruning the tree but less often starts new shoots. This is one of the reasons why conferences seem unproductive to some people, but if they merely help weed out obviously undesirable terms they perform a useful service.

There are some unhappily chosen terms that even the confirmed pedant would not attempt to ban, so long have they been used and so deeply have they burrowed into the literature. Examples from the field of ceramics that at once come to mind are temper and plumbate. Such words serve our purpose when the thing designated is perfectly familiar, but it may be a trifle embarrassing to explain them to the layman, and there is always a lurking chance that they harbor misunderstanding here and there within the profession. Plumbate, a chemical misnomer, suggests a lead glaze, and some people may still think the pottery has such a glaze. The only thing to do about such terms is to keep them from increasing by eliminating them before it is too late. It is reasonable to suppose that their use can be discouraged more effectively by calling attention to inappropriate derivation and false implication than by issuing formally certified systems of nomenclature. Periodic sessions on nomenclature can help purge our vocabulary of undesirable terms by catching them early and showing their faults.

The expression "unhappy choices" covers a multitude of poor terms. They are less bewildering if they are sorted according to the reasons why their use is ill-advised. In the process of analysis we should find bases for judging them. One of the easiest ways to obtain a precise term is to borrow it from another science. The danger is that we may acquire a cutting edge that we do not know how to use because the more strictly a term is defined, the greater the chances of misuse.

Analogies between phenomena may be assumed when actually superficial similarity covers fundamental differences. There is the same possibility of introducing false analogies when words from other industries are borrowed to describe ceramic techniques. Cloisonné as applied to a ceramic decorative technique is an extreme example that was rejected before it became fixed in the literature. There are also cases of incomplete analogy. For example, names of vessel shapes used in classical archaeology often designate function as well as form and consequently are not strictly applicable to comparable New World shapes of unknown function. False analogies can be subtle means of introducing misconceptions, but again the lack of correspondence may be obvious, and the term is used despite the incongruity out of sheer necessity or lack of resource for an appropriate word, and eventually a new meaning is established through usage.

More troublesome at times than borrowed scientific and technical terms are common words redefined to give them special meaning. The simplicity and familiarity of the word throws us off guard and, of course, it is especially confusing to the layman. Suppose, for example, that someone is describing pottery decoration in which vertical stripes are common. To spare himself the bother of repeatedly using the same adjective, he warns his readers that when he says stripe he means vertical stripe. The next step is for someone to publish a glossary including this definition of stripe. How is one to know thereafter whether the word stripe is used according to Webster or as "technically" defined for the convenience of someone describing a particular style? Unusual technical words may offend by their pretense or discourage by their unfamiliarity, but at least they stand as little flags to warn that something special is designated. Yet, a word of caution should not be mistaken for blanket condemnation. One cannot ignore the extent to which common words have been whittled to the needs of the scientist. The physicist defines work as "the product of the displacement produced by a force and the component of the force in the direction of the displacement," but context generally shows whether he means this or just plain labor.

The redefinition of common words for technical use may be related in origin to the tendency to give specific meanings to generic terms. It seems very likely that this tendency marks a phase in the development of a subject, the phase of intensive, detailed study in which generalization is neglected for specific description. The generic terms are there because the pioneers of the subject took a broad view and occasionally allowed themselves to indulge in a bit of philosophizing, whereas those who came after concentrated their attention on giving the subject detail and precision.

Another result of anxiety for precision is the adoption of arbitrary limits on range of dimensions indicated by certain words. "A vessel foot has a height-breadth ratio less than 0.5. For a leg, the same ratio is greater than 0.5." We are left to find a term for the support with a height-breadth ratio of 0.5, but the point is that the limit was not chosen as a result of a study of norms in the proportions of supports but merely because a half seems a natural figure to choose.

To counteract the negative impression the above remarks may have created, it will be well to summarize them in positive form. When adopting terms let us: (1) get behind words to establish facts and clarify ideas, (2) draw upon the wealth of terms offered by the sciences and technology and look carefully to the soundness of analogies, (3) accept standard definitions of familiar words from popular usage and as far as possible use words that are self-explanatory, (4) remember the value and need of generic as well as specific terms, and (5) base limiting terms on reliable statistical evidence.

A word regarding rules may be in order. There are those who do not care to be cramped by rules and principles. They have a point. When we draw up rules, we are handicapped by the same human limitations that were responsible for the faults of terminology we are endeavoring to correct. Our nomenclature will continue to grow in unpredictable ways; meanings will change and we will twist words to our purpose, despite the dour earnestness of the purist. To condemn the process is to berate human nature. A principle represents an attempt to generalize, and perhaps one has to go to mathematics for generalizations without exceptions. It does not follow, however, that we should give no thought to principles, but only that they should be examined critically and used as staves and not as tethers.

The short list of terms which follows obviously makes no pretense at comprehensiveness. It is a selected list and includes principally borrowed words which are none too familiar in archaeology. They present no need for modification of definition because they are completely applicable to our field. Also included are some more familiar words whose meanings I have re-examined.

ADSORPTION.   The adherence of one material on the surface of another, usually in monomolecular layers. A phenomenon to be distinguished from absorption. Water adsorbed by clay is held on the surface of particles by loose bonding force; when absorbed, it penetrates the pores between particles.

BASE EXCHANGE CAPACITY.   The maximum capacity of a material to adsorb ions (atoms or groups of atoms carrying electrical charges). It is expressed in milli-equivalents per 100 grams of clay. The clay minerals differ greatly in base exchange capacity, depending on their atomic structure. The nature of adsorbed ions has a marked effect on the properties of the adsorbing minerals.

Chroma. A color variable corresponding approximately to saturation or purity. Black, white, and gray (achromatic colors) have zero saturation. Chroma, the percentage of hue in a color, is proportional to departure of the color from gray of equivalent value. Chromas are described as weak, medium, and strong (cf. Hue and Value).

Clay minerals. A group of minerals forming extremely small crystalline particles and consisting essentially of hydrous aluminum silicate, although magnesium or iron partially or fully replaces alumina in some, and alkalies or alkaline earths are essential constituents of others. The principal groups of clay minerals are kaolin, montmorillonite, and illite. Clay may contain a single clay mineral or be composed of a mixture of several, and in addition, most clays contain varying amounts of nonclay minerals.

Colloid. This term does not distinguish material of a certain chemical composition but rather material whose particle size falls in the range between molecules and microscopic particles. There is no break between these three size ranges, but for convenience the limits of the colloidal range are defined as 500 and 1 millimicron (five thousandths and one millionth of a millimeter). The colloidal range is singled out because the reduction of coarser material to this state greatly increases surface area, in consequence of which special properties are developed. Clay not infrequently includes particles in the colloidal range, the effect of which is to increase plasticity and volume of water required to bring the clay to a plastic state, and also to lower fusion point. Colloids have the property of remaining in suspension in water for long periods. They therefore increase the body of a slip mixture and aid in its application, but high colloidal content will cause excessive shrinkage.

Compacted. A condition of surface, resulting from rubbing with a hard, smooth tool. The term *polished* is reserved for that surface quality which reflects light specularly and hence is characterized by glossiness or luster. The compacted surface is not necessarily glossy since tactual smoothness is retained after firing shrinkage has destroyed luster.

Curie Point. The temperature above which a ferromagnetic (highly magnetic) substance becomes paramagnetic (weakly magnetic). Each ferromagnetic substance has its characteristic Curie Point. The change is reversible and ferromagnetism increases with drop in temperature.

Deflocculation. The separation of aggregate particles into the individual particles of which they are composed. This can be accomplished with deflocculating agents such as ammonia and salts of alkali metals. Deflocculation improves the quality of slip by increasing the proportion of particles in suspension through reduction in particle size (cf. Flocculation).

Eutectic. The mixture of two or more substances in the proportions that give it the lowest melting point of any mixture of the given constituents. The composition is definite and the melting point sharp.

EVENNESS.   A condition of surface marked by absence of elevations and depressions. A leveled surface is produced by scraping with a firm tool but not by hand-shaping. Evenness should not be confused with smoothness, which refers to texture.

FLOCCULATION.   Clustering or coagulation of suspended particles. If a suspension is maintained by the repulsion of charged particles, neutralization of the charges will cause particles to gather into groups or flocks and precipitate.

FLUX.   Any substance that promotes fusion.

GRAINY.   A texture characterized by coarse temper particles. The term is proposed as a substitute for *granular*, which in common usage refers to the texture of material composed entirely of grains of approximately the same size range and is therefore inapplicable to tempered pottery.

HUE.   The variable that usually determines the position of a color in the spectrum. With reference to wave length of light, the spectrum forms a straight line progression. Hues are arranged in a full circle. If the spectrum is curved around the hue circle, there is a gap between the short wave lengths (violet) and the long (red). This gap is closed in the hue circle by purple, which combines the wave length of the two extremes of the visible scale. Hue is described by such basic color names as red, yellow, green, and blue, and is designated by reference to the wave length of the monochromatic light that it matches (cf. VALUE and CHROMA).

LEATHER-HARD.   The condition of a clay body or paste when it has become firm but not dry. It is not a state that is strictly defined, but clay workers judge it confidently from experience. A vessel in the leather-hard state can be handled without risk of deformation because the clay is no longer plastic and it can be carved or incised without chipping because it still retains considerable moisture.

MODULUS OF RUPTURE.   A measure of transverse strength expressed as breaking weight per unit cross section of a test bar.

OVERFIRED.   Fired to or above the point at which defects such as warping, bloating, and blistering occur. Either excessive temperature or too rapid firing can cause these defects. The term has at times been loosely applied to pottery that was assumed to have been fired higher than the average of its type, although the color difference on which judgment was based may have been due to more complete oxidation rather than higher temperatures. Ambiguity will be avoided if the expression is limited to pottery that shows firing defects.

OXIDIZED POTTERY.   Pottery in which the constituents in the paste have taken up as much oxygen as they can. The color of such pottery will depend on the amount, particle size, distribution, state and combination of impurities, of which iron compounds are by far the most important. The color will be white, buff, orange, or red. Pottery which has had only a short firing in direct contact with the gases formed in burning fuel is often incompletely oxidized. The interior of the vessel wall often contains unburned carbonaceous matter, even when the surface appears oxidized, or carbonaceous matter is burned out but the iron compounds are not brought to their highest state of oxidation. The surface itself frequently shows different degrees of oxidation from the effect on limited areas of jets of gas from smoking fuel. Oxidation can therefore be uniform but incomplete, or uneven. The unoxidized matter may be an original component of the clay or carbon from a smoky fire. The original condition of clay, and the temperature, atmosphere, and length of firing are all factors that affect the extent of oxidation. Adjectives can be used to indicate degree of oxidation, incompletely or partially when surface is oxidized and cores unoxidized, unevenly when there is surface variation. The expression *fired in oxidizing atmosphere* has been used to describe oxidized pottery. In so far as it suggests greater uniformity of firing conditions that are obtained by simple methods and tends to create an over-simplified concept of the factors that affect color, it is open to criticism. For pottery description, the term *oxidized* is preferable.

OXIDIZING ATMOSPHERE.   A firing atmosphere that contains free oxygen and promotes oxidation of substances in clay, principally carbonaceous matter and compounds of iron. An oxidizing atmosphere is obtained when there is good draft, but products of combustion from the burning of fuel are always mixed with the air and the proportion of oxygen in the gases surrounding pottery in a direct open fire is therefore highly variable. Rate of oxidation depends on the proportion of oxygen, temperature, density of the clay, and properties of the material oxidized.

PERMEABILITY.   A property which permits the flow of liquids or gases through a body. It differs from porosity in that not all of the pores enter into the system of connected capillaries that extends from one surface to the other. It is measured in terms of volume of fluid that will pass through a given area of unit thickness under specified head pressure.

POROSITY.   Volume of pores expressed as a percentage of total volume. *True porosity* is calculated from total pore volume, that is, volume of both open and sealed pores. *Apparent porosity* is calculated from volume of open pores alone— those pores which will absorb water when the piece is soaked. Sealed pores are negligible in low-fired pottery, hence apparent porosity closely approximates true porosity for such wares. Porosity should not be confused with permeability.

REDUCED POTTERY.   Pottery in which the iron oxide is present in the lower state of oxidation. The color is gray, but not all gray pottery is reduced. It may be colored by unoxidized carbonaceous matter or by carbon deposited in firing. Pottery cannot be positively identified as reduced without firing tests. The expression *fired in reducing atmosphere* has been used to describe reduced pottery and sometimes loosely extended as a blanket term for all gray pottery. It is open to the same criticisms as the expression *fired in oxidizing atmosphere* (see under OXIDIZED POTTERY).

RESIDUAL CLAY.   A clay occurring in the same position as the parent rock from which it was formed. Igneous rocks are the primary source of clay and residual deposits derived from them are classed as *primary clays*. The term "residual" is broader since it includes clays found in places where they have originated from the decomposition of a sedimentary rock.

SINTERING.   Heating to the point of incipient vitrification, at which some cementing of particles occurs as a result of the softening of constituents of the body.

SMOOTH.   A quality of surface texture. Since there are degrees of smoothness, and this quality is produced by different methods, the expression *tactually smooth* is proposed for the texture obtained by rubbing a leather-hard surface with a hard, extremely smooth tool. The carefully wiped surface of a fine-textured, plastic clay may appear smooth, but the burnished surface is much smoother to the touch.

SUSPENSION.   Dispersion of a finely divided solid in a solid, liquid, or gas. Contrasted with solutions which are characterized by molecular dimension of the dispersed matter. Used with reference to clay, dispersion of fine clay particles in water.

TEXTURE.   A property determined primarily by the particle size, shape, grading, and arrangement of particles. Surface texture is also influenced by finishing method. The expression *apparent texture* is proposed for paste descriptions based on unaided visual inspection since the finest grades cannot be seen and relative color contrast influences judgment. In defining particle size by microscopic methods, the Wentworth grade scale is used.

TUFF.   Indurated volcanic ash. This term should not be confused with tufa, which is a loose, porous form of calcium carbonate deposited from solution.

VALUE.   A color variable corresponding to lightness or brightness, the visually apparent reflectance of a surface under a given set of conditions. Values are described as dark, medium, and light (cf. HUE and CHROMA).

VITRIFICATION.   The formation of glassy material in a ceramic body. Vitrification is considered complete when pore spaces are filled and exterior volume is reduced to a minimum. *Vitrification range*, the time-temperature period between incipient vitrification, when glass can first be detected, and overfiring or deformation caused by increased fluidity of constituents of the body.

VOLCANIC ASH.   Uncemented volcanic ejecta consisting mainly of fragments under

4 cm. in diameter. *Vitric ash,* volcanic ash composed mainly of glassy fragments. *Crystal ash,* composed predominantly of crystals blown out during eruption. *Lithic ash,* composed largely of previously formed rock fragments.

WATER SMOKING.   Removal of mechanically held water during the early stages of firing. The term is derived from the fact that moisture in the form of condensed steam appears as white smoke issuing from the kiln. If the temperature is raised too rapidly, the evolution of steam may cause spalling or cracking. In commercial work, a temperature of 120°–130°C is commonly used for water smoking, and the time required for it varies, depending partly on density of clay. Native potters often recognize the importance of water smoking and pre-heat their pottery or warm it gradually.

YIELD POINT.   The shearing force that will just cause flow of a plastic mass. The more plastic clays have high yield points and long extension before fracture. Yield point is affected by the binding force of surface films and by extensibility which results from sliding on each other of platelike particles lubricated by water.

Notes on the Clay Minerals

THE definition and classification of the clay minerals is based on their atomic structure and chemical composition. Structure is not a matter of merely academic interest; it clarifies our understanding of the relationships and properties of the crystalline clay minerals—and all the clay minerals are crystalline except allophane, which is amorphous by definition. Allophane is somewhat variable in composition and has not been fully investigated, but the term is now more restricted in application than formerly because X-ray diffraction studies have shown that many clays once considered amorphous are actually crystalline.

The structure of the crystalline clay minerals is described by reference to two atomic configurations which the mineralogist compares to building blocks. One, the silica tetrahedron, has a silicon ion surrounded by four equidistant oxygen ions corresponding in position to the four corners of a tetrahedron. The other, the alumina or magnesia octahedron, has an aluminum or magnesium ion surrounded by six oxygens or hydroxyls corresponding in position to the corners of an octahedron. The force of the unsatisfied valence (combining power) of these atomic clusters is compared to a cement which binds the blocks together. Both types of clusters form sheets which enter into the structure of most of the clay minerals. Silica tetrahedra, with their bases in the same plane and their apexes pointing in the same direction, share oxygens at the basal angles to form a hexagonal net. When hydroxyls replace the oxygens at the apexes, the structure is balanced; that is, the valence is satisfied. This sheet is a unit of hydrated silica. The alumina octahedra join with their oxygens or hydroxyls in closest packing. The structure is balanced when aluminum ions occupy two-thirds of the central positions, or when magnesium ions occupy all the positions. A sheet of alumina octahedra with hydroxyls at the octahedral angles is the basic unit of the aluminum hydroxide mineral, gibbsite, and the corresponding sheet of magnesium octahedra is the basic unit of the magnesium hydroxide mineral, brucite.

A major class of clay minerals, the kaolin group, has a two-layer structure. A second important class, which includes the montmorillonite minerals and the illites, is distinguished by a three-layer unit. There are also clay minerals composed of two- and three-layer units regularly alternated. In addition, certain minerals distinguished by a chain structure are included in the general classification. Only the well-established and more important minerals need be reviewed here. For full descriptions and diagrams the reader is referred to Grim (1953).

The kaolinite group. Among the clay minerals, the members of this group are the simplest and most uniform in composition. They are hydrous aluminum silicates that differ from each other principally in structure. The silica-alumina molecular ratio is 2; bases other than alumina, if present, are impurities. Since kaolin clays, of which kaolinite is the chief constituent, are low in iron, they are white or near-white in color, a property that gives them commercial value for the manufacture of white ware. They are also important in the refractory industry because of their high proportion of alumina.

Kaolinite, which has long been recognized because it occurs in a relatively pure state in some residual clays and occasionally exhibits well-formed crystals of microscopic size, is the most important from the commercial standpoint because it is found in extensive deposits and meets the requirements of high-grade ceramic products. It is also present in many commercially low-grade clays and it has been recognized as a major constituent of soils that were once thought to be composed largely of amorphous oxides and hydroxides.

Structurally, a unit plate of kaolinite is composed of a silica sheet superimposed on a gibbsite sheet with the vertices of the silica tetrahedra pointing in and forming a common layer with the hydroxyls on the inner plane of the octahedral sheet. Two-thirds of the atoms in this layer are shared by both silicon and aluminum and they become oxygens instead of hydroxyls. An important characteristic of this structure is that charges are balanced; there are no unsatisfied bonds on the surfaces of plates. Consequently, kaolinite minerals do not absorb water between plates and expand as do some clay minerals, and their drying shrinkage is low. Their base exchange capacity is likewise low. Structure also influences their relatively low plasticity.

Other minerals of this group, dickite and nacrite, differ in the way in which unit layers are stacked above one another. These are both vein minerals formed by hydrothermal action. Although they are of slight interest commercially because their deposits are small, such deposits may well have been used by handcraft potters.

Halloysite, once considered an amorphous mineral, has the same silica-alumina molecular ratio as kaolinite and a two-layer structure, although it differs in form and is not classed by Grim with the kaolinite minerals. Two varieties are known, one of which is hydrated and alters readily to the other. Electron micrographs have shown that halloysite has a tubular form in contrast to the hexagonal plates of kaolinite. On dehydration, the tubes tend to flatten, unroll or break lengthwise, forming ribbons. Halloysite occurs in hydrothermal deposits and is present, though rare, in soils. When associated with kaolinite, it is difficult to distinguish.

The montmorillonite group. The minerals of this group have similar structure but are characterized by great variability in chemical composition. They have been difficult to investigate because they occur only in extremely fine particles. Electron micrographs of montmorillonite, the minerals from which the group takes its name, show fine plates of irregular outline. The generally accepted unit of montmorillonite structure consists of three sheets, an alumina sheet sandwiched between silica sheets. The vertices of the tetrahedra of both silica sheets point inward, forming on each side of the octahedral sheet a common layer with its hydroxyls. The common ions become oxygens instead of hydroxyls. In the stacking of these units, oxygen layers of adjacent units are opposed, forming a weak bond, which gives the mineral distinct cleavage. Water and other polar molecules are adsorbed between units, causing the swelling or expansion which is so characteristic of bentonite, in which montmorillonite is the chief clay mineral. Chemically, montmorillonite differs from kaolinite in having a higher silica-alumina ratio. According to the theoretical formula without lattice substitutions, it is 4. But montmorillonite always differs from the theoretic formula because of substitutions of aluminum for silicon in the tetrahedral sheet and/or magnesium, iron and other cations in the octahedral sheet. Substitution is limited in the tetrahedral sheet, but total replacement can occur in the octahedral sheet. The replacement of aluminum by magnesium yields the mineral saponite and replacement of aluminum by iron yields nontronite. Electron micrographs have shown that minerals with high substitutions have a lathlike or needle-like form.

Although the theoretical formula for montmorillonite is balanced, the mineral is actually always unbalanced because of substitution. The unbalanced state of one sheet may be partly compensated by that of another sheet of the unit, but only in part. There is always a net charge deficiency which is balanced by exchangeable cations adsorbed between unit layers. This explains the high base exchange capacity of the mineral. The bases generally adsorbed under natural conditions are sodium and calcium. A number of other ions have been substituted experimentally. The exchangeable base in a montmorillonite clay affects its wetting properties. The sodium clays form a gel-like mass when wet and remain in suspension indefinitely. The calcium clays are not as fully dispersed in water; they tend to soften to a granular mass, a large proportion of which settles quickly.

Montmorillonite is the common clay mineral of bentonites, which, as has long been known, are formed by the alteration of volcanic glass. Their origin was postulated from the absence of detrital minerals and presence of minerals characteristic of volcanic rocks even before they were studied in petrographic thin section. Later microscopic examination showed the distinctive structure peculiar to volcanic ash—fragments from the rims of glass bubbles or drawn-out vesicles— clearly preserved after alteration. Volcanic glasses vary in composition; chemically, each is the volcanic counterpart of a crystalline rock. Montmorillonite forms most readily from glasses less silicic than rhyolite although there is evidence that occasionally it is derived from these acid glasses.

Clays high in montmorillonite generally have excessive shrinkage and cannot be used alone for pottery, but this clay mineral also occurs in natural mixtures with kaolinite, and even a small amount—as little as 5 per cent—will have a pronounced effect on the properties of a clay, particularly its plasticity. Montmorillonite also affects the adsorptive power of clays, which fact suggests that the retention of organic paint by certain clays is explained by the presence of some montmorillonite which holds polar molecules between its units.

Illite minerals are mica-like in structure and resemble muscovite in that potassium is an essential constituent. Structurally, muscovite has a three-layer unit similar to that of montmorillonite, but part of the silicon of the tetrahedral layer is always replaced by aluminum and the resultant charge deficiency is balanced by potassium between units, fitting in the perforations of the oxygen sheets. Illites differ from muscovite in having less substitution of aluminum for silicon and partial replacement of potassium by other cations between layers. Although three-layered, the illites are electronically balanced and therefore nonexpandable. They are common in many clays and especially in sediments that predate the Mesozoic, marine sediments, and shales.

These notes will indicate how greatly modern research has changed our concept of the nature of clay. This new concept gives a clearer idea of the possible range of materials that may have been used by prehistoric potters and it offers means of specifically describing and distinguishing potter's clays. Applications are limited in the main to raw material, however, because atomic structure is destroyed in firing. Furthermore, the analysis of raw potter's clay is justified only if composition has special significance because fineness of particle size renders analysis difficult.

Criteria for the Identification of Varieties within Common Classes of Temper

POTTERS have used extensively as temper certain classes of material, such as sand, sherd, and igneous rock. Identification of the class tells something about technique—whether consolidated or unconsolidated material was selected and the relation of properties of the temper to strength, texture, and flaws of the pottery. In so far as classes of temper reflect aspects of technique, their distribution is also of interest. More specific identifications are necessary, however, if the sources of pottery are considered, and the question of the practicability of identifying varieties within widely distributed classes then arises. The following notes will give some idea of the possibilities with respect to four classes. Igneous rock is not included since mineralogical and textural differences clearly mark many types well established by petrographers.

Volcanic ash is widely distributed in several of the important pottery-making areas of America, especially in Mexico, Central America, and the Upper Rio Grande Valley in the Pueblo area. A consideration of the genesis of volcanic ashes will suggest possible means of distinguishing them. They are formed by the eruption of molten rock which, had it cooled at depths within the earth, would have formed a crystalline rock. Sometimes crystallization commences before the lava erupts. If the crystals (phenocrysts) make up a considerable percentage of the ejected material, it is called a crystal ash. Between the extremes of a vitric or glassy ash without mineral inclusions and a crystal ash there is an unbroken series defined by the ratio of glass to minerals. When such material is used as temper, it is not feasible to differentiate pastes by ratio of constituents because our methods of measurement are not applicable to the irregularly shaped particles of glass, but rough estimates of relative proportions can be made and may be useful for identification. For fine-textured ware, potters would choose an ash free from phenocrysts whenever it was available. Crystals combined in varying proportions with vitric ash are common in Mesoamerican pastes, however. The phenocrysts often have perfect crystal form because they developed in the fluid magma without interference from other crystals. When, in the process of weathering, they are separated from the glass and carried short distances in stream beds, they can be distinguished from ordinary stream sand even with the binocular microscope by their glassy clearness, their crystal faces, angularity, and absence of abrasion. The chief minerals that occur as phenocrysts in glass are quartz, sanidine (a form of orthoclase that has crystallized at high temperatures), and plagioclase. There are also many accessory minerals, chief of which in Central American ashes are horn-blendes, pyroxenes, micas, and olivine.

Some glasses contain incipient or skeletal crystals. There are also inclusions called crystallites which lack regular crystal boundaries and have been interpreted as representing a state between the amorphous and the crystalline. They appear as strings of minute globules, clusters of filaments, dendritic and other forms. Although they are not common in the glasses of Mesoamerica, they have diagnostic value when they do occur.

In addition to crystals, a vitric ash may contain rock fragments which constitute another distinctive feature. These are not formed from the glass but are torn from the rock through which the lava passes on its way to the surface.

A lava which contains gases will become a frothy mass when pressure is released as it reaches the surface. It may flow and cool as pumice or be blown into the air and, on cooling, shatter. The texture and structure of vitric ashes are determined largely by the size, shape, and distribution of gas bubbles. The bubbles may be irregularly distributed through a glass, or closely packed, forming a honeycomb-like structure, or drawn into long tubes by the movement of the lava, giving the pumice a fibrous structure. The possible variations are many, but often there are mixtures of different structures in a single deposit. Only experience with the volcanic tempers of a region will show how useful structure is for that region. For example, in the highlands of Guatemala, honeycomb and tubular pumice are both common, but neither has been found constituting a homogeneous temper. There is, however, one form of pumice distinguished by extremely fine vesicles; another is preponderantly tubular and has a silky luster. Each characterizes a particular pottery type or group of pottery types.

When volcanic glass is shattered or pumice is crushed either by natural agencies or by the potter, different textures and fragments of various shapes will be formed, depending on the original structure. If the bubbles are fairly coarse and closely packed, plates will be formed from their sides and multiflanged pieces from their junctures. Thin sections of a paste tempered with such a material show a very characteristic texture in which lunar, forked, and Y-shaped fragments of glass are prominent. If the vesicles of a pumice are very fine, grinding will only produce smaller particles of pumice and this fact affords basis for a major distinction in the vitric ash tempers. These two classes are easily distinguished with the binocular microscope, as well as in thin section. There is also a variety of vitric ash, called perlitic, which has fine concentric curvilinear cracks in a glass free of gas. Perlitic ash has been found in pottery from eastern Salvador and in intrusives in the eastern highlands of Guatemala. It also can be detected with the binocular microscope.

Vitric ashes are often transported long distances by air currents or water and become well sorted in the process. Thus the ash tempers of pottery from the lowlands of Peten, Guatemala, are readily distinguished from those, presumably primary in origin, which characterize pottery of the highlands. Some tempers are composed solely of very minute flakes, which could have been transported long distances by air and are appropriately called volcanic dust.

After deposition, vitric ash may be subject to sufficient pressure to consolidate it. The term "tuff" has been proposed (Wentworth and Williams, 1932) for ash thus hardened or indurated, although previously tuff had been used generically for all volcanic ash. I used it in this general sense up to 1940, and since then have followed the Wentworth-Williams terminology. Tuff that has been pulverized for temper can be recognized by the presence of lumps composed of flakes of ash of the same size and grading as the free flakes. A few aggregates will remain even when a tuff is soft and well pulverized.

Vitric ashes are decomposed in the process of weathering, but traces of the characteristic structure are often preserved in the altered material and can be detected with the petrographic microscope. When viewed with the binocular microscope, altered glass may have a pearly luster, or it may appear opaque and earthy and either white or discolored. Crystallization of glass (devitrification) is plainly visible in thin section and when once identified can often be detected with the binocular microscope by a peculiar sugary texture of the glass. In one instance, the mineral tridymite was identified in a glass. Both altered and devitrified ashes occur in homogeneous pastes unmixed with other volcanic material and afford means of differentiating and localizing the pottery in which they occur.

Finally there are certain foreign materials that occur with volcanic ash tempers that further aid in distinguishing them. In the limestone area of the Peten, vitric ashes are frequently impregnated with calcite, a condition not found in the highland ashes that have been examined to date. Another material sometimes associated with volcanic ash is opal, usually in minute, irregular or rodlike fragments. Siliceous fragments of organic origin, particularly diatoms and sponge spicules, also occur. Diatoms thrive in the siliceous waters of lakes in volcanic regions.

Features that may distinguish a glassy volcanic ash therefore include: (1) chemical composition of the glass, (2) structure of the glass, (3) condition of the glass—whether fresh, altered, or devitrified, (4) phenocrysts—mineralogical composition and relative proportion, (5) crystallites, (6) rock inclusions, (7) evidences of source of the glass—from a flow, an unconsolidated deposit, a tuff, etc., and (8) secondary materials. Obviously these criteria are not of equal value for identification; some are not invariably present, and some are more difficult to determine than others. It is not feasible, for example, to determine the composition of volcanic glass in pottery by chemical analysis. An indication of composition can be obtained from the refractive index of the glass, but since composition of volcanic glasses falls within a comparatively narrow range, this property is of limited value for identification. But reliance need not be placed on any single characteristic, and those that are most useful will differ from area to area.

This review should suggest the many possibilities of breaking down volcanic ash tempers into distinct classes marked by qualitative differences, classes that will distinguish the pottery of one locality from that of another. It may be a tedious task, and it takes experience and adequate sampling. There will always be some volcanic ash tempers of common and widely distributed types, but these seem more prominent and more discouraging when sampling is helter-skelter than when it is well planned and systematic.

Limestone or calcite temper is much more restricted in distribution than volcanic ash. Because of the defects resulting from calcination in firing, it was used mainly in areas where other materials were scarce. But since one such area— the Peten and the peninsula of Yucatan, a major portion of the lowland Maya area—is archaeologically important, it is worthwhile considering what consistent differences there are in this class of temper.

Limestones differ with respect to chemical composition, purity, crystalline structure, and the occurrence of fossil and mineral inclusions. A limestone may be composed entirely of calcium carbonate with impurities, but frequently it contains more or less magnesium, in which case it is classed as a magnesian or a dolomitic limestone. Dolomite contains one molecule of magnesium carbonate to one of calcium carbonate. There are simple chemical tests by which these limestones can be distinguished. Calcite is readily soluble in cold hydrochloric acid with strong effervescence, whereas dolomite is only slowly soluble in cold acid but effervesces strongly in warm acid. Only a small sample of powdered paste is required for this test. Another test, which can be performed as a check against the solubility test, is a microchemical one for magnesium using an organic reagent, Titan yellow (Feigl, 1937). If only calcium is present, the solution remains yellow; but if there is as little as 5 per cent magnesium, it turns pink. The solubility and spot tests together distinguish calcite and magnesian limestones, and dolomite. Calcite limestone will dissolve completely in the cold hydrochloric acid and cause no color change in the reagent; the magnesian limestone will also dissolve in cold acid but will turn the reagent pink, whereas dolomite will effervesce only in hot acid and will change the reagent deep pink.

The most common impurities in limestone are iron oxide, organic matter, silica and clay. Ferric oxide produces a pink or reddish calcite. Pink grains in a paste can be seen with the binocular microscope, when the thin slice examined in petrographic section appears colorless. The presence of organic matter in a limestone causes a gray or black color. Siliceous impurities are often collected in nodules of chert. Argillaceous or marly limestones are relatively common. They are characterized by a cryptocrystalline structure and can be tested chemically. The color is often gray or brownish in transmitted, as well as reflected, light.

Calcite crystallizes in several distinct forms, rhombs or "squashed cubes" being most characteristic, but scalenohedrons, familiar in the form of calcite known as dogtooth spar, also occur.

The calcium carbonate mineral, aragonite, which belongs to a different crystal system, is often fibrous or acicular. Crystalline form is usually clearly distinguishable in calcite even after it has been ground because the rhombic form has good cleavage and breaks into smaller rhombs. Only the relatively pure calcites are clear and crystalline. Some of these are composed of crystal mosaics, others have a saccharoidal texture. The latter may, upon grinding, break down into individual grains, giving the paste an exceedingly fine, uniform texture, though a few lumps indicating the original source will remain. Entirely distinct is calc-sinter or calc-tufa, a soft, porous material, generally opaque, that forms around springs or where lime-bearing waters are evaporating.

Various fossils occur in limestones, especially foraminifera, coral, and shells of mollusks. Pottery types tempered with foraminiferal ooze have been found in the Gulf Coast region and in Yucatan, but fossiliferous limestone tempers are not common in the lowland Maya area. Occasionally fragments of shell occur, but they are not an important diagnostic in this area.

Of the various mineral inclusions of limestone, two may be mentioned because they are so distinctive and so readily detected in thin section or with the binocular microscope. One is siliceous sinter, which forms about hot springs. It occurs in the limestone temper of certain British Honduras types. The other is quartz in short prisms with pyramidal terminations. This has been noted in a few types of pottery from Uaxactun but so far has been found abundantly only in sherds from Calakmul.

Fluorescence affords still another possible method of distinguishing calcite tempers. Many forms of calcite exhibit fluorescence, but since special equipment is required to test this property, it has not been used as a criterion in work on pastes of Maya pottery.

It is apparent that there are many features by which limestone-tempered pastes can be distinguished. Their value is variable; sometimes they mark the unusual intrusive, but often distinctions will be lacking in material of different localities because certain of these types of limestone are widely distributed. Consequently, no general rule as to what to observe and what to neglect can be laid down. The importance of having a large sample and of correlating paste characteristics with style cannot be overstressed because judgment of the value of a variable must be based on uniformity or homogeneity of a type, and such evaluations cannot be made with small samples.

Sand temper, though widely distributed, is more scattered in occurrence than is ash or limestone temper. Consequently, methods for differentiating sands have not been so fully exploited as have those for limestone and volcanic ash because the need for fine differentiation has not arisen as often, but the same general principles with respect to sampling and detail of analysis hold.

The chief variables of sands are composition of the major constituents, composition of the heavy minerals, and size, grading, and shape of grains. Quartz is generally the major constituent and occurs in various forms; especially distinctive are rounded aeolean grains, and grains with secondary deposits of silica that forms rims having the same crystallographic orientation as the original grain. Quartz also has many kinds of inclusions from gas bubbles to reticular crystallites of rutile. Sand temper derived from sandstone is recognized by uniformity of grading of grains, by adhering particles of cement, and by occasional particles of the parent rock. The cement may be argillaceous, ferruginous, or siliceous. Chalcedony and quartzite are not uncommon in sand, and the feldspars constitute another important constituent. Minerals of high specific gravity occur in fine grains as minor constituents. These so-called heavy minerals are often distinctive, but they are generally too small to detect with the binocular microscope and a thin section includes only a small sample of them. Ideally they should be separated by heavy liquids, and a quantitative, as well as qualitative, report made. But aside from the fact that this technique is time-consuming, it is not always feasible because of the difficulty of separating the clay from the minerals, particularly if the ware is well fired. This circumstance is not an invariable deterrent, but it is a limitation.

Sherd temper is the least distinctive as a class, yet the analyst has resources for differentiating varieties even here. He can detect differences in color and texture of sherd and, most important, he can identify the temper of the sherd temper. An illustration will serve to show that such identifications are more than idle entertainment with minutiae. A black-on-white type at Pecos has the same finish and style as the black-on-white pottery of the Galisteo Basin, some 30 miles away. Was the Pecos pottery imported or made locally? The potsherd temper seemed at first to offer little hope of answering the question, but thin sections showed that many of the temper particles were from culinary ware (blackened and coarse textured), tempered with rock—andesite or diorite. Galisteo culinary ware is tempered with this kind of rock, that of Pecos is sand-tempered. The sherd temper is, therefore, from Galisteo, for Pecos people obviously would not go 30 miles for sherds when there was an abundance of them on their own trash heaps, and this type of sherd-tempered pottery must have been brought into Pecos.

The purpose of this review has been to show the possibilities and the limitations of specific identification of varieties of these common, widely distributed tempers. In some instances distinctions are easily made, in others they are time-consuming and tedious. Before making analyses, therefore, one has to know what significance the data are likely to have, that he may judge how far it is desirable to break down material into subclasses.

Field Methods for the Identification
of Paints

Differentiation of carbon and black iron oxide paints by physical properties. In the Pueblo area these two classes of paint characterize particular pottery types and have different distributions. It is therefore an advantage to be able to recognize them by inspection, or at most with the aid of a binocular microscope. After having examined many thousands of black-on-white sherds and checked identifications repeatedly with chemical tests and by refiring, I am confident that the paints on the great majority of sherds can be classified reliably by inspection, provided one is thoroughly familiar with the range of colors and variations in surface features of each class, as well as the accidental effects that distinguish them. The field worker becomes familiar with the general appearance of the two classes of paint by handling sherds of well-established types, but many variations will prove puzzling to him unless he is familiar with the basic properties and understands the causes of unusual effects. One cannot rely on any single property for identification. Although some are more constant than others, there are exceptions to most of the generalizations regarding them, and judgment should be based on a combination of characteristics.

Theoretic considerations suggest that the primary difference between these paints is in color. Since the plant extract chars on heating, forming carbon, it can be burned out in firing; partial oxidation leaves it gray by dilution of color. Iron oxide, on the other hand, is at most merely changed in state of oxidation and with sufficient oxygen red ferric oxide is formed. Despite these fundamental differences, both kinds of paint often give near-blacks that are indistinguishable one from another. There are also occasional anomalous effects which will result in errors of classification when judgment is based on color alone. Certain types of clay turn red when they are painted with a plant extract and are subsequently well oxidized. The color is caused by the reaction of alkalies in the plant juice with the clay, which liberates ferric oxide originally masked by its chemical combination.

This accidental iron oxide color on a carbon paint specimen can be recognized by the fact that the paint surface has no relief and its smoothness and luster match those of the unpainted surface. The effect is observed only on sherds that are fully oxidized and generally the clay is buff-firing. A misleading color variation in the iron oxide paints is a gray, but this can be recognized as accidental because it occurs only under firing-clouds. In general, color is most useful for identifying those paints that have been subject to some oxidation in firing. The grays to which carbon paint turns under these conditions are not uncommon.

The physical state of the paint on application, rather than its composition, is responsible for the characteristics that are generally most useful. The organic paint, since it is applied as a solution, has no relief and its surface is similar in smoothness, texture, and luster to the unpainted surface. The variation in luster caused by filling of pores with carbon is slight and often imperceptible. The relation of these properties of organic paint to the vessel finish is therefore direct. If the clay surface is smooth and lustrous the paint will be also; if the vessel was unpolished or grainy, the paint will have the same roughness. There is no deposit on the surface; when the paint is scraped, one commences at once to cut into the clay.

In contrast to the organic paint, the iron oxide paint coats the surface, and its texture and luster are independent of those of the body. A powder can be scraped from it, and often it is more brown than the undisturbed paint. These are features that are readily recognized with a 10× lens in the majority of sherds.

Polishing strokes may appear to extend over a carbon paint, an effect that has sometimes led to misinterpretation of the differences in luster of the two classes of paint. It has been assumed that the organic paint was applied before polishing and the mineral paint, after polishing. Experimentation will satisfy one that this was not the case. It is not practicable to polish the organic paint. It smears when it is moist and becomes hard and horny when dry. Moreover, it is lustrous when applied on a polished surface and has the appearance of the prehistoric paints.

Certain peculiarities of each class of paint also aid in identification. The organic paint often has blurred or hazy outlines as a result of diffusion of the solution beyond the line of application. This same effect might occur with a mineral paint with which an organic vehicle had been used, but I have never noted an example. Diffusion seems to take place more readily with certain types of clays. Another occasional peculiarity of the organic paint is a scattering of white spots within the black. This is evidently due to the trapping of air bubbles when the paint is applied. The color of the organic paints is often uneven; not infrequently the center of the line is lighter than the margin. Since this paint is soluble, variation in color will be due primarily to difference in thickness or viscosity. A paint which is too thick does not penetrate well and will burn off in firing; a very thin one will not carry sufficient organic matter to stain the clay black. A hairline crack along the edge of the line is probably caused by the shrinkage of the clay that was wet by the gummy extract. A defect of the organic paint is chipping or spalling of the painted surface, which may again be due to weakening through contraction.

The black iron oxide paints are often distinguished by peculiarities of texture best seen microscopically. They are often hard and sintered or slightly vitrified, and under these conditions, crazing that exposes the gray paste is characteristic, although it may be so fine that it is only recognized microscopically. Incipient vitrification due to the formation of an iron-silica glass tends to cause beading. The poorly fired iron oxide paints are generally less completely reduced, and their tones are red or brown. They are soft and powdery and often worn; sometimes only the material that penetrated pores remains; in other cases color is patchy because of uneven abrasion or weathering.

Neither native iron oxides nor the plant extracts used on prehistoric pottery were uniform in composition and both were subject to varying firing conditions. The iron oxide paints differed in state of oxidation, in particle size and in their impurities. The plant extracts differed in concentration and they may have been obtained from different plants. Since they were not thinned uniformly, their viscosity, penetration, and effect on shrinkage of the clay varied. Clay bodies differed also and the extent of penetration of the paint and its adherence depended in no small measure on the structure, porosity, and adsorptive properties of the clay. The finish of the vessel affected texture and luster of soluble paints. Finally, differences in firing—time, atmosphere, and temperature—affected the extent of oxidation of both classes of paint, and the sintering or vitrification of the iron oxide paint. It is no wonder that each type shows considerable variation in color, texture, luster, and permanence and that the two are sometimes similar in appearance. Errors of judgment in classification are avoided when the causes of basic properties are understood. Many specimens can be classified at a glance; others should be examined with a binocular microscope; and a small number, perhaps 10 per cent of a sample and generally those that are poorly preserved, require chemical or thermal tests.

The oxidation test for iron and organic paints. The test commonly used to identify organic paint is indirect and dependent on the conversion of carbon to carbon dioxide gas on heating with sufficient oxygen. It was first proposed by Hawley (1929). The most satisfactory method of oxidation is to heat fragments of sherds in air in an electric resistance furnace to temperatures around 800°C. Chips from a large number of sherds can be handled in one firing in this way. The oxidizing flame of a blowpipe can also be used and, in the field, a small alcohol torch is a convenient source of heat. Heating alone, however, is often insufficient to test these paints because the carbon is adsorbed and protected by the clay, and it is therefore necessary to loosen the texture. A drop of hydrofluoric acid, which attacks silica and silicates, is used for this purpose. Because of its strong corrosive action, this acid must be handled with care, avoiding contact with the skin as well as with instruments it would attack. A matchstick is convenient for applying the acid. The drop should be allowed to dry completely before the specimen is heated. On heating, the carbon paint is burned out. If the paint is a black iron oxide instead of carbon, it will be converted to red ferric oxide by this test.

The organic paint we have considered was fired with the vessel. A paint of this type can also be used after firing and converted to carbon by applying it to the hot vessel as it comes from the fire or by reheating to a low temperature. Postfiring carbon paints are more easily oxidized than are fired ones, and we have proof of this technique if the carbon can be oxidized at a temperature lower than that at which the vessel was fired. Repeated tests are necessary to learn the minimum temperature at which a carbon paint can be oxidized, and the tests must be performed in the laboratory with a furnace and pyrometer.

Microchemical tests for major constituents of paints. These are short qualitative procedures that require only a few reagents and simple equipment, and the techniques of performing them can easily be acquired with practice.

To test for iron and manganese, a small sample of the paint is scraped from the surface, placed on the corner of a glass slide and 1:1 hydrochloric acid is added a drop at a time and after each addition gently heated over a small flame until evaporated. Three or four drops of acid are usually sufficient. To prevent the drop from spreading, the slide should be completely free of the oily film it acquires in handling. Some insoluble residue will remain undissolved if clay has been included with the sample or if the paint contains argillaceous or siliceous matter or is vitrified. Impurities reduce the concentration of the pigment, but vitrification will render it insoluble and it must then be fused with a flux before it can be tested. Vitrification can sometimes be judged by appearance of a paint and exceptional hardness is often an indication of it. The majority of iron and manganese paints, however, can be taken into solution in warm acid. If very much iron is present, the drop will turn yellow from the formation of ferric chloride ions. The residue that remains after leaching with acid is taken into solution with a drop of 1:7 nitric acid and can then be tested for either iron or manganese by adding appropriate reagents. A satisfactory reagent for manganese is sodium bismuthate, which, being an oxidizing agent, converts the manganese to the permanganate state in which it has a characteristic purplish pink color familiar in sodium permanganate. The depth of color obtained depends on the concentration of permanganate ions. If they are low, the color may not appear immediately but can be seen at the edge of the drop when it begins to dry. The slide should be held over white paper for viewing. The permanganate is not stable and begins to break down in a short time, leaving a brown powdery deposit of manganese dioxide. The color of the solution fades as the powder forms. The test is more sensitive and satisfactory than the borax bead test, the only advantage of which is that the borax fuses some of the rarer manganese minerals which are not soluble in hydrochloric acid. These minerals have not been reported in paints.

Most of the manganese-bearing paints also contain iron and a simple microchemical color test can be made with a sample prepared as for the manganese test. One of the best-known reagents is potassium ferrocyanide. When a small particle is added to the drop, the characteristic Prussian blue color of ferric ferrocyanide is formed. The principal disadvantage in this test is that other metals form precipitates with potassium ferrocyanide and may obscure the color of the iron compound. As a general reagent for iron, potassium mercuric thiocyanate is preferable. A drop of a 5 per cent solution is placed near the test drop and led into it with a fine glass rod. A red color indicates the presence of iron. A small fragment of the solid reagent can be used instead of the solution. These tests for iron are sensitive and will give positive results when iron is a minor constituent. Faint tests should therefore be disregarded. It is possible to leach red color from the potassium mercuric thiocyanate test with a reagent that unites with iron to form a colorless complex. The relative strength of the iron is judged by the amount of complexing agent required, but the test is complicated by the interference of acid and requires careful control of concentrations and maintenance of neutrality.

These color tests for iron and manganese are often performed in the depressions of a spot plate, but the sample cannot be heated in the spot plate and after solution there is no need to transfer them from the glass slide, since this involves loss of material.

A different technique can be used to advantage in testing for copper. Absorbent paper, such as filter paper, is impregnated with the reagent, a 2 per cent solution of α-benzoin-oxime, and dried. A drop of the unknown solution is then spotted on the paper and exposed to the vapour of ammonia. The presence of copper is shown by the development of a green color. The fibrous texture of the filter paper offers the advantage of a large surface area on which the reaction can take place.

It is often necessary to distinguish between cinnabar and ferric oxide in postfiring paints. Cinnabar, the sulfide of mercury, can be identified by a very satisfactory microchemical test for mercury. A sample of the pigment is placed in the lower end of a piece of glass tubing. On heating, the mineral decomposes to metallic mercury and sulfur dioxide. The tube is first heated just above the sample and then the sample is heated carefully and gradually to avoid driving off the black unoxidized sublimate of mercuric sulfide. As the sulfide is decomposed, mercury is deposited in the cool end of the tube in droplets that have a mirror-like appearance when viewed microscopically. To confirm mercury, a crystal of iodine is introduced into the tube. The iodine volatilizes and unites with the mercury to form characteristic rose-colored crystals of mercuric iodide. The reaction is interesting to observe microscopically because it is rapid and active; slender crystals lash about violently as they grow out from the walls of the tube.

These tests give an idea of simple, qualitative microchemical methods. They cover the elements which occur most commonly in paints and they are very useful in preliminary testing.

APPENDIX E

Classification of Vessel-forming Techniques

SINCE the section on ceramic processes was written, the need of a more explicit statement regarding methods of vessel building has been brought to my attention. Potters' diverse uses of the same tools, accomplishment of the same purpose with different tools, unexpected combinations of techniques, and seemingly endless quirks point up the question of how to obtain the order and consistency of designation, description, and classification necessary for sound and systematic comparison. Unfamiliar or rare and specialized features of technique have often been a snare to the student in so far as they have drawn his attention away from the basic aspects of method and led him to give undue emphasis to secondary features, to adopt inconsistent terminology, and to equate distinct aspects of technique or to assume linkage of independent steps.

The student must give his attention to the potter's manner of manipulating the clay, to the tools employed for the purpose, to the method of turning or working around the vessel during construction, and to the stages of construction and the order of completing vessel parts. Each of these aspects of construction affords the potter some independent choices, which means that, in description, one of them cannot designate another, nor can they be equated as criteria of classification. The error of contrasting paddle-and-anvil technique with coiling was apparent when it was pointed out that the paddle and anvil are sometimes used in finishing coiled vessels; the distinction, in this instance, is not between two building methods but between methods of thinning walls and shaping once the vessel is roughly formed. The basic error in logic, however, was that of equating a tool with a process. When we consider that the paddle and anvil may be used to pound out a vessel from a solid lump of clay, to bond elements of a coiled vessel, to thin walls and refine shape irrespective of building process, and that a paddle can be used in fitting clay onto a convex mold (the mold functioning as anvil), it should not be necessary to insist that the expression "paddle-and-anvil technique" is indefinite. The history and distribution of this specialized pair of tools may be quite significant, but the tool alone does not adequately define a technique. The same is true of specialized methods of turning the vessel while forming it. The use of a tournette, a kabal, or a "molde" resting on the convex base of an inverted vessel may raise important questions regarding the history of technique, but the means of rotating the vessel does not identify the method of building it.

The association of unusual methods which by their rarity suggest linkages is another possible pitfall in classification because each trait may be independent and may reappear in a very different trait cluster. An example of the grouping of unusual methods is the potter's custom of circling the vessel backward during the building process, of drawing up the vessel side from a ring of clay, and of first forming the upper half which is inverted to complete the vessel at its base. Although these processes are associated in several instances, they are not interdependent; and to designate a process by reference to any one alone would be misleading.

The first question to be determined in classification is the manner in which the clay is manipulated in building. Disregarding the advanced processes of wheel throwing and slip casting, we can distinguish freehand forming and molding (shaping by pressing clay into or onto a mold). In freehand forming the vessel may be built (1) by manipulating a solid lump of clay or (2) by joining elements such as coils, fillets, or slabs. For convenience we can refer to the first as *modeling*—although the term is not as specific as might be desired—and to the latter as *piece building*, of which coiling is by far the most familiar and frequent example. At least two distinct manipulations can be employed in modeling from a lump: direct impact with the hands or the paddle and anvil (punching, patting, slapping the lump into a hollow form); or drawing or dragging the clay upward between the lower edges of the hands after it is formed into a thick ring. Perhaps the simplest way of distinguishing these two processes is by the direction from which force is applied. In impact modeling it is approximately at right angles to the vessel wall; in drag modeling it is parallel to the wall.

This classification of basic techniques is relatively simple because distinctions are sufficiently clear to enable the student to avoid confusing one method with another, but in practice identification is complicated by the fact that two or more distinct techniques are often employed in succession for the same vessel; for example, the lower part of a jar may be formed on a one-part, convex mold and the upper part coiled or modeled freehand, or again the lower part may be modeled by impact and the upper part coiled. There is nothing mutually exclusive about these processes; they can be employed in all possible combinations. There are even records of part of a vessel being thrown on a wheel and the remainder finished by a freehand modeling process.

Combinations of techniques are interesting because of the question of their genesis: Do they represent the grafting of one technique on another, or the first stages in the development of a new technique, or are they traditional methods well established because they are efficient means of forming certain types of vessels?

In order to analyze the evidence relating to these questions it is important to distinguish primary and supplementary techniques: Is a distinct forming method used for a large section of the vessel body; for an accessory, such as a pedestal base; or for a small part of the body, such as the basal disc that is pressed into the "molde" at the start of a coiled vessel? Clearly the last example should not be classed as a combination of molding and coiling; the molded part is relatively small and its association with coiling is typical because it affords a convenient way of beginning the vessel. Relative ease or efficiency of manipulation is thus another factor to consider. It enters in the combination of an impact-modeled body and a coiled neck. To model the neck from the clay of the original lump of which the body was formed would be awkward; if clay must be added, a coil distributes it uniformly around the circumference. When clay is added, a distinction should be made between a single large roll to be shaped by impact or drag modeling and two or more coils to be bonded. In coiling, height of wall is obtained primarily by uniting a succession of elements; expanding occurs mainly in the final shaping. When a single roll intended for modeling is referred to as a coil, a confusion of techniques may arise. It is also well to bear in mind that the size of a vessel which can be formed by impact modeling from a single lump is influenced by the plasticity of a clay; furthermore, the size of a vessel and the strength of the plastic clay may determine whether the building process will be continuous or discontinuous. If a vessel base formed by impact modeling is so large that it must be allowed to stiffen before the upper part is formed, coiling may be the simplest way of raising the vessel wall.

These comments are intended to suggest some of the factors that should be weighed in judging the significance of "combined techniques". In order to avoid the confusion that would follow from loose usage, the expression might be limited to the employment of two methods of construction in forming major parts of the vessel body, and "supplementary techniques" could cover those used for minor or accessory parts. The main point, however, is to seek explanations and to differentiate associations which are strongly favored by practical considerations from those in which the potter could choose from several equally satisfactory procedures. Unless this is done, a study of trait distribution loses much of its precision and significance.

Suggestions regarding classification are outlined to stress the importance of defining primary manipulations and of maintaining uniformity of position of comparable criteria. The outline is oversimplified in so far as it is not inclusive or fully expanded. This is particularly true of III, for which only a few well-known illustrations are listed.

I. Single technique of freehand forming.
   A. Modeling.
       1. By impact from a solid lump.
          a. Hand-worked.
          b. Paddle-and-anvil–worked.
       2. By dragging clay upward from a ring.
   B. Piece building.
       1. With coils in rings or a spiral.
          a. Finger-bonded.
          b. Paddle-and-anvil–bonded.
       2. With patches.

II. Molding.
   A. One-part mold.
       1. Convex.
       2. Concave.
   B. Molds of two or more parts.
       1. Convex.
       2. Concave.

III. Two or more techniques combined.
   A. Freehand forming methods.
       1. Impact-modeled lower body.
          a. Coiled upper body.
          b. Drag-modeled upper body.
       2. Coiled upper body.
          a. Drag-modeled lower body.
   B. Molding and freehand forming combined.
       1. Molded lower body.
          a. Coiled upper body.
          b. Impact-modeled upper body.

The order of construction is followed in listing vessel parts under III.

For the archaeologist, the usefulness of an outline drawn up with reference to ethnological data will be limited by the difficulty of identifying basic techniques. Nevertheless, consistency of terminology in the two fields is desirable. General descriptive terms can be used in archaeology when needed; for example, "anvil-marked" is as specific as the evidence allows when there is uncertainty regarding the stage of construction in which the tool was employed. If analysis based on full ethnological data is accepted as the archaeologist's model, it will aid him in recognizing relations, maintaining consistency in comparison, and making meaningful interpretations.

References

AMBERG, C. R.
1948 Terra sigillata, forgotten finish. *Ceram. Industry*, vol. 51, no. 6, pp. 77, 90. Chicago.

AMSDEN, C. A.
1936 An analysis of Hohokam pottery design. *Medallion Papers*, no. 23, Globe.

ARKELL, A. J.
1939 Darfur pottery. *Sudan Notes and Records*, vol. 22, pt. 1. Khartoum.

ARROT, C. R.
1953 La ceramica moderna, hecha a mano en Santa Apolonia. *Antrop. e Hist. de Guatemala*, 5:3–10. Guatemala.

BAIR, G. J.
1936 The constitution of lead oxide-silica glasses: I, Atomic arrangement. *Jour. Amer. Ceram. Soc.*, 19:339. Easton.

BEALS, R. L., G. W. BRAINERD, AND W. SMITH
1945 Archaeological studies in northeast Arizona. *Univ. Calif. Pub. Amer. Archaeol. and Ethnol.*, vol. 44, no. 1. Berkeley.

BELOUS, R. E.
1953 The central California chronological sequence re-examined. *Amer. Antiquity*, 18:341–53. Salt Lake City.

BENEDETTI-PICHLER, A. A.
1942 Introduction to the micro-chemical technique of inorganic analysis. New York.

BINNS, C. F., AND A. D. FRASER
1929 Genesis of Greek black glaze. *Amer. Jour. Archaeol.*, 33:1–9. Concord, N. H.

BIRKHOFF, G. D.
1933 Aesthetic measure. Cambridge.

BORING, E. B., H. S. LANGFELD, H. P. WELD, AND COLLABORATORS
1939 Introduction to psychology. New York.

BRADFIELD, W.
1925 A new process for photographing the interior of Indian pottery bowls. *El Palacio*, vol. 14, no. 1, pp. 11–14. Santa Fe.
1929 Cameron Creek Village: a site in the Mimbres area in Grant County, New Mexico. Santa Fe.

BRAGG, W. L.
   1937   The atomic structure of minerals. Ithaca.
BRAIDWOOD, R. J., L. BRAIDWOOD, J. G. SMITH, AND C. LESLIE
   1952   Matarrah, a village of early farmers in Iraq, a southern variant of the Hassunan
          assemblage, excavated in 1948. *Jour. Near Eastern Studies*, 11:1–75. Chicago.
BRAINERD, G. W.
   1942   Symmetry in primitive conventional design. *Amer. Antiquity*, 8:164–66. Menasha.
   1946   Wheel-made pottery in America? *Masterkey*, 20:191–92. Los Angeles.
   1951   The place of chronological ordering in archaeological analysis. *Amer. Antiquity*,
          16:301–13. Salt Lake City.
BREW, J. O.
   1946   Archaeology of Alkali Ridge, southeastern Utah. *Papers Peabody Mus., Harvard
          Univ.*, vol. 21. Cambridge.
BUERGER, M. J., AND J. S. LUKESH
   1937   Wallpaper and atoms. *Technol. Rev.*, 39:338–42, 370. Concord, N. H.
BUNZEL, R.
   1929   The Pueblo potter. New York.
BUTEL-DUMONT, G. M.
   1753   Memoires historiques sur la Louisiane, 2:271. Paris.
BUTLER, M.
   1935   Piedras Negras pottery. *Piedras Negras Prelim. Papers*, no. 4. Philadelphia.
   1951   Genuine lost color. *Amer. Antiquity*, 16:260–61. Salt Lake City.
CASEY, R. S., AND J. W. PERRY, EDITORS
   1951   Punched cards: their applications to science and industry. New York.
CATTELL, R. B.
   1941   General psychology. Cambridge.
CHAPMAN, K. M.
   1936   The pottery of Santo Domingo Pueblo. *Mem. Lab. Anthropol.*, vol. 1. Santa Fe.
CLARK, J. G. D.
   1952   Prehistoric Europe; the economic basis. London.
COLE, FAY-COOPER, AND T. DEUEL
   1937   Rediscovering Illinois: archaeological explorations in and around Fulton county.
          Chicago.
COLTON, H. S.
   1939   Primitive pottery firing methods. *Mus. Notes, Mus. Northern Ariz.*, vol. 11,
          no. 10, pp. 63–66. Flagstaff.
   1939a The reducing atmosphere and oxidizing atmosphere in prehistoric southwestern
          ceramics. *Amer. Antiquity*, 4:224–31. Menasha.
   1951   Hopi pottery firing temperatures. *Plateau*, 24:73–76. Flagstaff.
   1953   Potsherds: an introduction to the study of prehistoric southwestern ceramics
          and their use in historic reconstruction. Flagstaff.
COLTON, M. R. F.
   1931   Technique of the major Hopi crafts. *Mus. Notes, Mus. Northern Ariz.*, vol. 3,
          no. 12, pp. 1–7. Flagstaff.

COMMITTEE ON STANDARDS, AMERICAN CERAMIC SOCIETY
1928 *Jour. Amer. Ceram. Soc.*, vol. 11, no. 6. Easton.
CURRY, H. J.
1950 Negative painted pottery of Angel Mounds site and its distribution in the New World. *Ind. Univ. Pub. Anthropol. and Ling.*, Mem. 5. Baltimore.
CUSHING, F. H.
1920 Zuni breadstuff. *Indian Notes and Monographs*, vol. 8. New York.
DEBEVOISE, N. C.
1934 The history of glaze and its place in the ceramic technique of ancient Seleucia on the Tigris. *Amer. Ceram. Soc. Bull.*, vol. 13. Easton.
DIGBY, A.
1948 Radiographic examination of Peruvian pottery techniques. *Actes du XXVIII Congrès International des Américainistes.* Paris.
DOUGLAS, F. H., AND F. R. RAYNOLDS, COMPILERS
1941 Pottery design terminology—final report on questionnaires. *Clearing House for Southwestern Museums, News-letter*, no. 35. Denver.
EVANS, R. M.
1948 An introduction to color. New York.
FARNSWORTH, M.
1951 Ancient pigments, particularly second century B.C. pigments from Corinth. *Jour. Chem. Educ.*, 28:72–76. Easton.
FEIGL, F.
1937 Qualitative analysis by spot tests. New York.
FEWKES, V. J.
1944 Catawba pottery-making, with notes on Pamunkey pottery-making, Cherokee pottery-making, and coiling. *Proc. Amer. Phil. Soc.*, 88:69–125. Philadelphia.
FORD, J. A.
1951 Greenhouse: a Troyville–Coles Creek period site in Avoyelles Parish, Louisiana. *Anthropol. Papers, Amer. Mus. Nat. Hist.*, vol. 44, pt. 1. New York.
1954 The type concept revisited. *Amer. Anthropol.*, 56:42–53. Menasha.
—— AND G. R. WILLEY
1949 Surface survey of the Viru Valley, Peru. *Anthropol. Papers, Amer. Mus. Nat. Hist.*, vol. 43, no. 1. New York.
FOSTER, G. M.
1948 Empire's children, the people of Tzintzuntzan. *Smithsonian Inst., Inst. Soc. Anthropol.*, Pub. 6. Washington.
1948a Some implications of modern Mexican mold-made pottery. *Southwest Jour. Anthropol.*, 4:356–70. Albuquerque.
GETTENS, R. J.
1938 The materials in the wall paintings of Bamiyan, Afghanistan. *Tech. Stud. Field Fine Arts*, 6:186–93. Lancaster.
1938a The materials in the wall paintings from Kizil in Chinese Turkestan. *Tech. Stud. Field Fine Arts*, 6:281–94. Lancaster.

GIFFORD, E. W.
    1928   Pottery-making in the Southwest. *Univ. Calif. Pub. Amer. Archaeol. and Ethnol.*, 23:353–73. Berkeley.
GILMORE, M. R.
    1925   Arikara uses of clay and other earth products. *Indian Notes, Mus. Amer. Indian*, 2:286–89. New York.
GREENMAN, E. F.
    1937   The Younge site. *Occasional Contrib., Mus. Anthropol., Univ. Mich.*, no. 6. Ann Arbor.
GRIFFIN, J. B.
    1935   Aboriginal methods of pottery manufacture in the eastern United States. *Pa. Archaeol.*, 5:19–24. Milton, Pa.
——, editor
    1951   Essays on archaeological methods. *Anthropol. Pap., Mus. Anthropol., Univ. Mich.*, no. 8. Ann Arbor.
—— AND A. D. KRIEGER
    1947   Notes on some ceramic techniques and intrusions in central Mexico. *Amer. Antiquity*, 12:156–68. Menasha.
GRIM, R. E.
    1953   Clay mineralogy. New York.
—— AND W. F. BRADLEY
    1940   Effect of heat on the clay minerals illite and montmorillonite. *Jour. Amer. Ceram. Soc.*, 23:242–48. Easton.
GUTHE, C. E.
    1925   Pueblo pottery making, a study at the village of San Ildefonso. *Papers Phillips Acad. Southwestern Exped.*, no. 2. New Haven.
HAMBIDGE, J.
    1920   Dynamic symmetry, the Greek vase. New Haven.
HARDY, A. C.
    1936   Handbook of colorimetry. Cambridge.
HARRISON, H. C., AND L. B. BASSETT
    1941   Emission spectroscopy and its application in the investigation and solution of problems in ceramics. *Jour. Amer. Ceram. Soc.*, 24:213–21. Easton.
HASLAM, R. T., AND R. P. RUSSELL
    1926   Fuels and their combustion. New York.
HAUSER, E. A.
    1941   Colloid chemistry in ceramics. *Jour. Amer. Ceram. Soc.*, 24:179–88. Easton.
HAWLEY, F. M.
    1929   Prehistoric pottery pigments of the Southwest. *Amer. Anthropol.*, n.s., 31:731–54. Menasha.
HILL, W. W.
    1937   Navajo pottery manufacture. *Univ. New Mex. Bull. Anthropol. Series*, vol. 2, no. 3. Albuquerque.

HOLMES, W. H.
   1888   Ancient art of the province of Chiriqui, Colombia. *Bur. Amer. Ethnol.*, 6th ann.
          rept., pp. 13–187. Washington.
HUNTER, R. S.
   1937   Methods of determining gloss. *Nat. Bur. Standards*, Research Paper RP958.
          Washington.
INSLEY, H., AND R. H. EWELL
   1935   Thermal behavior of the kaolin minerals. *Nat. Bur. Standards*, Research Paper
          RP792. Washington.
JONG, E. F. P. DE, AND A. J. RIJKEN
   1946   Surface decoration on terra sigillata and on Greek black painted vases. *Amer.
          Ceram. Soc. Bull.*, 25:5–7. Easton.
KELLY, I., AND A. PALERM
   1952   The Tajin Totonac, part 1. *Smithsonian Inst., Inst. Soc. Anthropol.*, Pub. 13.
          Washington.
KERR, P. F., M. S. MAIN, AND P. K. HAMILTON
   1950   Occurrence and microscopic examination of reference clay mineral specimens.
          Reference Clay Minerals, Amer. Petroleum Inst. Project 49, prel. rept. no. 5.
          New York.
KIDDER, A. V.
   1947   The artifacts of Uaxactun, Guatemala. *Carnegie Inst. Wash.*, Pub. 576.
          Washington.
——, J. D. JENNINGS, AND E. M. SHOOK
   1946   Excavations at Kaminaljuyu, Guatemala. *Carnegie Inst. Wash.*, Pub. 561.
          Washington.
—— AND A. O. SHEPARD
   1936   The pottery of Pecos, vol. 2. *Papers Phillips Acad. Southwestern Exped.*, no. 7.
          New Haven.
   1944   Stucco decoration of early Guatemala pottery. *Carnegie Inst. Wash., Div.
          Historical Research, Notes on Middle Amer. Archaeol. and Ethnol.*, no. 35.
          Cambridge.
KOENIG, J. H.
   1939   Physical properties of commercial dinnerware. *Ohio State Univ. Studies,
          Engineering series*, vol. 8, no. 3. Engineering Exper. Station, Bull. 101. Columbus.
KOFFKA, K.
   1935   Principles of Gestalt psychology. New York.
KRUMBEIN, W. C., AND F. J. PETTIJOHN
   1938   Manual of sedimentary petrography. New York.
LAUFER, B.
   1917   The beginnings of porcelain in China. *Field Mus. Nat. Hist.*, Pub. 192. Chicago.
LEWIS, D. R., AND W. BURKHARDT
   1951   Analytical data on reference clay minerals. Base exchange data. *Reference Clay
          Minerals, Amer. Petroleum Inst. Project 49*, prel. rept. no. 7, sec. 3. New York.

LINNÉ, S.
1925   The technique of South American ceramics. Göteborg.

LINTON, R.
1944   North American cooking pots. *Amer. Antiquity*, 9:369–80. Menasha.

LOTHROP, S. K.
1927   The potters of Guatajiagua, Salvador. *Indian Notes, Mus. Amer. Indian*, vol. 4, no. 2. New York.
1936   Zacualpa: a study of ancient Quiche artifacts. *Carnegie Inst. Wash.*, Pub. 472. Washington.

LUCAS, A.
1935–36   Glazed ware in Egypt, India, and Mesopotamia. *Jour. Egyptian Archaeol.*, vols. 21–22. London.
1948   Ancient Egyptian materials and industries. London.

MAERZ, A., AND M. R. PAUL
1930   A dictionary of color. New York.

MALINOWSKI, B.
1922   Argonauts of the western Pacific. London.

MARCH, B.
1934   Standards of pottery description. *Occasional Contrib., Mus. Anthropol., Univ. Mich.*, no. 3. Ann Arbor.

MATSON, F. R., JR.
1945   A technological study of the unglazed pottery and figurines from Seleucia on the Tigris. Ph.D. dissertation, Univ. Mich., 1939. *Univ. Mich., Univ. Microfilms*, Pub. 660. Ann Arbor.

MAXIMILIAN, PRINCE OF WIED-NEUWIED
1843   Travels in the interior of North America. London.

McBRYDE, F. W.
1943   The black lacquer mystery of the Guatemala Maya Indians. *Sci. Mo.*, 57:113–18. Lancaster.

MELLOR, J. W.
1916   Modern inorganic chemistry. London.

MERCER, H. C.
1897   The kabel or potter's wheel of Yucatan. *Bull. Mus. Sci. and Art, Univ. Pa.*, vol. 1, no. 2. Philadelphia.

MEYER, F. S.
1945   A handbook of ornament. Chicago.

MIELENZ, R. C., M. E. KING, AND N. C. SCHIELTZ
1950   Staining tests. *Reference Clay Minerals, Amer. Petrol. Inst. Project 49*, prel. rept. no. 7, sec. 6. New York.

MORRIS, E. H.
1939   Archaeological studies in the La Plata district. *Carnegie Inst. Wash.*, Pub. 519. Washington.

MUNSELL, A. H.
1942   Munsell book of color. Pocket ed., 2 vols. Baltimore.

MYER, W. E.
   1928   Two prehistoric villages in Tennessee. *Bur. Amer. Ethnol.*, 41st ann. rept. Washington.

NICKERSON, D.
   1940   History of the Munsell color system and its scientific application. *Jour. Opt. Soc. Amer.*, 30:575–86. Lancaster.
   1946   Color measurement and its application to the grading of agricultural products. *U. S. Dept. Agriculture*, Misc. Pub. 580. Washington.

NORTON, F. H.
   1952   Elements of ceramics. Cambridge.
—— AND S. SPEIL
   1938   The measurement of particle sizes in clays. *Jour. Amer. Ceram. Soc.*, 21:89. Easton.

PARMELEE, C. W.
   1946   Clays and some other ceramic materials. Ann Arbor.

PHILLIPS, P., J. A. FORD, AND J. B. GRIFFIN
   1951   Archaeological survey in the lower Mississippi alluvial valley, 1940–1947. *Papers Peabody Mus., Harvard Univ.*, vol. 25. Cambridge.

RALSTON, O. C.
   1929   Iron oxide and reduction equilibria: a critique from the standpoint of the phase rule and thermodynamics. *U. S. Bureau of Mines*, Bull. 296. Washington.

RENDON, S.
   1950   Modern pottery of Riotenco San Lorenzo, Cuauhtitlan. *Middle Amer. Research Records*, vol. 1, no. 15. New Orleans.

RIDGWAY, R.
   1912   Color standards and color nomenclature. Washington.

RIES, H.
   1927   Clays, their occurrence, properties and uses. 3d ed. New York.

ROBINSON, W. M.
   1951   A method for chronologically ordering archaeological deposits. *Amer. Antiquity*, 16:293–301. Salt Lake City.

ROGERS, M. J.
   1928   A question of scumming. *Ariz. Old and New*, vol. 1, no. 2, pp. 5, 18ff. Phoenix.
   1936   Yuman pottery making. *San Diego Mus. Pap.*, no. 2. San Diego.

ROSS, C. S.
   1943   Clays and soils in relation to geologic processes. *Jour. Wash. Acad. Sci.*, 33:225–35. Baltimore.
   1945   Minerals and mineral relationships of the clay minerals. *Jour. Amer. Ceram. Soc.*, 28:173–83. Easton.
—— AND S. B. HENDRICKS
   1945   Minerals of the montmorillonite group. *U. S. Geol. Survey*, Prof. Paper 205-B, pp. 23–79. Washington.
—— AND P. F. KERR
   1931   The kaolin minerals. *U. S. Geol. Survey*, Prof. Paper 165, pp. 151–80. Washington.

ROUSE, I.

1939   Prehistory in Haiti, a study in method. *Yale Univ., Pub. in Anthropol.*, no. 2. New Haven.

ROYS, R. L.

1943   The Indian background of colonial Yucatan. *Carnegie Inst. Wash.*, Pub. 548. Washington.

RUSSELL, R., JR.

1940   The effect of thermal process on properties. *Bull. Amer. Ceram. Soc.*, 19:1–12. Easton.

SEARLE, A. B.

1929–30   An encyclopaedia of the ceramic industries. Vols. I–III. London.

SEARS, P. B.

1950   Charles Darwin, the naturalist as a cultural force. New York.

SHEPARD, A. O.

1942   Rio Grande glaze paint ware. *Carnegie Inst. Wash.*, Pub. 528, Contrib. 39. Washington.

1948   Plumbate, a Mesoamerican trade ware. *Carnegie Inst. Wash.*, Pub. 573. Washington.

1948a   The symmetry of abstract design with special reference to ceramic decoration. *Carnegie Inst. Wash.*, Pub. 574, Contrib. 47. Washington.

SHOOK, E. M., AND A. V. KIDDER

1953   Mound E-III-3, Kaminaljuyu, Guatemala. *Carnegie Inst. Wash.*, Pub. 596, Contrib. 53. Washington.

SMITH, A. L., AND A. V. KIDDER

1943   Explorations in the Motagua Valley, Guatemala. *Carnegie Inst. Wash.*, Pub. 546, Contrib. 41. Washington.

1951   Excavations at Nebaj, Guatemala. *Carnegie Inst. Wash.*, Pub. 594. Washington.

SMITH, R. E.

1953   Pottery from Chipoc, Alta Verapaz, Guatemala. *Carnegie Inst. Wash.*, Pub. 596, Contrib. 56. Washington.

SPAULDING, A. C.

1953   Statistical techniques for the discovery of artifact types. *Amer. Antiquity*, 18:305–313. Salt Lake City.

STEVENSON, M. C.

1904   The Zuni Indians, their mythology, esoteric fraternities, and ceremonies. *Bur. Amer. Ethnol.*, 23d ann. rept. Washington.

STEWARD, J. H.

1954   Types of types. *Amer. Anthropol.*, 56:54–57. Menasha.

THOMPSON, E. H.

n.d.   The Maya potter of Yucatan. MS., Peabody Museum Library, Harvard Univ.

THOMPSON, J. E. S.

1939   Excavations at San Jose, British Honduras. *Carnegie Inst. Wash.*, Pub. 506. Washington.

TITTERINGTON, P. F.
  1933 Has the x-ray a place in the archaeological laboratory? *Amer. Anthropol.*,
        35:297. Menasha.
TRIAL DATA
  1939 Trial data on painting materials—pigment and inert materials. *Fogg Mus. Art,
        Harvard Univ., Technical Studies*, 8:12–60. Cambridge.
TSCHOPIK, H., JR.
  1950 An Andean ceramic tradition in historical perspective. *Amer. Antiquity*,
        15:196–218. Menasha.
VAN DE VELDE, P., AND H. R. VAN DE VELDE
  1939 The black pottery of Coyotepec, Oaxaca, Mexico. *Southwest Mus. Papers*,
        no. 13. Los Angeles.
WENDORF, D. F.
  1953 Archaeological studies in the Petrified Forest National Monument. *Mus.
        Northern Arizona*, Bull. 27. Flagstaff.
WENTWORTH, C. K.
  1933 Fundamental limits to the sizes of clastic grains. *Science*, 77:633–34. Lancaster.
—— AND H. WILLIAMS
  1932 The classification and terminology of the pyroclastic rocks. *Bull. Nat.
        Research Council*, no. 89. Washington.
WEYL, H.
  1952 Symmetry. Princeton.
WILLEY, G. R.
  1945 Horizon styles and pottery traditions in Peruvian archaeology. *Amer. Antiquity*,
        11:49–56. Menasha.
  1948 Functional analysis of "Horizon Styles" in Peruvian archaeology (in W. C.
        Bennett, A reappraisal of Peruvian archaeology). *Memoirs of the Society for
        Amer. Archaeol.*, 4:8–15. Menasha.
—— AND P. PHILLIPS
  1944 Negative-painted pottery from Crystal River, Florida. *Amer. Antiquity*,
        10:173–85. Menasha.
WILLIAMS, S. R.
  1942 Hardness and hardness measurements. Cleveland.
ZANDER, J. M., AND J. H. TERRY
  1947 Quantitative spectrographic analysis of powdered ceramic materials. *Jour.
        Amer. Ceram. Soc.*, 30:366–70. Easton.

SUGGESTED READING

This brief list of titles is appended for those who wish to follow the technical aspects of ceramics further.

CERAMICS

Among the many general works on ceramics, the one that incorporates the newer concepts of clays most fully and consistently is F. H. Norton, *Elements of Ceramics* (1952). Although it contains considerable technical material, the subject matter is clarified by extensive illustration. Many semipopular books on ceramics have been written in response to the growing popularity of pottery as a hobby. The archaeologist will find R. Homes, *Ceramics for the Potter* (1952), interesting for its historical and archaeological references. The discussion of properties of ceramic materials is written primarily for the hobbiest, emphasizes chemical composition and is drawn largely from texts antedating the new knowledge of the clay minerals.

CLAYS

The most recent general work on clays is R. E. Grim, *Clay Mineralogy* (1953). Another valuable reference is *Reference Clay Minerals*, American Petroleum Institute, Research Project 49 (1951). The student should also be familiar with the classic papers on the clay minerals: C. S. Ross and P. F. Kerr, "The Kaolin Minerals," U. S. Geological Survey, Professional Paper 165 (1931); C. S. Ross and P. F. Kerr, "Halloysite and Allophane," *ibid.*, Professional Paper 185-G (1934); C. S. Ross and S. B. Hendricks, "Minerals of the Montmorillonite Group," *ibid.*, Professional Paper 205-B (1945). C. S. Ross, "Minerals and Mineral Relationships of the Clay Minerals," *Journal of the American Ceramic Society*, 28:173–183 (1945), gives a semipopular summary of modern clay research and a discussion of the bearing of the newer knowledge of the clay minerals on their origin. A popular discussion of colloidal chemistry as applied in ceramics will be found in an article by E. A. Hauser, "Colloid Chemistry in Ceramics," *ibid.*, 24:179–88 (1941).

PRINCIPAL IMPURITIES IN CLAYS

Fundamental data on the iron oxides will be found in a technical paper, O. C. Ralston, "Iron Oxide Reduction Equilibria," U. S. Bureau of Mines, Bull. 296 (1929). F. B. Van Houton, "Origin of Red-banded Early Cenozoic Deposits in Rocky Mountain Region," *American Association of Petroleum Geologists*, 32:2083–2126 (1938), gives an interesting discussion of iron oxides in nature and the forces affecting their formation. Very little fundamental work has been done on the nature of organic matter in clays, but a suggestive paper is that of E. Sharratt and M. Francis, "The Organic Matter of Ball Clays," Part I, *Transactions of the British Ceramic Society*, 42:111 (1943).

GLAZES

The structure of glasses, a subject that is basic to an understanding of the properties of glazes, is considered in the following research papers: N. Kreidl and W. A. Weyl, "The Development of Low Melting Glasses on the Basis of Structural Considerations," *Glass Industry*, 1:335, 2:384, 3:426, 4:465 (1941); K. Sun, "Fundamental Condition of Glass Formation," *Journal of the American Ceramic Society*, 30:277 (1947); W. H. Zachariasen, "The Atomic Arrangement in Glass," *ibid.*, 3841 (1932).

COMBUSTION

A standard, general work which will clarify the question of the nature of firing atmosphere is R. T. Haslam and R. P. Russell, *Fuels and Their Combustion* (1926).

Index

Numerals in roman type designate text pages; those in italics indicate pages where illustrations appear.